Pascal for Studer

including Turbo Pascal

Third Edition

Brian
Departme
Universit
Rondebo
South Af

Ray Ke
Departme
Massey U
Palmerst
New Zea

Newnes

£22.99

Newnes
An imprint of Butterworth-Heinemann
Linacre House, Jordan Hill, Oxford OX2 8DP
225 Wildwood Avenue, Woburn MA 01801-2041
A division of Reed Educational and Professional Publishing Ltd

A member of the Reed Elsevier plc group

OXFORD AUCKLAND BOSTON
JOHANNESBURG MELBOURNE NEW DELHI

First published 1982
Second edition 1987
Third edition 1996
Reprinted 1998
Transferred to digital printing 2001

British Library Cataloguing in Publication Data
A catalogue record for this book is available from the British Library

Library of Congress Cataloguing in Publication Data
A catalogue record for this book is available from the Library of Congress

ISBN 0 340 64588 1

For information on all Newnes publications
visit our website at www.newnespress.com

FOR EVERY TITLE THAT WE PUBLISH, BUTTERWORTH-HEINEMANN
WILL PAY FOR BTCV TO PLANT AND CARE FOR A TREE.

Preface to the first edition

If you want to learn Pascal from scratch, particularly if it is your first programming language, then this is the book for you. The first part is based on a one semester introduction to programming that has been taught to first year degree students for several years. Most of the material in Section 2 has been used in a single semester follow-up course which covers the remaining features of Pascal, including all of the storage structures.

Experience has shown us that one of the most effective ways of teaching programming involves introducing one or two new constructions at a time and concentrating on these. The order in which these constructions are covered is also important and much thought has gone into this. Other, more general, features of programming that are often neglected are considered in detail. These include program debugging, testing and algorithm development.

This is very much a practical book with plenty of programs on a variety of topics including data validation, text manipulation, data processing and list processing. Throughout the first part, quick quizzes provide an opportunity to consolidate ideas that have been discussed; and, at the end of each chapter, there are graded programming exercises. All of the programs reproduced in the text have been tested on at least one mainframe computer and one microcomputer.

Pascal is one of the simplest and most versatile of the non-trivial programming languages and has a large following among computer multi-linguists, but be warned! You are likely to be hooked on the language by the time you finish this book.

Leicester   R Kemp
1981

Preface to the second edition

Pascal has come a long way since its beginnings as an obscure and little used programming language. Now, every self-respecting type of computer (including most micros) has at least one Pascal system available for it. More importantly the language has taken the educational world by storm. It has been recognised as an ideal language to teach the basics of problem-solving by computer and most institutions that teach programming seriously would not consider using any other language.

This book teaches you all you need to know about Pascal and incorporates the latest ISO and ANSI recommended modifications to the language. As in the first edition, new concepts are introduced carefully and in an order that experience has shown to be most effective in encouraging structured programming. The often neglected topics of program debugging, testing and algorithm development are discussed in some detail.

Students learn best from seeing plenty of programs that illustrate the points being made and this book has thirty-six of these – all solving useful and interesting problems. The problems tackled cover a wide range of general, business and scientific applications although none of them require any specialist knowledge. What the programs do have in common is that they have all been thoroughly tested on at least one mainframe and one microcomputer.

Although *Pascal for Students* is geared towards use on first and second level lecture courses on programming it is possible to learn the language from the book without additional tutoring (it has been used for extramural teaching in this way for several years). Quick quizzes in the first half of the book are placed at the end of each section and have answers supplied so you can check whether you are on the right track. The programming exercises are also graded, allowing you gradually to attempt more difficult problems as your confidence and experience increase.

As more and more user-friendly environments for running Pascal such as the Macintosh and Turbo Pascal systems become widespread the language will become even more popular and easier to learn. Don't miss out on the best introductory programming language around.

Massey University   R Kemp
1986

Preface to the third edition

The third edition includes two new sections. Turbo Pascal is one of the most widely used Pascal systems in the world. Section 3 covers the Turbo Pascal extensions and exceptions to standard Pascal, with separate chapters on Turbo Pascal file handling, and graphics. The information in this section will enable you to run any program in this book under Turbo Pascal.

Section 4 contains a number of applications of Turbo Pascal in a wide variety of areas: simulation, network theory, population modelling, Markov chains, linear equations, and numerical methods. Although the examples in this section are programmed in Turbo Pascal, those not involving graphics can easily be adapted to standard Pascal.

University of Cape Town 1995   Brian Hahn
Massey University 1995   Ray Kemp

Contents

Introduction

The computer revolution has come upon us in three stages. First, in the late 1950s and early 1960s, medium to large scale firms converted their operations to computers often causing great upheaval and sometimes chaos. These problems were caused not so much by the computer itself but by the need to organise all processes in a systematic manner for the machine to deal with. At that stage, although virtually everyone was affected by the computer, very few people actually saw one. Even most of the staff who were involved in writing material for the computer only saw large boxes with blinking lights through a window. The image of the computer as a god-like machine was in this way encouraged. Only the computer operators bustling around in the inner sanctum, flicking switches, changing tapes and typing in commands actually touched the machine.

All of this changed when computers with several terminals* attached came onto the market.# These terminals allowed several users to communicate with the computer at the same time. Better still the terminals did not have to be located inside the hallowed computer room but could be spread around a firm's premises. As time went on, of course, it became commonplace for staff to be able to enter information into a computer and receive back replies even though the machine itself could be located in another part of the country. When you withdraw money from a bank it's as likely as not that the cashier will be able to find out the state of your account immediately by typing information at a terminal even if the account is at a bank in another city.

The third stage in the humanisation of the computer came with the advent of microcomputers or 'micros'. These small computers are cheap and often portable enough for small firms and hobbyists to think of buying. Now many people have the opportunity to own their own computer and those that have taken this opportunity have been able to experience the excitement of using a machine that can simplify many jobs and that can be a lot of fun.

Sadly some of these micros are so small that they have little potential beyond game playing. Thus there is a danger of moving from one extreme of regarding the computer as a god-like device to the other extreme of thinking of it as merely for playing games that other people have devised. It is much more fun to be able to write your own software*.

If you have a computer that runs the programming language Pascal* then you can learn to write your own sets of instructions or computer programs*. This book tells you all about Pascal and assumes no previous knowledge of programming. All you need is a familiarity with some of the common computing terms and a rudimentary knowledge of how the computer works. A glossary of computing terms used in this book is supplied in appendix G and should give you some help, although if you are completely new to the subject you would be advised to have a general computing book to hand to fill in some of the background.

#Definitions of asterisked words and phrases may be found in the Glossary (Appendix G).

Fig. 0.1 (Photograph courtesy of IBM New Zealand Ltd)

Section 1

Pre-defined simple types and control structures

1

First steps

Introduction

The very simplest kinds of computer program are introduced in this chapter. Even so there is much to learn—the basic structure of Pascal programs, how to feed in data and layout results, but most of all how to get the computer to do what you want it to and find out what's going wrong when it doesn't.

1.1 Some simple programs

Computers, like the Delphic Oracle, are used to answer questions, but, as with the Oracle, you have to be careful how you phrase your request or you may get a misleading answer. In fact the computer may give you no answer at all if it doesn't like the question.

The first question we shall ask the computer is: 'given that a stone takes 3 seconds to reach the bottom of a well how deep is the well?' It would be nice if we could phrase the question exactly in this way and expect the computer to get the right answer. It will be a few years before that becomes possible. In the meantime the best way to get the computer to provide an answer is to write a computer program to do the job. Program 1.1 does just this. Before we examine the program in detail have a preliminary look at it to see if you can work out what's happening.

Ignoring much of the punctuation for now let's look at the program line by line. (Note that the line numbers that appear on the left-hand side are for reference only and are not part of the program.)

On the first line the program is given a title. The user chooses an appropriate name but, as with all Pascal names, there must be no break in the middle— Well depth would not work. The name output in parentheses, signifies that the answer that the computer gives should be transmitted to the device called output. This might be a printer*, vdu* or teletype*. Lines 3 to 10 contain a description of the purpose of the program. This description enclosed between braces '{' and '}' is known as a *comment*. In all programs, whatever the language, it is important to have a piece of text at or near the beginning describing the purpose of the program and, possibly, giving other information such as the name of the writer and the date of completion. In Pascal, any information enclosed between '{' and '}' is disregarded by the compiler* (even if it extends over several lines) and so explanatory text may be inserted at appropriate points*. In this example the rectangle of asterisks has no significance for the computer but helps to highlight the enclosed introductory description for the reader.

A blank line follows, and then, on lines 13 and 14, the constants to be used in the program are given values. In order to work out the depth of the well the computer needs to know how long a stone takes to reach the bottom and also how fast it is moving. The

---

In some implementations the symbols '(' and '*)' may be used to enclose comments. Further details concerning differences between implementations of Pascal are given in Appendix E.

```
 1      Program Welldepth ( output );
 2
 3      {*********************************************************************
 4       *                                                                  *
 5       * Program 1.1                                                      *
 6       * Given the time (in seconds) taken for a stone to reach the bottom *
 7       * of a well and the gravitational constant (in metres/sec/sec) the *
 8       * depth of the well (in metres) is calculated.                     *
 9       *                                                                  *
10       *********************************************************************}
11
12      const
13            timetaken = 3;
14            gravity   = 9.8;
15
16      var
17            depth : real;
18
19      begin
20
21         depth := 0.5 * gravity * sqr ( timetaken );
22
23         writeln ( 'Program 1.1  Calculation of well depth' );
24         writeln ( '======================================' );
25         writeln;
26
27         writeln ( 'time for stone to reach bottom =', timetaken , ' seconds' );
28         writeln ( 'gravitational constant         =', gravity , ' m/s/s' );
29         writeln ( 'depth of well                  =', depth , ' m' )
30
31      end.
```

Program 1.1

time taken was 3 seconds and a name timetaken has been invented to represent this. Note, again, that it would not be acceptable to have a name in two parts (time taken). There must be no spaces in the middle. The second constant 9.8 is given the name gravity. The stone actually falls because of the gravitational pull of the earth and if we are to determine the depth of the well this will be needed too.

After the next blank line, the word **var** (short for 'variable') indicates that the name following it denotes a variable in the program. The word that follows is depth and represents the depth of the well. At this point you may be wondering why depth is called a variable giving the impression that it is something that alters. Surely the depth remains unchanged in the same way that the time taken and the gravitational constant do? The distinction occurs because we know the values of the constants before we start but the value of the depth is to be calculated in the program itself. In Pascal any names used to denote values that are computed during the running of a program are designated as variables.

The fact that the depth will be a number which will probably contain a fractional part is indicated by placing the word real after the variable name.

None of the code up to line 17 actually commands the computer to carry out the task we are interested in. However, the directions on lines 12 to 17 are important to the organisation of information within the computer and to the execution of the code contained between the words **begin** and **end** in the 'statement part'.

The code on line 21 computes the depth from the given information using a formula.

The order of the elements on the line is misleading since it does not correspond to the order in which the computations are performed. First, the formula to the right of the ': = ' is evaluated using the values defined earlier in the program (note that multiplication is denoted by an asterisk and not by the more usual ' × ' symbol and that sqr indicates that the squaring operation is to be performed). The result is then assigned to the variable depth on the left-hand side. The assignment operator ': = ' may be read as 'becomes' or 'takes the value'.

The complete instruction on this line is called an *assignment statement* and tells the computer to halve the value of the gravitational constant, multiply this by the square of the time and assign the result to the variable called depth. When this instruction is executed the value of depth becomes approximately 44.1 (the result of $0.5 \times 9.8 \times 3 \times 3$) —this will be the computer's estimate of the depth of the well in metres. The actual precision of the result will vary from computer to computer. Note that the symbol ' = ' is not used for assignment as it was for giving values to constants. The link between a variable and its value is a looser attachment and we will return to this point later.

Even though the result has been computed, this is not the end of the problem: the value obtained will still be inside the computer. In order to inform the user of the result, the value must be transmitted to the output unit* and printed. The instructions on lines 23 to 29 tell the computer to send the result and other information to the printer.

When a writeln statement is carried out it has the effect of sending specified information to one line of the output device. The statement on line 23 has the effect of printing one item—a piece of text that is to be the title of the output. The second writeln causes another piece of text to be output on the next line, underlining the title. The word writeln on line 25 has no items in parentheses following it and simply causes a blank line to be output.

The statement on line 27 indicates that three items are to be output—a piece of text between quotation marks (quotes), the *value* of the constant timetaken and then another piece of text. If an item is not in quotes then its value is output rather than the actual word itself. The last two writeln statements will similarly cause three items to be printed —two pieces of text and a value.

Now you know *what* the program does but you may be wondering *why* it is written in this elaborate way. The result could be worked out with a calculator in much less time than it takes to read the program and certainly much less time than it takes to run it. There are two answers to this. Firstly, the program is purely illustrative and is included to show what a simple one looks like. Secondly, as we shall see later, the program needs only a slight modification to make it much more powerful.

Even for the task that it does you may feel that the program is too verbose. Certainly it could be shortened in several ways so let's examine each of these possible short cuts in turn. Before we do this though, let's be clear what the purpose of a program is. Principally it is for getting the computer to solve a problem. A small program may only take a few minutes to write but as you become more ambitious you may write programs that have hundreds or even thousands of lines and take several weeks or months to complete. It is quite likely that unless your program is carefully written and has adequate documentation* you will, over a period of time, forget what different parts of it are supposed to do and changes will therefore be very difficult to make. If you write software for a living then you will probably be writing programs that others have to amend and also modifying other people's programs. For these reasons it is important that as you write your program you spend as much time as possible making it easy to follow.

The first way the program could be shortened would be to remove those comments enclosed between '{' and '}'. Hopefully you will agree now that this is not a good idea. They don't make the program any less efficient and are of great assistance in helping the reader to find out what the program is supposed to do and in explaining the purpose of the names used.

What about those names though? Surely it would be possible to get rid of most of them. The assignment statement could then be abbreviated to

```
depth := 0.5 * 9.8 * sqr(3)
```

or (since everyone knows what 3 × 3 gives)

```
depth := 0.5 * 9.8 * 9
```

The usefulness of constant names like gravity and timetaken is not so obvious as that of the comments. In fact, in part, they fulfil a similar purpose, giving the reader some idea of what these numbers represent. The names for constants and variables should be chosen carefully. Names such as x, a, tmtkn and grvty should be avoided. They are more likely to confuse than help the reader.

All of these things help to document the program more effectively but that still doesn't explain why there are so many writeln statements. Only one of these is actually essential —the one that outputs the depth of the well. The others just make the results look tidy and output additional information (see below).

```
Program 1.1  Calculation of well depth
=======================================

time for stone to reach bottom =       3 seconds
gravitational constant         = 9.8 m/s/s
depth of well                  = 44.1 m
```
Output from Program 1.1

If it is important to make a program clear then it is doubly important to make its output readable and self-explanatory. A customer may not be interested in your program at all, but only in the results. Printing a single number may be at best meaningless and at worst misleading. The output from every program should consist of a title, information about the data used, and the results obtained. Some organisations may require further information, such as the date and the version of the program run.

In order to run Program 1.1 it must be read into a computer. You may be able to type it straight in at a terminal, onto a micro, or you may have to submit the program on coding forms or punch it onto cards. There are many different ways of entering a program onto the computer and even more variation in the instructions used to compile and run it. You will have to refer to the manual for your machine to find out the commands your system uses. Once the program has been compiled and run then the results should appear on your screen or printer in more-or-less the form shown above.

Now that we have determined that the depth of our well is about 44.1 metres the program could be thrown away, but there is still more that it can do for us. If we want a more accurate assessment of the depth then we could try to determine more precisely the time a stone takes to reach the well bottom or could use a closer approximation to the value of the gravitational constant. All that would be necessary then would be to change the constant definitions in the program and try it out again. We might have:

```
const
      timetaken = 2.7;
      gravity   = 9.81;
```

Having recompiled the program the new output might look like:

```
Program 1.1  Calculation of well depth
=======================================

time for stone to reach bottom = 2.7 seconds
gravitational constant         = 9.81 m/s/s
depth of well                  = 35.8 m
```

But why stop here? We could scour the country looking for wells and time stones dropped into them. Whenever a new well and time is found the program would be modified by changing the value of timetaken, and the depth of the new well calculated.

Having to change the program whenever a different time is to be entered is tedious and there is a better way to organise things—by making timetaken a variable and by supplying a value for it as data[*]. In this way the program can remain the same and won't need recompiling. The data is completely distinct from the program and depending on the system you are using may be entered via the keyboard or may be in a separate data file. In either case the values in the data may be input into the program using a read statement. This principle is illustrated in Program 1.2 where two values are read in as data.

```
1     Program Simpleinterest ( input, output );
2
3     {****************************************************************
4      *                                                             *
5      * Program 1.2                                                 *
6      * Calculation of simple interest on a principal at a given rate *
7      * of interest and over a given number of days.                *
8      *                                                             *
9      ****************************************************************}
10
11    const
12          rate = 10;  { per cent }
13          year = 365; { days }
14
15    var
16          principal, interest, amount : real;
17
18          time : integer;
19
20    begin
21
22        read ( principal, time );
23
24        interest := time / year * rate / 100 * principal;
25        amount   := principal + interest;
26
27        writeln ( 'Program 1.2  Computation of simple interest' );
28        writeln ( '============================================' );
29        writeln;
30
31        writeln ( 'principal              = $', principal :7:2 );
32        writeln ( 'interest rate          = ', rate :4, ' %' );
33        writeln ( 'term                   = ', time :4, ' days' );
34        writeln;
35        writeln ( 'interest               = $', interest :7:2 );
36        writeln ( 'new value of principal = $', amount :7:2 )
37
38    end.
```

Program 1.2

Before we look at the purpose of the program, compare its general format with that of Program 1.1. Again there is an initial comment; but this time, in addition, there are further comments interspersed with the text. Comments may appear anywhere except in a quoted piece of text or in the middle of a multi-character symbol (multi-character symbols include names, numbers and the assignment operator ': = '). Apart from the comments the general structure is the same as that of Program 1.1. There is a program heading followed by a set of *declarations*, i.e. lists of constant and variable names to be used. (Comparing a computer program with a recipe, the declarations can be likened to a list of ingredients preceding the instructions.) Then comes a set of statements to be executed, enclosed between the words **begin** and **end**—the statement part. All Pascal programs have these three parts: heading, declarations, and statement part and are terminated by '.'. The section of the program consisting of the declarations and statement part is known as the program body or *block*.

Certain words occur in both Program 1.1 and Program 1.2. These include **program**, **var**, **begin** and **end**, which always have a special meaning in Pascal. A full list of *reserved words* is given in Appendix B. In this text they are highlighted by bold lettering and if your are lucky your computer will do the same for you automatically. Otherwise your system may just display thes? words in normal print.

The title and names used to identify quantities within a program are invented by the user. Any suitable names may be chosen, except reserved words. Formally, a name (or 'identifier') in a program may consist of any sequence of letters or digits starting with a letter. This definition may be represented in a syntax diagram* as shown in Fig. 1.1.

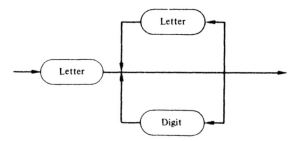

Fig.1.1

The purpose of Program 1.2 is to calculate the interest paid on a sum of money over a given number of days with a given rate of interest.

The first important difference from the previous program occurs in the heading. Program 1.1 is self-contained and needs no other values to be given, whereas Program 1.2 requires numbers to be read in from an input device and, for this reason, the word input occurs in the heading.

There are three real variables (principal, interest and amount) but, in addition, another variable time is declared to be of type integer. This means it will always have a whole number value. Variables that are always going to refer to whole number quantities should be declared in this way even though, in many circumstances, no error would result from making them real. The advantages of using integer variables are two-fold: their values are always stored exactly (which is not necessarily so for real variables); and if the programmer mistakenly tries to give an integer variable a value containing a fractional part, then this will be detected by the compiler and should cause an error message to be output.

Incidentally, note that the order in which variables appear in declarations is not important. In fact, the integer declaration could precede all of the real ones. However, any constant definitions must precede variable declarations and *all* user names must be declared.

On line 22 there is a read statement. When this is executed each of the variables within the parentheses is given a value transmitted from an input device. If the user is working at a terminal or at a micro then the computer will wait for her to type in two numbers; alternatively the data may be supplied in a separate file* or on cards. In any of these cases the data must consist of a real number (i.e. a number with a fractional part) followed by a whole number. There are only two restrictions applying to numbers in data: they must be separated by at least one space, and they must occur in the same order as the variables in the corresponding read statement. Other than that they may be separated by several spaces, or may even be on separate lines or cards.

The computations are performed in the assignment statements on lines 24 and 25. In the first of these there are two divisions to be performed as well as multiplications. Usually when division is written down on paper it takes up two or three lines—one line for the numerator and one line for the denominator with a line between. If we were setting out the formula for calculating the simple interest on paper it might be written as

$$\text{interest} = \frac{\text{time}}{\text{year}} \times \frac{\text{rate}}{100} \times \text{principal}$$

It is easier for the computer, however, if the information is written on a single line. In the program, the symbol '/' is used for division and the evaluated result is assigned to the variable interest.

The assignment on the next line uses the newly computed value of interest to find the new value of the principal (often called the 'amount'). It would not be possible to switch these assignments around, of course, since the statements are carried out from top to bottom. The computer could not work out the new value of the principal before calculating the interest anymore than you or I could.

As before there are a number of output statements, but a new feature has been used in some of them. In the earlier program we had no control over how the values output were to be formatted. The value of gravity, for example, could have been written in any number of ways including 9.8, 9.80, 9.800 and so on. It would be useful to be able to specify how many decimal places are to be printed (particularly in examples with money since anything other than two decimal places would be meaningless). Also, to make the layout neater it is necessary to be able to control the total amount of space that a number is to take up on the output line. Both of these requirements can be satisfied in Pascal by using a 'field width option'. By placing a colon followed by a number after an item in an output statement the total amount of space to be allocated for that item is indicated. If the item has a numerical value and takes up less space than that allocated then the space to the left is filled with blanks.

If the number is a real then you will probably want to specify the number of decimal places to be allocated as well as the total space for the number. This is done by attaching another colon followed by an integer. The second number is taken to be the number of decimal places required.

Looking at Program 1.2 we see that a total of seven positions has been allowed for printing out the value of principal of which two are to be to the right of the decimal point. Note the two decimal places are *part* of the seven and *not* additional to it. For rate there is only a single field width indicator since it is a whole number. If the data for this program was

     790.25   230

then the output might look like this:

```
Program 1.2  Computation of simple interest
============================================

principal                = $ 790.25
interest rate            =    10 %
term                     =   230 days

interest                 = $   49.80
new value of principal , = $ 840.05
```

This program is more flexible than Program 1.1 because it can be used to calculate the interest and amount for many different principals or terms without the need for recompilation. If the data is changed from run to run, although the same statements are executed, the values of the variables are different and so are the results.

Quick quiz 1.1   (solutions on p. 22)

1   What do you think would happen in Program 1.2 if the data was
(i)   − 12.05 and − 60
(ii)   t@**hj rt%

2   Why do you think rate was made a constant in Program 1.2 rather than a variable?

3   What do you think would happen if the number of digits in an integer output was greater than the amount of space allocated in the field width?

4   Write down the line of output produced by the following statement when age is an integer variable with value 27 and weight is a real variable with value 71.37445. Indicate the number of spaces between items.

writeln ('age □ = □', age :3, '□ □ □ weight □ = □', weight :8:3, '□ kilos')

The symbol '□' is used to denote a space.

1.2   Constructing a program

There are many different ways to approach the problem of producing a program from a possibly vaguely-worded specification. Ultimately, you must choose a technique that suits you. The one definite guideline is that the whole program should be planned and sketched out before individual sections are coded. The later you start coding, the more likely you are to produce a good, well-structured program.

The term algorithm* has come to be used for the initial sketch of the steps to be followed in order to solve a problem. Whether this takes the form of a structure diagram*, Nassi-Shneiderman diagram, pseudo-English description or whatever, it is important that the description should be clear and simple. A suitable approach for tackling larger problems is described in Chapter 3. To illustrate one approach for smaller examples the following problem will be used.

A car computer registers the time that a journey starts and the initial reading on the distance gauge. The time of the end of the journey and the corresponding distance reading are also noted. Write a program that inputs these values and works out

(i)   the total time for the journey
(ii)   the total distance travelled
(iii)   the average speed of the car

Assume that the journey starts and finishes on the same day and that the times are taken using the 24 hour clock.

If you are stuck at this point and don't know where to start then imagine that someone has asked you to solve this problem *without* using a computer. The first thing you would want to know would be the times and distances involved—this is equivalent to the computer reading in the values. Next you can compute the total time for the journey by subtracting the start time from the finish time. Similarly the total distance travelled can be calculated by subtracting the final distance reading from the initial one. The average speed can be computed by dividing the distance travelled by the time taken and then finally the person who set the question has to be told the answer and this is equivalent to the computer outputting the results. To summarise these steps in a pseudo-English algorithm:

read in the start time, finish time, start distance and finish distance
calculate the time taken (finish time − start time)
calculate the distance travelled (finish distance − start distance)
calculate the average speed (distance travelled/time taken)
output results

This algorithm could be easily transformed into a sequence of statements in any one of a number of computer languages, although in most of them (including Pascal) there are still one or two more problems to be solved before we get a final working program.

The first stage in converting the algorithm to Pascal could be to write out a list of suitable names for constants and variables that will be needed. An initial attempt might produce:

starttime
finishtime
totaltime
startdistance
finishdistance
totaldistance
averagespeed

An important point to bear in mind when choosing names is that some compilers only examine the first eight characters in a name and so if two names contain the same first eight characters then as far as the computer is concerned they may be indistinguishable. For example, the names distancestart and distancefinish would not be suitable for this reason.

All of the above names will be declared as variables since they are all to be read in or calculated during the running of the program, but when we come to relate the variables to the steps in the algorithm a problem can be seen. The start time will not be a single number but will consist of two numbers—the hours and minutes. Similarly the finish time and total time will each consist of two values. The way to get round this problem is to have two variables for each, which gives us a new set of time variables:

starthours
startminutes
finishhours
finishminutes
totalhours
totalminutes

A further headache is that the calculation of the total time taken is no longer simple, since each consists of two numbers. One answer is to convert each time to minutes, perform the subtraction and then convert back the result to give the hours and minutes of the total time taken. This is the approach taken to produce the final program (Program 1.3).

As usual the initial comment clearly sets out the purpose of the program and the assumptions made.

The declarations consist only of variables since no constants are needed, and all but one of these are defined to be of type integer since it is assumed that all times will be taken to the nearest minute.

The first four statements in the statement part of the program should be self-explanatory. The initial statement for reading in the data is so long that it has been extended onto a second line. There is no problem for the computer if this is done. The

```
Program Carstatistics ( input, output );

{********************************************************************
 *                                                                  *
 * Program 1.3                                                      *
 * It is required to calculate the distance a car has travelled, the *
 * time taken and the average speed, given the start and finish distance *
 * gauge readings and the start and finish time for the journey.    *
 * The assumptions are made that the journey starts and finishes on the *
 * same day and that times are taken (to the nearest minute) using the *
 * 24 hour clock.                                                   *
 *                                                                  *
 ********************************************************************}


var
      startdistance, finishdistance,  {    in      }
      totaldistance,                  { kilometers }
      starthours, startminutes,
      finishhours, finishminutes,
      totaltime,  { in minutes }
      totalhours, totalminutes     : integer;

      averagespeed : real;

begin

   read ( startdistance, finishdistance, starthours, startminutes,
                                  finishhours, finishminutes );

   totaldistance := finishdistance - startdistance;
   totaltime     := 60 * ( finishhours - starthours )
                      + finishminutes - startminutes;
   averagespeed  := totaldistance * 60 / totaltime;
   totalhours    := totaltime div 60;
   totalminutes  := totaltime mod 60;

   writeln ( 'Program 1.3  Statistics for a car journey' );
   writeln ( '=========================================' );
   writeln;

   writeln ( 'distance reading at start  =', startdistance :6, ' km' );
   writeln ( 'distance reading at finish =', finishdistance :6, ' km' );
   writeln ( 'total distance travelled   =', totaldistance :6, ' km' );
   writeln;
   writeln ( 'time of start of journey   =', starthours :4, ' hours',
                                 startminutes :3, ' minutes' );
   writeln ( 'time of end of journey     =', finishhours :4, ' hours',
                                 finishminutes :3, ' minutes' );
   writeln ( 'duration of journey        =', totalhours :4, ' hours',
                                 totalminutes :3, ' minutes' );
   writeln;
   writeln ( 'average speed              =', averagespeed :6:1, ' km/hr' )

end.
```

Program 1.3

programmer should position overflow material with care though because it can easily become untidy and difficult to read. The following three assignments calculate the distance travelled, time taken and average speed and again one of them has been extended carefully onto a second line (note that the average speed is multiplied by 60 since the time taken is in minutes).

The last two assignments are for converting the total time back to hours and minutes and use two features we haven't come across before—**div** and **mod**. When we want to divide one number by another one we can use the '/' operator but this always gives a real result even if both the values involved are integers (4/2 would not give 2 but 2.0). If a whole number result is needed then the operation **div** can be used. But beware—if there is any remainder when this operation is carried out then it is thrown away. The result of 13 **div** 5 is 2 not 2.6 or 3. Similarly the remainder on dividing one whole number by another is found by using **mod**. For instance 13 **mod** 5 is 3. These operations are complementary and have certain similarities. They can both be used only on integer values and they both need to be separated from other names by one or more blanks. (What would the computer make of applesdivchildren?—it would treat it as a rather long name, of course.)

Hopefully you can see how **div** and **mod** work in this program to give the right result. If not then try working through those last two assignment statements for a particular value of totaltime (400, say). Finally, the output statements produce the results we want with appropriate formatting of the values.

If the data supplied to the program was:

    10 243   10 596   9 20   14 25

then the results should look similar to those below:

```
Program 1.3  Statistics for a car journey
==========================================

distance reading at start  = 10243 km
distance reading at finish = 10596 km
total distance travelled   =   353 km

time of start of journey   =  9 hours 20 minutes
time of end of journey     = 14 hours 25 minutes
duration of journey        =  5 hours  5 minutes

average speed              = 69.4 km/hr
```

Output from Program 1.3

Once you have written your first algorithm, you will probably come across three main problems in trying to construct a corresponding program. These problems are as follows.

(i)   Punctuation—where should commas, colons and semicolons be inserted?
(ii) Layout—what restrictions are there on how the program is set out?
(iii) Expressions—how should arithmetic expressions be written?

Punctuation
The first problem is perhaps the most difficult to overcome. Initially, there may seem to be little logic about the positioning of punctuation symbols. Your early programs may contain several errors due to omitted or misplaced colons, semicolons and commas. You will be continually referring to other programs and syntax diagrams for guidance. Care and experience are the best teachers in this respect, though you should find the following summary helpful.

(a) The semicolon terminates the program heading, terminates each declaration, and separates each statement from the next. You do not need a semicolon between the last statement and **end** although one may be placed there if preferred.

(b) Commas are used to separate items in lists, such as the names in a real variable declaration or the items in a writeln statement.

(c) The colon is used in several situations but in elementary programs its main function is to separate a list of items in a declaration from the corresponding data type name. It is also used in field width specifications. (Note that the colon is not considered as a separate symbol in ': = '. It is part of the assignment operator.)

(d) The period '.' is used to terminate programs and always appears after the last **end.**

The full syntax of Pascal is set out in syntax diagrams in Appendix A although this includes many constructions that have not been mentioned yet. Figure 1.2 summarises the main structure of a Pascal program. You should be able to resolve any syntax problems that you have with the exercises at the end of this chapter by referring to Programs 1.1, 1.2 and 1.3 and, if necessary, by working through the relevant syntax diagrams.

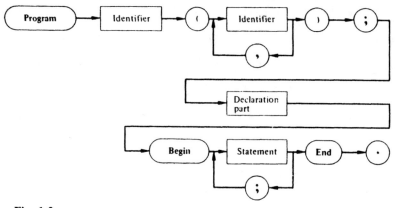

Fig. 1.2

Layout

Program layout is dangerously simple. It is simple because there are very few restrictions, and dangerous because there is a consequent temptation to place code anywhere on a line in an arbitrary fashion. The main rule is that any number of spaces may be placed *between* symbols but no spaces can occur *within* symbols. Symbols in Pascal include identifiers, numbers, reserved words, punctuation (;, :, ., etc.), and other multi-character symbols such as : = . In addition, identifiers, numbers, and reserved words must be separated from one another by at least one space if there is no other symbol between them. There is an imaginary space between the end of one line and the start of the next, and so the same rules apply here.

This freedom of layout can be used to improve the readability of programs. Neat and consistent layout of a program is as important to its comprehension as the use of comments. No internationally-agreed set of rules exists, although there are generally accepted conventions and these are described below.

(a) It is useful to separate different sections of program by blank lines. For example, the declarations may be separated from the statement part by a blank line.

(b)   Within the program body each statement is usually best placed on a separate line, although two or three associated statements may be placed on a single line where appropriate. If a statement cannot conveniently be written on a single line, then it should be carefully broken up to extend it onto two or more lines.

(c)   An important convention is that of indentation. Large programs usually have sections of code within other sections (each section is usually enclosed between **begin** and **end**). Each inner section should be further indented to distinguish it. In each of the programs considered so far there has been only a single **begin** and **end** pair, and code between has been indented three spaces. If there were further **begin**s and **end**s, each piece of code between the pairs could be indented a further three spaces. We shall see, in later chapters, how much this improves readability.

Expressions

Because programs are processed a line at a time, arithmetic expressions often cannot be set out in the normal algebraic fashion. For example, $\frac{a}{b}$ should be written as a/b. Since no subscripts or superscripts are allowed, x^2 should be written as sqr(x) or x*x. In more complicated expressions, ambiguity can arise unless formal rules are applied. Does $a + b/c$ mean $a + \frac{b}{c}$ or $\frac{a+b}{c}$? The rules that are used in Pascal follow, for the most part, the rules of precedence that apply in algebra. Operations are generally carried out from left to right, subject to these rules of precedence; and multiplying operators (**div**, **mod**, * and /) have priority over the adding operators (+ and −). For example, the computations in the expresssion

$$6 + 5 \textbf{ div } 4 * 3$$

would be performed in the following order:

5 **div** 4   (giving 1)
1 * 3   (giving 3)
6 + 3   (giving 9)

To assign higher precedence to a particular part of an expression, it should be enclosed in parentheses. Writing

$$6 + 5 \textbf{ div } (4 * 3)$$

for example, would ensure that 4 * 3 would be calculated before the **div** operation was executed.

Extra parentheses may be used to alter precedence, and also to improve clarity; for example,

a/((b **mod** c) * d)

The inner parentheses are not strictly necessary in this expression, since the **mod** operation (occurring before the multiplication) will be carried out first anyway. However, they do clarify the order of evaluation to anyone who is unsure of the precedence of operations. Redundant parentheses are ignored by the compiler, but don't let this go to your head. Too many of them can obscure the meaning of an expression.

Three further points

In scientific formulae, multiplication is often implicit, as in the expression *abc*. This would be confusing in Pascal, since identifiers may contain more than one character, and so multiplication must always be explicitly indicated.

Secondly, real and integer values may be mixed in an expression, but the type of the result depends on the situation, for example, a + i where a is real and i is integer gives a real result.

Lastly, we have met just one function so far—sqr. Most of the commonly used mathematical functions are available and some implementations may provide additional ones. The 'required functions' that should be available in every implementation of Pascal are listed in Appendix C.

There are three functions that we haven't met that are particularly useful. Two of these (called round and trunc) are complementary. They can both be applied to real values or to expressions that give real values and they have the result of rounding the value applied to and truncating the value applied to, respectively. For instance:

    round (4.2) gives 4
    round (4.6) gives 5
    trunc (4.2) gives 4
    trunc (4.6) gives 4

They are often used in assignments when the right-hand side is of type real but the variable on the left-hand side is of type integer. If you try to put an assignment of this sort into your program you will get an error message since it is not allowed in Pascal (although curiously enough the assignment of an integer value to a variable of type real is allowed.) To avoid this error you should decide whether the result of the computation is to be rounded or truncated and apply the corresponding function to the whole of the right-hand side of the assignment.

Take for example Program 1.3. If we had only wanted the average speed to the nearest kilometre per hour then we could have declared the variable averagespeed to be of type integer. The assignment

    averagespeed := totaldistance * 60 / totaltime

would then fail since '/' always gives a real result and the whole of the right-hand side is then of type real. To avoid this happening we could enclose the whole expression in parentheses and apply the round function making the modified assignment:

    averagespeed := round (totaldistance * 60 / totaltime)

A third handy function abs can be applied to real or integer values and gives the magnitude of the answer (i.e. its positive value). For example:

    abs (6) is 6
    abs (− 6) is 6
    abs (0) is 0

A common application of abs is for finding the difference between two values when it is not known (or does not matter) which is the larger. For instance the assignment

    heightdifference := abs (height1 − height2)

would give 0.1 if height1 was 1.8 and height2 was 1.7, but it would also give the same answer if height1 was 1.7 and height2 was 1.8.

Quick quiz 1.2   (Solutions on p. 22)

1   Given that a,b,c are real variables with values 0.5, 1.5 and 2.5 respectively, and i,j,k are integer variables with values 1,2, and 3 respectively, evaluate:

(i) a * b + c	(ii) a + b * c	(iii) a * b / c	(iv) a / b / c
(v) i **div** j + k	(vi) i **div** (j + k)	(vii) i / j + k	(viii) a + i **mod** j
(ix) round (j / k)	(x) trunc(a + j)	(xi) − abs (i − k)	

2 Express the following formulae in Pascal:

(i) $\dfrac{\ln(a+b)}{c+d}$ (ii) $\dfrac{1}{2}ab\sin c$ (iii) $\cos^2(e^x)$ (iv) $\dfrac{4}{3}\pi r^3$

(Only attempt this question if you are familiar with the mathematical functions used.)

1.3 Program errors and debugging

Basically there are two kinds of error that may occur in a program—syntax errors and logic errors.

(i) *Syntax errors*

These include mistakes such as misplaced punctuation, mis-spelt names, undeclared identifiers and badly-formed expressions. They are common errors for the novice programmer to make, but are usually detected by the compiler during translation. New programmers often become exasperated when seemingly trivial errors are picked up. Unless the syntax is perfect, however, the compiler will not translate your program. This may sometimes seem like fussiness on the compiler's part but it is actually necessary. If a program is incorrectly punctuated, it may be ambiguous and open to misinterpretation. For example, consider this mistyped statement:

```
writeln ( 'the values are, a, b, c )
```

Maybe you could guess where the missing quote should be, and certainly you would stand a better chance of being right than the compiler. Even so, you could not be sure without consulting the person who wrote the original program. It is difficult to make the computer into a good guesser, since there are so many different types of error (*bugs*) that may occur in a program. The compiler can easily detect that there *is* an error in this statement, since there should be an even number of quotes, but correcting the mistake is a difficult task and is usually left to the programmer.

Sometimes a compiler may detect an error but misinterpret the mistake. For example, if both quotes were omitted from the above writeln statement it would appear as

```
writeln ( the values are, a, b, c )
```

and some compilers might flag the error as

UNDECLARED AND BADLY FORMED IDENTIFIER 'the values are'

Confusion may also arise if an error in a program causes an error message not at the position that the mistake occurs but later on. For example, if a variable time is declared as **var** tine:real then the computer will not detect an error until corresponding references to time are found in the main part of the program. In each case time will be flagged as an undeclared identifier.

(ii) *Logic errors*

Once syntax errors have been corrected, a program may still fail to produce the expected results. If the algorithm is incorrect or has been miscoded then, even though there may be no punctuation errors, the program may still produce the wrong answers, or even no answers at all. These are logic errors, which become apparent at run-time in one of two ways: either the values output do not correspond to predicted results or the program execution is halted and an error message is output. In the first case, the computer has solved a problem; it just happens to be a different problem from the one the programmer intended to be solved! A careful examination of the code may indicate what is causing the error. If not, then the best procedure, in the case of a small program, is to trace through the statements with the given data until a discrepancy is found. The programmer must carry out the instructions in a mechanical way, noting intermediate results, to simulate the steps taken by the computer. This has to be done very carefully, since people are notorious for seeing what they expect to see rather than what is actually there.

Errors in larger programs cannot be effectively found using the method described above—it would take too long. Some installations have *debugging aids* which allow intermediate values of given variables to be output automatically during execution of a program, and sometimes an indication of the execution path traced through the program may be printed out. If these aids are not available, the programmer can place writeln statements at intermediate points in his program to give the same effect. Again, by checking through these intermediate results, he should be able to pinpoint where the program is starting to go wrong.

Sometimes an incorrect program will produce a run-time error. If the computer is instructed to perform a task that is impossible under the rules of the language or of arithmetic, then an error message will be output, usually giving some indication of the reason why execution has been stopped and the corresponding position in the program at which this occurred. If, for example, a programmer mistakenly coded the expression $\frac{a}{b+c}$ as a/b + c and, immediately prior to the evaluation of this expression, a, b and c had the values 2.0, 0.0 and 1.0 respectively, then the computer would first attempt to calculate 2.0/0.0. Most computers have built-in checks to avoid the attempted execution of this impossible task, and a message such as

ATTEMPTED DIVISION BY ZERO

will be output. This sort of information, together with an indication of where execution stopped, is usually very helpful in finding errors. Unfortunately, a mistake in the program often occurs at a completely different point from that at which the computer detects something going wrong. In fact, a bug is sometimes defined as an error that occurs somewhere else—otherwise it wouldn't be a bug! In these cases a trace procedure should be employed, as before.

Quick quiz 1.3 (Solutions on p. 23)

Find the errors in the following statements and indicate whether they would be detected during compilation or at run-time.

(i)   x + 1 : = 2 * y/3 + z * z
(ii)   i : = (j/k) **mod** 3
(iii)   y : = sqrt (− (sqr(x) + 1))
(iv)   writeln ('interest rate = ', rate: 3, 'per cent
                                                       per year')

1.4   Program testing

Once your program has been compiled, executed, and has given results, you should not be satisfied to leave it at that and move on to the next problem. For a start, are the results correct? The answers may be given to ten decimal places but that is no guarantee that they are right. You should check that the results obtained are approximately what you would expect.

Again it is important that your program should be tested for a range of input values, if appropriate. Devising suitable test data is an art in itself. It should check each of the distinct features of the program. Even for a short program, three or four sets of data may be needed to test the correctness of the computations. For example, look at Problem C2 at the end of this chapter (p. 25). This involves writing a program to calculate the distance between two points on the earth's surface. This program should be tested for at least four sets of data:

(i) two points on the same latitude but different longitudes;
(ii) two points on the same longitude but different latitudes;
(iii) two points within 9000 km of one another but in different hemispheres and on different longitudes;
(iv) two points more or less diametrically opposite on the earth's surface.

Incidentally, in order to check the answers, authentic positions of cities with known shortest distances could be used in addition to straight substitution in a formula. Results may be slightly out due to the equatorial bulge of the earth but would provide a rough cross-check on the formula itself in addition to verifying that it had been coded properly.

Some programmers give themselves a false sense of security by devising several sets of data that all test the same features of their program. To avoid this you should try to justify the use of each separate set of data. In addition it is a good idea to slip in one or two trivial cases. In the above program, for example, you could try calculating the distance from a place to itself. You might find it useful, in certain cases, to devise test data before the program (or even the algorithm) has been written. This can be helpful in ensuring that all possible alternatives are considered, and also facilitates the detection of snags at an early stage.

Quick quiz 1.4   (Solution on p. 23)

Look at problem C3 at the end of the chapter (p. 25) and, without constructing an algorithm, decide what data you would use to test the program.

Summary

In this chapter the writing of simple programs to perform arithmetic calculations has been considered. The basic structure of a Pascal program has been described essentially as consisting of heading, declarations and statements. Next the construction of programs was discussed, including the sketching out of the initial algorithms and the detailed rules and suggested layout of the code itself. Lastly, guidelines for program debugging and testing were given.

Now it is your turn to try constructing and running some programs. Those described in the problems at the end of this chapter are graded A, B and C, in increasing order of difficulty. If you are new to programming, you should attempt two or three A-grade problems first, and then a couple from section B. If you feel sufficiently confident you might then try one or two C-grade problems, although these are rather trickier and are aimed more at experienced programmers. If you are a computer multi-linguist, then you should still attempt one or two questions from each of sections A and B before trying any questions in the last section.

The section C questions are deliberately vaguely worded to simulate real-world problem solving. Obviously you don't have a customer to cross-question in order to resolve ambiguities or to tie down details, so you have to make your own assumptions and devise restrictions in order to produce a viable program. As in all programs, assumptions and restrictions should be clearly indicated in the documentation. Another difficulty in the section C problems is that formulae are not given. This does not mean that you have to derive them from first principles. It is not part of the programmer's task to re-invent the wheel. If you do not know a formula, look it up in a book or ask someone who might know.

Whatever your level of programming experience, remember that clarity and simplicity are most important. Saving a few microseconds of execution time by using a programming trick is simply not worth it if someone else has to spend several minutes, or hours, trying to work out what you have done. Always start your program with a comment describing its purpose, requirements and limitations in general terms. Other comments should be placed within the program to explain what identifiers stand for, if necessary, and also the purpose of different sections of code if this is not obvious. Lastly, even in these introductory exercises, get into the habit of producing tidy programs and output.

Solutions to quick quizzes

Quick quiz 1.1 (p. 12)

1 (i) The program would run but would produce meaningless results. It is the old *GIGO* principle (Garbage In, Garbage Out). If you feed rubbish into the computer you are liable to get rubbish out. Later we will see how the computer may be made to check for invalid input but for the moment we assume that all data provided is correct.
(ii) In this case the computer *can* check for us that something is wrong. When the read statement is executed and the computer finds something other than numbers in the data it will give a run-time error. That is, it will stop executing during the running of the program because it has found something wrong. Errors and their detection are discussed at greater length in Section 1.3.

2 The identifier rate could have been made a variable and in this case its value would need to be read in every time the program was run. However, if rate is going to stay the same for many runs of the program it is more convenient to make it a constant.

3 Here, you are being asked to make an intelligent guess as to what a sensible system should do (which is partly a matter of opinion). If you guessed that the program will fail during running or, at least, indicate in some way in the output that something has gone wrong then award yourself a point. Another possibility is that the computer will just allocate as much space as the number requires and carry on as if nothing has happened. If you guessed this then you win the prize since this is what Pascal systems are supposed to do. We could tell you what happens if a real is output with less space than is necessary but the rules are so complicated that it is better to avoid the situation altogether and make sure you allocate enough room. Incidentally, if you don't include a field width component at all for the output of numerically valued items then the computer will just allocate a default amount of space which will vary from system to system.

4 Col 1
|
age □ = □ □27 □ □ □ weight □ = □ □ □ 71.374 □ kilos

Quick quiz 1.2 (p. 18)

1 (i) 3.25   (ii) 4.25   (iii) 0.3
(iv) 0.13 (Remember—operations of equal precedence are performed from left to right and so a is divided by b giving 0.3 and this is then divided by 2.5.)
  (v) 3 (When **div** is used only the whole number part of the result is retained.)
 (vi) 0
(vii) 3.5 ('/' always produces a result of type real)
(viii) 1.5
 (ix) 1
  (x) 2
 (xi) − 2

2 (i) ln (a + b)/(c + d)

(ii) 0.5 * a * b * sin (c) (The value that a function operates on, its 'argument', must be enclosed by parentheses.)

(iii) sqr (cos (exp (x)))

(iv) 4 * pi * r * r * r/3 (Note that there is no function or operator in Pascal for raising a number to a given power and also that pi would probably be defined as a constant at the beginning of the program.)

Quick quiz 1.3 (p. 20)

(i) Only a variable can appear to the left of an assignment operator (you cannot assign a value to an expression). This would be detected during compilation.

(ii) **mod** and **div** can only be performed between integer values but j/k will always give a real value regardless of whether j and k are integer or real. Again, this can be detected during compilation.

(iii) There is nothing syntactically wrong with this statement but, when it is executed, sqr (x) + 1 will always be positive. So whatever the value of x, the computer will be asked to find the square root of a negative number. A run-time error will therefore occur.

(iv) A piece of text cannot be broken up in this way between lines. The desired effect could be obtained by writing

> writeln ('interest rate = ', rate :3, 'per cent',
>   'per year')

The error would be detected during compilation.

Quick quiz 1.4 (p. 21)

You should include one or two typical pieces of data, e.g.

> speed = 98.4 kph   angle = 20.2 degrees

Try out unusual cases, e.g.

> speed = 20 kph   angle = 90 degrees
> speed = 159 kph   angle = 0 degrees
> speed = 10 kph   angle = 135 degrees

and the trivial case with velocity = 0.

Don't forget to include real numbers in your data.

Exercises

A1 Write a program to input a temperature in degrees Fahrenheit and convert it to degrees Centigrade.

A2 The total resistance R of three resistors r_1, r_2, r_3 connected in parallel is given by the formula

$$\frac{1}{R} = \frac{1}{r_1} + \frac{1}{r_2} + \frac{1}{r_3}$$

Write a program to calculate the total resistance given the component resistances.

A3 I want to spread fertiliser on my lawn at the recommended rate of 50 grams per square metre. Given that the fertiliser costs $9.50 per kilogram write a program to input the length and width of the lawn in metres (to the nearest metre) and which calculates

  (i)   the area of the lawn (to the nearest square metre)
 (ii)   the amount of fertiliser I will need
(iii)   the total cost of the fertiliser

B1   The total inventory cost C in a large store is given by

$$C = \frac{c_s q}{2} + \frac{c_d r}{q}$$

where c_s is the unit storage cost per unit time, c_d is the cost per delivery, q is the number of items in each delivery (the lot-size), and r is the rate at which the item is sold (the demand rate).

The optimal lot-size q_o (i.e. the lot-size that minimises the total cost) is given by

$$q_o = \sqrt{\frac{2 c_d r}{c_s}}$$

Assuming that the unit storage cost per week and the delivery cost are constant, write a program to read in the current lot-size and demand rate and to calculate

(a)   the current inventory cost,
(b)   the optimal inventory cost,
(c)   the saving if the optimal lot-size is used.

B2   The annual rate of interest $r\%$ charged on a hire purchase debt can be calculated using the formula

$$r = \frac{200 \, mI}{B(n + 1) - I(n - 1)}$$

where
   n is the number of payments (excluding the down payment)
   m is the number of payments per year
   R is the amount paid in each instalment
   B is the unpaid balance (= cash price − down payment)
   I is the total interest paid (= $Rn - B$)

Write a program to calculate the annual rate of interest charged (to the nearest per cent) when the data consists of

  (i)   the number of payments to be made
 (ii)   the amount paid in each instalment (a real value)
(iii)   the cash price (a real value)
(iv)   the down payment (a real value)

Assume that the instalments are paid monthly.

B3   Given three points (x_1, y_1), (x_2, y_2), (x_3, y_3) write a program to calculate the area of a triangle with these points as vertices using the formula

$$\text{area} = \sqrt{s(s - a) \, (s - b)(s - c)}$$

where a, b, c are the lengths of the sides of the triangle and s is the semi-perimeter given by

$$s = \frac{1}{2}(a + b + c)$$

An alternative method of finding the area is to use the formula

$$\text{area} = \frac{1}{2} \left| (x_1 y_2 - x_2 y_1) + (x_2 y_3 - x_3 y_2) + (x_3 y_1 - x_1 y_3) \right|$$

Evaluate this as a cross-check on your answer.

C1   Write a program to input an amount, a period of time and a rate of interest and which computes the interest on the amount compounded quarterly.

C2   Write a program to calculate the distance between two given points on the earth's surface.

C3   Write a program to calculate the distance that a projectile will travel when fired at velocity V at an elevation of α degrees.

2
Comparisons and characters

Introduction

We need to be able to compare quantities since, as we shall see in later chapters, it is sometimes necessary to alter the sequence in which statements are executed, based on the results of comparisons. In addition, a high proportion of computer applications involve the handling of textual information. In this chapter, facilities are introduced to deal with both these situations.

2.1 Arithmetic comparisons

The arithmetic and logic unit* of the computer can be used to compare two quantities. This feature of the computer may be exploited in Pascal by setting up a condition that the computer then tests. The normal arithmetic conditions and their Pascal representations are given in Table 2.1.

Table 2.1

Condition	Algebraic representation	Pascal representation
i is equal to j	$i = j$	$i = j$
i is greater than j	$i > j$	$i > j$
i is greater than or equal to j	$i \geqslant j$	$i > = j$
i is less than j	$i < j$	$i < j$
i is less than or equal to j	$i \leqslant j$	$i < = j$
i is not equal to j	$i \neq j$	$i < > j$

The symbols that are used in Pascal to compare values are called **relational operators**; they do not quite correspond to the conventional mathematical symbols, since $\leqslant$, $\geqslant$ and $\neq$ are often not available in computer character sets. Depending on the relative values of i and j, the corresponding Pascal condition may be evaluated to give a value of true or false. The words true and false are required identifiers used in Pascal to represent so-called **truth values**. For example,

$4 = 4$ has the value true
$4 > 5$ has the value false
$7 > = 7$ has the value true
$-4 < 6$ has the value true
$7 < = 6$ has the value false
$5 < > 5$ has the value false

In practice, such comparisons would not be made in a program, since the results are obvious. This would not be so if the condition contained one or more variables. Thus, the result of the comparison

$\qquad$ x > 0

will depend upon the value of x. This value could have been read in as data, and might vary from run to run. Consequently, the value of the condition might be true on some runs (when x is positive) and **false** on others.

The conditions to be checked are often more complicated than this. For example, we might want to test whether a value lies between 0 and 10. In mathematical terms, this might be stated as $0 < x < 10$, but Pascal does not allow comparisons of this form. It must be split up into two relations: $0 < x$ and $x < 10$. In order to test both these relations in one expression, they may be linked by the word **and**, as shown below:

$\qquad$ (0 < x) **and** (x < 10)

The condition will only be true if x is between 0 and 10 when it is evaluated. To represent the opposite relationship (i.e. $0 \geqslant x$ or $x \geqslant 10$) the following expression could be used:

$\qquad$ (0 >= x) **or** (x >= 10)

There is no limit to the complexity of relationships that can be built up using this type of structure. So, for example,

$\qquad$ ((0 < x) **and** (x < 10)) **or** ((15 < x) **and** (x < 20))

is true when x has a value between 0 and 10 or between 15 and 20.

The use of operations involving **and** and **or** is by no means exclusive to Pascal. Logical operators were first proposed in the 19th century by George Boole and, for that reason, are often called Boolean operators. A third logical operator available in Pascal is **not**, which has the effect of changing the truth value of an expression. For example,

$\qquad$ **not** (x > 0)

is false if x is positive and true otherwise. It is equivalent to, and more conveniently written as,

$\qquad$ x <= 0

Constructions that give the values true or false are called *Boolean expressions*, and are similar to arithmetic expressions in two ways. Firstly, they may be evaluated to give a result; in this case the result is a Boolean value, true or false. Secondly, the order of evaluation in both types of expression is determined by the precedence of the operators used. Thus, in arithmetic expressions multiplication is performed before addition; in Boolean expressions **and** operations are carried out before **or** operations. In fact, since Boolean expressions may contain arithmetic expressions (e.g. $x * x > 20$), all types of operators need to have their relative precedences defined. For convenience, the operators are grouped together into four classes, as shown in Table 2.2 (higher numbers denote higher precedence).

Table 2.2

Class	Operators	Precedence
Negation	**not**	3
Multiplication	*, , **div**, **mod**, **and**	2
Addition	+ , -, **or**	1
Relation	= , < >, <, < = , > = , >	0

As in arithmetic expressions, parentheses may be used to override the normal precedence rules. In fact, in some cases, leaving out parentheses can invalidate an expression. If we had written

        0 >= x **or** x >= 10

then, since **or** has a higher precedence than the relational operators, the first operation that the computer would attempt to perform would be

        x **or** x

But Boolean operators can only act upon expressions that yield a value true or false, and so an error would be signalled. Incidentally, a common type of error is to try to use an expression such as

        x = 4 **or** 6

to represent the condition that is to be true when x has the value 4 or 6. Whichever operation is performed first, the expression does not make sense. The correct form is

        (x = 4) **or** (x = 6)

If you have not met Boolean algebra before, you may take a while to become familiar with the manipulation of **and**s, **or**s and **not**s. For the most part, however, Boolean expressions used in programs tend to be fairly simple, and self-explanatory.

Quick quiz 2.1   (Solutions on p. 38)

1   Given i = 4 and j = 4, calculate the values of:
(a)   i > j   (b)   **not** (j > i)   (c)   (i <> j) **or** (j > 0)

2   Express the following relationships, using Pascal:
(a)   a > b > c   (b)   i = j = k

3   Write a Boolean expression that is true if any two, or all three, of i, j and k are equal.

2.2   Boolean variables and functions

In the same way that an arithmetic expression can be evaluated and its value assigned to a variable, a Boolean expression can be evaluated and the result assigned to a Boolean variable. In this case, the variable will receive not a numerical value but one of the values true or false. So we may write

        toohot := temperature > 18

and

        toocold := temperature < 16

The values assigned to toohot and toocold for different values of temperature may be summarised in a table:

temperature	toohot	toocold
Below 16	false	true
Between 16 and 18 (inclusive)	false	false
Above 18	true	false

If, for example, the value of temperature was 17, then toohot and toocold would both be given the value false

The declaration of Boolean variables is straightforward. To declare toohot and toocold we would write

var toohot, toocold : boolean

Variables of type boolean may be manipulated in much the same way as arithmetic variables (one exception is that values of Boolean variables may not be input, as such). Once a value has been given to a Boolean variable, the variable may be used in a Boolean expression. If justright has been declared as of type boolean then, once toohot and toocold had been given values, we could write

justright := **not** toohot **and not** toocold

Notice that no parentheses are needed in this expression, since **not** has higher precedence than **and**.

The following are two further examples of contexts in which Boolean variables may be used:

numberfound := true

writeln (valid)

Execution of the second of these statements would cause either the word true or the word false to appear in the output, depending on the value of the Boolean variable valid.

Although Boolean variables are handled in a comparable way to arithmetic variables, care must be taken when mixing the two types of values. Thus.

toohot + 1

would be a meaningless expression, as would the application of any arithmetic operation to a Boolean variable.

All the Boolean expressions we need can be built up using **and, or** and **not**. Occasionally it is useful to be able to use two other Boolean operations: equivalence (denoted by ' = '), and implication (denoted by ' < = '). However, if you are not familiar with their usage in logic, it is best to ignore these operations. The fact that equivalence is represented by the same symbol as equality has an undesirable side effect: it permits the use of such statements as

nonnegative := (positive = true) **or** (zero = true)

and

outofrange := inrange = false

instead of the simpler

nonnegative := positive **or** zero

and

outofrange := **not** inrange

Remember that if you are using a Boolean variable in an expression, you do not need to compare it with true or false.

There are three standard functions in Pascal that give a Boolean result. The first is the function odd that operates upon an integer value and gives the result true if it is an odd number and false if it is even or zero. The other two provide a means of checking the state of the input. The function eoln (short for 'end of line') takes the value **true** if the last character on the current data line has just been read, and is false otherwise. The function eof ('end of file') is automatically set to true if the last character on the final line has been read, and is otherwise false. When used with the standard input device they may be written eoln (input) and eof (input) or may be abbreviated to eoln and eof.

Quick quiz 2.2   (Solutions on p. 38)

1 Given two Boolean variables dry and sunny, where dry is true and sunny is false, evaluate: (a) dry **and** sunny   (b)   dry **or** sunny   (c) **not** (dry **or** sunny)   (d) **not** dry **and not** sunny.

2 Given two Boolean variables tooearly and toolate, write an assignment statement for the Boolean variable ontime.

3 Simplify the following Pascal Boolean expressions: (a) found = false (b) **not** ((happy = true) **or** (sad = true)).

2.3 Two programs using Boolean variables

Program 2.1 checks whether it is meal-time or not. The time input is in hours and an indicator in the data is either 0 or 1 depending upon whether it is a.m. or p.m. For instance, if the data was 9   1 that would mean it was nine o'clock in the evening. Note that although it might be possible to make the program simpler by inputting a Boolean value (perhaps taking the value true or false depending upon whether or not it is before midday) standard Pascal does not allow the input of Boolean values from data.

If we assume 0 and 1 are the only two values indicator will take, it would have been equally valid to give afternoon a value using the assignment

        afternoon := **not** morning

since when morning is true afternoon will be false and vice versa.

There is what may appear to be an error in the writeln statement that prints out the time. There are two quote characters instead of one within 'o'clock'. If you think about it there is always going to be a problem with representing a quote symbol inside a quoted piece of text, since the computer may expect that the quote is not something to be written out but that it indicates the end of the text. In Pascal, if you actually want to output a single quote character you must type *two* adjacent quotes. The computer assumes, if it finds two adjacent single quotes, that this is what you want to do.

The rules for field width specification of Booleans are similar to those for integers except that if the space allocated for printing is insufficient then the word is truncated to that number of places. For instance if the writeln statement

        writeln (bankrupt :4)

was executed when bankrupt had the value true then the output would be

        true

whereas if it had the value false then the output would be

        fals

This assumes that the values are output in lower case. In some systems they might be upper case. Specimen output from Program 2.1 is given opposite

Program Mealtime (input, output);

```
{********************************************************************
 *                                                                  *
 * Program 2.1                                                      *
 * A time is read in and a check is made to see whether the time is  *
 * 8 a.m. or 9 a.m. (breakfast time), 12 a.m. or 1 p.m. (lunch time), *
 * 5 p.m. or 6 p.m. (tea time). The time read in consists of an hour *
 * in the range 1 to 12 and an indicator which is either 0 or 1 depending *
 * upon whether it is a.m. or p.m.                                  *
 *                                                                  *
 ********************************************************************}

var
        time, indicator : integer;

        morning, afternoon,
        breakfast, lunch, tea : boolean;

begin

    read ( time, indicator );

    morning   := ( indicator = 0 );
    afternoon := ( indicator = 1 );

    breakfast := ( ( time = 8 ) or ( time = 9 ) ) and morning;
    lunch     :=     ( ( time = 12 ) and morning )
                 or ( ( time = 1 )  and afternoon );
    tea       := ( ( time = 5 ) or ( time = 6 ) ) and afternoon;

    writeln ( 'Program 2.1  Is it meal time?' );
    writeln ( '=============================' );
    writeln;

    writeln ( 'time       = ', time :5, ' o'' clock' );
    writeln ( 'indicator  = ', indicator :5, '  ( 0 for a.m., 1 for p.m. )' );
    writeln;
    writeln ( 'breakfast?  ', breakfast :6 );
    writeln ( 'lunch?      ', lunch :6 );
    writeln ( 'tea?        ', tea :6 )

end.
```

Program 2.1

```
    Program 2.1  Is it meal time?
    =============================

    time       =    12 o' clock
    indicator  =     0  ( 0 for a.m., 1 for p.m. )

    breakfast?    FALSE
    lunch?        TRUE
    tea?          FALSE
```

Output from Program 2.1

Program Pythagoras (input, output);

```
{*****************************************************************************
 *                                                                          *
 * Program 2.2                                                              *
 * Pythagoras' theorem is used to determine whether three numbers could     *
 * form the sides of a right-angled triangle. The numbers (which are of type *
 * real) are assumed to be input in descending order of magnitude.          *
 *                                                                          *
 *****************************************************************************}

const
      tolerance = 1e-3;

var
      difference,   { the difference between the square of the first side
                      and the sum of the squares of the other two sides   }
      side1, side2, side3 : real;

      allpositive, rightangled : boolean;

begin

   read ( side1, side2, side3 );

   allpositive := ( side1 > 0 ) and ( side2 > 0 ) and ( side3 > 0 );
   difference  := abs ( sqr ( side1 ) - ( sqr (side2 ) + sqr ( side3 ) ) );
   rightangled := allpositive and ( difference < tolerance );

   writeln ( 'Program 2.2  Checking for a right-angled triangle' );
   writeln ( '==================================================' );
   writeln;

   writeln ( 'length of side 1 ', si.ªːJ :8:4 );
   writeln ( 'length of side 2 ', side2 :8:4 );
   writeln ( 'length of side 3 ', side3 :8:4 );
   writeln;
   writeln ( 'right-angled triangle?', rightangled :6 )

end.
```

Program 2.2

Program 2.2 determines whether three numbers could form the sides of a right-angled triangle. First, a check is made to make sure all the numbers are positive (we don't allow triangles with negative sides) and then Pythagoras' theorem is used to check whether the square of the longest side is equal to the sum of the squares of the other two sides. Thus 5   4   3 is a right-angled triangle since $5 \times 5 - (4 \times 4 + 3 \times 3) = 0$ but 3   2   1 is not since $3 \times 3 - (2 \times 2 + 1 \times 1) \neq 0$.

Unfortunately things aren't that simple if the numbers aren't integers. As mentioned in Chapter 1 numbers of type real are not necessarily stored exactly inside the computer and so even a simple sum like

$$2.0 - 1.0 - 1.0$$

won't always give the expected answer. Depending upon the computer in use the error could be 0.000 1 or 0.000 000 01. All that can be guaranteed is that the answer will be a 'very small' positive or negative value. Recall that the function abs always gives the magnitude of a result whether it is negative or positive and so

   abs (2.0 − 1.0 − 1.0)

will either give zero or a very small *positive* value.

It follows from the above argument that difference in Program 2.2 may not be quite zero but may be a small positive value and so, to ensure that right-angled triangles are not classified incorrectly because of small errors, we express this as

   rightangled := difference < tolerance

where tolerance might have a value of 0.0001.

The tolerance (effectively the degree of accuracy that is required) is defined as a constant at the beginning of the program. Here it is written in floating point* form.

Quick quiz 2.3   (Solutions on p. 39)

1   Assuming that x and y are real variables, and unequal is of type boolean, explain what is wrong with the following statement and suggest a better version:

   unequal := (x <> y)

2   Construct a writeln statement to output *two* quotation marks.

2.4 Characters

The character-processing facilities of the computer enable it to tackle such problems as

   compiling programs;
   processing files of names and addresses;
   verifying authorship of a book;
   translating from one natural language to another;
   formatting text in a newspaper.

It is not surprising, then, that most modern computer languages have facilities for explicitly handling characters. In Pascal, char is the fourth, and last, pre-defined data type (sometimes called *scalar* types) available in the language. As we shall see in a later chapter, other simple data types may be defined by the user, but real, integer, boolean and char are the only ones that are pre-defined. The values that are included in type char will vary from one computer to another. The particular characters available will depend upon the computer's character code. The two most commonly available codes are known as ASCII (pronounced 'askee': American Standard Code for Information Interchange) and EBCDIC (pronounced 'ebsadik': Extended Binary Coded Decimal Interchange Code). Their character sets are given in Appendix D.

The minimum working set of characters consists of the letters A to Z (or a to z), the digits 0 to 9, and the space character. In practice, many more are usually available, including all the characters that may be used to construct statements of the language: + , − , *, ;, ., etc.

The values we have met so far have all been numbers or truth values. A problem arises when we wish to denote character values, since programs are themselves built up from characters. If we have a variable called x, for instance, how can this be distinguished from the *character* x? Another example of a character is the *digit* 8. How is this to be distinguished from the *number* 8? To resolve possible ambiguities, character values referred to in programs are enclosed within quotation marks. Thus, 'x' represents a character value and x is an identifier; '8' represents a character value and 8 is a number.

Variables which take characters as values have to be declared as such:

var
```
     ch1, ch2 : char
```

One way in which character variables may be given values is by reading them in:

```
     read ( ch1 )
```

Input statements, when applied to variables of type char, do not operate in quite the same way as when they are applied to real and integer variables. When the read is executed, the character from the next position in the data becomes the new value of the corresponding character variable named in the read statement. Suppose the first part of the data consisted of the characters shown below.

    April showers

with the 'A' in column 1. The execution of the statement

```
     read ( ch1, ch2, ch3 )
```

would cause ch1, ch2 and ch3 to be given the values 'A', 'p' and 'r' respectively. Note that the characters in the data do not have to be enclosed in quotes—this is only necessary for character values in the program text itself. A further read statement

```
     read ( ch4 )
```

would assign the value 'i' to ch4.

Since a space is a valid character value, blanks are not ignored when they occur in the data, although they are when real or integer values are read in. Forgetting this distinction is a common oversight, and a frequent cause of run-time errors.

Suppose we have a program for updating a bank balance. We may wish to read in the account number (an integer), an indication of whether the transaction is a deposit or a withdrawal (denoted by 'd' or 'w' respectively) and the amount involved (an integer). The read statement could be

```
     read ( accountnumber, transtype, amount )
```

and the user might type in the data

    257926□ □w□500

At first sight it might appear that accountnumber, transtype and amount will be given the values 257926, 'w' and 500 respectively. It is clear on closer inspection that this is not so. Once the 257926 has been read in the next character is a blank, and this will be read in as the value of transtype. Consequently, when an attempt is made to read in the value of amount, the next non-blank character encountered is the 'w'. An attempt to read in this character as a number will normally produce a run-time error message.

One method of rectifying this would be to change the data so that the 'w' is in the position immediately following the '6'. Alternatively, a dummy character variable (blank, for example) could be used, effectively, to skip over the blanks. To read in data from the above data line, for instance, (assuming there are two spaces between the account number and the letter) we could write

```
     read ( accountnumber, blank, blank, transtype, amount )
```

Like the other simple variables, a character variable may be given a value by using an assignment statement. In the example given below, the variable ch is assigned the value of the space character (denoted by a space in quotes).

```
     ch := ' '
```

Program 2.3 involves reading in a character and comparing it with other character values.

```
Program Voweldetermination ( input,output );

{**************************************************
 *                                                *
 * Program 2.3                                     *
 * Determines whether input character is a vowel  *
 * (assuming character is lower case).             *
 *                                                *
 **************************************************}

var
      character : char;

      vowel     : boolean;

begin

    read ( character );

    vowel := ( character='a' ) or ( character='e' ) or ( character='i' )
                              or ( character='o' ) or ( character='u' );

    writeln ( 'Program 2.3  Vowel determination' );
    writeln ( '=================================' );
    writeln;

    writeln ( 'input character    =    ', character );
    writeln ( 'character is vowel ? ', vowel :7 )

end.
```

Program 2.3

In many applications of computing a conventional ordering of characters is useful. In particular, alphabetical ordering makes many computer tasks simpler as, of course, it does many clerical jobs. For example, it is easier to find someone's name in a list if the names are in alphabetical order. All character codes have an implicit ordering depending upon their representation inside the computer. This is called a *collating sequence*. Unfortunately, like the character sets themselves, the collating sequences vary between computer systems. The only conditions that are satisfied by all widely-used character sets are:

$$\text{'A'} < \text{'B'} < \text{'C'} < \ldots < \text{'Y'} < \text{'Z'}$$
$$\text{'a'} < \text{'b'} < \text{'c'} < \ldots < \text{'y'} < \text{'z'}$$

and

$$\text{'0'} < \text{'1'} < \text{'2'} < \ldots < \text{'8'} < \text{'9'}$$

These conditions are assumed in all Pascal implementations which conform to Jensen and Wirth's original definition of the language, and may be exploited in such statements as

```
    inorder := ( alpha1 < alpha2 )
```

and

```
    numeric := ( character >= '0' ) and ( character <= '9' )
```

In Program 2.4 the implicit ordering of digit characters is used to determine whether or not two input characters represent a number.

Program Numbercheck (input, output);

```
{******************************************************************
 *                                                                *
 * Program 2.4                                                    *
 * Reads in two characters and checks whether they represent a number. *
 *                                                                *
 ******************************************************************}

var
        firstdigit,                 { true if first character is a digit  }
        seconddigit,                { true if second character is a digit }

        validnumber : boolean;

        ch1, ch2 : char;           { first and second characters         }


begin

    read ( ch1,ch2 );

    firstdigit  := ( ch1>='0' ) and ( ch1<='9' );
    seconddigit := ( ch2>='0' ) and ( ch2<='9' );
    validnumber := (  ( ch1=' ' ) and seconddigit )
               or ( firstdigit and ( ch2=' ' ) )
               or ( firstdigit and seconddigit );

    writeln ( 'Program 2.4  Number check' );
    writeln ( '=========================' );
    writeln;

    writeln ( 'input characters =   ', ch1, ch2 );
    writeln ( 'valid number?        ', validnumber )

end.
```

Program 2.4

Occasionally it is more convenient to work with numbers associated with characters rather than with the characters themselves. In Pascal, each character is assumed to have a unique integer associated with it. This is its *ordinal value*. The ordinal value of a character may be found by applying the function ord to it. In addition to being different for each character, these ordinal values reflect the relative positions of the corresponding characters in the collating sequence. That is, ord(ch1) < ord(ch2) if and only if ch1 < ch2. In particular,

$$ord('a') < ord ('b') < \ldots < ord('z')$$

and

$$ord('0') < ord ('1') < \ldots < ord('8') < ord('9')$$

The obvious way of associating numbers with characters would be to give the first character in the set the value 1, the second the value 2, and so on. In most systems, however, the numbers chosen are dependent on their internal representations. Appendix D gives the ordinal values for ASCII and EBCDIC codes.

```
Program Charactercode ( input,output );

{*****************************************************************
 *                                                               *
 * Program 2.5                                                   *
 * A character is read in and its corresponding character code  *
 * is determined.                                               *
 *                                                               *
 *****************************************************************}

var
      character : char;

      code      : integer;

begin

   read ( character );

   code := ord ( character );

   writeln ( 'Program 2.5  Character code determination' );
   writeln ( '=========================================' );
   writeln;

   writeln ( 'character =   ', character );
   writeln ( 'code      =', code :4 )

end.
```

Program 2.5

In Program 2.5 the ordinal value of an input character is calculated. From the output (below), can you decide which character code is being used?

```
Program 2.5  Character code determination
=========================================

character =   a
code      =  97
```

Output from Program 2.5

A further condition imposed on character sets in Pascal is that the ordinal values of the digits '0' to '9' should be consecutive numbers. A consequence of this is that, for example,

$$\text{ord('5')} - \text{ord('0')} = 5$$

This property is useful when converting a sequence of digit characters into a number. But be careful: ord('0') is not the same as ord(0). The ordinal value of any integer is the integer itself and so if you miss out the quotes you won't get a syntax error, just the wrong answer.

To obtain the character corresponding to a given ordinal number (if it exists), an inverse function, chr, is available. For example, in the above system chr (97) would have the value 'a'.

There are two more functions that may be applied to characters; these are pred and succ. When applied to a particular character, they give the immediately preceding character and the immediately succeeding character, respectively, in the collating sequence. For example, succ('5') will be '6' and pred('8') will be '7'. For characters other than digits, the values produced by these functions will be implementation dependent.

Quick quiz 2.4   (Solutions on p. 39)

1   Why might the assignment of the Boolean variable letter, given by

letter : = (character > = 'a') and (character < = 'z')

fail to produce the expected result?

2   The first two positions in a data line contain a two-digit number. Write a piece of code to read the two digits as characters and to calculate the corresponding numerical value, assigning the result to an integer variable called number.

Summary

Two important concepts have been introduced in this chapter—Boolean values and character processing. Boolean expressions will appear again and again in subsequent chapters. They are essential to the writing of most programs, both technical and commercial. Their proper use makes programs easier to understand and debug. Character processing is becoming increasingly important as the computer is used for more and more non-numerical applications.

Solutions to quick quizzes

Quick quiz 2.1   (p. 28)

1   (a)   false (i is *not* greater than j)
   (b)   true (this is equivalent to j < = i)
   (c)   true (although i < > j is false, j > 0 is true, and this makes the whole expression true)

2   (a)   (a > b) and (b > c)   (b)   (i = j) and (j = k)

3   (i = j) or (j = k) or (i = k)

Quick quiz 2.2   (p. 30)

1   (a)   false (dry and sunny are not *both* true.)
   (b)   true (dry is true.)
   (c)   false (Opposite of (b) : 'neither dry nor sunny'.)
   (d)   false (Same as (c). Note this useful equivalence.)

2   ontime : = not tooearly and not toolate
   Alternatively, ontime : = not (tooearly or toolate)

3   (a)   not found   (b)   not (happy or sad)

Quick quiz 2.3 **(p. 33)**

1 If x and y have values computed at an earlier stage, then rounding errors in the computer may mean that, even if x and y are supposed to be equal in value, x < > y will be computed as true. Again, to avoid this, a tolerance should be decided upon, and the expression modified as necessary. For example:

```
unequal := ( abs ( x - y ) > epsilon )
```

unequal will only be set to true if the difference between x and y is greater than epsilon.

2 writeln (""""") Six quotes are needed—two for each quote character to be output and two for the quotes surrounding the text.

Quick quiz 2.4 **(p. 38)**

1 The expression on the right of the assignment will give the value true if character denotes a letter since the ordinal values of all letters lie in the range ord ('a') to ord ('z'). Some codes, however, contain other characters that have ordinal values in this range. Since, in the case of EBCDIC, these are non-printing characters and other commonly-used codes do satisfy the relationship, you will normally be safe in making this assumption. As with all assumptions you should include a comment at an appropriate point in your program to warn potential users.

2
```
read ( digitl, digit2 );

tens   := ord ( digitl ) - ord ( '0' );
units  := ord ( digit2 ) - ord ( '0' );
number := 10 * tens + units
```

Exercises

A1 Write a program to read in three integers a, b, c where $a > b > c$, and to determine whether they could represent the lengths of the sides of: (a) a triangle; (b) an isosceles triangle (a triangle with two sides equal).

A2 Write a program to read in a number representing a year and calculate whether: (i) it is a century year; (ii) it is a leap year. [Note: century years are only leap years if they are divisible by 400.]

A3 A CVC word, as used in recall tests, consists of a consonant, vowel and consonant. Write a program to read in three letters and determine if they form a CVC word.

B1 In the game of Scissors, Paper, Stone each of the two players chooses one of scissors (X), paper (P) or stone (O). If one chooses scissors and the other chooses paper then the first wins (scissors cut paper). If one chooses scissors and the other chooses stone then the second wins (stone blunts scissors). If one chooses paper and the other chooses stone then the first wins (paper wraps stone). If they both choose the same object then the result is a tie. Write a program that reads in two characters (X, O or P) representing the choice of the players and computes the result.

B2 In a certain examination scheme, four papers are set. These are paper 1 and paper 2 in each of Programming and Systems Analysis. In order to obtain a certificate a candidate must pass both paper 1 examinations and at least one paper 2. If he passes all four papers he obtains a merit award. If he passes both paper 1 examinations but does not pass either paper 2 he is allowed a resit. In all other cases he is given a fail grade.

The results obtained by each candidate are set out in the first four positions in the data, using the abbreviations:

P—pass in a paper;
F—fail in a paper;
N—paper not taken.

Write a program to input the results obtained by a student and classify his grade as one of merit, certificate, resit or fail.

B3   In the game of Brag, each player is dealt three cards and the hand is classified as follows:

pair—two cards of the same rank (e.g. 5H   7C   7S);
prial—three cards of the same rank (e.g. KH   KD   KS);
flush—three cards of the same suit (e.g. 2H   5H   9H);
run—three cards in rank sequence (e.g. 5H   6S   7C);
running flush—a run with all cards of the same suit (e.g 9S   TS   JS);
bust—none of these.

Write a program to classify an input hand, assuming that the cards are in ascending order of rank (ace counting low). The input hand should be represented by three pairs of characters, each pair separated by a space. The first character in each pair represents the rank (1 2 3 4 5 6 7 8 9 T J Q K) and the second one represents the suit (H C D S). For instance, 1H   5D   TC would represent a hand containing the ace of hearts, five of diamonds and ten of clubs and would be classified as bust.

C1   Write a program to read in two dates and determine whether they are in chronological order.

C2   Write a program to read in three coordinates of the vertices of a triangle and the coordinates of a point and determine whether the point lies inside, on, or outside the triangle.

C3   Write a program that reads in two words, each of up to four letters, and determines whether they are in dictionary order.

3

Repetition

Introduction

One of the facilities of the computer that has not been exploited in any of the previous examples is its speed. For most of the problems considered, results could just as easily have been worked out by hand. It is true that once a program has been written it can be run over and over again for different data, but in many practical applications computations have to be performed thousands or even millions of times. It is just not feasible to run a program repeatedly in order to do this. Fortunately, facilities exist in every modern programming language for indicating to the computer that sections of code are to be repeated as many times as required within a single run. In this chapter, three statements for performing repetition are considered. Different circumstances dictate which one is the most appropriate to use.

3.1 The *repeat* statement

There are many situations in which we wish to perform a set of computations until a condition is satisfied. For example:

Evaluate a formula for different sets of data until there is no data left.
Look through a file of information, examining each record, until a given name is found.
Compare and exchange pairs of numbers in a list until all the numbers are in ascending order.
Repeatedly improve a solution until the error is sufficiently small.

At the algorithmic level this type of operation may be described fairly simply. For example, one step in an algorithm might be:

Read in numbers until a negative value is found

Although this is a single step, it may involve the execution of a read statement many times before the next instruction is obeyed. We may not know (and may not need to know) how many times the read statement has been executed. What *is* important is that execution of the statement will terminate when a negative value has been read in.

The methods of representing this *cycling* or *looping* activity vary from language to language. The simplest way of representing it in Pascal is by use of the **repeat** statement. A construction for reading in numbers until a negative one is found could be coded as follows:

```
repeat
   read ( number )
until number < 0
```

During execution of this statement the read instruction would be executed repeatedly until the condition

    number < 0

became true. The computer would go through the sequence:

    read, compare, read, compare, . . .

Suppose that the following numbers are contained in the corresponding data:

        4   2   0   5   − 6   2   7   1   3

During execution of the **repeat** statement, number will take each of the values in turn (each value replacing the previous one) until it has the value − 6. Since the relation

    number < 0

will now be true, the execution of this statement will be terminated.

The question arises, 'what sort of object is number?'. It isn't a constant because it isn't given a value in the heading, and it isn't like any of the variables met so far because each of those was just given a single value at run-time. In fact, although all previous variables have each had one value their values *could* have been changed during the running of the program. What you actually get when you declare a variable is a location inside the computer with the name you have given it. Although you cannot change the name of this location you can change the value stored in it at any time (as long as it is a value of the appropriate type). Thus number, provided it is declared as a variable of type integer, can be assigned a new integer value at any stage or have a new integer value read in from the data. At any one time, of course, it will still only have one value.

The sequence of values that number takes in the above example may be recorded in a *trace table*, as shown below:

Variable	Successive values					
Number	?	4	2	0	5	-6

The value of number before the **repeat** statement is executed is unknown—this is indicated by a question mark. Then, successively, it takes the values 4, 2, 0, 5 and − 6.

A very useful operation in text processing may be described algorithmically as

    Read in characters until a non-blank is found

Again this has a simple Pascal representation:

```
repeat
    read ( character )
until character <> ' '
```

If the corresponding data was as shown in the data line below,

    □ □ □FIRST □ WORD

then a trace table for character would look like this:

Character	?	' '	' '	' '	'F'

Often we wish to perform a sequence of operations rather than a single statement. This is easily achieved by inserting the required statements between **repeat** and **until**. Statements within the 'body' of the **repeat** loop must be separated by semicolons. The full

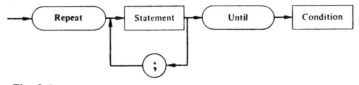

Fig. 3.1

syntax for the **repeat** statement is shown in Fig 3.1. Note that a semicolon is not needed immediately before **until**. As usual, the semicolon acts as a separator *between* statements. The reserved word **until** is not a statement in itself: it is part of the **repeat** statement. The **repeat** construction actually extends from the word **repeat** to the end of the condition. Although it may contain other statements, it counts as a single composite statement and so needs to be separated from other statements by a semicolon.

In the following example, for reading in and summing a set of numbers, two statements need to be repeatedly executed:

```
total := 0;

repeat
   read ( number );
   total := total + number
until number = 0;

writeln ( 'sum =', total )
```

First, a variable called total that is to be used to accumulate the sum of the input values is set to zero. In the body of the **repeat** loop there are two statements. The read statement is used for inputting successive numbers and the assignment statement is used for adding each number to the value of total. The form of this assignment may seem strange, and even illogical, since total occurs on both the left- and right-hand sides. In fact, executing this statement presents no problem to the computer. Remember that an assignment is executed by first evaluating the right-hand side with the current values of the variables and then assigning the result to the variable on the left-hand side. The effect of

```
total := total + number
```

will therefore be to take the old value of total, add number to it, and make this the new value of total. This results in increasing total by the value of number. (Note that total must be initialised, otherwise an error may occur—variables do not have default initial values.)

The terminating condition for the **repeat** loop is number = 0. In the corresponding data a zero will be used as an end marker. It is common practice to terminate data by using a value that cannot occur anywhere else in the data set.

Let us consider the effect of these statements on the following set of input values:

4   6   2   5   0

Again, a trace table is a good way of displaying the changing values of the variables. In this case, there are two variables and entries are made in a new column when either variable is given a value.

Number	?	?	4	4	6	6	2	2	5	5	0	0
Total	?	0	0	4	4	10	10	12	12	17	17	17

Follow through the execution of the code carefully to ensure that you understand the sequence of statements processed.

Note that the last time the assignment is executed, the value 0 is added to total. Stylistically this is unsatisfactory, although in practice it makes no difference to the result. If the end marker was changed to − 1 with a corresponding modification to the terminating condition then the result *would* be affected. That last − 1 would be added to total before the condition was tested. If it is not clear to you that this is so then substitute the condition number = − 1 in the previous piece of code and construct a trace table for

> 6   0   5   4   − 1

You should get the answer 14 which, of course, is not correct. (Remember − 1 is an end marker and not one of the numbers to be added.) The error could be rectified by adding 1 to total outside the loop, but this would be rather untidy. The real problem, and it occurs in many repetition sequences, is that we wish to leave the loop as soon as the terminating condition is satisfied, without executing any other instructions within the loop. This is not how **repeat** statements (and other repetition loops) work. Execution can only be terminated immediately after the condition has been reached and tested—in this case at the end of the loop. A solution that is often adopted in this situation is to have an initial read before the **repeat** construction and to insert another read within the **repeat** loop immediately before the end condition. Thus we have

```
read ( ... );

repeat
   .
   .
   .
   read ( ... )
until condition
```

This ensures that the loop condition is tested immediately after the second and any subsequent read statements. Program 3.1 uses this technique to sum a set of input values in order to calculate their mean. The writeln statement in the **repeat** loop is used for printing each value of number immediately after it has been read in. This is called *echo printing* and is of vital importance in program testing. We must be sure that the data we think is being input is the actual data being processed by the computer. This is particularly important when the value of a variable changes during the course of the program—in Program 3.1 the value of number is changed in every cycle of the **repeat** statement and so we need to output it each time before it is lost.

Quick quiz 3.1   (Solutions on p. 59)

1 Construct a trace table for the variables in Program 3.1 when the following data is input:

> 20   17   4   0   3   − 1

2 What do you think would happen in Program 3.1 if the data was that shown below?

> 5   2   7   − 2

```
Program Meancalculation ( input, output );

{*******************************************************
 *                                                     *
 * Program 3.1                                         *
 * The mean is calculated of a set of non-negative     *
 * integers read in as data.  There must be at least   *
 * one number before the end marker.                   *
 *                                                     *
 *******************************************************}

const
     endmarker = -1;

var
     itemno,                       { counts number of items }
     sum, number : integer;

     mean        : real;

begin

   sum    := 0;
   itemno := 0;

   writeln ( 'Program 3.1  Computation of mean' );
   writeln ( '=================================' );
   writeln;

   writeln ( 'input data : ' );

   read ( number );

   repeat

      writeln ( number );                 { echo print }
      itemno := itemno + 1;
      sum    := sum + number;

      read ( number )

   until number = endmarker;

   mean := sum / itemno;

   writeln;
   writeln;
   writeln ( 'number of items =', itemno :3 );
   writeln ( 'mean            =', mean :5:1 )

end.
```

Program 3.1

3.2 The *while* statement

The **repeat** statement is simple to use but suffers from one drawback—the body of the statement is executed at least once before the terminating condition is tested. What happens if the only number in the data list for Program 3.1 is the end marker?

This may seem like an academic question since there would appear to be no point in running a program if there is no data to process. However, it often happens in practice that part of a program, or even a whole program, has no data to analyse. A section of code may deal with the insertion of names of new employees onto a payroll. If there are no new employees to be dealt with on a particular run then no processing will be done. A program might analyse the performance of students in different options on a course. If a particular option was not taken by any student then again there would be no data to process.

The **while** statement, like the **repeat** statement, is used for repetition under a condition but differs in one important respect—the terminating condition is tested *before* the body of the statement is executed. If the terminating condition is initially false then the body of the **while** statement is not executed at all. Control just moves on to the following statement. The syntax diagram for the **while** statement is shown in Fig. 3.2.

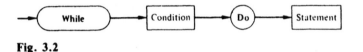

Fig. 3.2

If, as earlier (p. 41), we wanted to search through a set of data looking for the first negative number then this could be achieved by writing

```
while number >= 0 do
    read ( number )
```

The current value of number is first compared with zero. If it is non-negative then the read statement is executed. The condition is then tested again to see if another read should be carried out. These operations are repeated until the condition becomes false. The sequence is:

```
compare, read, compare, read, ...
```

number must, of course, have a value before the condition is first tested.

In the example above the most appropriate way of initialising number would be to read in its first value immediately before the **while** loop:

```
read ( number );

while number >= 0 do
    read ( number )
```

Compare this with the equivalent **repeat** statement:

```
repeat
    read ( number )
until number < 0
```

Note that the conditions tested in the two constructions are complementary and that, in this particular instance, the **repeat** statement gives a more concise description of the action to be taken.

Now take another look at the syntax graph for the **while** statement. Notice that there is no terminating symbol corresponding to the **until** of the **repeat** construction and that the body of the loop must be a single statement. This is not in any way restrictive, however, since in Pascal there is a construction called a *compound statement* that consists of any number of statements enclosed between the words **begin** and **end**.

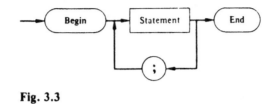

Fig. 3.3

Its syntax diagram is given in Fig. 3.3.

A compound statement may be placed anywhere within a program where a simple statement is allowed and acts as a composite unit. For example, if a compound statement follows the **do** of a **while** construction then the whole of it is governed by that **while** statement. The following example, for summing a set of values, illustrates this principle.

```
total := 0;
read ( number );

while number <> -1 do
   begin
      total := total + number;
      read ( number )
   end;

writeln ( 'sum =', total )
```

Here the body of the loop consists of two statements. This is again more cumbersome than the corresponding **repeat** version but has the advantage of being correct even if the first and only number in the data is − 1, whereas if you look again at Program 3.1 you will see that the **repeat** construction does not work in this case.

As with the **repeat** loop the statement affecting the terminating condition is located so that it will be executed immediately before that condition is tested. In this case, as soon as the read before **end** has been executed the computer returns to re-test the **while** condition.

All the repetition loops considered so far have contained read statements and have, in effect, been governed by them. Although this is a common type of application of these constructions there are many other ways of exploiting this facility. A frequently-occurring task is the summation of a series of terms until the total satisfies some criterion or until an individual term is smaller than some given value. If each of the terms to be accumulated is calculated in a similar way then a repetition loop is a suitable construction to use. For example, it is possible to sum the terms of the harmonic series until a term less than 0.0005 is found. The harmonic series is given by

$$1 + \frac{1}{2} + \frac{1}{3} + \frac{1}{4} + \frac{1}{5} + \ldots$$

A suitable piece of program might be

```
epsilon    := 0.005;
sum        := 0;
term       := 1;
termnumber := 1;

while term >= epsilon do
   begin
      sum           := sum + term;
      termnumber := termnumber + 1;
      term          := 1 / termnumber
   end
```

After any **repeat** or **while** loop has been constructed the terminating condition should be examined carefully to ensure that it is precisely what is wanted. Consider the following attempt to find the largest power of two that is smaller than or equal to a given positive integer number.

```
powervalue := 1;

while powervalue <= number do
   powervalue := 2 * powervalue
```

If we are uncertain whether the logic of our program is entirely correct, or if a run-time error occurs, then constructing a trace table for all or part of the program is invaluable. In this case number is assumed to have the value 100.

Powervalue	?	1	2	4	8	16	32	64	128
Number	100	100	100	100	100	100	100	100	100

The loop is terminated when powervalue is *greater* than 100. Effectively we have to go past the solution to know that we have found it. The mistake can easily be rectified by dividing powervalue by two at the end of the computation, but this would be poor programming practice. A better, but longer, solution would be to employ a 'look-ahead' feature to determine what the next value is before it is required.

```
powervalue := 1;
nextvalue  := 2;

while nextvalue <= number do
   begin
      powervalue := nextvalue;
      nextvalue  := 2 * nextvalue
   end
```

Remember that after its completion, the **while** loop terminating condition is false whereas the **repeat** loop terminating condition is true.

More complicated conditions than those used so far are sometimes needed to terminate loops. For example, in the piece of code for summing the harmonic series we may wish to place an upper limit on the number of terms added. In this case the first line of the **while** statement could be written as

```
while ( termnumber <= 1000 ) and ( term >= epsilon ) do
```

whereas if a **repeat** statement was used then its last line would be

until (termnumber > 1000) **or** (term < epsilon)

To end this section we have a program that uses both a **repeat** and **while** loop for processing a sequence of characters.

In some string processing problems it is useful to know how many characters there are in a string. Some languages (not Pascal) permit an 'empty' string containing no characters and so this possibility may need to be allowed for. Program 3.2 can be used to count the

```
Program Stringcount ( input, output );

{*****************************************************************
 *                                                               *
 * Program 3.2                                                   *
 * A line of data is read in containing a string of characters  *
 * between quotes (the string may be empty). The program        *
 * determines the number of characters in the string.           *
 *                                                               *
 *****************************************************************}

const
      quote = '''';

var
      charnumber : integer;

      character  : char;

begin

   charnumber := 0;

   repeat                                    { move to first quote }
      read ( character );                    {     on input line   }
   until character = quote;

   writeln ( 'Program 3.2  String length determination' );
   writeln ( '=======================================' );
   writeln;

   write ( 'string (enclosed in quotes)    : ', quote );
   read ( character );

   while character <> quote do
      begin
         write ( character );                      { echo print }
         charnumber := charnumber + 1;
         read ( character )
      end;

   writeln ( quote );
   writeln ( 'number of characters in string = ', charnumber :2 )

end.
```

Program 3.2

number of characters in a string read in as data. The program is largely self-explanatory but two points should be mentioned. Firstly, a character value appears in a constant definition. Both numbers and characters may be defined in this fashion. As mentioned in chapter 2, if a quotation mark is used as a character value in a program it is denoted by two quotes. It also has to be enclosed between quotation marks; consequently four quotes have to be typed. This device aids the compiler in its error detection but can be confusing to the programmer. If a quote character value appears several times in a program it is clearer (and safer) to define it as a constant.

The second point to be noted is that the program contains two write statements. These are used in a similar way to writeln statements but after execution they do not cause a new line to be output. This means that the next write or writeln statement will produce output on the next part of the same line. For example,

```
write ( x );
writeln ( y )
```

would have the same effect as

```
writeln ( x, y )
```

This property, together with the fact that the default field width for characters is one print position, greatly simplifies the output of sequences of characters, particularly for echo printing.

The output from a run of Program 3.2 illustrates this point.

```
Program 3.2  String length determination
==========================================

string (enclosed in quotes)    : 'zebra'
number of characters in string =  5
```

Output from Program 3.2

Although the characters of zebra are written out at different times they all appear together on one line. Many languages do not allow this 'stream' output, requiring each output statement to start a new line. This is because some output devices (notably the line printer) print a line at a time anyway. In Pascal, the compiler handles this problem by temporarily storing the symbols to be output until a writeln statement is executed. With certain compilers this can produce problems.

The first difficulty may have already occurred to you: what happens when an attempt is made to output more material on one line than the output device can handle? You may be lucky and find that the excess information is printed on the next line, but there is no guarantee that this will happen. Alternatively, a 'line overflow' error message may be printed. The third and least desirable possibility is that some or all of the excess output will be ignored. It is best not to leave things to the discretion of the compiler writer—instead ensure that the situation does not arise by interspersing your write statements with writeln statements to avoid line overflow.

A second problem is that after your program has completed execution (either naturally or because of a run-time error) there might still be part of a line stored ready for output but awaiting a writeln statement. Again, some compilers automatically output any part line when execution has terminated, while others just forget about the information. You can ensure that the last line of output *is* printed when the program terminates normally by placing writeln statements at appropriate points.

The problem of loss of output due to premature termination is not so easy to deal with.

When you look at the output from a program that has failed at run-time there is a natural tendency to assume that the last piece of information output will pin-point the last output statement processed. This may not be so; further write statements may have been processed but the information lost. There is little to be done about this except perhaps to write and complain to the suppliers of the compiler. At least being aware of the problem should help. When your program is going wrong and you suspect that some output is being lost, try placing extra writeln statements at appropriate points before the suspected failure point to force the computer to disgorge its contents.

One last point about repetition statements before we consider a larger program: since the code in the body of one of these statements may be executed thousands of times it may be vital to ensure that it is as efficient as possible. After writing a program, examine the code within each **repeat** and **while** statement to see if any redundant operations are being performed. In particular, check to see if any code inside a loop could be removed from that loop altogether.

Quick quiz 3.2   (Solutions on p. 59)

1   An alternative solution to the power value problem (p. 48) is shown below. Comment on it.

```
powervalue := 1;

while 2 * powervalue <= number do
    powervalue := 2 * powervalue
```

2   When a certain ball bounces it reaches three quarters of its previous height. Given the initial height and target height, write a piece of program to calculate and print out the number of bounces the ball will have made the last time it reaches the target height (assume that the initial height is greater than the target height and that both are positive).

3.3   Developing a program

The repetition statements, particularly the **while** statement, greatly increase the range of problems that may be solved by computer. As we develop more complex programs, the corresponding techniques for program design need to be more sophisticated. In this section a more elaborate technique for developing algorithms is introduced.

The problem to be considered is one that occurs in compilers. Compilers, remember, have the task of reading in a program and translating it into a suitable form for the computer to execute. This involves, among other things, recognising the basic constructions in the user's program such as reserved words, variable names and numbers. In this particular example, we assume that syntax diagrams are given to define valid forms of unsigned numbers. From this definition a program is to be written to check whether a given sequence of characters represents a permissible unsigned number. The definition to be used is shown in two parts in Fig. 3.4. Note that this is a simplified version of the Pascal definition, since no exponent part is allowed.

In the method of program development we are going to use the main steps will be outlined in algorithmic form. Each step is then elaborated, if necessary, into a sub-algorithm. If any step in a sub-algorithm cannot easily be written as a piece of code then a further sub-algorithm may be required. This is called *step-wise refinement* and is continued until each individual step in the algorithmic description is sufficiently detailed to allow a single program statement or sequence of simple program statements to be written from it.

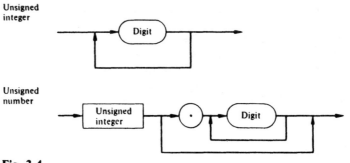

Fig. 3.4

Referring back to Fig. 3.4, the way the definition is split into two parts gives an idea of how to start. An unsigned integer is a special case of an unsigned number and any checking procedure should test for this first, and then go on to check for a fractional part. Assuming, for simplicity, that the string of characters has been typed somewhere on an otherwise blank data line, an initial outline might be as follows.

   1 Skip any initial blanks.
   2 Check for an unsigned integer or integer part.
   3 Check for a fractional part.
   4 Determine whether the string represents an unsigned number.
   5 Output results.

All but the last of these steps requires further elaboration before any coding is attempted.

The first step involves reading in characters until a non-blank character is found. As we have already seen, this can easily be coded as a **repeat** statement. However, we can make it more like the final code to be produced by rephrasing the description as follows.

   1.1 Read in characters until a non-blank is found.

In step 2 we need to check for an initial string of digits. This involves reading in characters until a non-digit is found. If the first non-digit is a blank then the string represents an unsigned integer. If this character is a decimal point then the string, so far, is the integer part of an unsigned number.

From these observations the following sequence of steps can be constructed.

   2.1 Read in characters until a non-digit is found.
   2.2 Determine whether the string is a valid unsigned integer (i.e. whether the last character read in is a blank).
   2.3 Determine whether the string, so far, represents a valid integer part (i.e. whether the last character read in is a decimal point).

Using the same approach, steps 3 and 4 can be expanded as below.

   3.1 Read in characters until a non-digit is found.
   3.2 Determine whether this part of the string is a valid fractional part (i.e. the last character read in is a blank).

   4.1 Determine whether the string represents a valid unsigned number (i.e. it is either an unsigned integer or a valid integer part followed by a valid fractional part).

At this point it would be a good idea to devise some suitable test data and check through the steps with it to see whether all possible situations have been considered. In order to test the algorithm thoroughly examples of four types are needed:

    (i)   valid unsigned integers;
    (ii) invalid unsigned integers;
    (iii) valid numbers with fractional parts;
    (iv) invalid numbers with fractional parts.

For (ii) and (iv) we shall want some examples that are almost correct. Suitable test data might be as shown in Table 3.1.

Table 3.1

Valid integers	Invalid integers	Valid numbers with fractional part	Invalid numbers with fractional part
2	A	0.6	.2
56	A2	2.94	6.
974	2A	31.8	A.2
597042	2A3	478.0416	2A.2
			26A.2
			4.2B6
			250.*
			94.72?

Each of the strings in Table 3.1 tests a different feature of the proposed program. The fact that the string may occur anywhere on the input line has been ignored—the starting column can be varied when the data is typed in.

Carefully working through the algorithmic steps developed so far with each of the pieces of test data there appear to be no problems until .2 is reached. If we are not careful this will be recognised as a valid number since the first non-digit found is the decimal point. Remember that, according to the syntactic definition, a number must start with a digit and so we shall have to modify the algorithm slightly to incorporate a check for this. Expanding each of the instructions in step 2 and incorporating this modification gives the following.

    2.1.1 Determine whether the first non-blank is a digit.
    2.1.2 Read in further characters until a non-digit is found.

    2.2.1 Determine whether the string is a valid unsigned integer (i.e. the leading non-blank is a digit and the last character read in is a blank).

    2.3.1 Determine whether the first part of the string is a valid integer part (i.e. the leading non-blank is a digit and the last character read is a decimal point).

This solves the problem of detecting the error in .2, but the next invalid string (6.) produces a similar difficulty in the checking of the fractional part. Again, unless a check is made that there is at least one digit, a blank will be accepted as a valid fractional part! In order to deal with this problem, steps 3.1 and 3.2 may be expanded as below.

    3.1.1 Read in a character (the leading fractional character).
    3.1.2 Read in further characters until a non-digit is found.

    3.2.1 Determine whether this is a valid fractional part (i.e. whether the leading fractional character was a digit and the last character read is a blank).

The algorithm is now almost ready to convert to code but before doing this let's look at the structure of the problem solving method that has been used. It is perhaps best represented by a diagram, as shown in Fig. 3.5. This is called a tree structure since, turned

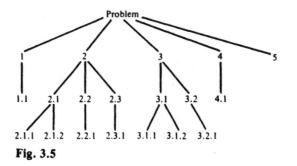

Fig. 3.5

upside down, the links between stages look like the branches of a tree. As in a tree, none of the branches link up again once they have separated. Each step at each stage becomes a separate sub-problem that is expanded independently of the other steps. This type of elaboration is often the most effective technique for solving complicated problems.

Back to the problem: a minor amendment that should be made, in order to check results, is that code should be included for echo printing the data. At the moment, once an invalid character is found, no further processing is done. In this situation a piece of code to print out the remainder of the string should be executed.

Before coding the program it is a good idea to list the main variables that will be needed. In addition to a variable for reading in the characters, several Boolean variables will be used for checking the following conditions:

(i)   whether the leading character is a digit;
(ii) whether the string represents an unsigned integer;
(iii) whether the first part of the string is a valid integer part;
(iv) whether the fractional part starts with a digit;
(v)   whether the string represents an unsigned number.

The steps in the algorithm that are to be coded are the ones at the tips of the branches in the tree diagram. These are 1.1, 2.1.1, 2.1.2, 2.2.1, 2.3.1, 3.1.1, 3.1.2, 3.2.1, 4.1 and 5.

```
Program Numberrecogniser ( input, output );

{**************************************************************
 *                                                            *
 * Program 3.3                                                *
 * Classifies the input string as either a valid unsigned integer, *
 * a valid unsigned number or neither.  The string may be preceded *
 * by spaces and must be terminated by at least two spaces.   *
 *                                                            *
 **************************************************************}

var
      ch : char;

      leaddigit,            { true if first character is digit         }
      unsinteger,           { true if string is valid unsigned integer }
      integerpart,          { true if first part of string is valid
                              integer followed by a decimal point      }
      leaddecdigit,         { true if decimal point is followed by digit }
      fractionpart,         { true if fractional part is valid         }
      unsnumber : boolean;  { true if string is valid unsigned number  }
```

Program 3.3 (continued opposite)

```
begin

    writeln ( 'Program 3.3  Number recogniser' );
    writeln ( '==============================' );
    writeln;
    write ( 'input string    :   ' );

    repeat                                          {   skip   }
       read ( ch )                                  {  initial }
    until ch <> ' ';                                {  blanks  }

    write ( ch );

    leaddigit := ( ( ch >= '0' ) and ( ch <= '9' ) );   {  check   }
                                                        {   for    }
    while ( ch >= '0' ) and ( ch <= '9' ) do            {  valid   }
       begin                                            { unsigned }
          read ( ch );                                  { integer  }
          write ( ch )                                  {   or     }
       end;                                             {  valid   }
                                                        { integer  }
    unsinteger  := ( leaddigit and ( ch = ' ' ) );      {   part   }
    integerpart := ( leaddigit and ( ch = '.' ) );

    read ( ch );
    write ( ch );

    leaddecdigit := ( ( ch >= '0' ) and ( ch <= '9' ) );

    while ( ch >= '0' ) and ( ch <= '9' ) do
       begin                                            {   check    }
          read ( ch );                                  {   for      }
          write ( ch )                                  {   valid    }
       end;                                             { fractional }
                                                        {   part     }
    fractionpart := ( leaddecdigit and ( ch = ' ' ) );

                                                        { unsigned }
    unsnumber := unsinteger                             {  number  }
              or ( integerpart and fractionpart );      {  check   }

    while ch <> ' ' do
       begin                                            { echo print }
          read ( ch );                                  { any extra  }
          write ( ch )                                  { characters }
       end;                                             { in string  }

    writeln;
    writeln ( 'unsigned integer  :  ', unsinteger :5 );
    writeln ( 'unsigned number   :  ', unsnumber :5 )

end.
```

Program 3.3 (continued)

The final coded version is shown in Program 3.3 on the previous page. Here the main steps in the process have been separated out and individually commented. The comments down the right-hand side almost read like a 'top-level' algorithm for the program. The advantage of placing them on the right-hand side is that they occur near to the pieces of code to which they refer without interrupting the flow of the program.

Results from three runs of the program are as follows.

```
Program 3.3  Number recogniser
================================

input string      :    294
unsigned integer  :  true
unsigned number   :  true
```

```
Program 3.3  Number recogniser
================================

input string      :    2.94
unsigned integer  :  false
unsigned number   :  true
```

```
Program 3.3  Number recogniser
================================

input string      :    a.2
unsigned integer  :  false
unsigned number   :  false
```

Outputs from Program 3.3

Quick quiz 3.3   (Solution on p. 60)

Why must the input string be followed by at least two blanks?

3.4 The *for* statement

The third construction used for representing repetition is the **for** statement. It is more specialised than the other two repetition statements in that it is a counting loop. The terminating condition is based on the value of a counter variable, which is sometimes called the *control*, or *controlled variable*. There are two forms of the statement, depending on whether the count is ascending or descending. Their structure is shown in Fig. 3.6.

If we wished, for example, to calculate n factorial (i.e. $1 \times 2 \times 3 \times \ldots \times (n-1) \times n$) where n is read in, the following piece of code would achieve this:

```
read ( n );
factorial := 1;

for number := 1 to n do
   factorial := factorial * number
```

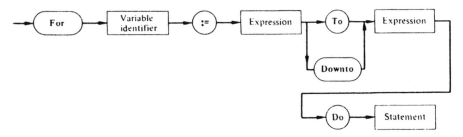

Fig. 3.6

number takes the values $1, 2, \ldots, n$ in turn as the body of the statement is executed. In fact, this is just a simpler way of writing

```
read ( n );
factorial := 1;
number    := 1;

while number <= n do
   begin
      factorial := factorial * number;
      number    := number + 1
   end
```

Note that in neither version is the repetition loop executed if n is zero, but, since 0 factorial is conventionally set to 1, this is exactly what we want.

The **for** statement is not, however, just a shorthand way of writing certain **while** constructions. It has been designed to translate into efficient machine code for many machines that have fast registers for counting. For this reason only unit increments (using **to**) and decrements (using **downto**) are allowed and the control variable may be of any simple type except real. In addition, the lower and upper limits are fixed on first entering the loop and the value of the control variable cannot be modified by statements in the body of the loop. Lastly, on normal exit from a **for** statement the value of the control variable is undefined.

Some languages have only one type of repetition statement—one similar to the **for** statement. If you have previously studied such a language, you might be tempted to use the **for** statement rather more than is necessary. It should only be used, for the most part, when a counting operation is required and there are no other terminating conditions on the loop. **for** statements are most useful for manipulating the array—a structured data type that will be introduced in Chapter 6.

Quick quiz 3.4   (Solutions on p. 60)

1   Use a **for** statement in a piece of code to calculate the sum of the natural numbers from n1 to n2.

2   Use a **for** statement in a piece of code to calculate and print out x and sin x for

$$x = -\pi\left(\frac{\pi}{6}\right) \pi \text{ radians.}$$

(Only attempt this problem if you are familiar with radian measurement.)

3.5   Use of *eoln* and *eof* in repetition statements

It is sometimes useful to have eoln (end of line) or eof (end of file) as a terminating condition for a repetition loop, although care must be taken with both of them.

As mentioned in Chapter 2, eoln is set to true when the last character of a line has just been read. A special value called the 'end-of-line component' marks the end of each line (including the last one) of all files. This value will not appear on your screen or on the output from a printer because it is just a signal to the computer to start a new line (at a terminal it will usually be signalled by the user pressing the 'return' key).

Consider the piece of code shown below for counting the number of characters remaining on the current data line.

```
charsleft := 0;

while not eoln do
   begin
      read ( ch );
      charsleft := charsleft + 1
   end
```

After execution of this code the read mechanism will be between lines. In order to move it to the start of the next line the instruction readln could be used. In fact, whatever part of the current data line is about to be read, readln will move the read mechanism to the start of the next one.

eof must also be used carefully. When numbers are being processed, for example, eof will not be set to true when the last number on the last data line has been read (unless it ends in the last column) and so eof cannot be used in an obvious way. One method of getting over this problem would be to have one number per line and to use readln, effectively, to detect the last line. In the next piece of code a set of numbers is being summed.

```
sum := 0;

while not eof do
   begin
      read ( number );
      readln;
      sum := sum + number
   end
```

read and readln may be merged and so

```
read ( number );
readln
```

could be simplified to

```
readln ( number )
```

The correspondence between this usage and write and writeln should be obvious.

The advantage of using eof in the way described above is that no end marker is needed. The disadvantage is that there can be only one item or set of items per data line.

Quick quiz 3.5   (Solution on p. 61)

Write a piece of code to count the number of data lines left after the current one.

Summary

The two main statements for performing repetition described in this chapter are the **while** and **repeat** statements. The **while** construction is the more useful of the two, since it includes the possibility of non-execution of the statement body. In circumstances where at least one cycle through the loop is required, the **repeat** statement usually gives a more natural representation. The main differences between the two are as follows.

(i) The body of the **repeat** statement is executed at least once, whereas that of the **while** loop is not necessarily executed at all.

(ii) The body of the **repeat** statement consists of any number of statements. The body of the **while** loop must be a single statement (although this may be compound).

(iii) The **repeat** statement is executed *until* a condition is true (and therefore while it is false). The **while** statement is executed *while* a condition is true (i.e. until it becomes false).

The second major topic that was introduced in this chapter was the method of stepwise refinement for planning programs in a systematic way. Try to use this technique wherever possible in the development of larger programs. *Don't be too anxious to start coding.* Mistakes in an algorithm are far easier to rectify than those in a program, particularly if there is a major logical inconsistency. If, when you produce data to test your algorithm, you find it needs a lot of patching up then it may be better to abandon your design and start again from scratch.

The **for** statement was then introduced. This is a useful construction when a statement or group of statements needs to be executed a specific number of times and the number of repetitions does not depend upon the effect of statements within the loop.

Lastly, the use of eof and eoln to control data input was discussed.

Solutions to quick quizzes

Quick quiz 3.1 (p. 44)

1

itemno	?	?	0	0	1	1	1	2	2	2	3	3	3	4	4	4	5	5	5	5
sum	?	0	0	0	0	20	20	20	37	37	37	41	41	41	41	41	41	44	44	44
number	?	?	?	20	20	20	17	17	17	4	4	4	0	0	0	3	3	3	-1	-1
mean	?	?	?	?	?	?	?	?	?	?	?	?	?	?	?	?	?	?	?	8.8

2 After adding − 2 to sum, giving 12, the next read statement will be executed. Since there is no more data you might expect a run-time error message to this effect to be printed. Unfortunately, not every compiler will do this. Some compilers might assign a value of zero to number in this situation and consequently the **repeat** statement body will be executed indefinitely, since the terminating condition will never be satisfied. It is not uncommon for programs containing repetition of pieces of code to get into an *infinite loop*. If, as a result of an error in logic or data, the terminating condition of a loop is never satisfied then the program will carry on looping for ever. Fortunately, 'for ever' is not a very long time on most computers and you are likely to get a run-time error message such as

EXCEEDED PROCESSOR TIME

pretty quickly. Most computer systems place a fairly low limit on the amount of time for which your job is allowed to run, but it is usually sufficient to do all but the most complex computations. You should always suspect, therefore, when you get this kind of message, that your program is in an infinite loop.

Quick quiz 3.2 (p. 51)

1 This looks simpler than the previous version but closer inspection reveals that twice as many multiplications are being performed since 2 * powervalue is computed twice in each cycle. This is unnecessarily inefficient and so the previous version is to be preferred.

2   A suitable piece of code is shown below.

```
bounces          := 0;
currentheight    := initialheight;
nextheight       := 0.75 * initialheight;

while nextheight > targetheight do
   begin
      bounces       := bounces + 1;
      currentheight := nextheight;
      nextheight    := 0.75 * currentheight
   end;

writeln ( 'initial height     =', initialheight );
writeln ( 'target height      =', targetheight );
writeln ( 'number of bounces =', bounces )
```

A **repeat** loop is not appropriate here since the ball may not reach the target height after the first bounce.

Quick quiz 3.3   (p. 56)

For certain inputs the program reads in two characters beyond the end of the string (e.g. when reading in an unsigned integer).

Quick quiz 3.4   (p. 57)

```
1      sum := 0;
       for number := n1 to n2 do
          sum := sum + number

2      angle := -6 * piby6;
       writeln ( '       angle           sin' );

       for i := 1 to 13 do
          begin
             sinangle := sin ( angle );
             writeln ( angle :7:3, ' radians', sinangle :10:3 );
             angle := angle + piby6
          end
```

piby6 should be defined as a constant to an appropriate number of decimal places. The variable i counts the number of values to be calculated and output. An alternative approach would be to use the control variable as a multiplier to calculate each term. In this case the code might be:

```
       writeln ( '       angle           sin' );

       for m := -6 to 6 do
          begin
             angle    := m * piby6;
             sinangle := sin ( angle );
             writeln ( angle :7:3, ' radians', sinangle :10:3 )
          end
```

This version might take slightly more execution time but is less susceptible to rounding errors and is, perhaps, easier to follow than the previous one.

Quick quiz 3.5   (p. 58)

```
lines := 0;

while not eof do
   begin
      readln;
      lines := lines + 1
   end
```

Exercises

A1   Frequency data has been collected and is arranged in the form

$$x_1 f_1 \quad x_2 f_2 \quad x_3 f_3 \quad \ldots \quad x_n f_n$$

where each observed value x_i occurs f_i times. Assuming that the last pair of observations is followed by the pair $-1 \quad -1$, write a program to calculate the mean $\bar{x}$ given by

$$\bar{x} = \frac{f_1 x_1 + f_2 x_2 + \ldots + f_n x_n}{f_1 + f_2 + \ldots + f_n}$$

A2   A sequence of positive integers, terminated by -1, is given. Write a program to determine whether these numbers are in ascending order. Assume that there are at least two numbers.

A3   A car depreciates at 20% per year; that is, its value at the end of a given year is 20% less than at the start of that year. Given its initial value write a program to compute and print out its value at the beginning of each of the first ten years.

B1   In the programming language FORTRAN, a string represents a valid variable name if it contains six or fewer characters and if the characters consist of a letter followed by up to five alphanumeric characters. Also the first letter, by default, determines whether the identifier represents a variable of type real (A–H, O–Z) or of type integer (I–N). Write a program that reads in a string of non-blank characters and determines whether the string represents a valid variable name and, if so, what its default type is. Assume that the string may occur anywhere on the data line, which otherwise contains only blanks.

B2   In order to improve the reliability of a section of an electronic system, several identical units are often placed in parallel so that, even if one or two fail, at least one is likely to work. The reliability of a device may be quantified as a value between 0 and 1, representing the likelihood that the device will work. If R is the reliability of a given unit then the reliability R_n of a system of n identical independent units in parallel is given by $R_n = 1 - P_n$ where P_n, the probability that all the units fail, is given by $P_n = (1 - R)^n$. Write a program that reads in a value for R and uses a repetition statement to calculate the minimum number of parallel units required to achieve this reliability. (Note that the answer can also be computed by a formula. If you know this formula then use it to check your results.)

B3   Write a program to compute $\cos x$ to a given accuracy using the Taylor series given below.

$$\cos x = 1 - \frac{x^2}{1.2} + \frac{x^4}{1.2.3.4} - \frac{x^6}{1.2.3.4.5.6} + \ldots$$

B4   Write a program to process scores from a golf tournament. Each line of data consists of a golfer's name followed by a colon and then a list of the scores obtained on each of the 18 holes. Assuming the golfers' names contain up to 35 characters write a program to input the data and produce a table of scores neatly laid out.

For instance, if the data was:

Tom Watson: 4 3 4 4 3 4 3 5 4 4 4 4 3 4 5 4 5 4
Severiano Ballesteros: 3 3 3 4 4 4 3 4 6 5 7 2 3 3 4 4 4 4
Ben Crenshaw: 4 4 4 4 3 4 4 5 4 4 5 4 4 3 4 4 4 4

the output might look like:

Player   Score
========   =======

Tom Watson   71
Severiano Ballesteros 70
Ben Crenshaw   72

(Hint: use a variable to count how many characters each golfer's name contains and note that the field width component in an output statement doesn't have to be a number, it may be a variable or even an expression as long as the result is of type integer.)

C1   Write a program to input two numbers and determine whether they are relatively prime.

C2   Write a program to calculate the square root of a given number without using the standard function.

4

Conditional execution and transfers

Introduction

There are many occasions when it is necessary to indicate alternative courses of action within a program, the one selected depending upon the data given. Pascal provides two constructions—the **if** statement and the **case** statement—for describing this 'conditional execution'.

Control may be transferred to another part of a program by using a **goto** statement. The **goto** statement may also be used in conjunction with other statements to define alternative courses of action.

4.1 The *if* statement

Sometimes a point is reached in a program at which we want a piece of code to be performed only if a particular condition is satisfied. Examples of this kind of situation are as follows.

 (i)   If x is positive, calculate $\sqrt{x}$.
 (ii) If the number examined is greater than the largest one found so far then make this one the largest.
 (iii) If the given mark is less than 0 or greater than 100, write out an error message.

In Pascal these might be expressed as

```
if x > 0 then
    y := sqrt ( x )
```

```
if number > maximum then
    maximum := number
```

```
if ( mark < 0 ) or ( mark > 100 ) then
    writeln ( 'invalid data' )
```

The general form of this type of statement is shown in Fig. 4.1.

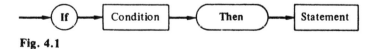

Fig. 4.1

In general, if the condition is true then the corresponding statement is executed, otherwise not. In either case control then moves to the statement following. A piece of program incorporating an **if** statement is as follows.

```
maximum := 0;
read ( number );

repeat
   writeln ( number );
   if number > maximum then
      maximum := number;
   read ( number )
until number = 0;

writeln ( 'maximum value = ', maximum )
```

This reads in a set of positive numbers and finds the largest one. The value of maximum is initially set to zero and is changed every time the condition number > maximum is satisfied. Consequently the final value of maximum will be the largest of the values read in. In this example the number zero is used as an end marker.

If the corresponding data line contained the numbers

| 4 | 2 | 7 | 5 | 6 | 3 | 0 |

then the trace table would be:

Number	?		4		2	7		5	6	3	0
Maximum	?	0		4			7				

The trace table is slightly different in form from earlier examples. An entry need only be made in a column when the value of the corresponding variable is changed. This reduces the number of entries that have to be made, without causing confusion. If there is no entry in a given position, the current value of the corresponding variable may be found by scanning to the left until an entry is found.

In Program 4.1 an **if** statement is used for counting the frequency of occurrence of a given character.

If more than one action is to be carried out when a given condition is satisfied then this can be achieved by including a compound statement. For example, if we want to ensure that the values of two variables are in ascending order, then the following piece of code has this effect:

```
if number1 > number2 then
   begin
      copy     := number1;
      number1 := number2;
      number2 := copy
   end
```

After execution of this **if** statement the value of number1 will be less than or equal to the value of number2. The compound statement to exchange the values of number1 and number2 is only executed if number1 is initially greater than number2.

Note that, in order to perform the exchange, a third variable is used. The piece of code

```
number1 := number2;
number2 := number1
```

would not have the desired effect. In fact, after execution of these two statements number1 and number2 would have the same value!

Program 4.2 illustrates the use of this type of construction for computing the sum of two weights.

```
Program Lettercount ( input, output );

{*****************************************************************
 *                                                               *
 * Program 4.1                                                   *
 * A data line is read in containing a letter in column one.     *
 * The next line contains a sentence terminated by a period.     *
 * The program determines the number of times the given letter   *
 * appears in the sentence.                                      *
 *                                                               *
 *****************************************************************}

const
      period = '.';

var
      givenletter, character : char;

      frequency : integer;

begin

   frequency := 0;

   readln ( givenletter );

   writeln ( 'Program 4.1  Letter frequency count' );
   writeln ( '====================================' );
   writeln;

   writeln ( 'given letter = ', givenletter );
   write ( 'sentence : ' );
   read ( character );

   repeat

      write ( character );
      if character = givenletter then
         frequency := frequency + 1;
      read ( character )

   until character = period;

   writeln ( period );
   writeln ( 'letter frequency =', frequency :3 )

end.
```

Program 4.1

It is often useful to be able to specify alternative actions to be taken depending upon a condition. This may be represented by the flowchart[*] construction shown in Fig. 4.2.

An example of an algorithmic step that requires this type of construction is as follows.

If the number is less than zero then print an error message otherwise print that the number is valid.

```pascal
Program Weightadd ( input, output );

{***********************************************************
 *                                                         *
 * Program 4.2                                             *
 * Two weights in kilograms and grams are added together.  *
 *                                                         *
 ***********************************************************}

var
      kilos1, grams1, kilos2, grams2,
      kilosum, gramsum : integer;

begin

   read ( kilos1, grams1, kilos2, grams2 );
   kilosum := kilos1 + kilos2;
   gramsum := grams1 + grams2;

   if gramsum >= 1000 then
      begin
         kilosum := kilosum + 1;
         gramsum := gramsum - 1000
      end;

   writeln ( 'Program 4.2   Weight addition' );
   writeln ( '============================' );
   writeln;

   writeln ( 'first weight  =  ', kilos1 :2, ' kilos ',
                                  grams1 :3, ' grams' );
   writeln ( 'second weight =  ', kilos2 :2, ' kilos ',
                                  grams2 :3, ' grams' );
   writeln ( 'total weight  = ', kilosum :3, ' kilos ',
                                  gramsum :3, ' grams' )

end.
```

Program 4.2

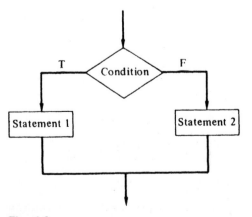

Fig. 4.2

This may be coded in Pascal by using an **if-then-else** construction, as follows:

```
if number < 0 then
    writeln ( 'out of range' )
else
    writeln ( 'ok' )
```

Its general structure is shown in Fig. 4.3.

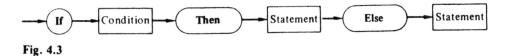

Fig. 4.3

As before, either or both statements may be compound:

```
if overtime then
    begin
        read ( hoursover, overrate );
        overpay := hoursover * overrate;
        writeln ( 'overtime pay = $', overpay :8:2 )
    end
else
    writeln ( 'no overtime worked' )
```

Observe that there is no semicolon after the **end** since it is followed by the rest of the statement. There is no situation in which **else** may be immediately preceded by a semicolon.

if-then-else statements are often used to check for an error condition before processing data. The general form of this type of structure is:

```
if validdata then
    begin

        { process valid
            data          }

    end
else
    writeln ( 'error in data' )
```

By making the statement after **else** into another **if** statement the number of conditions that may be tested can be increased:

```
if temperature < 16 then
    write ( 'too cold' )
else if temperature > 18 then
    write ( 'too hot' )
else
    write ( 'just right' )
```

The first condition is tested and if it is satisfied then the first write statement is executed; otherwise the second condition is checked. If this is found to be true then the second write statement is executed; otherwise the third write statement is carried out. Note that exactly one of the write statements is executed whatever the circumstances. The fact that only one of the write statements is executed is seen more clearly by re-ordering the tests, as shown below:

```
if temperature < 16 then
   write ( 'too cold' )
else if temperature <= 18 then
   write ( 'just right' )
else
   write ( 'too hot' )
```

At first glance it may appear that 'just right' is printed even if the temperature is below 16. Further examination shows that this test is not even made if the temperature is below 16, since the first write is executed and the remainder of the statement is then ignored.

If there is more than one alternative to be tested then we will normally be able to choose the order in which these tests are to be made. From the point of view of efficiency it is best to check for the most commonly occurring condition first. For example, if most of the temperatures to be tested by the above **if** statement were higher than 18°C then it would be more efficient to use the form

```
if temperature > 18 then
   write ( 'too hot' )
else if temperature >= 16 then
   write ( 'just right' )
else
   write ( 'too cold' )
```

Examine Program 4.3. This contains three variations of the **if** statement. The first of these is the only type we have not met before. This is an **if-then-else** statement that contains an **if-then** statement. If neither of the two conditions tested is true then neither corresponding statement is executed.

There is no limit to the number of if statements that may be joined together. Look for example, at the piece of code below for reading in two dates and determining whether they are in chronological order:

```
read ( month1, day1, year1, month2, day2, year2 );

if year1 < year2 then
   inorder := true
else if year2 < year1 then
   inorder := false
else if month1 < month2 then
   inorder := true
else if month2 < month1 then
   inorder := false
else if day1 < day2 then
   inorder := true
else if day2 < day1 then
   inorder := false
else
   inorder := true                        { dates are the same }
```

The dates are compared, component by component, starting with the years. If neither of the first two conditions is satisfied then the years must be equal and the months are compared. If these are equal, the day numbers are compared. Only if the year, month and day numbers are equal does control reach the last statement that sets inorder to true.

```
Program Checkparentheses ( input, output );

{**********************************************************************
 *                                                                    *
 * Program 4.3                                                        *
 * An arithmetic expression is read in and the balance of parentheses *
 * is checked. No other checks are performed and it is assumed that   *
 * there are no spaces within the expression. The expression must be  *
 * terminated by a space.                                             *
 *                                                                    *
 **********************************************************************}


var
        leftparentheses,                   { to count left and right }
        rightparentheses : integer;        {         parentheses     }

        symbol : char;

        balance : boolean;                 { true if parentheses balance }


begin

    leftparentheses  := 0;
    rightparentheses := 0;
    balance := true;

    writeln ( 'Program 4.3  Parenthesis check' );
    writeln ( '==============================' );
    writeln;

    write ( 'arithmetic expression : ' );
    read ( symbol );

    while balance and ( symbol <> ' ' )  do
       begin
          write ( symbol );
          if symbol = '(' then                          {    count    }
             leftparentheses := leftparentheses + 1      {  left and   }
          else if symbol = ')' then                      {    right    }
             rightparentheses := rightparentheses + 1;   { parentheses }

                                                         {   check for      }
          if leftparentheses < rightparentheses then     { right parenthesis }
             balance := false;                           { without matching  }
                                                         { left parenthesis  }

          read ( symbol )
       end;

    balance := ( leftparentheses = rightparentheses );

    write ( symbol );
```

Program 4.3 (continued overleaf)

```
while symbol <> ' ' do
   begin
      read ( symbol );                    {   echo print any     }
      write ( symbol )                     { remaining characters }
   end;

writeln;

   if balance then
      writeln ( 'parentheses balance' )
   else if leftparentheses > rightparentheses then
      writeln ( 'left parenthesis without matching right parenthesis' )
   else
      writeln ( 'right parenthesis without matching left parenthesis' )

end.
```

Program 4.3 (continued)

Another way of determining whether the two dates are in order would be to use an assignment of the form

```
inorder := . . .
```

where the right-hand side would consist of a complicated Boolean expression. This second form might take fewer lines to write out but would normally take longer to execute. Speed could be crucial if the order test was to be repeated many times (perhaps in a program for sorting a large set of dates). If most of the dates had different year numbers then only two conditions at most would need to be tested in the **if** statement. Only in a few cases would execution pass to the last part of the statement that checks for equal day numbers. Whatever the data the Boolean assignment would take the same amount of time to evaluate. It will normally, therefore, take longer to execute than the **if** statement.

One last type of **if** construction that is sometimes useful is

```
if condition then
   if condition then
      statement
   else
      statement
```

The indentation suggests, correctly, that the **else** is associated with the second **if**. Slack indentation, such as that shown below, would give the impression that the **else** belonged to the first **if**.

```
if condition then
   if condition then
      statement
else
   statement
```

In general, each **else** is associated with the most recent unmatched **if**. To override this precedence a **begin-end** pair may be used:

```
if x > 0 then
   begin
      if y > 0 then
         z := 0
   end
else
   z := 1
```

Earlier, we considered an example of a situation in which an **if** statement was more appropriate than a Boolean assignment. Sometimes a Boolean assignment is the simpler and more effective form to use. Compare, for example, the two statements below for assigning a value to the Boolean variable positive:

```
if a > 0 then
   positive := true
else
   positive := false
```

```
positive := a > 0
```

Conditional statements and Boolean assignments can often be interchanged to achieve the same effect. Clearly, simplicity and efficiency will be the main considerations when deciding which to use.

Quick quiz 4.1   (Solutions on p. 84)

1   The input contains a sequence of two or more positive integers terminated by -1. Write a piece of code to count the 'incidences' in this sequence (i.e. the number of pairs of equal, adjacent numbers). For example, the following sequence contains 4 incidences:

4	2	9	9	3	7	7	7	3	3	-1

2   In the game of buzz-fizz each player adds one to the previous player's number and calls out that number unless it divides exactly by three or five. If it divides by three he calls out 'buzz' instead and if it divides by five he calls out 'fizz'. If it divides by both three and five he calls out 'buzz fizz'. Construct a piece of code to output the numbers one to one hundred, in figures, substituting 'buzz', 'fizz', or 'buzz fizz', if appropriate.

3   Given two integer variables, i and j, write a statement to set a Boolean variable b to true if i is zero or if j is an exact multiple of i, and to false otherwise.

4   Now you have conditional statements available there is no need in many cases to output values of Boolean variables—a more natural form can be used. For instance instead of using the statement

```
writeln ( 'character is vowel ? ', vowel :7 )
```

for indicating whether an input character is a vowel (see Program 2.3) the statement

```
if vowel then
   writeln ( 'character is vowel' )
else
   writeln ( 'character is not vowel' )
```

could be used. Apply the same idea to Program 2.1 and produce a statement to indicate which meal time it is (if it isn't a meal time then nothing should be output).

4.2 The *case* statement

It may be very inefficient to use an **if** statement when there are several alternatives, dependent upon similar conditions and with the same likelihood of occurrence. For example, a piece of program to print out a month name given its number could be written as

```
if monthnumber = 1 then
    write ( 'January' )
else if monthnumber = 2 then
    write ( 'February' )
else if monthnumber = 3 then
    write ( 'March' )
else if monthnumber = 4 then
    write ( 'April' )
else if monthnumber = 5 then
    write ( 'May' )
else if monthnumber = 6 then
    write ( 'June' )
else if monthnumber = 7 then
    write ( 'July' )
else if monthnumber = 8 then
    write ( 'August' )
else if monthnumber = 9 then
    write ( 'September' )
else if monthnumber = 10 then
    write ( 'October' )
else if monthnumber = 11 then
    write ( 'November' )
else if monthnumber = 12 then
    write ( 'December' )
```

These alternatives could be described more concisely by a **case** statement of the form:

```
case monthnumber of
   1 : write ( 'January' );
   2 : write ( 'February' );
   3 : write ( 'March' );
   4 : write ( 'April' );
   5 : write ( 'May' );
   6 : write ( 'June' );
   7 : write ( 'July' );
   8 : write ( 'August' );
   9 : write ( 'September' );
  10 : write ( 'October' );
  11 : write ( 'November' );
  12 : write ( 'December' )
end
```

At the head of the **case** statement is an expression (here it is a simple variable—monthnumber). This is the *selector*. Following this is a list of statements, each preceded by a number and a colon. The numbers are called **case** labels.

The first step in the execution of a **case** statement is the evaluation of its selector.

Depending upon this value, control jumps to the statement in the **case** list with the corresponding label. After this has been executed control moves to the end of the **case** statement. Consequently only one of the statements in the **case** list is executed.

The **case** labels do not have to be consecutive integers, nor do they have to be in ascending order. In fact, there may be any number of them associated with each statement. The only restriction is that the **case** labels within the body of a **case** statement must all be distinct.

In the last example a suitable selector was already available. This is not always so. For instance, we may have a set of examination marks that have to be classified according to the following guidelines:

Mark	70–100	60–69	50–59	40–49	0–39
Assessment	very good	good	fair	poor	fail

A suitable selector is mark **div** 10, since this will give a value between 0 and 10 (remember that **div** truncates the result). The corresponding **case** statement could be

```
case mark div 10 of
   7, 8, 9, 10 : write ( 'very good' );
             6 : write ( 'good' );
             5 : write ( 'fair' );
             4 : write ( 'poor' );
   0, 1, 2, 3 : write ( 'fail' )
end
```

In both of the previous examples the selector and labels have had integer values. In general, they may have any scalar value except real. A situation where a selector of type char might be useful is shown below.

```
case answer of
   'a' : score := score + 1;
   'b' : score := score + 6;
   'c' :                    ;
   'd' : score := score + 10
end
```

answer is a character variable representing the choice made by a student in a multichoice question in which the alternatives were labelled a–d. Depending upon his answer the student may get 1, 6, 0 or 10 marks added to his score. Notice that since no marks were awarded for c, no action is required. This is permissible since the 'empty' statement is a valid statement. It implies the absence of a statement and, in fact, the semicolon in case c could have been placed next to the colon. A space has been left between the two symbols to make the meaning clear.

In Program 4.4 a **case** statement is used to simplify output of days of the week. A test of the validity of the data has not been included although, of course, in any program to be used commercially or as an interactive demonstration program, such a check would be essential. A user who is informed that the 31st day of April 1979 was a Thursday is liable to lose faith in your program. The quick quiz at the end of Section 4.4 (p. 83) asks you to supply suitable validation code.

One question you may have already asked yourself regarding **case** statements is, 'What happens if there is no label corresponding to a selector value?' The answer is that the result is undefined—the compiler writer can effectively choose what should happen in this situation. You might find one compiler gives a run-time error message while another

```
Program Daysofweek ( input, output );

{********************************************************************
 *                                                                 *
 * Program 4.4                                                     *
 * A set of dates is read in using month number, day number,      *
 * year number form. The day of the week on which each date occurs *
 * is computed using Zeller's formula. The date numbers need      *
 * to be modified in the program since the formula treats March   *
 * as month 1, April as month 2 and so on. The calendar was last  *
 * adjusted on September 14th 1752 and so any date read in must   *
 * not precede this date.                                         *
 *                                                                 *
 ********************************************************************}

var
     month, day, year, daynumber,

     century, yearincentury : integer;

     validdate : boolean;


begin

   writeln ( 'Program 4.4  Day of the week determination' );
   writeln ( '==========================================' );
   writeln;
   writeln ( '   date        day of week' );

   repeat
      readln ( month, day, year );       { code for validation could }
      validdate := true;                 {      be included here      }

      if validdate then
         begin
            write ( month :3, day :3, year :5 );
            century        := year div 100;
            yearincentury := year mod 100;

            if month >= 3 then                 { since March = month 1 }
               month := month - 2              { April = month 2  etc  }
            else
               begin
                  month := month + 10;
                  if yearincentury > 0 then
                     yearincentury := yearincentury - 1
                  else
                     begin
                        yearincentury := 99;
                        century        := century - 1
                     end
```

Program 4.4 (continued opposite)

```
                end;

            daynumber := ( trunc ( 2.6 * month - 0.2 )   + day   { Zeller's }
                        + yearincentury + century div 4       { formula  }
                        + yearincentury div 4
                        - 2 * century )  mod 7;

        case daynumber of
            0 : writeln ( '    Sunday' );
            1 : writeln ( '    Monday' );
            2 : writeln ( '    Tuesday' );
            3 : writeln ( '    Wednesday' );
            4 : writeln ( '    Thursday' );
            5 : writeln ( '    Friday' );
            6 : writeln ( '    Saturday' )
            end
        end
    else
        writeln ( 'this is not a valid date' )

    until eof

end.
```

Program 4.4 (continued)

compiler simply ignores all the statements in the **case** list. Neither of these possibilities is desirable and so you should always test the selector value, if necessary, before the corresponding **case** statement is executed. A typical construction might be:

```
    if validselector then
        case selector of
            .
            .
            .
        end
    else
        write ( 'invalid selector' )
```

Lastly, any statement in the case list may be compound. This means that, if required, a sequence of statements may be associated with any alternative.

Quick quiz 4.2   (Solution on p. 85)

An integer variable, number, is known to have a value in a given range. A piece of code is required to print out that value in words; for example, 24 is to be printed as twenty-four. Write a suitable piece of code for when number is in the range (a)   1–10; (b)   1–99.

4.3   The *goto* statement

The **goto** statement is used to transfer control from the current position in a program to another point. Its syntax is given in Fig. 4.4.

   The label must be an unsigned integer in the range 0–9999 and there must be a

Fig. 4.4

statement somewhere in the program that is labelled with the same number. For example, corresponding to

goto 20

there might be a statement elsewhere in the program

```
20 : writeln ( 'error in data' )
```

After **goto** 20 has been executed, control will jump to label 20 and the writeln statement will be obeyed. Execution then continues with the statement following the writeln. Although there must be a unique destination for each **goto**, there may be several **gotos** with the same destination. There may be several **goto** 20 statements but there must be only one statement labelled 20 that may be reached from them.

At first sight the **goto** seems a very attractive feature. It is simple to understand, and provides an easy method of controlling the sequence of statements executed. In practice, the indiscriminate use of **gotos** makes programs difficult to follow and debug. A moment's thought should convince you that the objective of separating out the different processes in a program is liable to be undermined by allowing frequent transfers from one section to another. A program containing a large number of **gotos** is sometimes disparagingly referred to as 'spaghetti code' and this analogy gives a good idea of the tangled state that programs can get into. It is difficult to appreciate the overall structure of a program if there is a criss-cross flow between its various parts.

If you develop your programs using the techniques described in Section 3.3, then you will find that **gotos** are rarely needed. If you do discover that the only way out of a situation is to use a **goto** then perhaps the overall design is wrong and you should reconsider the structure of your program. You may still find that a **goto** is necessary; the only alternative may be to have awkward or very inefficient code. If so, go ahead and use it. We will now look at the kinds of situation in which this might occur.

The simplest case is when a search is being carried out for a particular value (the *target*) in a list of values. For example, given a thousand numbers in a file, we wish to determine whether a particular number is present. Using a **repeat** loop we might write:

```
count := 0;

repeat
    count := count + 1;
    read ( number )
until ( count = 1000 ) or ( number = target );

numberfound := ( number = target )
```

whereas a version using a **goto** statement might look like this:

```
for count := 1 to 1000 do
    begin
        read ( number );
        if number = target then
            goto 10
    end;

10:
    numberfound := ( number = target )
```

There is not much to choose between the two versions. The second one uses a **for** statement and so might execute rather faster but purists could complain that the code is misleading—the loop is not necessarily executed 1000 times as the **for** statement implies.

The advantage of using a **goto** statement is more obvious when we wish to exit from a loop within another loop. This is the situation that occurs in Program 4.5. Here the numbers that are being scanned are library book numbers. The book numbers for each branch of the library are stored in ascending order in a file and so, if the number of the

```
Program Booksearch ( input, output );

{************************************************************************
 *                                                                    *
 * Program 4.5                                                        *
 * Each library book in an area is identified by a six digit number.  *
 * Each branch has a list of its book numbers stored in ascending     *
 * order in a file - one number per line. The last entry for each     *
 * branch is followed by a line containing an end marker (a number    *
 * larger than any book number). The book number to be located is     *
 * read in and then the book numbers for the branches are examined    *
 * until a copy of the book is found or all branches have been searched. *
 *                                                                    *
 ************************************************************************}

label
      10;

const
      maxbranches = 5;
      endmarker   = 1234567;

var
      branchnumber, booknumber,
      targetnumber : integer;        { book to be found }

begin

   read ( targetnumber );

   for branchnumber := 1 to maxbranches do
      begin
         read ( booknumber );

         while booknumber <> endmarker do
            if booknumber < targetnumber then
               read ( booknumber )                      { try next book }
            else if booknumber = targetnumber then
               goto 10                                  {  book found    }
            else
               repeat                               { book not at this }
                  readln ( booknumber )             {  branch - skip   }
               until booknumber = endmarker         {  to end marker   }
      end;
```

Program 4.5 (continued overleaf)

```
10:
   writeln ( 'Program 4.5  Library book search' );
   writeln ( '==================================' );
   writeln;
   writeln ( 'required book number = ', targetnumber :6 );

   if booknumber = targetnumber then
      writeln ( 'book found in branch #', branchnumber :2 )
   else
      writeln ( 'book not found' )

end.
```

Program 4.5 (continued)

target book is smaller than that of the current book being examined, we can deduce that this branch does not have a copy and skip to the end of the books for that branch. Since there are a number of branches to be examined the corresponding program may have a *nested* loop structure as shown.

When testing the program, of course, all the book numbers should be echo printed, but this facility will probably not be required in the final version. Notice that when labels are used in a program (with the exception of **case** labels) they must be declared. The label declaration precedes all other declarations in the program block and consists of the word **label** followed by a list of labels to be used separated by commas.

As an exercise you might try rewriting Program 4.5 without using a **goto** statement. If you use the same nested loop structure then the code becomes rather untidy, since the condition booknumber = targetnumber has to be tested in both the outer and inner loop. With a certain amount of restructuring, however, a perfectly acceptable **goto**-less version may be produced.

Another situation in which we may wish to transfer control from a particular part of a program is when an error in the data has been found. For example, if the sum of a set of numbers read in from data is being calculated then there is no point in carrying on with the process if one of the numbers is found to be obviously wrong. Using a **goto** statement to move control to another part of the program is often the simplest solution. The problem of data validation and how to deal with errors is considered in the next section.

One last point to note regarding the use of **goto**s is that a jump into a structural statement such as a conditional statement or **for** loop is illegal.

Quick quiz 4.3   (Solution on p. 86)

Write a piece of code to check whether a set of input numbers is in ascending order:
(a)   using a **goto** statement; (b)   without using a **goto** statement. (Assume that there are at least two numbers and that the list is followed by an end marker.)

4.4   Data validation

Up to this point we have usually assumed that the data provided for each program is valid. This is a dangerous assumption to make, since it is quite common for information to be typed incorrectly at a terminal. If there is only a small set of data, it should be checked through carefully before running. When the amount of data becomes large, the visual checking process becomes tedious and is best left to the computer which is, in any case, much better suited to this kind of routine task than we are.

A small error may be impossible to detect by computer. If an examination mark is typed as 56 instead of 65, the only way of detecting the mistake is to check the typed marks against the original data. The type of error a computer *can* check for would include the typing of obviously impossible marks, such as 105 or − 6, or the occurrence of alphabetic characters where numeric ones are expected. If a value 'A7' were typed by mistake, this could be detected at run-time by the computer. If an attempt were made to read this as the value of a variable of type integer, the computer would normally issue a run-time message to the effect that there was a mis-match between the type of the data item and that of the variable in the read statement.

It is often unsatisfactory to leave the detection of this sort of error to the compiler. There are two main reasons for this, and in both cases the difficulty arises because the program has to hand control over to the computer's operating system. Firstly, once a run-time error occurs, execution of the program is terminated, although in many cases we might prefer it if the program were to continue and look for further errors. Secondly, if the person using the program is not a programmer, we may wish to ensure that he is not confronted by a run-time error message produced for programmers with an intimate knowledge of the workings of the machine. Such messages may relate to statements in our program that the user neither knows about nor wants to know about!

It is particularly important to bear these points in mind when preparing interactive programs to be run from terminals. A user may be asked to input, for example, a number between 0 and 9. If he presses '?' by mistake, he might get the reply:

        data er no label

A naïve user receiving this message could be forgiven for deducing that computers are indeed inscrutable machines. A much more suitable response from a computer would be:

```
you have depressed the '?' key by mistake
please input a number between 0 and 9
```

Such a scheme is easy to implement:

```
writeln ( 'please input a number between 0 and 9' );
readln ( ch );

while ( ch < '0' ) or ( ch > '9' ) do
    begin
        writeln ( 'you have depressed the ''', ch, ''' key by mistake' );
        writeln ( 'please input a number between 0 and 9' );
        readln ( ch )
    end
```

In practice, it would be better to ensure that this loop does not get repeated indefinitely. For example, many keyboards have a SHIFT key which must be held down when a digit key is depressed, and this is often forgotten by beginners. If a new user was working at such a keyboard, he might well be confused by the consequent repeated request for a number. If he cannot get it right in, say, three attempts then maybe he should be referred to his tutor. The code to do this could be:

```
      writeln ( 'please input a number between 0 and 9' );
      readln ( ch );
      attempts := 1;

      while ( ( ch < '0' ) or ( ch > '9' ) ) and ( attempts < 3 ) do
         begin
            writeln ( 'you have depressed the ''', ch, ''' key by mistake' );
            writeln ( 'please input a number between 0 and 9' );
            readln ( ch );
            attempts := attempts + 1
         end;

      if ( ch < '0' ) or ( ch > '9' ) then
         begin
            writeln ( 'please refer to your tutor' );
            goto 99                               { program termination }
         end
```

The label 99 would probably be at the end of the program. This is perhaps the best way of dealing with the situation using the facilities described so far. Incidentally, when it has been confirmed that ch represents a digit character then it could be converted to the corresponding integer by using the expression

```
      ord ( ch ) - ord ( '0' )
```

Writing code to validate data which has been input from a terminal can be messy. The problem is that at each point where values are input they have to be checked, and this can spoil the flow of the program. The situation is rather better when using batch facilities, since the data can be pre-checked, if required, by a separate 'data vet' program. The main program for processing the data can then be run with the minimum of data checks. It should thus be simpler to write and debug.

Program 4.6 is a validation program for a file of data. Each entry is on a separate line and the layout of each line is described in the initial comment of the program. An entry is said to be *left justified* if it starts in the left-most column of the field.

Notice that no error is castastrophic. Once a mistake is found, a note is made of its position and the next field is examined.

Program Validate (input, output);

```
{*******************************************************************************
 *                                                                            *
 * Program 4.6                                                                *
 * A set of records is checked for validity.                                  *
 * The format of each line should be                                          *
 *                                                                            *
 *        columns                        information                          *
 *                                                                            *
 *        1 - 30             surname field   (alphabetic and hyphen           *
 *                                            characters left justified)      *
 *        31 - 38            initials field (upto four initials               *
 *                                            each followed by a blank)       *
 *        39 - 44            year of birth   (four digits left justified)     *
 *        45 - 46            sex field       ('M ' or 'F ')                    *
 *        47                 marital status field ('M' or 'S')                 *
 *                                                                            *
 *******************************************************************************}
```

Program 4.6 (continued opposite)

```
var
        colnumber : integer;          { column number on current line }

        ch, ch1, ch2, ch3, ch4, ch5, ch6 : char;

        surnameerror, initialserror, yearerror, sexerror,
        maritalerror, letterblank : boolean;

begin
    writeln ( 'Program 4.6  Validation of data file' );
    writeln ( '====================================' );
    writeln;

    writeln ( 'input data : (asterisks beneath a field denote ',
            'an error in that field)' );
    writeln;

    while not eof do
        begin
        { check surname field }
            colnumber    := 0;
            surnameerror := false;

            repeat
                read ( ch );
                write ( ch );
                colnumber := colnumber + 1;
                if ( ch <> ' ' )  and ( ch <> '-' )
                    and ( ( ch < 'A' )  or ( ch > 'Z' ) )  then
                        surnameerror := true
            until ( colnumber = 30 )  or surnameerror or ( ch = ' ' );

            if ( ch = ' ' )  and ( colnumber = 1 )  then      { field must start }
                surnameerror := true;                          {  with non-blank  }

            for colnumber := colnumber + 1 to 30 do
                begin
                    read ( ch );
                    write ( ch );
                    if ( ch <> ' ' )                    { only spaces }
                        and not surnameerror then       { allowed at  }
                            surnameerror := true        { end of field }
                end;


        { check initials field }
            colnumber := 30;
```

Program 4.6 (continued overleaf)

```
repeat
   read ( ch1, ch2 );
   write ( ch1, ch2 );
   colnumber   := colnumber + 2;
   letterblank := ( ch1 >= 'A' ) and ( ch1 <= 'Z' ) and ( ch2 = ' ' )
until ( colnumber = 38 ) or not letterblank;

initialserror := not letterblank and
               ( ( ch1 <> ' ' ) or ( ch2 <> ' ' )
                              or ( colnumber = 32 ) );

for colnumber := colnumber + 1 to 38 do
   begin
      read ( ch );
      write ( ch );
      if ( ch <> ' ' )                        { only spaces   }
         and not initialserror then           { allowed at end }
            initialserror := true             {   of field    }
   end;

{ check year field }
   read ( ch1, ch2, ch3, ch4, ch5, ch6 );
   write ( ch1, ch2, ch3, ch4, ch5, ch6 );
   colnumber := 44;
   yearerror := ( ch1 <> '1' ) or ( ( ch2 <> '8' ) and ( ch2 <> '9' ) )
            or ( ch3 < '0' ) or ( ch3 > '9' )
            or ( ch4 < '0' ) or ( ch4 > '9' )
            or ( ch5 <> ' ' ) or ( ch6 <> ' ' );

{ check sex field }
   read ( ch1, ch2 );
   write ( ch1, ch2 );
   colnumber := 46;
   sexerror := ( ( ch1 <> 'F' ) and ( ch1 <> 'M' ) ) or ( ch2 <> ' ' );

{ check marital status field }
   read ( ch1 );
   write ( ch1 );
   colnumber   := 47;
   maritalerror := ( ( ch1 <> 'M' ) and ( ch1 <> 'S' ) );
   writeln;

{ indicate error(s) underneath each output line }
   if surnameerror then
      write ( '******************************' )
   else
      write ( ' ' :30 );
   if initialserror then
      write ( '********' )
   else
      write ( ' ' :8 );
   if yearerror then
      write ( '******' )
   else
      write ( ' ' :6 );
```

Program 4.6 (continued opposite)

```
         if sexerror then
            write ( '**' )
         else
            write ( '  ' );
         if maritalerror then
            write ( '*' )
         else
            write ( ' ' );
         writeln;
         readln
      end

end.
```

Program 4.6 (continued)

Sample output from this program is shown below:

```
Program 4.6  Validation of data file
=====================================

input data : (asterisks beneath a field denote an error in that field)

BRITTEN                      B E      1913  M S
DOBBIE                       G S      1763  F S
                                      ******
HOWE                         D R      194?  M M
                                      ******
LANGE                        D R      1942  M M
MC ENROE                     J        1959  M 5
*****************************                **
ORWELL                       G        1903  M M
```

Output from Program 4.6

Quick quiz 4.4   (Solution on p. 86)

To make the Zeller's congruence program (Program 4.4) foolproof, code should be inserted to validate the input date. This validation could be in two parts—first a check could be made that the input consists of a string of digits (converting them to numbers if so); secondly, these numbers could be checked to ensure that they represent a valid date (for example, neither 4 31 72 nor 20 2 73 would be allowed). Assuming that the first part of this validation has been performed and the resultant numbers are stored using integer variables month, day and year, write a piece of code to check that the given date is a valid calendar date.

Summary

This chapter has introduced three methods of altering the normal flow of control in a computer program. The most useful of these is the **if** statement, since we often wish to specify one or two alternative courses of action, depending upon circumstances. If there are several equally likely possibilities, then a **case** statement may be the most appropriate construction to represent them. The **goto** statement represents a simple way of getting out of a tight corner. However, if a **goto** refers to a statement earlier in the program, it is almost certain that the same effect could be achieved more simply by using other statements. Forward-referencing **goto** statements are occasionally useful for terminating a computation when something goes wrong, but think very carefully before using this statement. All of the exercises in this book can be programmed quite easily without using the **goto** statement at all.

Solutions to quick quizzes

Quick quiz 4.1   (p. 71)

1
```
        incidences := 0;
        read ( number, nextnumber );

        repeat
          if number = nextnumber then
              incidences := incidences + 1;
          number := nextnumber;
          read ( nextnumber )
        until nextnumber = -1;

        writeln ( 'number of incidences = ', incidences :3 )
```

2
```
        for number := 1 to 100 do
          begin
              buzz := number mod 3 = 0;
              fizz := number mod 5 = 0;
              if buzz then
                  write ( 'buzz ' );
              if fizz then
                  write ( 'fizz' );
              if not buzz and not fizz then
                  write ( number );
              writeln
          end
```

There are a number of variations on this, some more and some less efficient. Ensure that your version works for the four distinct cases.

3   To check whether j is an exact multiple of i the relation

    j mod i = 0

may be used. This is true if i divides exactly into j, and false otherwise. If i is zero, however, then this is liable to cause a run-time error message since j **mod** i will normally be computed by dividing j by i. The assignment

        b := (i = 0) or ((j mod i) = 0)

would therefore be incorrect. An **if** statement may be used to separate out the two tests, as shown by the following code.

```
        if i = 0 then
            b := true
        else
            b := ( ( j mod i ) = 0 )
```

```
4      if breakfast then
          writeln ( 'breakfast time' )
       else if lunch then
          writeln ( 'lunch time' )
       else if tea then
          writeln ( 'tea time' )
```

Quick quiz 4.2 (p. 75)

(a)
```
    case number of
       1 : writeln ( 'one' );
       2 : writeln ( 'two' );
       3 : writeln ( 'three' );
       4 : writeln ( 'four' );
       5 : writeln ( 'five' );
       6 : writeln ( 'six' );
       7 : writeln ( 'seven' );
       8 : writeln ( 'eight' );
       9 : writeln ( 'nine' );
      10 : writeln ( 'ten' )
    end
```

(b)
```
    if ( number < 10 ) or ( number >= 20 ) then
       begin
          case number div 10 of
             0 :                 ;              { number less than ten }
             2 : write ( 'twenty' );
             3 : write ( 'thirty' );
             4 : write ( 'forty' );
             5 : write ( 'fifty' );
             6 : write ( 'sixty' );
             7 : write ( 'seventy' );
             8 : write ( 'eighty' );
             9 : write ( 'ninety' )
          end;

          if ( number mod 10 <> 0 ) and ( number > 20 ) then
             write ( ' - ' );

          case number mod 10 of
             0 : writeln;
             1 : writeln ( 'one' );
             2 : writeln ( 'two' );
             3 : writeln ( 'three' );
             4 : writeln ( 'four' );
             5 : writeln ( 'five' );
             6 : writeln ( 'six' );
             7 : writeln ( 'seven' );
             8 : writeln ( 'eight' );
             9 : writeln ( 'nine' )
          end
       end
    else
```

```
case number of
   10 : writeln ( 'ten' );
   11 : writeln ( 'eleven' );
   12 : writeln ( 'twelve' );
   13 : writeln ( 'thirteen' );
   14 : writeln ( 'fourteen' );
   15 : writeln ( 'fifteen' );
   16 : writeln ( 'sixteen' );
   17 : writeln ( 'seventeen' );
   18 : writeln ( 'eighteen' );
   19 : writeln ( 'nineteen' )
end
```

The code would be even more tedious to write, of course, if the value of number had to be validated.

Quick quiz 4.3   (p. 78)

(a)   read (number, nextnumber);

```
repeat
   if number > nextnumber then
      goto 10;
   number := nextnumber;
   read ( nextnumber )
until nextnumber = endmarker;
```

```
10:
   ascending := ( nextnumber = endmarker )
```

(b)   read (nextnumber);

```
repeat
   number := nextnumber;
   read ( nextnumber )
until ( nextnumber = endmarker ) or ( number > nextnumber );
```

```
   ascending := ( nextnumber = endmarker )
```

Note that the assignment

```
   ascending := ( nextnumber > number )
```

might not work if the end marker is smaller than the last number in the list.

Quick quiz 4.4   (p. 83)

```
readln ( month, day, year );

if ( year < 1752 ) or ( ( year = 1752 ) and ( month < 9 ) )
   or ( ( year = 1752 ) and ( month = 9 ) and ( day < 14 ) )
   or ( month < 1 ) or ( month > 12 ) or ( day < 1 ) then
      validdate := false
```

(continued overleaf)

```
    else
        case month of
            1, 3, 5, 7, 8, 10, 12 : validdate := ( day <= 31 );
                                2 : if year mod 4 <> 0 then
                                        validdate := ( day <= 28 )
                                    else if year mod 100 <> 0 then
                                        validdate := ( day <= 29 )
                                    else if year mod 400 <> 0 then
                                        validdate := ( day <= 28 )
                                    else
                                        validdate := ( day <= 29 );
                4, 6, 9, 11 : validdate := ( day <= 30 )
    end
```

Exercises

A1 Write a program to process deposits and withdrawals for a bank account. The input should consist of the initial balance followed by a set of deposits and withdrawals, each represented by the letter 'd' or 'w' followed by an amount. Each entry starts on a new line. The output should consist of a statement with the heading

   deposit withdrawal credit debit

where an entry is made in the third or fourth column, depending upon whether or not the account is overdrawn.

A2 Write a program to determine the number of ascending sequences (runs) in a list of positive numbers, assuming that the list is terminated by a negative value.

B1 A file of names has been set up where each line contains a surname, starting in column 1, followed by a list of forenames separated by spaces. Write a program to input this file and output a list of surnames, each followed by initials; for example,

   Brown Alan David

would be printed as

   Brown A D

B2 Write a program that inputs another Pascal program and outputs the program with comments removed (replaced by spaces).

B3 If your Pascal implementation has a function for generating pseudo-random numbers then you may use this to obtain an approximation to π. The procedure involves generating a random point in a unit square (by generating two random numbers between 0 and 1), and determining whether this point is inside or outside the circle of diameter 1 with centre at $(\frac{1}{2}, \frac{1}{2})$ see Fig. 4.5). This process is repeated for a large number of points

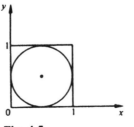

Fig. 4.5

(5000, say). The proportion of 'hits' (i.e. points lying inside or on the circle) to the total number of attempts will be roughly equal to the ratio of the area of the circle to that of the square (i.e. $\pi/4$). Use this technique in a program for approximating π. See how accurate the result is for various numbers of attempts.

C1   Write a program to convert an input number from decimal to hexadecimal (base 16).

C2   Write a program to calculate the number of days between two given dates.

C3   Write a program to input a number in decimal form and output the corresponding Roman numeral.

5
Subprograms

Introduction

We have already considered the breaking down of problems into sequences of steps in order to produce programs in which the different activities are separated out. It is often useful to consider these distinct pieces of program as self-contained *subprograms*, each with its own name and declarations. A subprogram may be defined and given a name in one part of a program and may then be called into action from another point. There are several good reasons for using subprograms:

(a) the structure of a program becomes easier to appreciate;
(b) the clarity of a program is improved by being able to refer to the *name* of a subprogram at the point at which it is to be executed, instead of having to write out the code at that point;
(c) when writing large programs, each subprogram can be developed and tested separately (perhaps by different programmers);
(d) since activities are isolated and localised, debugging becomes simpler;
(e) subprograms performing commonly-occurring tasks may be transferred from program to program;
(f) if a piece of code is to be used in several places in a program then it can be written out once and *called* from these points by referring to its name.

In relatively small programs the last of these features is the easiest to appreciate and demonstrate. In practice, the other advantages are at least as important.

There are two kinds of subprograms available in Pascal: the *procedure* and the *function*. They are similar in structure but are used in slightly different circumstances. We have already met the required functions in Pascal and so user-defined functions will be considered first, although procedures are perhaps more generally useful.

5.1 Functions

In order to use a standard function in Pascal we need only write down a function name followed by a *parameter* or *argument* (the value that the function acts upon) and the computer does the rest. If we required the square root of 5 we could write

```
y := sqrt ( 5 )
```

Someone has to write a piece of code to evaluate square roots, but this is the compiler writer's problem and the code does not appear in our program. We now consider the task of writing our own functions which may then be used in a similar way.

A common operation that is not provided in Pascal is exponentiation (raising a number to a power). If we have a program in which this operation occurs frequently then it will normally be worth defining a function to carry out the computation. The simplest case is the raising of a number to a positive integral power. The definition of a function to perform this is given as follows:

```
function power ( number : real; index : integer ) : real;

{**************************************************
 *                                                *
 * Raises number to positive integer power index  *
 *                                                *
 ************************************************}

var
     i : integer;

     product : real;

begin { power }

   product := 1;

   for i := 1 to index do
      product := product * number;

   power := product

end;   { power }
```

Notice that the structure of this definition is similar to that of a complete program, consisting of a heading, declarations and a statement part.

The heading of a function gives it a name, describes its parameters and specifies the type of the result. In this case the function operates upon two values represented by the *formal* parameters number and index, of types real and integer respectively. The result of the computation will be real—this is indicated by the ': real' following the right parenthesis of the parameter list.

The rest of the function definition looks like a program block and, in fact, has the same form. Any constants or variables to be used within the function body (but not outside it) may be declared at the head of this block—in which case they are *local* to this subprogram definition. The function value is computed within the statement part and assigned to the function name, in this case power.

It is important to distinguish between the purpose of formal parameters and locally declared variables. number and index represent quantities that are supplied to the function in order to compute the result, and they are therefore included in the parameter list. i and product are variables that are used to aid the computation and the quantities they represent have no relevance outside the function block. For this reason, they are declared within the function block.

Once defined, a function may be used in any context where a value of the corresponding type is expected. If p was a real variable then the following would be a valid assignment:

```
p := power ( 5.3, 4 )
```

When the power function is executed the *actual parameter* values (5.3 and 4) become the initial values of the corresponding formal parameters, number and index. The actual parameters are not constrained to be numbers. They may be variables or even expressions so long as, when evaluated, they produce values of the appropriate type. The call in the following statement would be perfectly acceptable if diameter was of type real or integer.

```
volume := 4 * pi * power ( diameter / 2, 3 ) / 3
```

Many other functions that are needed, particularly in numerical computations, are not standard in Pascal. These include tan, arcsin, arccos, sinh, cosh and random (the last of these gives a random number between 0 and 1). Once a user has defined a function to perform a computation it can easily be moved from program to program.

A function that would be useful for business applications is one to calculate compound interest. The basic idea is that interest is paid on the principal at a specific time (as in simple interest) but then the interest is added to the principal and next time the interest is computed it is calculated using this new principal and so on.

We will simplify the problem by assuming that the interest is paid annually. The method used involves first computing the factor (1 + rate / 100). This factor when multiplied by the principal will give the new principal after one year. By multiplying the new principal by this factor again the new principal for the following year is found. The process continues for the appropriate number of years. By subtracting the initial principal from the final amount the total interest is found. A function for performing these calculations is given below:

```
function compoundinterest ( principal, rate : real;  time : integer ) : real;

{*********************************************************************
 *                                                                 *
 * Computes the compound interest on the given principal over a given *
 * (whole) number of years assuming interest is compounded annually   *
 *                                                                 *
 *******************************************************************}

var
      factor, newprincipal : real;

      yearnumber : integer;


begin { compoundinterest }

   newprincipal := principal;
   factor := 1 + rate / 100;

   for yearnumber := 1 to time do
      newprincipal := newprincipal * factor;

   compoundinterest := newprincipal - principal

end;   { compoundinterest }
```

The function has three parameters—two of type real and one integer. As in the previous example the final result will be a real value.

Function definitions in Pascal, as in most Algol-like languages, are regarded as declarations, and for this reason are included in the declaration section of programs. They are placed after variable declarations and before the statement part. The definition and use of the function compoundinterest is illustrated in Program 5.1. Note that execution starts at the beginning of the main program and that the function is not executed until a reference is made to it from within the main program.

Incidentally, a good habit to get into is to write an explanatory comment in every function heading, and another short comment at the end to indicate its completion. Also leave line spaces before and after the definition to make it easily distinguishable as a separate piece of code.

```pascal
Program Compinterest ( input, output );

{*******************************************************
 *                                                     *
 * Program 5.1                                         *
 * Tests a function for computing compound interest.   *
 *                                                     *
 *******************************************************}

var
      money, interest,  { dollars }
      rateofinterest : real;

      numberofyears : integer;



function compoundinterest ( principal, rate : real;  time : integer ) : real;

{****************************************************************************
 *                                                                        *
 * Computes the compound interest on the given principal over a given     *
 * (whole) number of years assuming interest is compounded annually       *
 *                                                                        *
 ****************************************************************************}

var
      factor, newprincipal : real;

      yearnumber : integer;


begin { compoundinterest }

   newprincipal := principal;
   factor := 1 + rate / 100;

   for yearnumber := 1 to time do
      newprincipal := newprincipal * factor;

   compoundinterest := newprincipal - principal

end;  { compoundinterest }

begin  { main program }

   writeln ( 'Program 5.1  Compound interest' );
   writeln ( '==============================' );
   writeln;
```

Program 5.1 (continued opposite)

```
      write ( ' principal      interest rate (%)      period (years)' );
      writeln ( '   interest ($)' );
      writeln;

while not eof do
   begin
      readln ( money, rateofinterest, numberofyears );
      interest := compoundinterest ( money, rateofinterest, numberofyears );
      writeln ( money :8:2, rateofinterest :17:2, numberofyears :17,
               interest :19:2 );
   end
```

Program 5.1 (continued)

A function may take any scalar value. In Program 5.2 the function has a value of type char.


```
Program Encode ( input, output );

{*********************************************************************
 *                                                                   *
 * Program 5.2                                                       *
 * A message is read in and encoded using a simple coding function. *
 *                                                                   *
 *********************************************************************}

var
      character, symcode : char;



function code ( ch : char ) : char;

{***********************************************************************
 *                                                                     *
 * ch is encoded by taking its successor in the character code.  The last *
 * character in the character set is encoded by the first character.     *
 *                                                                     *
 ***********************************************************************}

const
      firstchar = ' ';        { first and last printable }
      lastchar = '~';         { characters in ascii code }

begin { code }

   if ch = lastchar then
      code := firstchar
   else
      code := succ ( ch )

end; { code }
```

Program 5.2 (continued overleaf)

```
begin   { main program }

    writeln ( 'Program 5.2   Encoding a message' );
    writeln ( '================================' );
    writeln;
    writeln ( 'coded message :' );
    writeln;

    while not eof do
        if eoln then
            begin
                readln;
                writeln
            end
        else
            begin
                read ( character );
                symcode := code ( character );
                write ( symcode );
            end
end.
```

Program 5.2 (continued)

The encoding function is just a single statement that is only called from one point and it may seem hardly worthwhile to separate out the definition from the main program. If, however, we wish to substitute a different encoding function at a later date then this can be simply done without changing the main program at all—an important feature of subprograms.

Quick quiz 5.1   (Solutions on p. 110)

1 Construct a function cash that has two integer parameters dollars and cents representing the dollars and cents of a cash amount and that produces a real value with the dollars as the whole number part and the cents as the fractional part.

2 Construct a function fieldwidth that takes a single integer parameter and calculates the number of characters the number contains.

5.2 Procedures

A procedure is similar to a program in that it is a piece of code with an associated name. In the same way that a program has parameters (usually the file parameters input and output) that provide a link with the external environment, a procedure may have parameters for receiving information from and for transmitting information to the rest of the program.

Two aspects of a procedure need to be considered—its definition and its execution. Procedure definitions, like function definitions, are regarded as declarations in Pascal and are included in the same part of the heading.

An example of a procedure definition might be as follows.

```
procedure copyline;

{***********************************************************
 *                                                         *
 * A line of text is copied from the input device to the   *
 * output device                                           *
 *                                                         *
 ***********************************************************}

var
      character : char;

begin { copyline }

   while not eoln do
     begin
        read ( character );
        write ( character )
     end;

   readln;
   writeln

end;   { copyline }
```

Recall that eoln is a standard function that takes the value true when the last character of the current line has been read. The effect of the execution of this procedure will be to copy the contents of the current data line straight to the output device.

The syntax of the definition is straightforward. The word **procedure** is followed by the procedure name and any formal parameters (in this case, none are needed). The rest of the procedure has the same structure as a program block.

The procedure is *called*, or *invoked*, when another reference is made to the procedure name from within the program. In this case, the placing of the name copyline in any position where a statement is expected will cause the procedure to be executed when control reaches that point. For example:

```
writeln ( 'the first input line is' );
copyline;
writeln ( 'the second input line is' );
copyline
```

When such a *procedure statement* is executed, control is transferred to the procedure definition. The code in this definition is executed and then control is returned to the statement following the procedure statement.

If an error is discovered in the data to a program then we may wish just to print out the remaining data. The statement

```
while not eof do
   copyline
```

would achieve this.

copyline uses no information from the rest of the program and calculates no values that are used elsewhere. For this reason it needs no parameters. The next procedure, newline, *does* have a parameter.

```
procedure newline ( n : integer );

{*******************************************
 *                                         *
 * The output device moves on by n lines   *
 *                                         *
 *******************************************}

var
       linenumber : integer;

begin {newline }

   for linenumber := 1 to n do
       writeln

end;   { newline }
```

In any corresponding procedure statement an actual parameter would be needed to specify the number of lines to be skipped.

```
newline ( 4 )
```

and

```
newline ( number )
```

might be typical calls. In the second example number must be of type integer and must be given a value before the call is made.

Program 5.3 uses newline and two functions in order to control the layout of text to be copied from a file. Note the use of the required procedure page for indicating that a new page should be started on the output device. On a vdu this might cause the screen to be cleared.

```
Program Textformatter ( input, output );

{**********************************************************************
 *                                                                    *
 * Program 5.3                                                        *
 * Text is copied from a file to lineprinter. Special control characters *
 * indicate newline, new page of output and end of text.              *
 *                                                                    *
 **********************************************************************}

const
      linemarker = '#';
      pagemarker = '&';
      endmarker  = '%';

var
      number : integer;

      character : char;
```

Program 5.3 (continued opposite)

```
function control ( ch : char )  : boolean;

{******************************************************
 *                                                    *
 * Returns true if 'ch' is new line or page indicator *
 * or terminator                                      *
 *                                                    *
 ******************************************************}

begin { control }

   control := ( ch = linemarker )  or ( ch = pagemarker )
                                   or ( ch = endmarker )

end;  { control }


function nextchar : char;

{*****************************************************
 *                                                   *
 * Takes as its value the next character on input *
 *                                                   *
 *****************************************************}

var
     c : char;

begin { nextchar }

   if eoln then
      readln;
   read ( c );
   nextchar := c

end;  { nextchar }


procedure newline ( n : integer );

{******************************
 *                            *
 * Gives n new lines of output *
 *                            *
 ******************************}

var
     linenumber : integer;

begin { newline }

   for linenumber := 1 to n do
      writeln

end;  { newline }
```

Program 5.3 (continued overleaf)

```
begin { main program }

    writeln ( 'Program 5.3  Text formatter' );
    writeln ( '============================' );
    writeln;

    character := nextchar;

    while character <> endmarker do
      begin

          while not control ( character )  do
            begin
               write ( character );
               character := nextchar
            end;

          if character = linemarker then
            begin
               read ( number );
               character := nextchar;                { line marker }
               newline ( number );
               character := nextchar
            end
          else if character = pagemarker then
            begin
               page ( output );
               character := nextchar
            end

      end;

    writeln

end.
```

Program 5.3 (continued)

Sample data is shown below:

&   East Virginia#2#I was born in East Virginia#1#North Carolina I did go#1#
There I met a fair young maiden#1#And whose name I did not know.#2#Well her hair
was dark of color#1#Cheeks they were a rosy red#1#On her breast she wore white
lilies#1#Where I longed to lay my head.%

The corresponding output would appear as:

```
        East Virginia

    I was born in East Virginia
    North Carolina I did go
    There I met a fair young maiden
    And whose name I did not know.

    Well her hair was dark of color
    Cheeks they were a rosy red
    On her breast she wore white lilies
    Where I longed to lay my head.
```

More elaborate text processors than this are becoming popular for controlling textual output in newspapers, books and other publications.

Quick quiz 5.2   (Solutions on p. 111)

Write a procedure skip such that a call skip(n) will cause n character positions on the input stream to be skipped (don't forget to allow for the line separator between input records).

5.3   Value and variable parameters

Parameters have only been used, so far, for transmitting values *to* subprograms. If values are computed *by* a subprogram then these values may be transmitted to the calling program by using parameters.

For example, we may wish to write a procedure to break down a time given in seconds into hours, minutes and seconds. The procedure timeconversion carries this out.

```
procedure timeconversion ( totalseconds : integer;
                           var hours, minutes, seconds : integer );

{***********************************************************
 *                                                         *
 * Converts time in seconds to hours, minutes and seconds  *
 *                                                         *
 ***********************************************************}

begin { timeconversion }

   hours   := totalseconds div 3600;
   minutes := ( totalseconds mod 3600 ) div 60;
   seconds := ( totalseconds mod 3600 ) mod 60

end; { timeconversion }
```

The parameter totalseconds supplies a value to the procedure and its description has a similar form to that used in earlier examples. This kind of parameter is called a *value parameter*. The other three parameters are used to compute results within the procedure and pass these values back to the main program. They are called *variable parameters* and are distinguished from value parameters by placing the word **var** before their names in the procedure heading. This notation makes the parameter list seem more than ever like a declaration, but do not confuse the two. Declarations create memory space for variables, whereas a parameter list only indicates what type each corresponding actual parameter must be and how it will be treated inside the subprogram.

Once defined, the procedure can be called, in the normal way, by referring to the procedure name and giving a list of actual parameters. A typical call of timeconversion could be:

```
timeconversion ( t, hrs, mins, secs )
```

where t,hrs, mins and secs are variables that have been declared in the main program, and 't' has been given the value 4700. The first parameter is a value parameter and may therefore be a number, variable or expression. This is evaluated before entry into the procedure. The other three actual parameters must be names of variables—since they are going to contain results computed in the procedure they can be nothing else. To place a constant or expression in any of these positions would be meaningless.

Unlike value parameters, variable parameters are not evaluated on entry into a procedure. In this case, hrs, mins and secs need not have been assigned a value at all. On exit from the procedure they *will* have values—the values of the corresponding formal parameters. In the above call, hours, minutes and seconds will be given the values 1, 18 and 20, respectively. hrs, mins and secs will therefore take these same values.

When a subprogram is executed, the variable parameters are treated differently from value parameters. The first thing that happens when a call is made is that each variable formal parameter name becomes an alternative name (*alias*) for the corresponding actual parameter. For example, hours and hrs refer to the same location during the execution of timeconversion. Consequently, any change in hours causes a similar change in hrs.

A different mechanism is used for value parameters. Their formal parameters act rather like variables declared locally to a procedure. The only purpose of the corresponding actual parameters is to give them initial values. After this, any changes in the values of the formal parameters do not affect the values of the actual parameters. This is a safety mechanism. If we wish to ensure that a variable used as an actual parameter is not affected by that procedure then it should be made a value parameter. To see the effects of these processes for the timeconversion procedure look at the following diagram.

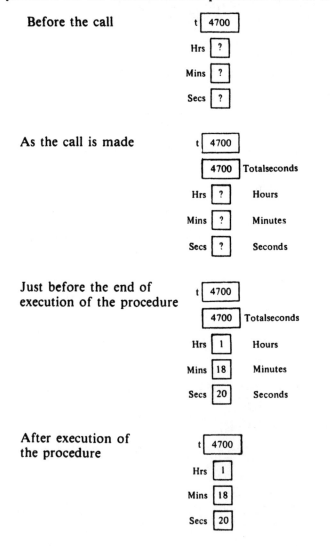

```pascal
Program Reactiontime ( input, output );

{*****************************************************************
 *                                                              *
 * Program 5.4                                                  *
 * The start and finish times of a chemical reaction are read in. *
 * The reaction time in seconds is calculated and all three times *
 * are converted to hours, minutes and seconds prior to output. *
 *                                                              *
 *****************************************************************}

var
      starttime, stoptime, reacttime,      { three times in seconds }
      starthour, startminute, startsecond,
      stophour, stopminute, stopsecond,
      reacthour, reactminute, reactsecond : integer;


procedure timeconversion ( totalseconds : integer;
                           var hours, minutes, seconds : integer );

{*********************************************************
 *                                                      *
 * Converts time in seconds to hours, minutes and seconds *
 *                                                      *
 *********************************************************}

begin { timeconversion }

   hours   := totalseconds div 3600;
   minutes := ( totalseconds mod 3600 ) div 60;
   seconds := ( totalseconds mod 3600 ) mod 60

end;  { timeconversion }


begin { main program }

   read ( starttime, stoptime );
   reacttime := stoptime - starttime;

   timeconversion ( starttime, starthour, startminute, startsecond );
   timeconversion ( stoptime, stophour, stopminute, stopsecond );
   timeconversion ( reacttime, reacthour, reactminute, reactsecond );

   writeln ( 'Program 5.4  Reaction time computation' );
   writeln ( '=====================================' );
   writeln;

   writeln ( 'start time    =', starthour   :4, ' hours',
                                startminute :4, ' minutes',
                                startsecond :4, ' seconds' );
   writeln ( 'stop time     =', stophour    :4, ' hours',
                                stopminute  :4, ' minutes',
                                stopsecond  :4, ' seconds' );
   writeln ( 'reaction time =', reacthour   :4, ' hours',
                                reactminute :4, ' minutes',
                                reactsecond :4, ' seconds' )

end.
```

Program 5.4

Actual parameter names have been placed to the left of the location boxes and formal parameter names to the right. Note that the formal parameters have no meaning outside the procedure. Even within the procedure, hours, minutes and seconds have no substance except as aliases for the corresponding actual parameters.

timeconversion is seen in operation in Program 5.4. This is a program for monitoring the progress of a chemical reaction. The times, in seconds, at the start and at the end of the reaction have been registered (perhaps by some monitoring device). The computer inputs these times, calculates the reaction time and outputs the results in hours, minutes and seconds.

The syntax of parameter lists containing variable and value parameters is shown in Fig. 5.1.

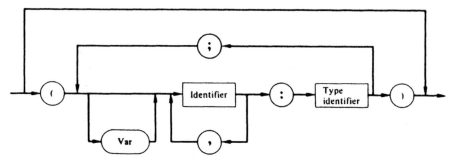

Fig. 5.1

Parameters of similar type and having the same parameter-passing mechanism can be listed together, separated by commas. Parameter descriptions of different types or having different mechanisms are separated by semicolons. For example,

        procedure p1 (**var** a : real; i : integer)

would define one variable parameter a of type real and one value parameter i of type integer. To make i a variable parameter the following description could be used.

        procedure p2 (**var** a : real; **var** i : integer)

Similarly, if i and j were both of type integer but i was a variable parameter and j was a value parameter, the procedure heading might be

        procedure p3 (**var** i : integer; j : integer)

There are occasions when a parameter supplies a value to a procedure but we may also wish to change its value inside the procedure. In this case the parameter should be made variable:

```
procedure swap ( var a, b : real );

{**********************************
 *                                *
 * Exchanges the values of a and b *
 *                                *
 **********************************}

var
     copy : real;

begin { swap }

   copy := a;
   a    := b;
   b    := copy

end;  { swap }
```

Suppose that two real variables x1 and x2 have been declared in the main program; then the sequence of statements

```
x1 := 2.4;
x2 := 3.6;
swap ( x1, x2 );
writeln ( x1, x2 )
```

would cause the values 3.6 and 2.4 to be output in that order.

It is important to decide, for each parameter, whether it should be made value or variable. Making what should be a variable parameter into a value parameter, or *vice versa*, is quite a common error which is sometimes difficult to spot. If you have an inexplicable error involving the passing of values to or from a subprogram then check that the parameters are of the right kind. In addition, check that the parameters used in each call of a subprogram are in the same position as in the subprogram declaration. It is the *order* in which parameters are listed that provides the link between formal and actual parameters, not their names.

Do not worry if you have found the material in this section difficult to grasp first time through. For most applications of procedures you can use the following criteria to decide upon parameter type.

(1) If a parameter represents a *result* computed *in* the procedure to be used elsewhere in the program then make it a variable parameter.
(2) If a parameter is used only to transmit a *value to* the procedure then make it a value parameter.

All the features of procedure parameter lists described apply equally to functions, although functions are normally used when only one result is to be computed.

Quick quiz 5.3   (Solutions on p. 112)

1   If, in the swap procedure, a and b had been made value parameters, and x1 and x2 had the values 2.4 and 3.6 respectively, what would be the effect of the call

```
swap ( x1, x2 )
```

(Draw a diagram similar to the one on p. 100 to show the values of the actual and formal parameters at different stages.)

2   Write a procedure called order with three integer parameters i, j, k such that after the call

    order (n1, n2, n3)

the integer variables n1, n2 and n3 satisfy the condition n1 ⩽ n2 ⩽ n3 .

5.4   Further features of subprograms#

You can get by perfectly well by using just the features of subprograms described so far. However, if you wish to exploit their full potential then you need to know about their other properties, and other ways of using them. In this section we have collected together three other aspects of subprograms.

(1)   *Scope of identifiers*
The body of a subprogram is a block, possibly with its own declarations. As mentioned earlier, any declarations made in a subprogram are valid only within that subprogram. In this way it becomes possible to have blocks within blocks, each with its own set of declarations. Corresponding to the declaration of an identifier is a section of program within which the declaration applies. This is called the *scope* of that identifier. Normally the scope of an identifier extends from the point in a block at which it is declared to the end of that block.

For example, a variable declared at the beginning of a program may be referred to in an appropriate context from that point until the end of the program. Examine the program skeleton opposite. On the right-hand side the scope of each identifier is indicated.

The constant a and the variables b, c and d may be used anywhere in the program and are known as *global* identifiers. Since they may be referred to within any procedures and functions in the program, global variables may be used in many cases to pass information to and from subprograms. However, it is usually preferable to let parameters do this, for several reasons.

(i)   In a subprogram call, all the expressions and variables used in the subprogram are set out in the parameter list. This makes it clear exactly what information the subprogram uses and also what results it calculates. There will be no so-called *side-effects* caused when a variable that is global to a subprogram is changed within that subprogram.

(ii)   Debugging is made easier since as much information as possible has been made local to the subprogram. (This is one reason why identifiers should be declared local to a subprogram, if possible.)

(iii)   The safeguard on value parameters makes it less likely that something will go wrong.

(iv)   The transfer of a subprogram from one program to another is made simpler.

As can be seen from the skeleton program the scope of a subprogram parameter is the whole of that subprogram. The scope of subprograms themselves (i.e. the section of the

---

This section may be omitted on first reading

Program example1 (input, output);

label
    500;

const
    a = 10;

var
    b, c, d : integer;

procedure e (f, g, h : real);

var
    i, j : char;

begin { e }
   .
   .
end;   { e }

function k (**var** l : integer) : boolean;

var
    m : boolean;

begin { k }
   .
   .
end;   { k }

begin { main program }
   .
   .
   .
end.

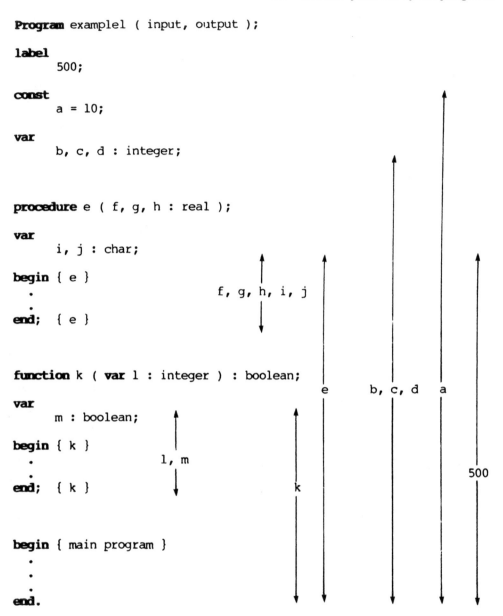

program from which they may be called) extends from their definition to the end of the block in which they are defined. A method of increasing their scope will be described later in this section.

Since any block may contain further subprogram declarations, each with its own block, there is no limit to the 'nesting' of declarations and scopes. The situation is further complicated by the fact that an identifier declared in one block may be redefined in an inner block:

```
Program example2 ( input, output );

var
      a, b : real;



procedure c ( d, e : integer );

var
      a : char;
begin { c }
   .
   .
end;  { c }



begin { main program }
   .
   .
   .
end.
```

Here, any reference to a in the main program will use the main program declaration and a will be of type real. Any reference to a in the procedure c will be governed by the declaration at the head of c and therefore a is of type char in this block. A call of c within the main program will cause the real a and its value to become temporarily inaccessible. After execution of c the previous value of a will be restored.

If the same name is used in more than one declaration in a program then you can always tell, by inspecting the program, which declaration governs a particular reference. Follow the blocks outwards from the innermost one containing the reference, examining the declarations at the head of each block. The first declaration of that name that you find is the one that corresponds to that identifier.

Usually it is inadvisable to use the same name to describe two different objects. An occasion when this technique *can* be used safely is in the naming of formal parameters. It is often convenient to give formal parameters the same names as the corresponding actual parameters (if the actual parameter names do not change from call to call). This emphasises the correspondence between them, and avoids the problem of trying to think of suitable alternative names. For example, in Program 5.2 the formal parameter of code might just as well have been called character. Remember, though, that the actual parameters are still distinct variables and need to be declared at the head of the program.

The last point that should be mentioned is that scope rules for labels are slightly different from those for other declarations. The statement identified by a label must occur in the statement part of the block in which the label is declared. Label 500 in this program can only prefix one statement and that must be between the **begin** and **end** of the main program. However, **goto** 500 may occur anywhere in the block (including the subprograms e and k). A consequence of this rule is that a **goto** can be used to transfer control *out of* a subprogram but not *into* a subprogram.

(2) *Recursion*
The scope of a subprogram identifier extends from its heading to the end of the block in which it is defined. This means that one subprogram can be called from inside another

one or even from inside itself. If a procedure or function contains a call to itself from within its own statement part it is said to be *recursive*.

Defining a process in terms of itself may seem strange, but there are many instances where recursion provides the most simple and concise description. You have already met an example of a recursive definition, perhaps without realising it. Look at the syntactic description of Pascal given in Appendix A. The construction called 'factor' has several alternative forms, one of which consists of the word **not** followed by the construction 'factor'. So 'factor' occurs within its own definition. If you were writing a compiler for Pascal it might be appropriate to use a recursive procedure to process factors.

Many types of computations may be described fairly easily using recursion and there is evidence to suggest that recursion is a more fundamental operation than repetition. Several common mathematical functions may be defined concisely using recursion. Three examples are given below.

$$factorial(n) = n \times factorial(n - 1) \quad n \geqslant 1$$
$$factorial(n) = 1 \qquad\qquad\qquad\qquad n = 0$$

$$comb(n,r) = comb(n - 1, r) + comb(n - 1, r - 1) \quad n > r > 0$$
$$comb(n, r) = 1 \qquad\qquad\qquad\qquad\qquad\qquad n = r$$
$$comb(n, r) = 1 \qquad\qquad\qquad\qquad\qquad\qquad r = 0$$

$$fib(n) = fib(n - 1) + fib(n - 2) \quad n \geqslant 2$$
$$fib(n) = 1 \qquad\qquad\qquad\qquad\qquad n = 1$$
$$fib(n) = 0 \qquad\qquad\qquad\qquad\qquad n = 0$$

The first function, n factorial, we have already met. The second formula gives the number of combinations of n objects taken r at a time (i.e. the number of distinct sets of r items that can be chosen from n items). The last function calculates the terms in a Fibonacci series, where, for $n > 1$, each term is calculated by adding together the two immediately preceding terms.

These definitions, like all recursive definitions, have two features in common: firstly, there is an element of counting in each of the functions; secondly, there is always a 'get-out' condition—that is, at least one situation in which a recursive call is not made—otherwise the process would never terminate. Since Pascal allows a subprogram to call itself there is no problem in representing a recursive definition:

```
function factorial ( n : integer ) : integer;

{************************************
 *                                  *
 * Computes n factorial recursively *
 *                                  *
 ***********************************}

begin { factorial }

   if n = 0 then
      factorial := 1
   else
      factorial := n * factorial ( n - 1 )

end;  { factorial }
```

Keeping track of the execution of a recursive function can be a problem. Each call causes the function to be executed again with a different parameter. When execution of a call is completed, control returns to the point following the point at which the call was made.

For example, a call factorial(3) would, during its execution, involve a call to factorial(2). Similarly, to calculate factorial(2), factorial(1) needs to be evaluated. Next, during the computation of factorial(1), a call to factorial(0) is made. The value of factorial(0) is 1 and so, once this has been found, the execution of factorial(1) can continue by computing 1×1. Now factorial(2) may be computed giving $2 \times 1 = 2$. Lastly, factorial(3) can be calculated by evaluating 3×2.

One point that can cause confusion is that the same function identifier factorial and parameter name n are used to represent different values during the computation. This presents no problems to the computer, however, since each call initiates a new *activation* of the function and the new declarations of the identifiers temporarily override the earlier ones.

Although the three mathematical examples mentioned earlier are good examples of recursive definitions, they produce inefficient programs. There are two reasons for this. Firstly, nested subprogram calls on computers are usually inefficient in terms of time and space used. Secondly, there are often repeated computations that are difficult to limit. For example, when evaluating comb(5,2), comb(2,1) is computed 3 times.

Unless a process can be expressed very much more easily in recursive rather than iterative (i.e. repetitive) terms it is usually advisable to use iteration. For example, a perfectly acceptable iterative definition of factorial(*n*) was given in Section 3.4. Where recursion really comes into its own is in the processing of recursive data structures, such as syntax diagrams and other structures that we will meet in the second part of this book.

One last aspect of recursion should be mentioned at this point. A subprogram a may be declared which contains a call to a second subprogram b. If b contains a call to a then this is known as *mutual recursion*. In fact, more than two definitions may be involved. Refer again to the syntax diagrams in Appendix A. A 'factor' may consist of an 'expression' enclosed within parentheses. An 'expression' may be a 'simple expression', an example of which is a 'term'. Finally, a 'term' may be a 'factor'. Whenever this *indirect recursion* is used, it is inevitable that at least one of the subprograms will be called before it is defined (think of the simplest case of a calls b and b calls a). To overcome this problem, a *forward reference* may be used. This gives the heading of a subprogram without its code. Later on, the subprogram body can be defined.

```
procedure a ( i : integer; r : real ); forward;



procedure b ( ch : char );

var
      j : integer;

      s : real;

begin { b }
      .
      .
   a ( j, s );          { call of a }
      .
end;  { b }
```

(continued opposite)

```
procedure a;        { note that the parameter list is not repeated }

var
      c : char;

begin { a }
      .
      .
    b ( c );           { call of b }
      .
end;  { a }
```

(3) *Subprograms as parameters*

In addition to value and variable parameters there are two other kinds of formal parameter that a subprogram may have. If a subprogram contains a reference to another subprogram that may change from call to call then this subprogram may be made into a parameter.

We may wish to write a procedure that will tabulate values of functions for a given set of arguments. By making one of the parameters of the tabulation procedure a function, different functions can be tabulated by just changing the function name in the call. A suitable procedure declaration might be

```
procedure tabulate ( function f ( i : integer ) : real;
                     lower, upper : integer );

var
      argument : integer;

begin { tabulate }

    for argument := lower to upper do
      writeln ( argument :3, f ( argument ) :8:2 )

end; { tabulate }
```

The function f may have any number and types of parameters but the parameter names have no significance. In this example the parameter i could be renamed without affecting any other part of the program. Two possible calls of tabulate are given below and you will note that the parameters of thisfunction and thatfunction are not given in the heading. The parameters are specified indirectly in the references to f in the procedure body.

```
tabulate ( thisfunction, 0, 10 )


tabulate ( thatfunction, -5, 25 )
```

thisfunction and thatfunction must be declared within the program itself and so could not be required functions. In this example they must also each have a single value parameter of type integer and give a result of type real.

In a similar way a procedure can be made into a parameter. The full syntax for subprogram parameters is given in the parameter list description given in appendix A.

The syntax for both function and procedure parameters has been modified by the ISO standard from the original Wirth specification. If the compiler you are using conforms to the old standard then you are not likely to have to include the parameters of a subprogram in its specification and tabulate, for instance, would have the heading

procedure tabulate (**function** f : real; lower, upper : integer);

However, the subprogram parameter (in this case f) would only be permitted to have value parameters.

Quick quiz 5.4   (Solution on p. 94)

Write a recursive function to compute comb(n,r).

Summary

Effective and appropriate use of subprograms is a vital part of structured programming. Ideally, the main program should have a very simple structure, consisting largely of calls to subprograms. When first working at a program you should start by reading this section to get a general appreciation of the main steps involved. If a subprogram performs a complicated process then this, in turn, should be described by a sequence of further subprogram calls.

At first, the use of subprograms may increase rather than decrease the number of errors in your programs. Once you have mastered their use, however, particularly the handling of value and variable parameters and the scope rules, you will find that they make the writing of large programs much easier.

Solutions to quick quizzes

Quick quiz 5.1   (p. 113)

1   **function** cash (dollars, cents : integer) : real;

```
{**********************************************************
 *                                                        *
 * Converts dollars and cents into a single real value    *
 * with the integer part representing the dollars and     *
 * the fractional part representing the cents             *
 *                                                        *
 **********************************************************}
```

begin { cash }

```
   cash := dollars + cents / 100
```

end;   { cash }

2   **function** fieldwidth (n : integer) : integer;

```
{******************************************************************
 *                                                                *
 * Calculates the number of characters contained in the integer n *
 *                                                                *
 ******************************************************************}
```

(continued opposite)

```
var
      number, { this is initially set to abs(n) and repeatedly divided }
              { by 10 until it is a one digit number                    }

      charnumber : integer;

begin { fieldwidth }

   if n >= 0 then
      begin
         charnumber := 1;
         number := n
      end
   else
      begin
         charnumber := 2;  { one for the '-' sign }
         number := -n
      end;

   while number >= 10 do
      begin
         charnumber := charnumber + 1;
         number := number div 10
      end;

   fieldwidth := charnumber

end;  { fieldwidth }
```

Quick quiz 5.2   (p. 99)

```
procedure skip ( n : integer );

{****************************************
 *                                      *
 * Skips n positions on the input stream *
 *                                      *
 ****************************************}
var
      i : integer;

      ch : char;

begin { skip }

   i := 0;

   while i < n do
      if eoln then
         readln
      else
         begin
            read ( ch );
            i := i + 1
         end

end;  { skip }
```

Quick quiz 5.3   (p. 103)

1 Before the call

x1 `2.4`

x2 `3.6`

As the call is made

x1 `2.4`

x2 `3.6`

`2.4` a

`3.6` b

Just before the end
of the procedure

x1 `2.4`

x2 `3.6`

`3.6` a

`2.4` b

After execution of
the procedure

x1 `2.4`

x2 `3.6`

If a and b are value parameters then, during a call of the procedure, they act like locally declared variables with initial values of 2.4 and 3.6 respectively. During the execution of swap their values are interchanged, but this has no effect on x1 and x2. After execution of the procedure, a and b disappear leaving x1 and x2 unchanged. This, of course, is unlikely to be what the programmer intended.

2

```
procedure order ( var i, j, k : integer );

    {**************************************************
     *                                                *
     * Orders the parameter values so that i <= j <= k *
     *                                                *
     **************************************************}

    begin { order }
        if i > j then
            swap ( i, j );
        if j > k then
            swap ( j, k );
        if i > j then
            swap ( i, j )

    end;   { order }
```

There is no problem about using swap as long as its declaration precedes that of order. If you have followed the same steps but have not used swap then that is fine. The final test, i > j, is necessary in case k was initially the smallest value. You could make the code slightly more efficient by noticing that the third test is not necessary if the result of the second test is false. The procedure body could thus be written as

```
begin { order }

   if i > j then
      swap ( i, j );
   if j > k then
      begin
         swap ( j, k );
         if i > j then
            swap ( i, j )
      end

end;   { order }
```

In most circumstances the time saved in execution would not be worth the additional complexity of this second version.

Quick quiz 5.4   (p. 110)

```
function comb ( n, r : integer ) : integer;

{*****************************************************************
 *                                                               *
 * Computes the number of combinations of n objects selected     *
 * r at a time                                                    *
 *                                                               *
 *****************************************************************}

begin { comb }

   if ( n = r ) or ( r = 0 ) then
      comb := 1
   else
      comb := comb ( n - 1, r ) + comb ( n - 1, r - 1 )

end;   { comb }
```

Exercises

A1 The number of combinations of n objects chosen r at a time, ^nC_r, is given by the formula

$$^nC_r = \frac{n \times (n-1) \times \ldots \times (n-r+1)}{r \times (r-1) \times \ldots \times 1} \qquad n \geqslant r > 0$$

Write a function to compute ^nC_r using this formula and test it in a program that prints out ^nC_r for all values of n and r between 1 and 10 for $n \geqslant r$. The results should be output in a table.

A2 Write and test an iterative function $f(n)$ that takes the value of the nth Fibonacci number.

A3   Write and test a Boolean function prime(n) that is set to true if n is a prime number and to false otherwise.

B1   The cost of a telegram is a fixed amount multiplied by the number of words it contains. Any word of over ten letters counts as two words, over twenty letters as three words and so on. Write a program to input a telegram and compute its cost. Include a procedure that reads in a word and computes the number of words it is equivalent to for costing purposes. The procedure should also have a parameter endofmessage that is set to true if there are no words left. Assume that there may be any number of blanks between words and that the last word is followed immediately by a period.

B2   Write a procedure to read in a six-digit date of the form $m_1m_2d_1d_2y_1y_2$. The procedure should read in the date in character form and check its validity. If it is valid then the integer values of the month, day and year number should be calculated. Write a Boolean function that is set to true if a given date (in numerical form) is a true calendar date and is set to false otherwise. (Assume that 00 represents the year 2000.) Incorporate these two subprograms into a program that inputs a set of dates (one per line) and checks their validity.

B3   In a scheme for performing computations with fractions, each fraction is represented by a pair of integers denoting the numerator and denominator. Write and test procedures for performing the following operations: (i)   reducing a fraction to irreducible form; (ii)   adding two fractions; (iii)   multiplying two fractions.

C1   Write and test a procedure to plot a graph of a given function in a given range.

C2   In certain dice games the aim is to have as many dice as possible showing the same face within a certain number of throws. After each throw, any number of dice that have not been previously saved may be taken up and thrown again. Write and test a procedure to calculate the probability that *m* of a kind may be achieved with *n* dice within *r* throws.

C3   Write a computer program that inputs an arithmetic expression composed of integers, simple operators (e.g. $+$, $-$, $*$, $/$) and parentheses and that works out the result of the evaluated expression.

Section 2

Structured and enumerated data types

In Section 2 the emphasis will be upon the organisation of data before and during its processing.

The relationship between data components may be represented in a form that is independent of both the computer and computer language to be used. Such a representation is called a *data structure*, and may be illustrated diagrammatically, described in English or formally defined in a mathematical notation. To do justice to this topic would require a separate book, and there are indeed many texts that deal exclusively with data structures and their properties. Once a data structure has been decided upon it must then be represented in the chosen computer language using a *storage structure* available in that language. The rest of this book is devoted to the description and usage of the storage structures available in Pascal. It is therefore suitable for a second course in Pascal or as a supplementary text to a course on data structures.

The wider the range of storage structures a computer language provides, the more likely it is that a particular data structure can be accurately represented. Pascal is particularly rich in storage structures and these may often be combined giving even greater flexibility. Before deciding the form in which a particular set of data is to be stored the following questions need to be considered.

(a) What operations are to be performed on the data?
(b) Can a reasonable upper limit on the amount of space needed for data be estimated *before* the program is compiled?
(c) What media are to be used for input of data and output of results?

Choosing the appropriate data structures often simplifies the development of the corresponding program, and so, in many cases, it is useful to develop data and storage structures in parallel with the algorithm and control structures.

6

Arrays

Introduction

An array contains an ordered set of components, all of the same type. By using a suitable selector, individual components may be accessed and modified. Arrays are simple to use and are implemented efficiently on almost all present-day computers.

6.1 Arrays of scalars

The simplest kinds of array contain only scalar components. For example, a set of marks for 500 students can be stored in an array containing 500 components, each of type integer. An appropriate selector for referring to individual marks would be the candidate number—an integer in the range 1 to 500. This structure could be described in Pascal by the following definition:

```
type
    results = array [1..500] of integer
```

type definitions are placed immediately before variable declarations in programs but should not be confused with them. Only four data types are predefined in Pascal: real, integer, boolean and char. A **type** definition allows the user to increase the number of types of variable that may be declared and used in his program. When **var** declarations are processed, space is allocated for the variables, whereas a **type** definition describes a new kind of structure that may be later used in a declaration. For example, now that the structure of results has been described we can declare variables of that type:

```
var
    exammark, coursemark, modulemark : results
```

Within the scope of this declaration individual elements from any of these arrays may be referred to. This is done by writing the array name, followed by a selector value (or *index*) enclosed in brackets; thus

```
exammark [5]
```

represents the examination mark of student number five. Any element of an array behaves in exactly the same way as a simple variable of the same type. For example, it may be given a value using an assignment:

```
coursemark [203] := 47
```

or it may be compared with another value of the same type:

```
if modulemark [342] < 50 then
    write ( 'fail' )
```

Obviously, the use of arrays simplifies declarations: instead of declaring 500 separate variables, the whole structure can be declared in two lines. Of more significance is that an index may be represented by an expression, most commonly a variable. The power of this facility can be seen in the following statement:

```
for s := 1 to 500 do
    read ( exammark[s], coursemark[s] )
```

Each time the read statement is executed, s will have a different value. After the completion of the **for** statement, 500 numbers will have been read into each array, in the order exammark[1], coursemark[1], exammark[2], coursemark[2],... exammark[500], coursemark[500].

If the module marks were computed by weighting examination marks to coursework marks in the ratio 2:1, the computation could be performed by using the statement

```
for s := 1 to 500 do
    modulemark[s] := round ( ( 2 * exammark[s] + coursemark[s] ) / 3 )
```

The indices of these three arrays are integers. More precisely, the *index type* of each array is the integer *subrange* 1..500. As long as an index expression produces a value of type integer in this range there is no problem. Any attempt to use a non-integer index in a reference to one of these arrays should produce a compile-time error message. For example, a reference

```
exammark[x]
```

where x is real would be invalid. However,

```
exammark[ round ( x ) ]
```

would be perfectly acceptable, although, of course, there is no guarantee that round(x) will produce a value in the range 1..500 when the program is run.

In general, no check is made during compilation to ensure that all index expressions produce values within the given index ranges—in many cases this would be impossible to do. Any self-respecting compiler will perform checks at run-time to avoid references to non-existent array elements and should give an error message if such a situation arises.

In the examination results example it was not necessary to store the complete set of marks in order to compute and print out the module marks. The piece of code shown below would have been sufficient:

```
for s := 1 to 500 do
    begin
        read ( exammark, coursemark );
        modulemark := round ( ( 2 * exammark + coursemark ) / 3 );
        writeln ( s, modulemark )
    end
```

where exammark, coursemark and modulemark could have been declared as integer variables.

If, however, the data had to be scanned more than once, then it *would* be appropriate to read it into an array. This would be the case if, for example, the marks were to be sorted into ascending order, or if an elaborate results layout was required. In Program 6.1, examination marks are read in and their mean is computed in the first scan. In the second scan each mark is output together with ' + ' if the mark is above the mean or a ' − ' if it is below the mean.

```
Program Examresults ( input, output );

{******************************************************************
 *                                                                *
 * Program 6.1                                                    *
 * A set of student examination marks is input and its mean is    *
 * computed.  Each mark is output followed by '+' if the mark     *
 * is above the mean or '-' if it is below the mean.              *
 *                                                                *
 ******************************************************************}

const
      totalstudents = 100;

type
      results = array [1..totalstudents] of integer;

var
      exammark : results;

      student, sum : integer;

      mean : real;

begin

   sum := 0;

   for student := 1 to totalstudents do
      begin
         read ( exammark[student] );
         sum := sum + exammark[student]
      end;

   mean := sum / totalstudents;

   writeln ( 'Program 6.1  Examination mark analysis' );
   writeln ( '=======================================' );
   writeln;
   writeln ( 'student  exam' );
   writeln ( 'number   mark' );

   for student := 1 to totalstudents do
      begin
         write ( student :4, exammark[student] :8 );
         if exammark[student] < mean then
            write ( ' -' )
         else if exammark[student]>mean then
            write ( ' +' );
         writeln
      end;

   writeln;
   writeln ( 'mean = ', mean :5:1 )

end.
```

   Program 6.1

Program Textcopy (input, output);

```
{*********************************************************************
 *                                                                   *
 * Program 6.2                                                       *
 * A piece of text is copied from a file to the printer where the   *
 * maximum width of output lines is specified and no words are to be *
 * split. It is assumed that each word on each input line is followed *
 * by at least one space or by punctuation character(s) and space(s). *
 * For simplicity, punctuation characters are considered as part of  *
 * the preceding word. Redundant spaces are removed.                 *
 *                                                                   *
 *********************************************************************}
```

const
```
      maxoutputwidth = 50;
      blank          = ' ';
      maxwordlength  = 32;    { including possible punctuation }
```

type
```
      string = array [1..maxwordlength] of char;
```

var
```
      word : string;

      character : char;

      charsleft,                            { space left on current line }
      letternumber, lettercount : integer;
```

procedure getchar (**var** character : char);

```
{****************************************************************
 *                                                              *
 * Finds next character in input stream returning blank if no   *
 * characters left (i.e. eof is true) or if end of line reached *
 *                                                              *
 ****************************************************************}
```

begin { getchar }

```
   if eof then
      character := blank
   else if eoln then
      begin
         readln;
         character := blank
      end
   else
      read ( character )
```

end; { getchar }

Program 6.2 (continued opposite)

```
begin { main program }

    writeln ( 'Program 6.2  Text copier' );
    writeln ( '=========================' );
    writeln;

    repeat                                          { skip    }
       getchar ( character )                        { initial }
    until ( character <> blank ) or eof;            { blanks  }

    charsleft := 0;                             { force output of  }
                                                { initial new line }

    while not eof do
       begin

          lettercount := 0;

          while character <> blank do
             begin
                lettercount := lettercount + 1;     { read next }
                word[lettercount] := character;     { word into }
                getchar ( character )               {   array   }
             end;

          if charsleft > lettercount then
             begin
                write ( ' ' );                   { ready to output }
                charsleft := charsleft - 1       {   on same line  }
             end
          else
             begin
                writeln;                         { ready to output }
                charsleft := maxoutputwidth      {   on next line  }
             end;

          for letternumber := 1 to lettercount do    { output }
             write ( word[letternumber] );           {  word  }
          charsleft := charsleft - lettercount;

          while not eof and ( character = blank ) do   { skip   }
             getchar ( character )                     { blanks }

       end;

    writeln

end.
```

Program 6.2 (continued)

Notice that the number of candidates has been declared as a constant and used as a limit in the array type definition. This is quite common, since we often wish to change the limits of arrays from run to run, depending on the amount of data to be processed. The amount of space to be used is determined at compile-time in Pascal and so the index range description must not contain expressions or variables. If a reasonable upper limit cannot be placed on the number of elements to be stored in an array, one of the other storage structures, to be described in later chapters, should be considered.

In Program 6.2 an array is used in a slightly different way. A piece of text is to be read in from a file having lines of one length and output to a printer with lines of a different length. The maximum width of each output line is specified as a constant. In order to avoid splitting a word between lines it is necessary to look ahead to the end of each word, before deciding whether to print it on the current line or on the next one. An array called word is declared, in which each word is temporarily stored.

Sample output from this program is shown below (reproduced from *Kinflicks* by Lisa Alther, by permission of the author and Chatto and Windus Limited).

```
Program 6.2  Text copier
===========================
```

```
My family has always been into death. My father,
the Major, used to insist on having an ice pick
next to his placemat at meals so that he could
perform an emergency tracheotomy when one of us
strangled on a piece of meat. Even now, by running
my index fingers along my collarbones to the
indentation where the bones join, I can locate the
optimal site for a tracheal puncture with the same
deftness as a junky a vein.
```

6.2 Sorting and searching

Two of the most important operations that may be performed on arrays are sorting the elements into order and searching for a given element.

Many techniques have been developed for sorting the elements of an array. One of the simplest is the *selection sort*. In this method the smallest elements are interchanged with elements at one end of the array and in this way a list of numbers in ascending order is built up. Initially the whole array is scanned to find the smallest element. This is then interchanged with the first element. The sublist consisting of all but the first element is now scanned to find the next smallest number which is then interchanged with element two. Next the sublist containing all but the first two elements is searched and so on. This process is continued with sublists of decreasing size, terminating with the sublist containing the last two elements in the array.

The piece of program below shows the sorting of an array containing n integers using this technique.

```
for subliststart := 1 to n - 1 do

  begin

      minvalue := a[subliststart];      { set current minimum to  }
      minposition := subliststart;      { first number in sublist }
```

(continued opposite)

```
     for i := subliststart + 1 to n do
        if a[i] < minvalue then
           begin
              minvalue := a[i];        { find position of smallest }
              minposition := i         { element in sublist         }
           end;

        if minposition <> subliststart then
           begin
              copy := a[subliststart];            { perform }
              a[subliststart] := a[minposition];  {  swap   }
              a[minposition] := copy
           end

end
```

The process may obviously be modified so that the largest element is chosen during each scan and placed at the end of the array.

Program 6.3 shows the selection sort method applied to the problem of determining positions of competitors in a sporting event. Competitor numbers and corresponding times are input and the times need to be sorted. One extra point to be remembered is that, when times are interchanged, the corresponding competitor numbers must also be switched.

```
Program Timesort ( input, output );

{*********************************************************************
*                                                                   *
* Program 6.3                                                       *
* A set of competitor numbers and times is read in and sorted       *
* by times using a selection sort. Times are given to the nearest   *
* 1/100 second. To avoid rounding errors each time is multiplied    *
* by 100 and rounded before the sort is performed.                  *
*                                                                   *
*********************************************************************}


const
      entries = 10;

var
      competitor, itime : array [1..entries] of integer;

      i, copynumber, copytime, subliststart,
      mintime, minposition, position : integer;

      time : real;


begin

   for i := 1 to entries do
      begin
         read ( competitor[i], time );
         itime[i] := round ( 100 * time )
      end;
```

Program 6.3 (continued overleaf)

```
for subliststart := 1 to entries - 1 do

  begin

      mintime := itime[subliststart];   { set current minimum to  }
      minposition := subliststart;      { first number in sublist }

      for i := subliststart + 1 to entries do
        if itime[i] < mintime then
          begin
            mintime := itime[i];      { find position of smallest }
            minposition := i          { element in sublist         }
          end;

      if minposition <> subliststart then
        begin
          copytime := itime[subliststart];               { perform }
          copynumber := competitor[subliststart];        {   swap  }
          itime[subliststart] := itime[minposition];
          competitor[subliststart] := competitor[minposition];
          itime[minposition] := copytime;
          competitor[minposition] := copynumber
        end

  end;

writeln ( 'Program 6.3  Time sort' );
writeln ( '======================' );
writeln;
writeln ( 'position  competitor  time' );
writeln ( 1 :5, competitor[1] :11, itime[1] / 100 :10:2 );

position := 1;

for i := 2 to entries do
    begin
      if itime[i] > itime[i - 1] then
          position := i;
        writeln ( position :5, competitor[i] :11, itime[i] / 100 :10:2 )
    end

end.
```

Program 6.3 (continued)

Program 6.3 uses a new method for declaring arrays. Instead of having separate **type** definitions the range and element type are described inside the **var** declarations themselves. Often either form of declaration may be used.

One of the fastest sorting methods for randomly distributed data is known as *quicksort*. In this method, a central value is chosen and exchanges are performed so that all the elements to one side are smaller than or equal to it and all the elements on the other side are greater than or equal to it. This should produce two equal length sublists to the left and right of the chosen element. Each of these is then partially sorted in a similar way. In turn each of the four resultant sublists is sorted and so on. The effectiveness of quicksort (as of most other sorting methods) is dependent upon the degree of ordering already present. For example, although quicksort is comparatively fast for a large set of randomly distributed data, it takes about the same amount of time as a selection sort for data that is almost in order.

A common requirement is to take two lists that are already sorted and produce from them a single ordered list. This is called *merging* the lists. In Program 6.4, two sets of ordered numbers are read in and merged.

```
Program Merge ( input, output );

{**************************************************************
 *                                                            *
 * Program 6.4                                                *
 * Reads in two lists of ordered numbers, a and b, and merges *
 * them into a third list c.                                  *
 *                                                            *
 **************************************************************}

const
      alength   = 7;
      blength   = 9;
      comblength = 16;

var
      a : array [1..alength] of real;
      b : array [1..blength] of real;
      c : array [1..comblength] of real;

      i, j, k : integer;

begin

   for i := 1 to alength do
      read ( a[i] );

   for j := 1 to blength do
      read ( b[j] );

   i := 1;
   j := 1;
   k := 1;

   while ( i <= alength ) and ( j <= blength ) do
      if a[i] < b[j] then
         begin
            c[k] := a[i];
            i := i + 1;
            k := k + 1
         end
      else
         begin
            c[k] := b[j];
            j := j + 1;
            k := k + 1
         end;

   while i <= alength do               { b exhausted - }
      begin                            {  add tail of  }
         c[k] := a[i];                 {  a to list    }
         i := i + 1;
         k := k + 1
      end;
```

Program 6.4 (continued overleaf)

```
            while j <= blength do
               begin                        { a exhausted - }
                  c[k] := b[j];             {   add tail of  }
                  j := j + 1;               {   b to list    }
                  k := k + 1
               end;

            writeln ( 'Program 6.4  Merge sort' );
            writeln ( '========================' );
            writeln;

            write ( 'list a  ' );

            for i := 1 to alength do
               write ( a[i] :6:1 );

            writeln;
            writeln;
            write ( 'list b  ' );

            for j := 1 to blength do
               write ( b[j] :6:1 );

            writeln;
            writeln;
            write ( 'merged list  ' );

            for k := 1 to comblength do
               write ( c[k] :6:1 );

            writeln

      end.
```

Program 6.4 (continued)

Note that in any particular run only one of the last two **while** loops will be entered, depending upon which list is first exhausted.

A problem related to sorting is that of searching through a list for a given item. This has obvious applications—searching for stock, looking for someone's name in a register, looking up the meaning of a word in a computer dictionary, and so on. The simplest approach is to work systematically through the list, examining each item in turn until the required one is found, or until the list is exhausted. Care must be taken when using this method. The following piece of code apparently performs the task of searching for a cheque number in an array containing a list of cheque numbers.

```
      i := 0;

      repeat
         i := i + 1
      until ( i > totalcheques ) or ( cheque[i] = targetcheque )
```

Assuming that cheque has been declared as an array of type integer with index range 1..totalcheques then there is no problem as long as the target number is in the list. If this is not so then a run-time error will occur when the terminating condition at the end of the last cycle is tested, since i will be greater than totalcheques and an attempt to calculate cheque[i] will fail. An obvious solution to this problem is to increase the length of the array (but *not* totalcheques) by one. If, in addition, the target value is placed in this last position then the search procedure can be simplified:

```
cheque[maxindex] := targetcheque;
i := 0;

repeat
   i := i + 1
until cheque[i] = targetcheque
```

Since a 'sentinel' has been posted at the end of the array the terminating condition is bound to be satisfied at least once. If the first occurrence of the target cheque number is in this last position then we may deduce that it does not occur anywhere else in the list. We could therefore write

```
chequefound := ( i <> maxindex )
```

This technique of examining successive elements of a list in turn is known as *linear*, or *sequential*, searching. It is slow in operation unless the most frequently accessed elements are near the front of the list, or unless the list is relatively small. A generally much faster method is the *binary* search. This technique may only be used if the elements are ordered, and so more work may be needed to perform an initial sort of the data. Once this has been done, however, an item in even a long list (of, say, 1000 elements) can be found by examining at most 10 of them. The target item value is compared with the element in the middle of the list. If we are lucky, then this is the one we want and the search is complete. If not, then we can tell which half of the list the target item will be in by comparing its value with that of the central item. If the target item value is less than the middle value, we need to look in the first half of the list; otherwise the second half must be searched. This *binary chop* is then repeated for the appropriate half-list, and so on. By successively halving the search area, the required item may quickly be found. If a given sublist contains an even number of elements then one of the two central items is chosen arbitrarily. The complete process may be described by the following piece of code:

```
lowindex := 1;
highindex := maxindex;
numberfound := false;

repeat

   index := ( lowindex + highindex ) div 2;

   if targetnumber < number[index] then
      highindex := index - 1
   else if targetnumber > number[index] then
      lowindex := index + 1
   else
      numberfound := true

until numberfound or ( lowindex > highindex )
```

lowindex and highindex denote the limits of the current search list. If the target item is not found at a particular point, then either the lower limit or the upper limit is modified, as necessary.

In most sorting and searching problems, the information to be processed will have a more complex structure than that in the examples considered here—it may contain names, dates, addresses, and so on. Usually only one part of the information stored for each item will be used to order the elements, or to look for particular items. This is called a *key*. If the items are bank accounts, the key might be the account number. It is clear that the techniques described apply equally well to this type of data, as long as a suitable key is defined.

6.3 Manipulating complete arrays

In certain circumstances, it is possible to refer to a complete array by name rather than to its individual elements. The simplest case is that of assignment—the complete contents of one array (b) may be copied into another array (a) by using the statement

```
a := b
```

In this case, the *base types* of a and b (i.e. the types of their elements) and their index ranges must be identical. However, care is needed—there are certain other statements, which appear on the surface to be similar, that are *not* allowed. Some examples are as follows.

```
a := b + c
```

```
a := 2 * b
```

We often wish to be able to pass array data to and from a subprogram. This may be achieved by making an array a parameter of the subprogram. For example, a sort procedure might have this heading:

```
procedure sort ( var a : list; n : integer )
```

where list has been described in a **type** definition of the form

```
type
      list = array [1..maxno] of integer
```

This is one situation in which a type definition is essential, since a parameter type in a procedure heading *must* be a simple name.

The facility for passing array information *en bloc* to and from procedures makes tidy programs easier to write. Consider, for example, the problem of reading in a set of temperatures, validating them, calculating their mean and then printing the results. This could be programmed without the use of arrays but, in this case, all of the above tasks would have to be carried out concurrently. A more natural structure for the program is sketched out below.

```
      Read in temperatures
      Validate temperatures
      If valid then
          Compute mean temperature
          Output results
      Else
          Output error message
```

The corresponding main program could be

```
begin { main program }

   readin ( temperature, n );
   validate ( temperature, n, valid );
   if valid then
      begin
         computemean ( temperature, n, mean );
         outresults ( temperature, n, mean )
      end
   else
      writeln ( 'error in data' )

end.
```

In addition to being easier to follow than the composite version of mean calculation, it would probably execute more efficiently, since no calculations are performed at all if any item in the data is invalid.

We shall look at the declaration of just one of these procedures:

```
procedure computemean ( var temperature : templist; n : integer;
                                            var mean : real );

{*****************************************************
 *                                                   *
 * Calculates mean of elements in temperature array  *
 *                                                   *
 *****************************************************}

var
      i : integer;

      total : real;

begin { computemean }

   total := 0;

   for i := 1 to n do
      total := total + temperature[i];

   mean := total / n

end;   { computemean }
```

As an exercise, you could write the other procedures and run the program.

One last point about this example—you may have noticed that the array in computemean was made a variable parameter, although none of its values were changed in the procedure. For reasons of efficiency it is usual to make all array parameters variable. If an array is made a value parameter then the computer has to make a copy of the whole array, in addition to setting up a mechanism inside the procedure for accessing the elements of this copy. There are no such problems if the array is made a variable parameter, since the formal parameter identifier becomes just an alternative name for the original array.

A controversial restriction in Pascal has been the requirement to specify array type names in procedures since, although it makes the compiler writer's job easier, it effectively means that the size of an array cannot be changed from call to call. For instance, the sort procedure declared earlier in this section would only be useful for sorting an array with bounds 1 to maxno where maxno is some constant. This obstacle can be surmounted (or at least side stepped) by introducing another parameter (n in the sort example) which can take any value in the range 1 to maxno and which specifies the upper bound of the section of the array to be sorted. The lower bound could similarly be indicated.

To some people's minds this is a crude device and, after much debate, the ISO Pascal committee decided to allow an optional feature in compilers called 'conformant array parameters'. If a formal array parameter is specified in a special way then the corresponding actual parameter may contain any number of elements as long as it has the same base type and the subscripts are of the type specified in the formal parameter part.

For example, a procedure for sorting an array of real numbers could have the heading

```
procedure sort ( var a : array [lower..upper : integer] of real )
```

lower and upper are called 'bound identifiers' and may be referred to in the body of the procedure. When a call of the procedure is made they take on the values of the lower and upper bounds of the actual array parameter.

So if a1 to a4 were declared as

```
var
        a1 : array [-5..10] of real;

        a2 : array [0..500] of real;

        a3 : array ['a'..'z'] of real;

        a4 : array [1..10] of boolean;
```

then sort (a1) and sort (a2) would be valid calls (in the first case lower and upper would be automatically set to -5 and 10, respectively, and in the second case to 0 and 500). The call sort (a3) could not be made because the subscripts of a3 are of the wrong type and sort (a4) would also be incorrect because the base type of a4 is not real.

The ramifications of a such a scheme may be imagined and for a fuller description of this facility see *Standard Pascal* by D Cooper published by Norton.

If the contents of two arrays are to be compared or if a complete array is to be transmitted using the standard input/output devices then these operations must normally be performed on each element in turn. It is not possible, for example, to output the contents of an array by just referring to the array name. The only exception occurs when the array is a string. In standard Pascal 'string' is not a reserved word but any 'packed' array with a lower bound of unity and containing two or more characters has special properties and is referred to as a string-type.

Placing the word **packed** before any structured type description tells the compiler that it may compress the elements of the structure in order to save space. This will often increase access time for individual elements in the structure, but this may be unimportant. For example, if we wish to store a word from a piece of text in an array then, once it has been read in, we would not normally wish to access individual letters of the word. Usually a scalar is stored in a single computer word and so, on most computers, a lot of space would be wasted by storing an array of characters using one computer word for each character. Referring back to Program 6.2, there was an array declaration of the form

type

        string = **array** [1..maxwordlength] **of** char;

var

        word : string

If the first word read in had been **programs**, and the particular computer in use could hold 6 characters per computer word, the first part of the array might look like Fig. 6.1.

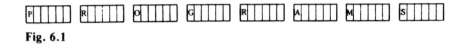

Fig. 6.1

If, instead, the declaration had been

type

        string = **packed array** [1..maxindex] **of** char;

var

        word : string

the information could be compressed as shown in Fig. 6.2.

```
|P|R|O|G|R|A| |M|S| | | | |
```

Fig. 6.2

In this instance, the saving in space is hardly worth bothering about. However, if we wish to compare two strings it is obviously much faster to compare two computer words rather than eight. If this comparison is repeated thousands of times, a substantial saving in time can be made.

In Pascal, comparisons may be made directly between arrays when they are string-types;

        found := (word1 = word2)

would be a valid statement as long as word1 and word2 were packed arrays of type char and had index ranges starting with 1. In fact any of the relations $<$, $<=$, $=$, $>=$, $>$, $<>$, may be used between two such arrays. For example:

```
if word1 <= word2 then
    write ( 'words are in alphabetical order' )
else
    write ( 'words are not in alphabetical order' )
```

The results of comparisons will depend upon the collating sequence in use but, of course, for strings of letters or strings of digits the results will be consistent from machine to machine.

A string contained in quotes is regarded as a packed array of characters of the appropriate length, which means that constructions such as

        word := 'animal '

and

        if word = 'cracker' then...

would be acceptable as long as word contained seven packed elements.

A string may also be printed by referring to the array by name:

```
write ( word )
```

Some installations would also allow

```
read ( word )
```

but this is not standard Pascal, and the safer form would be

```
for i := 1 to maxindex do
    read ( word[i] )
```

Access time for individual elements of a packed array may be substantially greater than that for elements from an unpacked array. Ideally, one might wish to work with an unpacked array when individual elements are being processed, and then pack the information when manipulation of the whole array is required. Pascal provides required procedures for packing and unpacking arrays. The statement

```
pack ( a, index, b )
```

compresses the elements of a into a packed array b starting with a[index]. All three parameters must be declared as variables of the appropriate types, and there must be at least enough space in b to accommodate all the elements of a. The inverse operation is

```
unpack ( b, a, index )
```

In this case the unpacking starts from the beginning of the packed array b and the first character is placed in a[index].

Since the packing and unpacking operations themselves are likely to be rather slow, it is preferable—for most applications—to work with one kind of array throughout.

To complete this section we include a procedure from a program for analysing a piece of text. Prior to a full analysis of text, such as in the concordance example of Chapter 7, it may be useful to perform a preliminary examination. In this case the procedure processwords (opposite) analyzes a piece of text to determine the longest word, the distribution of words in the alphabet, and the first and last words taken in alphabetical order.

readin is a procedure for reading a word into the word array (a packed array of characters). endword is a Boolean variable that is set to true if the word just read in was the last. The array frequency is used for storing the frequencies of words starting with each letter of the alphabet. For this reason its index type is declared as the subrange 'a'..'z'. The array type list could be declared at the beginning of the program as

```
type
    list = array ['a'..'z'] of integer
```

In all of the previous examples, arrays have had integer subscripts. It is occasionally useful, as in this example, to have non-integer index types. Any scalar type except real may be used in this context.

```
procedure processwords ( var firstword, lastword, longestword : string;
                          var wordnumber : integer; var frequency : list );

{*********************************
 *                               *
 * Reads in and processes words  *
 *                               *
 *********************************}

var
     word : string;

     length, maxwordlength : integer;

     endword : boolean;

     firstletter : char;

begin { processwords }

   for firstletter := 'a' to 'z' do
      frequency[firstletter] := 0;

   readin ( word, length, endword );

   firstword := word;
   lastword := word;
   longestword := word;
   firstletter := word[1];
   frequency[firstletter] := 1;
   maxwordlength := length;
   wordnumber := 1;

   while not endword do
      begin
         readin ( word, length, endword );
         wordnumber := wordnumber + 1;
         firstletter := word[1];
         frequency[firstletter] := frequency[firstletter] + 1;
         if word < firstword then
            firstword := word
         else if word > lastword then
            lastword := word;
         if length > maxwordlength then
            begin
               maxwordlength := length;
               longestword    := word
            end

      end

end;   { processwords }
```

Procedure processwords

6.4 Arrays of arrays

The base type of an array may be any type, either pre-defined or user-defined. It is even possible to make each element an array. For example, we described earlier a structure for storing temperatures. These may be temperatures on the same day in different places, and the array type definition might be

```
type
        templist = array [1..maxplaces] of real
```

In addition, it may be necessary to store the temperatures for these places over a period of time (a month, say) in which case a table of values would need to be represented. A variable to store this information could be declared as

```
var
        temperature : array [1..daysinmonth] of templist
```

As in earlier examples the complete structure could be described in a separate **type** statement or in the variable declaration itself. So we could have

```
type
        temptable = array [1..daysinmonth] of
                            array [1..maxplaces] of real;

var
        temperature : temptable
```

or alternatively

```
var
        temperature : array [1..daysinmonth] of
                            array [1..maxplaces] of real
```

All three of these methods of declaring temperature have the same effect. Individual elements of the array may be referred to in the normal way. For example, the reference

```
        temperature[12]
```

would represent all of the temperatures on day 12 of the month. More commonly, it is necessary to refer to individual temperatures. This may be done by using a logical extension of the notation for simple element references. For example,

```
        temperature[12][5]
```

would denote the temperature on day 12 in place number 5.

To conform with the convention in other computer languages, and to simplify references, the notation may be modified by using a comma to separate indices. For the previous example this would give

```
        temperature[12, 5]
```

A similar modification may be made to abbreviate array descriptions:

```
var
        temperature : array [1..daysinmonth,
                                1..maxplaces] of real
```

Since this type of structure is often used to store tabular data, it is called a *two-dimensional array*, whereas an array of unstructured elements is *one-dimensional*.

In the same way that many operations on one-dimensional arrays are governed by single **for** statements, operations on elements of two-dimensional arrays often use two nested **for** loops. For example,

```
for dayno := 1 to daysinmonth do
    for placeno := 1 to maxplaces do
        read ( temperature[dayno, placeno] )
```

A piece of code to calculate the mean temperature per day, and print out this information in addition to the original table, is given below.

```
write ( ' ' :7, 'place' );

for placeno := 1 to maxplaces do
    write ( placeno :7 );

writeln ( '    mean' );
writeln ( 'day number', 'temperature' :(7 * maxplaces + 14) );

for dayno := 1 to daysinmonth do
    begin
        totaldaytemp := 0;
        write ( dayno :6, ' ' :7 );

        for placeno := 1 to maxplaces do
            begin
                temp := temperature[dayno, placeno];
                write ( temp :7:1 );
                totaldaytemp := totaldaytemp + temp
            end;

        writeln ( totaldaytemp / maxplaces :7:1 )

    end
```

Notice that a real variable, temp, was used in the inner loop to avoid a second reference to the array element. Accessing an element of a two-dimensional array is a relatively slow operation on most computers, because of the linear nature of their addressing systems. Consequently, references to these elements in frequently executed code, such as in nested loops, should be reduced to a minimum if speed of execution is important. Part of the output from a program containing the above piece of code is shown below.

place	1	2	3	4	5	6	mean
day number							temperature
1	15.1	17.9	14.3	16.0	18.6	16.9	16.5
2	15.8	15.6	18.0	14.2	16.0	18.4	16.3
3	16.7	15.8	15.0	18.5	15.0	16.5	16.3
4	18.0	15.5	14.9	16.5	17.0	16.1	16.3
5	15.9	17.6	15.4	15.3	16.9	17.2	16.4
6	16.3	16.6	17.9	16.3	16.0	17.0	16.7

All two-dimensional arrays in Pascal are rectangular in structure. That is, if we regard the first subscript as representing a row number, and the second subscript as a column number, every row has the same number of elements and every column contains the same number of elements; see Fig. 6.3.

```
x x x x x x x x x x x x
x x x x x x x x x x x x
x x x x x x x x x x x x
x x x x x x x x x x x x     Fig. 6.3
```

Sometimes the system we wish to represent does not have this convenient form. For instance, if you are familiar with matrices (usually represented by two-dimensional arrays), you may have met the 'triangular' form. An example of a lower triangular matrix is as follows:

$$\begin{bmatrix} 5 & 0 & 0 & 0 & 0 \\ 6 & 2 & 0 & 0 & 0 \\ 3 & 2 & 5 & 0 & 0 \\ 4 & 3 & -1 & 7 & 0 \\ 2 & 1 & 15 & 2 & 6 \end{bmatrix}$$

The elements above the leading diagonal in this kind of matrix always have the value zero. It would therefore be convenient to be able to store the elements of the lower triangle in a triangular array, and so avoid wasting space. This type of structure does not exist in Pascal, but certain tricks may be used for saving space when storing this and other types of 'sparse' matrices (i.e. those containing a high proportion of zeros). Most books on data structuring describe these devices.

In the next example, the data has an irregular structure. A two-dimensional array is used for storage, and so some space is wasted, but the scheme described uses an additional array to aid validation. The problem involves checking and accumulating returns of sales representatives from different areas. There are five areas (denoted a, b, c, d and e), and each area has a certain number of representatives. The largest area has seven salespersons, whereas the smallest has only one. If a two-dimensional array is used to store sales by individuals then $5 \times 7 = 35$ locations will be allocated, although only a small proportion of these might be needed.

The first line of input data contains five numbers, indicating the number of representatives in each area. Each of the succeeding lines contains a sales date (which, for the purpose of this example, will be ignored), an area identification letter, a salesperson's number and an amount. The file has been sorted into date order. If, on a certain day, a particular agent made no sales, there will be no entry for him, and so, in a given batch (for sales over the period of a week, say), one person may have several entries while another has none at all.

Program Salesprocessing (input, output);

```
{*****************************************************************************
 *                                                                         *
 * Program 6.5                                                             *
 * Sales for individual salespersons in a set of areas are validated      *
 * and totalled. First a list of numbers of agents per area is read       *
 * in. If these numbers are valid then the individual entries,            *
 * each consisting of a date (ignored), an area, a salesperson            *
 * number and number of items sold, are validated. Sales for              *
 * individual agents are accumulated and results are output in            *
 * tabular form.                                                          *
 *                                                                         *
 *****************************************************************************}
```

Program 6.5 (continued opposite)

```
const
      firstarea       = 'a';     { area  }
      lastarea        = 'e';     { names }
      numberofareas = 5;
      maxagents       = 7;       { maximum number of agents per area }
      maxitems        = 20;      { maximum feasibie number of items
                                   sold per day by one salesperson   }

type
      agentslist = array [firstarea..lastarea] of integer;
      salesinfo = array [firstarea..lastarea, 1..maxagents] of integer;

var
      agents : agentslist;

      sales : salesinfo;

      validagents, validsales : boolean;




procedure readagents ( var agents : agentslist; var validagents : boolean )

{****************************************:*******
 *                                          *
 * Read and validate salespersons per area *
 *                                          *
 ********************************************}

var
      agentnumber : integer;

      area : char;

begin { readagents }

   validagents := true;
   area := firstarea;

   while ( area <= lastarea ) and validagents do
     begin
        read ( agentnumber );
        if ( agentnumber < 0 )  or ( agentnumber > maxagents ) then
           validagents := false
        else
           agents[area] := agentnumber;
        area := succ ( area )
     end;

   readln

end;  { readagents }
```

Program 6.5 (continued overleaf)

```
procedure processsales ( var agents : agentslist; var sales : salesinfo;
                                        var validsales : boolean );

{************************************************************************
 *                                                                    *
 * Reads in and validates entries, accumulating total items sold for  *
 * each salesperson                                                   *
 *                                                                    *
 ********************************************************************** }

var
      month, day, year, agentnumber, itemssold, entrynumber : integer;

      area, blank : char;


begin { processsales }

    for area := firstarea to lastarea do
      for agentnumber := 1 to agents[area] do
        sales[area, agentnumber] := 0;

    validsales := true;
    entrynumber := 0;

    while not eof do
      begin
        readln ( month, day, year, blank, area, agentnumber, itemssold );
        entrynumber := entrynumber + 1;
        if ( area < firstarea ) or ( area > lastarea )
          or ( agentnumber <= 0 )  or ( itemssold < 0 )
          or ( itemssold > maxitems )  then
          begin
            validsales := false;
            writeln ( 'error in entry', entrynumber :4 )
          end
        else if agentnumber > agents[area] then
          begin
            validsales := false;
            writeln ( 'error in entry', entrynumber :4 )
          end
        else if validsales then
          sales[area, agentnumber] := sales[area, agentnumber] + itemssold
      end

end; { processsales }

procedure writeresults ( var agents : agentslist; var sales : salesinfo );

{**************************************
 *                                    *
 * Writes out results in tabular form *
 *                                    *
 ************************************** }
```

Program 6.5 (continued opposite)

```
var
      agentnumber : integer;

      area : char;

begin { writeresults }

   writeln ( ' ' :15, 'Program 6.5  Processing of agent returns' );
   writeln ( ' ' :15, '=========================================' );
   writeln;
   writeln;

   writeln ( ' ' :15, 'the table shows total items sold for each' );
   writeln ( ' ' :15, '          salesperson in each area' );
   writeln;
   writeln ( ' ' :20, 'salesperson number' );
   write ( ' ' :14 );

   for agentnumber := 1 to maxagents do
      write ( agentnumber :4 );
   writeln;
   writeln;

   for area := firstarea to lastarea do
      begin
         if area <> 'c' then
            write ( area :13, ' ' )
         else
            write ( '     area    ', area, ' ' );

         for agentnumber := 1 to agents[area] do
            write ( sales[area, agentnumber] :4 );

         writeln
      end

end; { writeresults }


begin { main program }

   readagents ( agents, validagents );
   if validagents then
      begin
         processsales ( agents, sales, validsales );
         if validsales then
            writeresults ( agents, sales )
      end
   else
      writeln ( 'error in agent numbers' )

end.
```

Program 6.5 (continued)

In Program 6.5 on page 136 the entries are read in, validated, and the total sales of each representative is calculated. Notice how the one-dimensional array **agents** containing the number of salespersons per area is used in checking for illegal entries and in aiding layout of results.

The table produced from a typical run is shown below.

Program 6.5 Processing of agent returns
===

the table shows total items sold for each
salesperson in each area

		salesperson number						
		1	2	3	4	5	6	7
	a	5	12	6	0			
	b	13						
area	c	0	4	7				
	d	6	4	1	5	1	4	18
	e	0	2					

Output from Program 6.5

Tables of words may often be conveniently stored in two-dimensional arrays. For example, given the declaration

var
        month : **array** [1..12]
                        of packed array [1..9] **of** char

we could store the month names using assignments of the form:

```
month[1]    := 'January  ';
month[2]    := 'February ';
month[3]    := 'March    ';
month[4]    := 'April    ';
month[5]    := 'May      ';
month[6]    := 'June     ';
month[7]    := 'July     ';
month[8]    := 'August   ';
month[9]    := 'September';
month[10]   := 'October  ';
month[11]   := 'November ';
month[12]   := 'December '
```

In this case, a piece of code for reading in a date using month number form and writing it out using month names becomes:

```
read ( monthnumber, day, year );
write ( month[monthnumber], day :3, year :5 )
```

This is, perhaps, neater than using a **case** statement; and, of course, validity tests can easily be incorporated. Whenever your first thought is to use a **case** statement in a particular situation check whether an array might be used as an alternative; if so, consider whether it might produce a less cumbersome piece of code.

Arrays of three or more dimensions are represented by extending the notation in an obvious way, although particular implementations may have a limit on the number of dimensions allowed.

Summary

By using arrays, large amounts of information may be stored and manipulated efficiently and simply. Individual elements are accessed by using an index, where the index type may be a range of integers or of any other simple type except real. The base type of an array may be any required or user-defined type, including an array. One-dimensional arrays are suitable for storing linearly-structured data. Two-dimensional arrays are particularly suitable for storing tabular data, matrices and lists of words.

Exercises

1 Write a program to simulate a simple stock control system. There are ten different types of item, with item numbers 1 to 10, and the initial stock of each is to be read in together with its reorder level. This is followed by a list of requests of the form:

> item-number   quantity-required   item-number   quantity-required . . .

It may be assumed that the data has been validated. The program should output a table giving the following information for each request:

  (i)   item number requested;
 (ii)   quantity required;
(iii)   quantity supplied;
 (iv)   new stock level (after order met);
  (v)   whether the item should be reordered;
 (vi)   whether the item is out of stock.

2 Write a program to recognise palindromes (i.e. words that read the same backwards as forwards). Some examples are:

  A   MADAM   HANNAH   REDIVIDER

You could then extend your program to allow palindromic sentences. For example:

ABLE WAS I ERE I SAW ELBA
EVIL RATS ON NO STAR LIVE
A MAN, A PLAN, A CANAL, PANAMA!

3 Write a program to check whether an $N \times N$ table of numbers represents a magic square (i.e. each of the numbers 1 to N^2 occurs exactly once, and the row, column and diagonal totals are equal).

4 Write a program to compute all of the distinct partitions of a given number. A partition of a number consists of a set of numbers that add up to the original number. For example, all of the partitions of 5 are:

  5
  4   1
  3   2
  3   1   1
  2   2   1
  2   1   1   1
  1   1   1   1   1

(The order in which these have been written down may suggest a method of solution.)

5 Write and test procedures for adding and multiplying together two matrices.

6 Find out how to write your own pseudo-random number generator. One of the methods of checking a pseudo-random number generator is the poker test. The generator is used to give five digits in the range 0 to 9 and the set of digits is classified as if it was a poker hand (e.g. full house, three of a kind, run etc.). This is repeated a large number of times and a distribution is obtained of the number of times each type of hand occurs. This can be compared with the theoretical probabilities of the hands occurring. Write a program to test a pseudo-random number generator in this way.

7 Write a program to find all the prime numbers up to a certain value using the method of Eratosthenes' sieve.

7

User-defined values, subranges and record structures

Introduction

In Pascal, the user may define new data values and then declare variables that can take these values. For example, a variable may have as a value the name of a day of the week, or the name of an article in a store. This feature, together with a facility for defining subranges of values, provides a useful way of making programs more readable and more reliable.

Another feature that is not essential, but aids clarity and reliability, is the record structure. Using this construction, components of possibly different types may be brought together and manipulated as a single object.

7.1 Enumerated types

Three of the four 'required' types in Pascal (integer, boolean and char) are similar in that they can be counted. The odd one out is real since its values cannot be listed in order (what, for instance, is the value of succ(9.12)?). This is why a real value cannot be used for controlling a **for** loop, or as a subscript of an array. Integer, boolean and char are called 'ordinal' types and the user can introduce other simple ordinal types as necessary by enumerating their values in a definition.

Why should we want to introduce other types of values? The object is to represent as naturally as possible the features of the problem being solved. The four required simple data types in Pascal are sufficient to describe information in most numerical and textual processing problems in a straight-forward way. In other types of problem the objects we are dealing with are often neither numbers nor characters. The only solution in many languages is to use some artificial encoding. For example, if a variable is to represent items stocked in a store then we could define

```
const
      envelopes = 0;
      erasers   = 1;
      pens      = 2;
      pencils   = 3;
```

and then refer to the item names instead of the numbers. In this way,

```
quantity[pencils]
```

might represent the number of pencils to be ordered. There would be no problem as long as the array quantity had an index range of 0..3.

One disadvantage of this technique is that things are not quite what they seem. The computer would accept expressions such as pens + 2 or even sqr(envelopes) which would be meaningless in real terms. One of the reasons for distinguishing and declaring data types is to permit compile-time checks to be made on expressions and assignments, and to weed out the meaningless ones such as

    true + 2

For this reason, Pascal allows the programmer to define his own data types, leaving the compiler to check that he has used them in the correct way.

For the above example we could define

    type
            stock = (envelopes, erasers, pens, pencils)

with a corresponding **var** declaration:

    var
            item : stock

The name item can now be associated with any of the 'values' in the definition of stock. A particular value may be given to item using an assignment statement such as

    item := erasers

It may also be used in such statements as

    if item = pencils **then**
        writeln ('order more pencils')

whereas a compilation error would result from using the expression

    erasers + 2

Remember that envelopes, erasers, pens and pencils are now names of items and *not* numerical values.

In addition to indicating a set of identifiers that are to denote values, a **type** definition imposes an ordering on these values. This is determined by the order in which the identifiers appear in the definition. Adjacent values may now be referred to by using the predecessor and successor functions. Both of the following expressions would give erasers as their value:

    pred (pens)

    succ (envelopes)

whereas

    succ (pencils)

and

    pred (envelopes)

would be undefined. The position of a value in the value list may be determined by using the ord function, where the position of the first item is conventionally 0. So, for example,

    ord (pens)

would give the value 2.

Enumerated values may be used as subscripts of an array. The declaration of such an array for storing the stock of items could be

```
var
        quantity : array [envelopes..pencils] of integer
```

Since the subscript range includes all of the values in the defined type this could have been written as

```
var
        quantity : array [stock] of integer
```

The elements may be set to zero using the statement

```
for item := envelopes to pencils do
    quantity[item] := 0
```

One restriction on enumerated values is that they may not be transmitted using the standard 'textual' input/output devices. This problem may be overcome by using a construction such as the following:

```
case item of
    envelopes : write ( 'envelopes' );
    erasers   : write ( 'erasers' );
    pens      : write ( 'pens' );
    pencils   : write ( 'pencils' )
end
```

Alternatively, an array of strings could be set up with appropriate assignments:

```
name[envelopes] := 'envelopes';
name[erasers]   := 'erasers  ';
name[pens]      := 'pens     ';
name[pencils]   := 'pencils  '
```

In this case, the following write statement could be used to output the name of an item:

```
write ( name[item] )
```

Neither of the above techniques, of course, is entirely satisfactory.

We now look at a program that contains enumerated types. An important class of problems involves finding a path between two given points. An example is the guiding of a robot around obstacles to some destination. Program 7.1 is used to tackle the problem in one of its simplest forms. A subject is to be guided around a maze to find a target square. The maze is surrounded by a wall but has one access point in a corner. In addition there are no circular paths. In this case, all the subject has to do is follow a wall around and she will eventually have covered the whole of the accessible part of the maze and so will find the target square (as long as it is accessible).

In our program the subject always keeps to the left-hand wall. Enumerated values are introduced to represent the direction in which she is travelling (north, east, south or west) and, relative to this, the directions she examines (left, ahead, right and back). The use of these types does not improve the efficiency of the program but makes the code easier to follow.

The main procedures in the program are choosemove and makemove. We have relaxed our rule of passing information to these procedures by using parameters since they

```
Program Mazesearch ( input, output );

{********************************************************************
 *                                                                  *
 * Program 7.1                                                      *
 * The plan of a maze is read in and an attempt is made to find a   *
 * path from the top left hand corner to the target square (assuming *
 * these positions do not coincide). The left hand wall of the maze *
 * is followed until either the target square is found or the start *
 * square is returned to.                                           *
 *                                                                  *
 ********************************************************************}

const
     maxrows = 11;
     maxcols = 16;
     space   = ' ';

type
     relposition = ( left, ahead, right, back );
     points      = ( north, east, south, west );
     adjustment  = array [points, relposition] of integer;
     maze        = array [1..maxrows, 1..maxcols] of char;

var
     onrow, oncol,             { square occupied by subject }
     nextrow, nextcol,         { square to be moved to      }
     targetrow, targetcol : integer;

     orientation : points;     { compass direction subject is facing }

     direction : relposition;  { direction of square adjacent to      }
                               { subject relative to his orientation }
     square : maze;

     rowchange,                { changes in row and column numbers     }
     colchange : adjustment;   { when moving between adjacent squares }

     backatstart, targetreached : boolean;

procedure readmazeplan ( var square : maze );

{********************************************************************
 *                                                                  *
 * Reads in and prints out a plan of the maze. The walls are        *
 * represented by asterisks and clear paths by space characters.    *
 * The maze must be completely surrounded by a wall except at the   *
 * start position ( row 2, column 1 ) and there must be no cycles   *
 * in the maze.  A '?' is printed out in the target square position. *
 *                                                                  *
 ********************************************************************}

var
     row, col : integer;
```

Program 7.1 (continued opposite)

```
begin { readmazeplan }

    writeln ( '   plan of maze' );
    writeln;

    for row := 1 to maxrows do
       begin

          for col := 1 to maxcols do
             begin
                read ( square[row, col] );
                if ( row = targetrow ) and ( col = targetcol ) then
                   write ( '?' )
                else
                   write ( square[row, col] )
             end;

          readln;
          writeln
       end

end;   { readmazeplan }


procedure initialize ( var rowchange, colchange : adjustment );

{*****************************************************************
 *                                                              *
 * Stores in arrays rowchange and colrange, respectively, the row *
 * and column adjustments that have to be made when in any      *
 * orientation and moving in any direction                      *
 *                                                              *
 *****************************************************************}

begin { initialize }

    rowchange[north, left]  :=  0; colchange[north, left]  := -1;
    rowchange[north, ahead] := -1; colchange[north, ahead] :=  0;
    rowchange[north, right] :=  0; colchange[north, right] :=  1;
    rowchange[north, back]  :=  1; colchange[north, back]  :=  0;
    rowchange[east, left]   := -1; colchange[east, left]   :=  0;
    rowchange[east, ahead]  :=  0; colchange[east, ahead]  :=  1;
    rowchange[east, right]  :=  1; colchange[east, right]  :=  0;
    rowchange[east, back]   :=  0; colchange[east, back]   := -1;
    rowchange[south, left]  :=  0; colchange[south, left]  :=  1;
    rowchange[south, ahead] :=  1; colchange[south, ahead] :=  0;
    rowchange[south, right] :=  0; colchange[south, right] := -1;
    rowchange[south, back]  := -1; colchange[south, back]  :=  0;
    rowchange[west, left]   :=  1; colchange[west, left]   :=  0;
    rowchange[west, ahead]  :=  0; colchange[west, ahead]  := -1;
    rowchange[west, right]  := -1; colchange[west, right]  :=  0;
    rowchange[west, back]   :=  0; colchange[west, back]   :=  1

end;   { initialize }
```

Program 7.1 (continued overleaf)

```
procedure choosemove;

{******************************************************************
 *                                                                *
 * Given the position and orientation of the subject, each of the *
 * adjacent squares is examined in the order left, ahead, right   *
 * and back until a space is found. This becomes the chosen       *
 * next square to move to.                                        *
 *                                                                *
 ******************************************************************}

var
      rowfound, colfound : integer;

   procedure findsquare;

   {**************************************************************
    *                                                           *
    * Given the position and orientation of the subject and     *
    * the relative direction of the square to be examined the   *
    * co-ordinates (row number and column number) of this square *
    * are computed                                              *
    *                                                           *
    **************************************************************}

   begin { findsquare }

      rowfound := onrow + rowchange[orientation, direction];
      colfound := oncol + colchange[orientation, direction]

   end;  { findsquare }



begin { choosemove }

   direction := left;
   findsquare;

   while square[rowfound, colfound] <> space do
      begin
         direction := succ ( direction );
         findsquare
      end;

   nextrow := rowfound;
   nextcol := colfound

end;  { choosemove }
```

Program 7.1 (continued opposite)

```
procedure makemove;

{**********************************************************
 *                                                        *
 * Moves the subject to the next position. If this is the *
 * target square or the subject is back at the start then *
 * appropriate booleans are set otherwise the orientation *
 * of the subject is changed as necessary.                *
 *                                                        *
 **********************************************************}

begin { makemove }

   onrow := nextrow;
   oncol := nextcol;

   writeln ( onrow :2, oncol :6 );

   if ( onrow = targetrow ) and ( oncol = targetcol ) then
      targetreached := true
   else if ( onrow = 2 ) and ( oncol = 1 ) then
      backatstart := true
   else
      case direction of

         left  : case orientation of
                    north : orientation := west;
                    east  : orientation := north;
                    south : orientation := east;
                    west  : orientation := south
                 end;

         ahead :   { no change }                  ;

         right : case orientation of
                    north : orientation := east;
                    east  : orientation := south;
                    south : orientation := west;
                    west  : orientation := north
                 end;

         back  : case orientation of
                    north : orientation := south;
                    east  : orientation := west;
                    south : orientation := north;
                    west  : orientation := east
                 end

      end

end; { makemove }
```

Program 7.1 (continued overleaf)

```
begin { main program }

    initialize ( rowchange, colchange );

    writeln ( 'Program 7.1  Maze search' );
    writeln ( '=========================' );
    writeln;

    readln ( targetrow, targetcol );
    readmazeplan ( square );

    if square[2, 2] = '*' then
       writeln ( 'maze is blocked' )
    else

       begin
          onrow        := 2;           { start position  }
          oncol        := 1;           { and orientation }
          orientation  := east;        {   of subject    }
          backatstart  := false;
          targetreached := false;

          writeln;
          writeln ( 'row column' );

          repeat
             choosemove;
             makemove
          until backatstart or targetreached;

          if backatstart then
             writeln ( 'no path to target square' )
          else
             writeln ( 'target reached' )
       end

end.
```

Program 7.1 (continued)

both use so much information that including a long list of parameters would be counter-productive. The variables that these procedures use are declared globally.

Let's examine makemove in more detail (see previous page). Its main inputs are the current and next positions of the subject, her orientation (i.e. whether she is facing North, East, West or South and the direction she is to move in. The procedure is to move the subject to a new square and also to change her orientation if necessary.

The first two assignments in makemove change the square in which the subject is located. Then checks are made to see whether she has reached the target or moved back to the start square. If neither of these apply then it may be necessary to change the direction she is facing. For instance if the subject is facing North and moves to the square on her left then she will naturally turn to face West. If she moves to the square on her right then she will turn to face East. All the possible directions and orientations are covered in the **case** statement that completes the procedure makemove.

The main **case** statement distinguishes the different directions that the subject may move in—these are left, ahead, right and back. So we have

```
case direction of
    left  : . . .
    ahead : . . .
    right : . . .
    back  : . . .
end
```

If the subject is just continuing in the same direction then no change needs to be made. In each of the other cases the new direction will depend upon her current orientation. So for each of these situations a further **case** statement is included to account for all the possibilities. If the subject moves back to the square she just came from, for example, she will turn around and be facing in the opposite direction:

```
back  : case orientation of
            north : orientation := south;
            east  : orientation := west;
            south : orientation := north;
            west  : orientation := east
        end
```

Sample output from a run of the complete program is shown below.

```
Program 7.1  Maze search
========================
    plan of maze

****************
        **    ***
** **  * *  ****
*  ?*** * *   *
*        *******
*  ** *   **   *
*  ** *** ** ***
*  ****** *   *
*  ***** *** ***
*             *
****************
row column
  2    2
  2    3
  2    4
  2    5
  2    6
  2    7
  3    7
  3    6
  2    6
  2    5
  2    4
  2    3
  3    3
  4    3
  4    4
target reached        Output from Program 7.1
```

7.2 Subranges

Frequently, the full range of data values defined for a particular data type will not be needed. A month number may only take one of the values 1 to 12; the characters processed by a particular program might include only letters; the days considered as part of the working week might include only Monday to Friday. In each of these examples it might be useful to narrow down the range of values referred to. For ordinal types *subranges* of either required or user-defined ordinals can be defined. Some examples are as follows:

```
type
      studentnumbers = 1..50;
      percentages    = 0..100;
      letters        = 'a'..'z';
      workdays       = monday..friday
```

The last of these would only be valid if a type definition had occurred earlier containing both monday and friday, in that order.

We have already met subranges, although not explicitly defined as such. The index type of an array with integer subscripts will normally be a subrange of integer. Usually it is more convenient to place the subscript range in the actual array declaration, but it could be defined separately:

```
type
      golfholes = 1..18;

var
      score : array [golfholes] of integer
```

There are three other reasons for defining subranges. Firstly, they effectively act as extra comments within the declarations, indicating to the reader the values that variables are permitted to take:

```
var
      partnumber : 1000..9999
```

Secondly, certain compilers incorporate run-time checks into the code to determine whether values of variables are within a given range, outputting an error message if they are not. This facility is not necessarily desirable. It could be argued that a good programmer will ensure that validity checks of this nature are incorporated into his program so that it does not break down. In addition, the resultant code would inevitably be executed more slowly if these checks were made.

Lastly a clever compiler may be able to economise on space allocated if a variable has a limited range specified in its declaration.

7.3 Records

An array is a suitable structure to use if we have a set of elements of the same type that we wish to consider as a unit. If the elements are of different types, or if we wish to distinguish elements by name rather than by an index, a *record* is likely to be more appropriate.

An example of a situation in which data of different types may be considered together is in the representation of a date. We may want the day and year numbers to be subranges of integer, and the months to be represented by an enumerated type containing abbreviated month names. This could be described by the **type** definition:

```
type
    date =
        record
            month : ( jan, feb, mar, apr, may, june,
                      july, aug, sept, oct, nov, dec );
            day   : 1..31;
            year  : 1900..1985
        end
```

The definition provides a pattern or *template* for any variable subsequently declared to be of this type. The components of the record are known as *fields*, and each field has a field identifier and corresponding type. A variable having this structure could be set up using the declaration

```
var
    birthday : date
```

A component of a record is referred to by writing down the record name followed by a dot and the appropriate field identifier. The component accessed may be used in the same contexts as a simple variable of the same type:

```
birthday.month := feb
```

```
if birthday.year = 1960 then . . .
```

In the date example, each field has a simple type but, in general, fields may be of any type, including arrays or even other record types:

```
type
    personinfo =
        record
            name      : packed array [1..50] of char;
            birthdate : date;
            sex       : ( female, male );
            married   : boolean
        end
```

This definition would only be valid if date had been defined earlier. We may now create variables of type personinfo using the declaration

```
var
    subject, nextsubject : personinfo
```

To refer to a structured element within a record the notation is extended in an obvious way:

```
firstletter := subject.name[1]
```

```
yearofbirth := subject.birthdate.year
```

Often we wish to access a particular record and perform operations on several or all of its fields. In this case it would be tedious to precede each reference with the name of the record. In Pascal, a record name may be omitted from field references by using a **with** statement. For example:

```
with subject do
    begin
        sex           := female;
        married       := true;
        birthdate.year := 1958
    end
```

Several records, or record fields within the same record, can be governed by a **with** statement. The general structure is shown in Fig. 7.1.

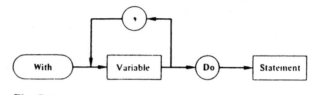

Fig. 7.1

A complete record can be copied using an assignment statement:

```
subject := nextsubject
```

and a record name may be a parameter of a subprogram but, as with arrays, a complete structure can neither be read from the standard input device nor written to the standard output device. Also any comparison of records has to be carried out element by element.

An example of a procedure to output the contents of a record is shown opposite. This again highlights a disadvantage of employing enumerated types. If the month had been coded as an integer, or as a string, then the output procedure could have been simpler.

Note that there is one **with** statement nested within another. In fact the leading part of the outer **with** statement could have been written as

```
with subject, birthdate do
```

and the inner **with** construction removed.

7.4   Arrays of records

One method of storing a large number of records of similar type is to use an array. Any individual record may then be accessed by referring to its index. For example, given the definition

```
type
    register = array [1..maxpersons] of personinfo
```

with a corresponding variable declaration

```
var
    p : register;
    index : integer
```

```
procedure writerecord ( var subject : personinfo );

{*********************************************
 *                                           *
 * Outputs contents of the subject record    *
 *                                           *
 *********************************************}

begin { writerecord }

   with subject do
      begin
         writeln ( name );

         with birthdate do
            begin
               case month of
                  jan  : write ( ' jan ' );
                  feb  : write ( ' feb ' );
                  mar  : write ( ' mar ' );
                  apr  : write ( ' apr ' );
                  may  : write ( ' may ' );
                  june : write ( ' june' );
                  july : write ( ' july' );
                  aug  : write ( ' aug ' );
                  sept : write ( ' sept' );
                  oct  : write ( ' oct ' );
                  nov  : write ( ' nov ' );
                  dec  : write ( ' dec ' )
               end;

               writeln ( day :3, year :6 )
            end;

         if sex = male then
            write ( 'male' :8 )
         else
            write ( 'female' :8 );
         if married then
            writeln ( 'married' :12 )
         else
            writeln ( 'single' :12 )
      end

end;  { writerecord }
```

then p[index] will denote a particular record in the list and so may be used in the same context as any other record reference. Some examples of references to fields of an array element are as follows:

```
p[index].married := true

if p[index].birthdate.year = 1920 then . . .

with p[index] do . . .
```

The use of the **with** construction in this context is particularly valuable for improving efficiency since the record only has to be found once—at the beginning of the construction.

We now apply these ideas in a program for performing concordance analysis.

In order to verify authorship of a book, manuscript, or any piece of text, a frequency count of words used has been found to be effective. A given author will tend to use the same words with about the same relative frequency from book to book, and statistical analysis of these 'concordances' can be very helpful. In this section, a computer program is developed for processing input words and counting their frequencies.

A suitable structure for storing a set of words is a table or, in Pascal, a two-dimensional array of characters. For our purposes, each entry will contain not only a string of characters representing a word but also a number representing the frequency with which that word has occurred. In addition, we wish to be able to check quickly whether an entry has been made in a particular position in the table. Considering these factors, a suitable record structure for an entry is

```
type
        string = packed array [1..maxwordsize] of char;

        wordinfo =
          record
            word : string;
            frequency : integer;
            empty : boolean
          end
```

The corresponding table structure could be defined as:

```
table = array [1..tablesize] of wordinfo
```

and a corresponding array of entries set up by the declaration

```
var
        entry : table
```

Having defined the storage structure to be used we can now sketch out the program.

```
Initialise table entries to empty
While not eof do
  Read in next word
  If this word is not already in the table then
    Insert
  Else
    Increase frequency by 1
Sort words
List words and frequencies
```

Initialising the table is a straightforward process since only the 'empty' indicator in each entry needs to be set. At any stage, this will be tested before any other information in a record is accessed.

```
procedure initialise ( var entry : table );

{****************************************
 *                                      *
 * Initialises table entries to empty   *
 *                                      *
 **************************************}

var
     i : integer;

begin { initialise }

   for i := 1 to tablesize do
      entry[i].empty := true

end;   { initialise }
```

The procedure for finding the next word will depend upon the form of the input text. For simplicity we shall assume that each word has been read in from a separate line. A more realistic version of getword will be described in Chapter 8.

```
procedure getword ( var inword : string );

{*****************************************************************
 *                                                              *
 * The next word on the input stream is read into inword,       *
 * assuming that each word starts in column 1 of a new line.    *
 * If a word is longer than maxwordsize then the extra          *
 * characters are ignored.                                      *
 *                                                              *
 *****************************************************************}

var
     i : integer;

begin { getword }

   i := 0;
   while not eoln and ( i < maxwordsize ) do
      begin
         i := i + 1;
         read ( inword[i] )
      end;

   for i := i + 1 to maxwordsize do
      inword[i] := ' ';

   readln

end;   { getword }
```

Inword will be padded out with blanks and the next line will be positioned ready for the next call of getword. If there is no next line then eof will be set to true.

To what value should maxwordsize be set? If it is made too small, a lot of words are going to be cut short. If it is made too large, a great deal of space is going to be wasted. The value chosen will therefore depend upon the amount of space available and the importance of distinguishing between long words. As a compromise, we have chosen the value 15.

The simplest procedure to write next is one for outputting the results. All that needs to be done is to search through the table and, whenever a non-empty record is located, print the corresponding word and frequency.

```
procedure list ( var entry : table );

{**********************************
 *                                *
 * Lists   entries in the word table *
 *                                *
 **********************************}
var
     i : integer;

begin { list }

   writeln ( ' word             frequency' );

   for i := 1 to tablesize do
     with entry[i] do
       if not empty then
           writeln ( word, frequency :6 )
end;   {* list *}
```

None of the procedures written so far assumes a particular strategy to be used for inserting items into the table. Before developing this last part of the program it might be wise to test these earlier procedures. This is just what Program 7.2 does. The procedure to initialise entries is first called, and then a set of test entries is read in and the output procedure is called.

Perhaps the simplest method of inserting items is to place the first word found in the first position in the table, the second in the second position, and so on. As each word is read in, it must be checked against all the other words in the table in case it is already present.

First we develop a Boolean function to determine whether a given word is present in the table. One possibility that was not considered in the initial algorithm is that the table might be full. The way we handle this situation depends on the circumstances. If space is no object we might declare tablesize to be large enought to cope with any likely set of data. Another approach would be to argue that any words that occur for the first time only when the table has been filled will occur so infrequently that they may be safely ignored. The most drastic course of action would be to signal an error and stop the processing altogether once the table is full. We will choose the second of these alternatives and so modify the repetition loop of the algorithm as follows.

```
While not eof do
   Read in next word
   If this word is not already in table then
      If table is not full then
           Insert
   Else
      Increase frequency by 1
```

```
Program Concordtest ( input, output );
```

```
{**************************************************************
 *                                                            *
 * Program 7.2                                                *
 * Tests the initialisation, word reading and listing procedures *
 * for concordance analysis. A set of specimen table entries are *
 * read in.                                                   *
 *                                                            *
 **************************************************************}
```

```
const
      maxwordsize = 15;
      tablesize   = 50;
```

```
type
      string = packed array [1..maxwordsize] of char;

      wordinfo =
         record
            word      : string;
            frequency : integer;
            empty     : boolean
         end;

      table = array [1..tablesize] of wordinfo;
```

```
var
      entry : table;

      entrynumber, freq : integer;

      inword : string;
```

```
procedure initialise ( var entry : table );
```

```
{**************************************
 *                                    *
 * Initialises table entries to empty *
 *                                    *
 **************************************}
```

```
var
      i : integer;

begin { initialise }

   for i := 1 to tablesize do
      entry[i].empty := true

end; { initialise }
```

Program 7.2 (continued overleaf)

```
procedure getword ( var inword : string );

{*****************************************************************
 *                                                               *
 * The next word on the input stream is read into inword,        *
 * assuming that each word starts in column 1 of a new line.     *
 * If a word is longer than maxwordsize then the extra           *
 * characters are ignored.                                       *
 *                                                               *
 *****************************************************************}

var
     i : integer;

begin { getword }

   i := 0;

   while not eoln and ( i < maxwordsize ) do
     begin
       i := i + 1;
       read ( inword[i] )
     end;

   for i := i + 1 to maxwordsize do
     inword[i] := ' ';

   readln

end;   { getword }




procedure list ( var entry : table );

{***********************************
 *                                 *
 * Lists  entries in the word table *
 *                                 *
 ***********************************}

var
     i : integer;

begin { list }

   writeln ( ' word           frequency' );

   for i := 1 to tablesize do
     with entry[i] do
       if not empty then
         writeln ( word, frequency :6 )

end;   { list }
```

Program 7.2 (continued opposite)

```
begin { main program }

   initialise ( entry );

   while not eof do
      begin
         readln ( entrynumber, freq );
         getword ( inword );

         with entry[entrynumber] do
            begin
               word := inword;
               frequency := freq;
               empty := false
            end
      end;

   writeln ( 'Program 7.2  Concordance procedures test' );
   writeln ( '=======================================' );
   writeln;

   list ( entry )

end.
```

Program 7.2 (continued)

A suitable Boolean function for testing whether a given word is in the table is shown below.

```
function wordintable (var entry : table;
                      var inword : string;
                      var position : integer;
                      var tablefull : boolean)
                                          :boolean;

{****************************************************************
 *                                                              *
 * A linear search is made for inword in the word table.        *
 * If it is found then position takes the value of the index of *
 * the corresponding table entry, otherwise it takes the value  *
 * of the first empty element.  The boolean variable tablefull  *
 * is set to true if the table is full.  The last position in   *
 * the table is kept empty to facilitate the search.            *
 *                                                              *
 ****************************************************************}

var
     wordfound : boolean;

begin { wordintable }

   entry[tablesize].empty := true;
   position := 1;
   wordfound := false;
```

(continued overleaf)

```
      while not entry[position].empty and not wordfound do
        if entry[position].word = inword then
          wordfound := true
        else
          position := position + 1;

      wordintable := wordfound;
      tablefull := not entry[tablesize - 1].empty

  end;  { wordintable }
```

By using a sentinel the code is simplified, but we lose one storage location at the end of the table.

The insertion procedure is simple, since the search procedure provides the required information.

```
  procedure insert ( var inword : string; var entry : table;
                                           position : integer );

  {**********************************************************
   *                                                        *
   * If inword is in the table then frequency is increased  *
   * otherwise the new word is entered                      *
   *                                                        *
   ***********************************************************}

begin { insert }

    with entry[position] do
      if not empty then
        frequency := frequency + 1
      else
        begin
          word := inword;
          frequency := 1;
          empty := false
        end

  end;  { insert }
```

Once an appropriate sort procedure has been included the main program (opposite) will look very similar to the algorithmic version. Besides being easy to follow, the structured nature of the main program makes modifications easy to carry out. It has already been mentioned that getword is not very convenient in its present form. The other candidate for modification is wordintable.

In Chapter 6, a binary search strategy was described as an alternative to the linear search. In some cases even faster access may be achieved by using a variation of the linear search. The main problem with the simple linear search is that, since each search starts at the beginning of the list, the search time grows in proportion to the size of the list. A more effective approach would be to use different start positions for different words. For example, a search for words beginning with 'A' could be started at position 1, those starting with 'B' at position 101, those starting with 'C' at position 201 and so on. Obviously the start positions would depend upon the size of the table; and, in addition, the space provided for a given letter could be adjusted depending upon the expected relative frequency of words starting with that letter. This cuts down the size of

```
begin { main program }

    initialise ( entry );
    tablefull := false;

    while not eof do
      begin
        getword ( inword );
        if not wordintable ( entry, inword, position, tablefull ) then
          begin
            if not tablefull then
                insert ( inword, entry, position )
          end
        else
          entry[position].frequency := entry[position].frequency + 1
      end;

    sort ( entry );
    list ( entry )

end.
```

Main program to insert word in table

```
    function hash ( var inword : string ) : integer;

    {***************************************************************
     *                                                             *
     * Computes a number in the range 1 to tablesize by adding     *
     * the ordinal values of the non-blank characters in inword    *
     *                                                             *
     ***************************************************************}

    var
          hsum, i : integer;

    begin { hash }

        hsum := 0;

        if inword[maxwordsize] = ' ' then    { length of word is less }
          begin                              { than array length      }
            i := 1;

            repeat
              hsum := hsum + ord ( inword[i] );
              i := i + 1
            until inword[i] = ' '

          end
        else
          for i := 1 to maxwordsize do
            hsum := hsum + ord ( inword[i] );

        hash := hsum mod tablesize + 1

    end;   { hash }
    Function hash
```

```
function wordintable ( var entry : table;
                       var inword : string;
                       var position : integer;
                       var tablefull : boolean ) : boolean;

{***********************************************************************
 *                                                                     *
 * A search is made for inword in the word table using a hash function *
 * technique. If it is found then position takes the value of the index*
 * of the corresponding table entry, otherwise position takes the value*
 * of the first empty element found.  The variable tablefull is set to *
 * true if the table is full and the word is not found.                *
 *                                                                     *
 ***********************************************************************}

var
     startposition : integer;
     wordfound : boolean;


   function hash ( var inword : string ) : integer;

      .
      .
      .

   end;  { hash }


begin { wordintable }

   wordfound := false;
   startposition := hash ( inword );
   position := startposition;
   tablefull := false;

   if not entry[startposition].empty then
      if entry[startposition].word <> inword then    { collision }
         begin
            entry[startposition].empty := true;  { marker for start }
                                                 {    of search     }
            position := startposition mod tablesize + 1;

            while not entry[position].empty and not wordfound do
               if entry[position].word = inword then
                  wordfound := true
               else
                  position := position mod tablesize + 1;

            if position = startposition then
               tablefull := true;
            entry[startposition].empty := false  { remove marker }
         end;

   wordintable := wordfound

end;  { wordintable }

Function wordintable
```

the problem significantly, since there is now only one of twenty six shorter lists to look through. The search time may be reduced even further by taking into account all the letters of the input word in order to determine a start position for searching. The words do not have to be inserted in alphabetical order, but we do have to ensure that the start position for searching for a particular word is always the same.

Essentially, a process is required that produces from a given word a number in the range 1 to **tablesize**. A function that produces a number from a string of characters is called a *hash function*. It is not necessary that a hash function should give a different value for each word; but the more widespread the values are, the more effective the function will be. Another consideration is that the function should be simple, since it may be called many thousands of times. A possible function definition for our problem is given on page 163 (function hash).

Once the start position has been computed for a given word, the search is continued as in the linear search, except that once the end of the table is reached the search may be continued from the beginning of the table. Tablefull is set to true only if the search returns to the original position without the word being found.

The definition of the modified form of wordintable is given on page 164. This function may now be substituted directly into the program above without any modification being required elsewhere.

7.5 Record variants*

When every item in a set of values has exactly the same structure it is convenient to define an array of records to describe that structure. In some cases items have essentially the same form but differ in one or two details. For example, in a set of records containing information about individuals, there may be a field in each record stating whether or not the person is married. If the person is married, there may be another field for personal details of the spouse, whereas this field is redundant if the person is single.

As another example, consider records containing information about stock in a warehouse. There might be three fields common to all items—item number, item description, and an indication of whether there are any items of that type in stock. If an item is in stock we may require a further field indicating the quantity held, otherwise a field denoting the reorder date may be included. There will be no situation in which both of these fields will be needed, and so to provide for both in every record would be wasteful of space. Pascal provides a method of dealing with this situation by allowing the user to include a *variant part*. A suitable structure for stock information is given below.

```
type
    iteminfo =
       record
          catalogno    : 10000..99999;
          description : packed array [1..80] of char;
          case instock : boolean of
             true  : ( stock : integer );
             false : ( reorderdate : date )
       end
```

The compiler may now arrange for stock and reorderdate to share the same space. The value of instock will indicate which one is being stored in a given record. It distinguishes between the two variants and is called the *tag field*. References to fields of variables having

---

*This section may be omitted on first reading

this structure follow the normal rules. If item is declared as

```
var
        item : array [1..stocknumber] of iteminfo
```

then the following statements would be valid:

```
if item[i].catalogno = targetno then
    writeln ( item[i].description )



with item[i] do
    if instock then
        read ( stock )
    else
        with reorderdate do
            begin
                month := jan;
                day   := 20;
                year  := 1980
            end
```

The value of the tag field should always be checked before referring to one of the case constants to ensure the appropriate one is in operation. Compilers can be made to check for this at run-time but many don't.

Another variation on the same theme is to leave the tag field out altogether:

```
type
        iteminfo =
            record
                catalogno     : 10000..99999;
                description   : packed array [1..80] of char;
                case boolean of
                    true  : ( stock : integer );
                    false : ( reorderdate : date )
            end
```

This increases the flexibility of the record structure allowing the user to store a value as one type and access it as another. The disadvantage is that the protective shield of type checking that Pascal provides in other circumstances is lost. The programmer takes the responsibility for ensuring that each variant is used in an appropriate context.

The tag-type in either variant form must be defined using a type identifier—it cannot be a new type created at that point. Also each of the possible values of the tag-type must occur in the constant list although one or more of them may have an empty variant (as in the example of the spouse information). An empty variant is shown as below:

```
v : ( )
```

A record can have only one variant part, and this must follow all other field definitions. However, the number of variants within this is not restricted to two—there may be several, each with its own field type. Also, if a variant is a record, then this record may, itself, contain a variant part. Care should be taken when defining field names since all the field names in a record must be distinct, even if they occur in different variants.

Summary

Enumerated types are valuable for improving the readability of programs. In addition, since their values cannot be mixed with values of other types, compiler checks may be performed for correct usage.

Declaring a variable to be of a subrange type effectively acts as a comment on the range of values that the variable may take. Certain compilers perform run-time checks on the values of these variables, but this facility has to be used carefully.

Record structures are available in one form or another in many computer languages, and are indispensable for most commercial applications. Once you start using record structures you will wonder how you ever managed without them.

Exercises

1   Write a program to sort a set of dates into chronological order where months are represented by the symbols jan, feb, mars, april, may, june, july, aug, sept, oct, nov, dec.

2   Assuming an 8 × 8 two-dimensional array is to be used to represent the contents of a chess board, write a record description to represent the contents of a single square (remember that it may be empty). Write and test procedures to input and to output the current board position, and a procedure that inputs a move and checks its validity.

3   Write a program for searching a maze that may contain circular paths.

4   Write a program to represent a crossword, incorporating procedures for reading in a template, checking if a word may be placed in a given position, inserting a word, deleting a word, and outputting a representation of the crossword.

5   Write a program that inputs another Pascal program as data and counts the frequency of occurrence of each of the reserved words.

8

Files

Introduction

In this chapter we consider how information may be written to and read from backing storage devices. Space and permanence are the main reasons for using magnetic disk and tape storage. For most practical purposes, there is no limit to the amount of storage space available on these media. In addition, information can be copied to disk or tape and left there until required again, perhaps by another program, whereas information stored in arrays effectively disappears when the program that created them has terminated.

The structure used in Pascal for representing information stored on an external medium is the sequential file.

8.1 Defining a sequential file

A sequential file consists of a sequence of components of similar type. There is no indexing facility such as is provided for arrays. Items may only be accessed by scanning through the elements one by one, and new ones may only be added to the end of the file.

Components may be of any allowable Pascal type except files or any structure containing a file definition. For example, files of integers, arrays, or records, may be defined. One of the most useful file types is the file of records. The following piece of code shows how a variable, accountfile, representing a file of records containing bank account information could be declared.

```
type
    accinfo = file of
            record
                accnumber : packed array [1..10] of char;
                name      : packed array [1..40] of char;
                address   : packed array [1..80] of char;
                balance   : integer
            end;

var
    accountfile : accinfo
```

Operations on files are much more restrictive than on other structures we have met. Implicit copying, or amendment, using such statements as

```
f1 := f2
```
or
```
f1 := f2 + f3
```

are *not* permitted.

Fig. 8.1

Data can only be processed by the computer when it is in the main memory. Most computers will transfer a small block of items at a time from an external medium into main memory. The number of items transferred will vary from system to system and so, for simplicity, Pascal allows just one component of a file to be accessible from a program at any one time. Similarly, items may only be transferred to a file one at a time. The currently accessible item is called the *current file component* and is stored in a *file buffer*. Conceptually, we can think of the file buffer as the link between the secondary storage device and main memory, as illustrated in Fig. 8.1.

When writing information to a file, each item must be transmitted in turn using the file buffer. When reading information from a file, one item at a time becomes accessible via the file buffer.

To refer to the current file component, the file variable name is followed by the character '↑'; so, for example, a reference to the current record from the accounts file defined earlier would be written.

```
accountfile↑
```

This *buffer variable* may be used in two different ways, depending upon whether information is being written to or read from the file.

8.2 Initialising and writing to a file

The number of records in a file may vary during the running of a program. It is the first *dynamic* storage structure that we have met in Pascal, so far. When a file is created it is, initially, empty. Its size may be *increased* as items are added but may not be *decreased* at any stage except by erasing the complete contents of the file. To initialise the file described earlier, we would use the instruction

```
rewrite ( accountfile )
```

An end-of-file marker is provided which is initially coincident with the start of the file. Any information contained in accountfile prior to the execution of this statement would effectively be erased.

Placing information in the file may be performed in two stages. First, the buffer variable is given a value:

```
accountfile↑ := thisaccount
```

This information is then transmitted to the file using a put instruction:

```
put ( accountfile )
```

In addition to placing a record of information on the file, execution of the put statement causes the end-of-file marker to be moved along one record position. It is useful to think in terms of an indicator to denote the current file component; this indicator is called a *file window*. When writing to a file, the file window is always over the end-of-file marker. A piece of code for setting up a file of integers, ifile, and for writing to it, is shown

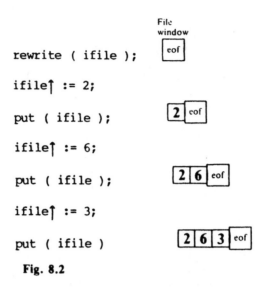

```
rewrite ( ifile );

ifile↑ := 2;

put ( ifile );

ifile↑ := 6;

put ( ifile );

ifile↑ := 3;

put ( ifile )
```

Fig. 8.2

in Fig. 8.2, together with a diagrammatic representation of the file contents and file window after each file operation has been performed.

The file could have initially been declared as

var
```
      ifile : file of integer
```

In Program 8.1 opposite an accounts file is created and information is read into it from data. The first point to note is that, since accountfile is to be preserved after the program has terminated, its name must appear in the list of program parameters. This would also oe the case for a program accessing a pre-existing file but would not be necessary when a temporary file is created by a program (i.e. a file that is no longer needed once the program has terminated). *

Secondly, references are made to fields of accountfile↑. This is no problem since a buffer variable may be treated in the same way as a normal variable of the corresponding component type. The only restriction is that, after execution of a put statement, the value of the corresponding buffer variable is undefined.

The operations of assigning a value to a buffer variable and transmitting this value to the corresponding file often occur together and so a shorthand form is permitted; for example

```
      write ( ifile, i )
```

is equivalent to

```
      ifile↑ := i;
      put ( ifile )
```

To further simplify things write may contain a list of items to be added to the file.

Lastly, note that accountfile is made a variable parameter of setup—file parameters in a subprogram must always be made variable.

---

*Some implementations of Pascal have non-standard conventions for declaring and saving files. Check your User Manual on these points.

```
Program Createaccounts ( input, accountfile );

{**************************************************************
 *                                                            *
 * Program 8.1                                                *
 * An accounts file is created containing information read in *
 * from the standard input device.                            *
 *                                                            *
 **************************************************************}

type
      accinfo = file of
                    record
                        accnumber : packed array [1..10] of char;
                        name      : packed array [1..40] of char;
                        address   : packed array [1..80] of char;
                        balance   : integer
                    end;

var
      accountfile : accinfo;



procedure setup ( var accountfile : accinfo );

{**********************************************************************
 *                                                                    *
 * Sets up accounts file. Each account record is contained in two     *
 * lines with the following layout:                                   *
 *                                                                    *
 *         line 1                                                      *
 *                 cols  1 - 10    account number (alphanumeric)       *
 *                      14 - 53    name (alphabetic - left justified)  *
 *                      56 - 70    balance (integer)                   *
 *                                                                    *
 *         line  2                                                     *
 *                 cols  1 - 80    address (alphanumeric)              *
 *                                                                    *
 **********************************************************************}

var
      colnumber : integer;
      blank : char;

begin { setup }

   rewrite ( accountfile );

   while not eof do
      begin

          with accountfile↑ do
              begin
```

Program 8.1 (continued overleaf)

```
        for colnumber := 1 to 10 do
           read ( accnumber[colnumber] );

        read ( blank, blank, blank );

        for colnumber := 1 to 40 do
           read ( name[colnumber] );

        readln ( balance );

        for colnumber := 1 to 80 do
           read ( address[colnumber] );

        readln

     end;

   put ( accountfile )

  end

end;  { setup }


begin { main program }

  setup ( accountfile )

end.
```
Program 8.1 (continued)

8.3 Reading from a file

After setting up a file, we may wish to read elements from that file, either in the same program or in a different one. In order to start reading items from a file, the file window must be located at the beginning of that file. This is achieved by using the reset command. For the accounts file we would write

```
reset ( accountfile )
```

The name accountfile would also have to appear in the program parameter list if the file had been set up by a previously run program. In this case a check should be made that the file has exactly the same structure in both programs.

Information is read from a file by using the get statement. For example,

```
get ( accountfile )
```

moves the file window along to the next component and accountfile↑ takes the value of this new component.

For simplicity, we demonstrate this mechanism for the file of integers created in the last section (see Fig. 8.3). The effect of each file processing statement is shown on the right. The values 2, 6, 3 would be printed by the output device. Incidentally, notice that a get statement is *not* needed directly after the reset statement, because the file window is initially placed over the first item in the file.

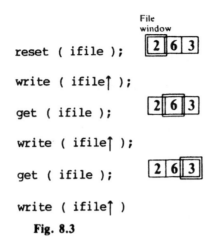

reset (ifile);

write (ifile↑);

get (ifile);

write (ifile↑);

get (ifile);

write (ifile↑)

Fig. 8.3

The question arises—what would happen if another get statement was executed for the above file? To answer this we have to introduce another operation familiar from another context—the eof function. The value of eof, when applied to a file, is false as long as the file window is over a component of the file. As soon as the file window is moved beyond the end of the file, eof becomes true. In the above example, a further statement

    get (ifile)

would leave ifile↑ undefined (and a reference to it may produce an error) but would change the value of

    eof (ifile)

to true.

A suitable piece of code for summing the contents of ifile is shown below.

```
reset ( ifile );
isum := 0;

while not eof ( ifile ) do
   begin
      isum := isum + ifile↑;
      get ( ifile )
   end
```

This piece of code will give the value of isum as zero if the file is initially empty, since the loop will not be entered. Many file processing algorithms involve processing each component of a file in a similar fashion until the end of the file is reached, and so will have the same basic structure as the above example.

Program 8.2 overleaf processes the accounts file created earlier, printing out the account numbers and deficits of accounts that are overdrawn.

There are circumstances when it is convenient to mix reading and writing operations on a file. For example, we may wish to extract an element from a file, modify it and then put back the amended record in the same place. Unfortunately this cannot be done in standard Pascal. A file is either in reading mode ('inspection state') or writing mode ('generation state'). A file is put into reading mode only when a reset command has been executed (which takes the file window back to the beginning of the file). It is put into

```
Program Checkbalance ( accountfile, output );

{**************************************************************
 *                                                            *
 * Program 8.2                                                *
 * accountfile is searched for accounts that are overdrawn.   *
 * The corresponding account numbers and balances are output. *
 *                                                            *
 **************************************************************}

type
      accinfo = file of
                      record
                          accnumber : packed array [1..10] of char;
                          name      : packed array [1..40] of char;
                          address   : packed array [1..80] of char;
                          balance   : integer
                      end;

var
      accountfile : accinfo;

begin

    writeln ( 'Program 8.2  Search for overdrawn accounts' );
    writeln ( '==========================================' );
    writeln;

    writeln ( 'account number    balance' );
    reset ( accountfile );

    while not eof ( accountfile ) do
       begin
          with accountfile↑ do
              if balance < 0 then
                  writeln ( accnumber :12, balance / 100 :11:2 );
          get ( accountfile )
       end

end.
```

Program 8.2

writing mode when a rewrite instruction is carried out which, of course, erases the previous contents of the file. Since a file cannot be in reading mode and writing mode at the same time it will be seen that there is no way to alternate the two operations on a file and achieve anything useful. The only way of 'updating' a file is to process each record of the old file in turn, and put into a new file containing the amended records. An example of this technique is given in Section 8.4.

Pascal allows the use of a read statement for combining the copying of the value of a buffer variable and the moving on of the file window; for example

```
read ( ifile, i )
```

would be equivalent to

```
i := ifile↑;
get ( ifile )
```

8.4 File update

The problem of updating a file is sometimes regarded as the *only* data processing problem. Although this is not quite true, it appears in many guises in commercial installations—stock control, customer accounts at a store, payroll computations, and so on. We shall continue with the bank account example and consider the updating of the file of accounts (the *old master* file) using a *transaction* file to produce a *new master* file.

The transactions will be of three types:

(a)   insertion—placing a new account on the account file;
(b)   amendment—adjusting the balance of an account;
(c)   deletion—removing an account from the account file.

We assume that both the account file and the transaction file have been sorted into ascending account number order and that the transaction file has been validated to ensure that all entries have the correct format. This allows all the modifications to be made in one scan, processing the two files in parallel. The new master produced will contain only valid entries and will also be in ascending order of account number.

There may be several transactions with the same account number, and so a temporary 'current' record should be set up to hold intermediate information relating to the account currently being processed. The last of these transactions could be a deletion, in which case nothing will be transferred to the new master. To deal with this situation we need to be able to check whether the current record is empty (a Boolean variable will be used for this in the final program). The initial solution procedure may now be described at the top level as follows.

> While not eof(oldmaster) or not eof(transaction) do
>   Set up the current record
>   Process transactions with the same key
>   If the current record is not empty then
>   Transfer the contents of the current record to the new master file

As the two files are being processed there are three distinct situations that can occur. Which of these applies will affect the way in which the current record is set up. The situations are as follows.

(i)   The old master record key is less than the transaction record key (see Fig. 8.4). Since both files are in ascending order of key we may infer that there are no transactions for this master file record. It may therefore be copied to the current record, ready to be transferred to the new master. The next master record may then be placed in position ready to be examined.

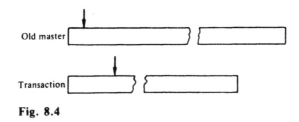

Fig. 8.4

(ii)   The old master record key is equal to the transaction record key (see Fig. 8.5). This will be the first of a possible sequence of transactions on the same account. The old master record should therefore be copied to the current record and the old master file moved on to the next record.

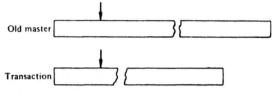

Fig. 8.5

(iii)   The old master record key is greater than the transaction key (see Fig. 8.6). This transaction must have a key that is not in the old master file and so a new account is to be processed. In this case, a new empty current record is set up ready for processing the transactions with this key.

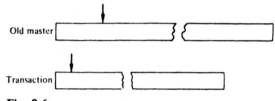

Fig. 8.6

The first two possibilities involve the same action and can be combined. The process for setting up the current record can therefore be described as follows.

> If old master key ≤ transaction key then
>   Copy old master record to current record
>   Set current record to not empty
>   Get next old master record
> Else
>   Copy transaction account number to current record
>   Set current record to empty

We now come to the kernel of the algorithm—processing transactions with the same key. An extra complication that needs to be considered at this stage is the possibility of an illegal transaction—an amendment or deletion of a nonexistent record or the attempted insertion of an account that is already present. We shall use an error file to note any illegal transactions. In fact there is no real problem in detecting these errors since once we have distinguished the three legitimate cases:

(i)   amendment and current record not empty;
(ii)   insertion and current record empty;
(iii) deletion and current record not empty;

then anything else must be an error.

The algorithm for processing transactions with the same key now becomes

> While current record key = transaction key do
>   If transaction type = amendment and current record not empty then
>   Add transaction amount to current record balance
>   Else if transaction type = insertion and current record empty then
>   Copy transaction information to current record
>   Set empty record to false
>   Else if transaction type = deletion and current record not empty then
>   Set empty record to true
>   Else note error type and account number in error file
>   Get next transaction record

The program is now nearly ready for coding. One last point needs to be considered—what happens when the end of either file is reached? If the end of the old master file is encountered first then the remaining legal transactions must all involve new accounts. If the transaction file is the first to be exhausted then the remainder of the program involves copying old master records across to the new master file. Both of these situations can be dealt with within the existing framework by including a dummy record at the end of each file, with a key that is greater than any valid account number. Two small modifications now need to be made to the algorithm . First, the termination test for processing records should now refer to the dummy keys instead of eof. Secondly, a dummy key should be inserted at the end of the new master, ready for the next time the program is run.

Program 8.3 performs the complete file update as described here. This formulation is only one of many approaches to the problem and is based on the algorithm developed by E W Dijkstra in his book *A Discipline of Programming* (see p. 247). Various modifications to include situations such as a change of address or printing out the balance in each deleted record can easily be incorporated without changing the main algorithm.

```
Program fileupdate ( oldmaster, transaction, newmaster, errorfile );

{**********************************************************************
 *                                                                    *
 * Program 8.3                                                        *
 * A bank accounts file is updated using a transaction file to produce *
 * a new master file. It is assumed that the input files have been    ·   *
 * validated and that entries in both the oldmaster and transaction   *
 * file are in ascending order of key. Both files end with a dummy    *
 * record containing the same account number  -  maxkey. Any attempt  *
 * to amend or delete a non-existent record or to insert a record     *
 * with an account number that is already present is signalled as     *
 * an error -  this information is sent to an error file.             *
 *                                                                    *
 **********************************************************************}

const
      maxkey = 'zz99999999';

type
      accstring   = packed array [1..10] of char;

      namestring  = packed array [1..40] of char;

      addstring   = packed array [1..80] of char;

      operation = ( insertion, amendment, deletion );

      entry =
         record
            accnumber : accstring;
            name      : namestring;
            address   : addstring;
            balance   : integer
         end;
```

Program 8.3 (continued overleaf)

```
var

    emptycurrentrecord : boolean;

    currentrecord : entry;

    oldmaster, newmaster : file of entry;

    transaction :
        file of
            record
                accnumber : accstring;
                case transtype : operation of
                    insertion : ( name          : namestring;
                                  address       : addstring;
                                  initialbalance : integer );
                    amendment : ( amount : integer );
                    deletion  : ( )
                end;

    errorfile : file of
                    record
                        accnumber : accstring;
                        errortype : operation
                    end;

procedure setupcurrentrecord;
```

```
{**************************************************************************
 *                                                                      *
 * The key of the next record to be processed is determined. This will  *
 * be either the account number of the next record in the old master    *
 * file or of the next record in the transaction file whichever is the  *
 * smaller. Its value is placed in currentrecord.accnumber.             *
 * In addition, if the next record to be processed is from the old       *
 * master file, a copy of this is placed in currentrecord, otherwise     *
 * emptycurrentrecord is set to true.                                    *
 *                                                                      *
 **************************************************************************}
```

```
begin { setupcurrentrecord }

    if oldmaster↑.accnumber <= transaction↑.accnumber then
        begin
            currentrecord := oldmaster↑;
            emptycurrentrecord := false;
            get ( oldmaster )
        end
    else
        begin
            currentrecord.accnumber := transaction↑.accnumber;
            emptycurrentrecord := true
        end

end;  { setupcurrentrecord }
```

Program 8.3 (continued opposite)

```
procedure processtranswithsamekey;

{**********************************************************************
 *                                                                    *
 * All transactions with the same key are processed using currentrecord *
 * to store the result. Any errors are noted in errorfile.            *
 *                                                                    *
 **********************************************************************}

var
     t : operation;

begin { processtranswithsamekey }

   while currentrecord.accnumber = transaction↑.accnumber do
     begin
        t := transaction↑.transtype;
        if ( t = amendment ) and not emptycurrentrecord then
           currentrecord.balance := currentrecord.balance +
                                               transaction↑.amount
        else if ( t = insertion ) and emptycurrentrecord then
           begin
              emptycurrentrecord      := false;
              currentrecord.name      := transaction↑.name;
              currentrecord.address := transaction↑.address;
              currentrecord.balance := transaction↑.initialbalance
           end
        else if ( t = deletion ) and not emptycurrentrecord then
           emptycurrentrecord := true
        else  { transaction error }
           begin
              errorfile↑.accnumber := currentrecord.accnumber;
              errorfile↑.errortype := t;
              put ( errorfile )
           end;
        get ( transaction )
     end

end;  { processtranswithsamekey }




begin { main program }

   reset ( oldmaster );
   reset ( transaction );
   rewrite ( newmaster );
   rewrite ( errorfile );

   while ( oldmaster↑.accnumber <> maxkey )
         or ( transaction↑.accnumber <> maxkey ) do
     begin
        setupcurrentrecord;
        processtranswithsamekey;
```

Program 8.3 (continued overleaf)

```
        if not emptycurrentrecord then
            begin
                newmaster↑ := currentrecord;
                put ( newmaster )
            end
    end;

newmaster↑ := oldmaster↑;                    { dummy key at end }
put ( newmaster )                            { of newmaster      }

end.
```

Program 8.3 (continued)

8.5   Textfiles

Files in which each component is of type char and which have special properties making
them compatible with the standard input and output devices are called *textfiles*. An
example of a textfile declaration is given below.

```
    var
            progfile : text
```

Any sequence of characters from the character set in use may then be entered into
progfile. In addition, an extra line separator character is available for denoting the end
of a line.

Let's assume that progfile already contains a copy of a computer program, and we wish
to count the number of lines in the program. The following piece of code would do the
trick.

```
lines := 0;
reset ( progfile );

while not eof ( progfile ) do
    begin
        lines := lines + 1;
        readln ( progfile )
    end
```

readln is a special function, available for use with textfiles, for skipping to the character
beyond the next end-of-line symbol. In addition, progfile↑ takes the value of the first
character on this new line. If we wish to make a copy of progfile, the following piece of
code could be used:

```
rewrite ( pcopy );
reset ( progfile );

while not eof ( progfile ) do
    begin
        while not eoln ( progfile ) do
            begin
                read ( progfile, character );
                write ( pcopy, character )
            end;
        readln ( progfile );
        writeln ( pcopy )
    end
```

This piece of code introduces several features of textfiles. Firstly, the function eoln may be used to test for an end-of-line since it becomes true if and only if the file window is over a line separator. Next there are read and write statements which, in this instance, have a similar effect to the read and write statements for general files. Lastly, the procedure writeln has the effect of placing a line separator on the file.

You may wonder why the copying operation is not simpler. For instance, why not use the following piece of code?

```
rewrite ( pcopy );
reset ( progfile );

while not eof ( progfile ) do
   begin
      read ( progfile, character );
      write ( pcopy, character )
   end
```

The answer is that the line separators may not be treated as ordinary characters. Although progfile↑ conventionally has the character value ' ' when the file window is over a line separator, its representation is implementation-dependent.

In Program 8.4 the common operation of *squashing* a file is carried out. We assume that tfile is a textfile with constant line length, and we wish to create a new file with redundant blanks removed from the end of each line, in order to save space. The array called line temporarily stores a line of text before it is processed. This is scanned from right to left in order to detect redundant blanks. The non-redundant characters are then copied to the new file.

```
Program Squashfile ( tfile, tsquash );

{*********************************************************************
 *                                                                  *
 * Program 8.4                                                      *
 * tfile contains the text of a program. This is copied to the file *
 * tsquash with redundant blanks at the end of each line removed.   *
 *                                                                  *
 *********************************************************************}

var
      tfile, tsquash : text;


procedure squash ( var tfile, tsquash : text );

{*****************************************************************
 *                                                              *
 * tfile is copied into tsquash with redundant blanks           *
 * removed from the end of each line.                           *
 *                                                              *
 *****************************************************************}
```

Program 8.4 (continued overleaf)

```
const
      maxlinelength = 100;   { maximum length of lines of tfile }
      linemarker    = '%';
var
      line : array [0..maxlinelength] of char; { used to store each }
                                               { line of tfile      }
      character : char;

      charnumber, i : integer;

begin { squash }

   rewrite ( tsquash );
   reset ( tfile );

   line[0] := linemarker;   { needed in case of blank line }

   while not eof ( tfile ) do
      begin
         charnumber := 0;

         while not eoln ( tfile ) do
            begin                              { a line of tfile }
               charnumber := charnumber + 1;   {  is read into   }
               read ( tfile, line[charnumber] ) { the line array  }
            end;

         while line[charnumber] = ' ' do     { line array is scanned from }
            charnumber := charnumber - 1;     { right for first non-blank  }

         for i := 1 to charnumber do                     { copy to }
            write ( tsquash, line[i] );                  { tsquash }

         readln ( tfile );
         writeln ( tsquash )
      end

end;   { squash }



begin { main program }

   squash ( tfile, tsquash )

end.
```

Program 8.4 (continued)

8.6 *input* and *output*

The read and write statements for textfiles are as versatile as those used in normal input/output. For example, a sequence of characters may be read from a file in a single statement:

```
read ( f, c1, c2, c3 )
```

In addition, values of certain other types may be stored in textfiles. real and integer values may be read from a textfile, whereas values of type real, integer, boolean and packed array of char may be written to one.

It is no coincidence that read and write statements for these files look similar to those for standard input and output. In fact, input and output are just ordinary textfiles associated with the main input and output devices. The statement read(ch), for example, is short for read(input,ch).

get and put may be used, in the same way as they are used with other files. An example of input/output without read and write statements is given below.

```
while not eof do
   begin

      while not eoln do
         begin
            output↑ := input↑;
            put ( output );
            get ( input )
         end;

      readln;
      writeln

   end
```

Compare this with the code for copying a program given in Section 8.5 (p. 180). The only apparent advantage of the above version is that an extra variable is not required. In fact, on most computers, the above version would be much faster since get and put are usually more efficient than read and write. This is not to suggest that you should go through all your programs replacing the read and write instructions: in most cases using read and write will make your programs easier to understand.

Occasionally, to achieve a particular effect, there is no choice but to use get or put. For example, if we require a program to process words in a piece of text where the words are separated by one or more blanks, then a skipblanks procedure would be useful. An attempt to code this using a normal read statement is shown below.

```
repeat
   read ( character )
until ( character <> ' ' ) or eof
```

There are two problems with this formulation. For a start the value of character may not be defined when the file window is between lines (i.e. when eoln is true) or at the end of the file. Secondly even if it is defined it will have the value of the first non-blank and not the last blank. Although we can get around the first problem by checking for eoln and eof before performing the read statement there is no way we can avoid the second difficulty without using get to look ahead and examine the next character without reading it in. A version of skipblanks using get is shown overleaf.

```
procedure skipblanks;
```

```
{******************************************************************
 *                                                                *
 * Skips over any non-blanks in the input stream stopping in front *
 * of the next non-blank or at the end of the file if this occurs first. *
 *                                                                *
 ******************************************************************}
```

```
var
      blank : boolean;
```

```
begin { skipblanks }

   blank := true;

   while not eof and blank do
      if input↑ = ' ' then
         get(input)
      else
         blank := false

end;   { skipblanks }
```

After this procedure has been executed the file window will be over the next non-blank character and so the effect of

```
read ( character )
```

will be to make the value of character this first non-blank (assuming the end of file has not been reached). Referring back to the concordance analysis problem of Section 7.4 (p. 156), the procedure getword could be modified to allow for any number of words per input line by incorporating skipblanks:

```
procedure getword ( var inword : string );
```

```
{*********************************************************
 *                                                       *
 * The next word on the input stream is read in to inword *
 * assuming that words are separated by one or more blanks *
 *                                                       *
 *********************************************************}
```

```
var
      i : integer;

      ch : char;

      endofword : boolean;


   procedure skipblanks;
      .
      .
      .
   end;   { skipblanks }
```

(continued opposite)

```
begin { getword }

   i := 1;
   endofword := false;
   repeat
      if i <= maxwordsize then
         begin
            read ( inword[i] );
            i := i + 1
         end
      else
         read ( ch );        { if more than maxwordsize characters in }
                             {  word then these are ignored           }
      if eof then
         endofword := true
      else if input↑ = ' ' then
         endofword := true

   until endofword;

   for i := i to maxwordsize do      {  fill out   }
      inword[i] := ' ';              { with blanks }

   skipblanks

end;  { getword }
```

Here we assume that the first word starts in column 1 of the first input record. If this is not necessarily so then an initial call of skipblanks would be needed. Obviously, there is no problem in generalising this technique to allow skipping of any punctuation characters.

One difference between input and output and other textfiles is that reset(input) and rewrite(output) are automatically performed by the system. Any further calls to reset or rewrite for these files should produce an error, for obvious reasons.

Summary

Files are an important feature of modern computing, particularly in the commercial world. File operations in Pascal are very elementary and rather restrictive; there is no provision, for example, for indexing file elements to allow faster access when using disk storage. Sequential file access is rather slow. However, the language does provide a useful introduction to file manipulation, and all the most common sequential operations, such as file updating, may be carried out.

Exercises

1 Programs that are used regularly are often stored on disk. In a large computer the operating system may control the storage of program files—removing files that have not been used since a given date. Write a procedure that creates a file containing a list of program names (up to 12 characters) and the date when each of the programs was last run. Write a second procedure to output the contents of this file. Incorporate these procedures into a program that inputs a cut-off date and creates a new file containing the names of only those programs that have been run since the cut-off date.

2 resultsfile contains the results of candidates in examinations. Each record consists of a candidate name (up to 30 characters), a candidate number (6 characters) and an examination mark. Write procedures to create and print out the contents of resultsfile. Write a program to produce three new files containing lists of candidates obtaining distinctions (over 80%), candidates who passed but did not obtain a distinction (50–79%) and candidates who failed. Assume that all the information has previously been validated.

3 Write a program to update a stock file using a sales file. You should first write procedures for setting up a stock file and for outputting the contents of the file. Each entry will consist of a five digit item number and the quantity in stock. The output should contain an indication of which items are out of stock. Next, write a procedure to create a sales file where each record contains the item number and the quantity sold. Write a program to update the stock file using the sales file. Assume that both files are ordered by item number and that there may be several requests for the same item. Unfulfilled requests should be stored in a separate file. If you wish, you may simplify the problem by assuming all item numbers in the sales file also occur in the stock file.

4 Write a program to sort a file of numbers.

5 Write a program to compare two textfiles to check if they contain the same information.

6 Text editing facilities often include a feature that allows a user to find all of the occurrences of a particular string of characters in a program. Write a procedure to create a textfile containing a Pascal program. Write and test another procedure find for listing all of the line numbers on which a given string occurs (assume the maximum length of a string is equal to the maximum line length of a program).

7 Write a program to merge two files of sorted integers.

9
Pointer structures

Introduction

The two structures we have used so far for storing large amounts of information—the array and the file—are both rather inflexible. The size of an array must be decided before compilation and so arrays are of limited use when the amount of data varies significantly from run to run or even within a single run. The file does not have this restriction but, because of the nature of the physical storage devices used, file operations are rather slow and limited. A system is needed that allows flexible run-time management of storage; it should also permit items to be added and removed quickly and allow the development of interrelations between items. In Pascal these facilities are provided by the use of *pointer variables*.

9.1 Lists and pointers

We first consider the problem of setting up and maintaining a list of items when no reasonable estimate on the upper limit of the length of the list is available. For instance, if we wanted a program to find the mode (most commonly occurring value) of a set of numbers, a simple approach would be to set up, at run-time, a list of those values that actually occur in the data and increment their frequencies as necessary.

Each item in the list would consist of a number and its associated frequency. A suitable storage structure could be defined by

```
type
      iteminfo =
         record
            number,
            frequency : integer
         end
```

The sequence of numbers that have been found at any particular time must be accessible in some way so that we can decide if the next number in the data has already been found or whether it must be added to the list. The method we shall use is to link each new item to another one already in the list. The structure we get is shown in Fig. 9.1 and is known as a *singly-linked list*.

Once one item has been located, the next can be found by following the pointer. In computing terms, this means that the address of the next item in the list will be stored with each item. As long as the address of the first item is known, each of the others may

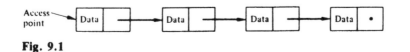

Fig. 9.1

be accessed in turn. A pointer to another object is indicated, in Pascal, by using the '↑' symbol. Each element or *node* of the list will have two components—information about the item and a link to another node. A suitable *type* definition is as follows:

```
type
      element =
        record
          data : iteminfo;
          link : ↑element
        end
```

A snag with the above formulation is that the field link has an anonymous type so no other variable with a similar type could be declared. This would mean, for instance, that the value in the field could not be assigned to another variable. A more useful way to define the structure is shown below.

```
type
      pointer = ↑element;

      element =
        record
          data : iteminfo;
          link : pointer
        end
```

This requires a reference to element before it has been defined, but that is permitted in this context.

In order to create and manipulate a list containing items having this structure, we first need to declare variables of the type pointer.

```
var
      list, p : pointer
```

list will indicate the position of the beginning of the list, and p will point to the particular item that is being processed. Initially there will be no items in the list, and so we can write

```
list := nil
```

where **nil** is a reserved word denoting a pointer to an empty list.

Space for storing items is created as required, at run-time, by using a required procedure called new. The execution of the statement

```
new ( p )
```

would cause space to be allocated for storing whatever type of information p may refer to, and also associates p with this space. This situation is illustrated in Fig. 9.2.

What is the name of this object we have just created? It is not p, since p denotes a position, not a value. In fact, we identify it by saying it is 'the object p is pointing to', or, in the notation of Pascal,

```
p↑
```

In this case p↑ is a record of type element.

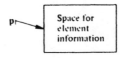

Fig. 9.2

As each number is read in (represented by a variable value) a search is made to determine if that number has previously occurred. If it has not, we first create space for a new item, place the new number in the node and then set its frequency to 1; thus

```
new ( p );

with p↑.data do
    begin
        number    := value;
        frequency := 1
    end
```

Since p↑ is a record, we may refer to any of its fields in the normal way. In this case the data field is itself a record containing two components—the number and its frequency.

Now we have to insert this node into the current list; the simplest strategy here is to place the item at the beginning. The code to perform this, and its effect on the list, is shown in Fig. 9.3.

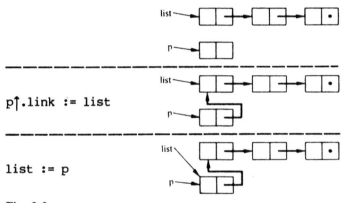

Fig. 9.3

The effect is to insert the new item at the start of the list while still retaining the chain of links to other items. In Fig. 9.3 the last item has a dot in its pointer field as a terminator. On the computer the last item will be distinguished by having a pointer to the empty list, **nil**. This ensures that the insertion procedure works, even when the list is initially empty.

The code for searching the list for a particular number has to be constructed carefully. There are two terminating conditions for the search—either the number is found or the end of the list is reached—and, as with arrays, we must ensure that a comparison with a non-existent element does not take place. A terminating condition of the form

```
( p↑.data.number = value ) or ( p = nil )
```

is incorrect since, if p is equal to **nil** then p↑ data does not exist and a run-time error will occur. The coding below shows how this problem may be avoided.

```
p := list;
found := false;

while not found and ( p <> nil ) do
    if p↑.data.number = value then
        found := true
    else
        p := p↑.link
```

By posting a sentinel at the end of the list, the code can be made less cumbersome.

In Program 9.1 the method outlined here is applied to the problem of finding the mode of a set of numbers that have been read in.

You may already have sketched out a method of solving this problem using an array or a file, but both have their disadvantages. If you use an array you need to have prior knowledge of the range of values to be processed or, at least, a reasonable upper limit on the number of distinct values. A solution that uses a file is also simple to code but would, in practice, be very slow running.

```
Program Modedetermination ( input, output );

{*********************************************
 *                                           *
 * Program 9.1                               *
 * A sequence of integers is read in and     *
 * the mode of the sequence is determined.   *
 *                                           *
 *********************************************}

type
      iteminfo =
        record
          number,
          frequency : integer
        end;

      pointer = ↑element;

      element =
        record
          data : iteminfo;
          link : pointer
        end;

var
      list, p : pointer;

      value, mode : integer;

      found : boolean;


procedure search ( list : pointer; value : integer;
                   var found : boolean; var p : pointer );

{*************************************************************************
 *                                                                      *
 * Searches list for value. The variable found is set to true           *
 * if value is found and p then points to the element containing value, *
 * otherwise found is set to false and p points to the empty list.      *
 *                                                                      *
 *************************************************************************}
```

Program 9.1 (continued opposite)

```
begin { search }

   p := list;
   found := false;

   while not found and ( p <> nil ) do
      if p↑.data.number = value then
         found := true
      else
         p := p↑.link

end;  { search }


procedure insert ( var list : pointer; value : integer );

{**********************************************
 *                                            *
 * value is inserted at the head of the list  *
 *                                            *
 **********************************************}

var
      p : pointer;

begin { insert }

   new ( p );
   p↑.link := list;
   list    := p;

   with p↑.data do
      begin
         number    := value;
         frequency := 1
      end

end;  { insert }


procedure findmode ( list : pointer; var mode : integer );

{*********************************************************
 *                                                      *
 * Finds the mode of the numbers in list. If there are  *
 * two or more modes then the first in list is chosen.  *
 * If the list is empty, mode is set to zero.           *
 *                                                      *
 *******************************************************}

var
      maxfrequency : integer;

      p : pointer;
```

Program 9.1 (continued overleaf)

```
begin { findmode }

    maxfrequency := 0;
    p := list;
    mode := 0;

    while p <> nil do
        begin
            with p↑.data do
                if frequency > maxfrequency then
                    begin
                        maxfrequency := frequency;
                        mode := number
                    end;
            p := p↑.link
        end

end;  { findmode }

begin { main program }

    list := nil;

    while not eof do
        begin
            readln ( value );
            search ( list, value, found, p );
            if found then                          { place    }
                with p↑.data do                    { numbers  }
                    frequency := frequency + 1     {   in     }
            else                                   {  list    }
                insert ( list, value )
        end;

    findmode ( list, mode );

    writeln ( 'Program 9.1  Mode determination' );
    writeln ( '================================' );
    writeln;

    writeln ( 'number   frequency' );
    p := list;

    while p <> nil do
        begin
            with p↑.data do
                writeln ( number :4, frequency :10 );
            p := p↑.link
        end;

    writeln;
    writeln ( 'mode =', mode :4 )

end.
```

Program 9.1 (continued)

None of the three methods would be very effective once the number of items to be stored became large—more than 500, say. In this case a more elaborate pointer system might be appropriate; alternatively, each number could be inserted in such a position that the values are in ascending order. This last type of scheme, and other features of lists, are described in Section 9.2.

9.2 Ordered lists

If we have imposed some ordering scheme on the elements of a list, it may be necessary to insert items in some position other than the beginning. As an example of this type of situation, we shall consider the representation of a *queue*. A queue is formed when there is a line of people (or, more generally, objects) waiting for service. This might be a queue of people at a checkout in a store, or a line of components waiting to be processed by a machine. The analysis of the behaviour of queues is a very complicated mathematical problem, unless certain simplifying assumptions are made. It is often more convenient to model, or *simulate*, this behaviour on the computer.

If the queue length never exceeds some fairly low maximum value, and the customers are served on a 'first come, first served' basis, then an array provides the most convenient representation. In other circumstances (where certain customers may have priority, for example) a linked list might be more appropriate.

As an illustration we shall consider the simulation of a system in which files in a large computer are being transmitted to a printer. These files may have to be queued until the printer is available, and we shall assume that each file has a priority value associated with it that allows it to jump ahead of other files of lower priority. We wish to measure the amount of time that files are spending in the queue, and so a suitable structure could be defined as follows:

```
type
    iteminfo =
      record
         filenumber : integer;
         priority   : ( low, middle, high );
         timeinq    : integer
      end;

    pointer = ↑filenode;

    filenode =
      record
         data : iteminfo;
         link : pointer
      end
```

As a new file enters the queue, we create space for it by using the function new. So, if a variable pnew of type pointer has been declared then the statement

```
new ( pnew )
```

has this effect. The corresponding record, pnew↑, must then be assigned a filenumber and priority. In addition, timeinq should be set to zero.

Since, dependent upon its priority, a new file may be placed anywhere in the queue, we need a more general insertion algorithm than that described in Section 9.1. This task can be split into two parts—finding the position in which the element is to be placed and then linking it into the list. A procedure for finding the correct position for pnew↑ (or, more precisely, for locating its predecessor) is shown overleaf.

```
procedure locate ( var ppred : pointer; pnew, flist : pointer );

{*****************************************************************
 *                                                               *
 * Locates ppred, the pointer to the node that will precede      *
 * pnew↑ in the list flist. If pnew↑ is to be inserted at the    *
 * beginning of the list, ppred is set to nil.                   *
 *                                                               *
 *****************************************************************}

var
      p : pointer;

      searching : boolean;

begin { locate }

   ppred := nil;
   p := flist;
   searching := ( flist <> nil );   { if flist is empty then position }
                                     { for insertion has been found    }
   while searching do
      if pnew↑.data.priority <= p↑.data.priority then
         begin
            ppred := p;                    { move down }
            p := p↑.link;                  {   list    }
            if p = nil then
               searching := false          { end of list }
         end
      else                                 { correct position found }
         searching := false

end;  { locate }
```

Since we have already covered the insertion of an item at the beginning of a list, we will not consider the case when ppred has been set to **nil**. Code for inserting pnew in another position, together with a diagram showing the effect of each statement, is given in Fig. 9.4.

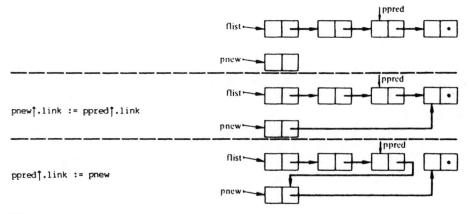

pnew↑.link := ppred↑.link

ppred↑.link := pnew

Fig. 9.4

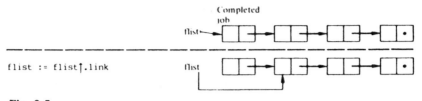

Fig. 9.5

Notice that these two statements have the desired effect, even when the new item is to be added to the end of the list. Inserting an item in a list is simpler than the corresponding operation on an array or file. This is because items in a list are not necessarily stored physically next to one another, and so inserting a new one does not involve moving those already in the structure.

When the line printer has completed the printing of a file, that item is then deleted from the queue. Again, because of the linked storage system, this operation is easy to represent and execute; see Fig. 9.5.

The completed job is effectively by-passed. The only problem with this operation is that there is now unneeded (and inaccessible) storage space containing information about the printed file. If no attempt were made to reclaim space, the matter would soon get out of hand, with hundreds of blocks of inaccessible store scattered around main memory. The reclaiming of space used by deleted items is always a problem in languages that allow dynamic storage allocation. One solution is to have a special *garbage collector* program that intermittently gathers up storage space that is no longer accessible from the program. On a computer with a single processor, this means that all other operations must stop while the garbage is collected. The Pascal solution is to make the user perform his own storage management. Once space is no longer needed he can instruct the computer to reclaim the space by using the dispose procedure. In the above example, we could have written

```
oldp := flist;
flist := flist↑.link;
dispose ( oldp )
```

Note that certain compilers may ignore the dispose instruction completely, and this might be a consideration when deciding upon a storage structure for a particular application.

If the set of files to be printed had not been ordered, then deletion might have been necessary from the middle of the list. This, again, is no real problem (as long as you remember to treat deletion of the first item as a special case). It is just a matter of linking the predecessor of the item to be deleted to its successor, as illustrated in Fig. 9.6.

If insertions and deletions tend to be concentrated in one part of a list at a time, the singly-linked structure can be rather inefficient. An example is the storage of lines of a file in a text editing system. Most terminal systems offer the user facilities for editing programs and data files. Instructions are usually included for inserting and deleting complete lines of text, and for modifying a particular line identified by a line number. A suitable storage structure is therefore a linked list in which each node contains a line

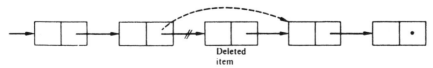

Deleted
item

Fig. 9.6

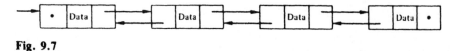

Fig. 9.7

number and the corresponding line of text. In addition to a pointer to the beginning of the list, it is useful to have one pointing to the line the user is currently working on, since modifications and corrections tend to be localised. The singly-linked list works perfectly well as long as the user works systematically through the file, making all his corrections in increasing order of line number. If, however, he wishes to go back a couple of lines then there is no way the system can cope with this (unless several pointers are used), other than to start searching from the beginning of the file. For a large file this would take an unacceptable amount of time. A common solution to this problem is to use a *doubly-linked list*, in which each node contains a pointer to the immediately preceding node as well as to the one immediately following it. As can be seen from Fig. 9.7, this structure allows movement up or down the list with equal facility.

For the text editing system, suitable storage structure definitions might be as follows.

```
type
    lineinfo =
        record
            linenumber : integer;
            linetext   : packed array [1..72] of char
        end;

    node =
        record
            predecessor : ↑node;
            data        : lineinfo;
            successor   : ↑node
        end
```

9.3   Recursion revisited

Structures that may be built up using pointers can often be described by recursive definitions. For example,

> A singly-linked list is either empty or consists of a node containing a pointer to a singly-linked list.

The 'get-out' condition occurs when the pointer refers to an empty list. The value of such a definition is not only that it is concise but also that it aids the construction of recursively-defined functions and procedures to operate upon the structure. Consider the following procedure for printing out the contents of a list of integers.

```
procedure printlist ( l : ipointer );

{***********************************************
 *                                             *
 * Prints out contents of list l using recursion *
 *                                             *
 ***********************************************}
```

(continued opposite)

```
begin { printlist }

    if l <> nil then
        begin
            write ( l↑.data );
            printlist ( l↑.link )
        end

end; { printlist }
```

The call printlist(ilist) where ilist points to the first item will cause the whole list to be output. As in the recursive definition of the list the 'get-out' condition is provided by the empty list.

Like many recursive subprograms, this procedure is not as trivial as might appear. In fact, if we interchange the write statement and procedure call to printlist the list is printed out in reverse! We formalise this as a separate procedure:

```
procedure reverseprint ( l : ipointer );

{*******************************************************
 *                                                     *
 * Uses recursion to print out the list l in reverse   *
 *                                                     *
 *******************************************************}

begin { reverseprint }

    if l <> nil then
        begin
            reverseprint ( l↑.link );
            write ( l↑.data )
        end

end; { reverseprint }
```

When the call reverseprint(ilist) is made this causes a sequence of further calls to reverseprint before any other operations are carried out. Only when the end of the list is reached do the recursive calls terminate. At that point the parameter of reverseprint is the last item in the list, and this is then printed. The previous call to the procedure is then completed by printing the next-to-last item, and so on. In this way a path is traced back from the last to the first item in the list as if by magic, since there are no pointers going in this direction. It is not magic, of course, since the computer has 'remembered' the address of each previous item in the list as each call is temporarily suspended.

Although operations on these linear structures may be simply expressed using recursion, it is usually more effective, in terms of both time and storage space, to employ iterative methods. There are many non-linear structures, however, for which this is not so. One example is the binary tree. A recursive definition of this type of construction is as follows.

A binary tree is a finite set of nodes that is either empty or consists of a root with two disjoint binary trees called the left and right subtrees of the root.

The root is usually the access node for a binary tree. Figure 9.8 shows a typical binary tree structure. Note the important word 'disjoint' in the definition. Two subtrees must contain distinct sets of nodes—there is no recombining of branches.

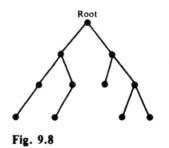

Root

Fig. 9.8

If we only ever wish to scan down the tree (i.e. away from the root), a suitable storage structure would allow for two pointers for each node—one to point to each subtree. If each item of data was an integer then the following node description could be used.

```
type
    pointer = ↑tnode;

    tnode =
        record
            lchild : pointer;
            data   : integer;
            rchild : pointer
        end
```

The relationships between nodes are usually expressed in terms of family tree relationships. So, for example, the nodes below a given node and directly connected to it are called its *children*. In this case, we distinguish the left and right child.

Using the recursive definition of a binary tree, we can construct a concise description of tree traversal, i.e. the accessing of each element. There are several methods of traversal depending upon the order in which we wish to examine the elements. We shall use the *in-order* traversal method which may be described as follows:

> traverse the left subtree
> visit the root
> traverse the right subtree

Since each left and right child is itself the root of a tree, and traversal of an empty tree involves doing nothing, these instructions could be implemented using a recursive procedure. In particular, if we wished to list the contents of the tree, we could use the following procedure:

```
procedure printtree ( t : pointer );

{*****************************************************
 *                                                   *
 * Prints out the tree elements using in-order traversal *
 *                                                   *
 *****************************************************}
```

(continued opposite)

```
begin { printtree }

    if t <> nil then
        with t↑ do
            begin
                printtree ( lchild );
                write ( data );
                printtree ( rchild )
            end

end; { printtree }
```

The call printtree(root) would cause each element to be printed in turn. Verify that, for the tree structure in Fig. 9.9, the numbers 1 to 10 would be printed out in ascending order.

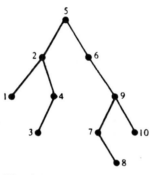

Fig. 9.9

Another operation that would be awkward to code without the use of recursion is the comparison of trees. For example, we may wish to check whether two trees have exactly the same structure with the same data values in corresponding nodes. A function for performing this test is shown below.

```
function equal ( t1, t2 : pointer ) : boolean;

{************************************************************
 *                                                          *
 * Returns the value true if the two trees with roots t1 and t2 *
 * are identical in structure and content                   *
 *                                                          *
 ************************************************************}

begin { equal }

    if ( t1 = nil ) or ( t2 = nil ) then
        equal := ( t1 = t2 )
    else if t1↑.data = t2↑.data then
        equal := equal ( t1↑.lchild, t2↑.lchild )
                and equal ( t1↑.rchild, t2↑.rchild )
    else
        equal := false

end; { equal }
```

Again the structure of the operations reflects the structure as described in the recursive definition. This function would only be worth using if the two trees were relatively small, since in many cases the process does not immediately terminate once a mismatch has been found. Verify that this is so for the two trees in Fig. 9.10 and try to construct a more efficient recursive version.

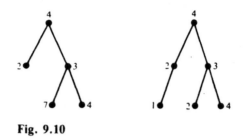

Fig. 9.10

9.4 Binary search trees

Using the binary tree storage structure described in Section 9.3 would be no help in improving access time for individual elements. We would still need to look for any given item by examining elements one by one, as with a linear list. To aid searching, we need a structure with a suitable ordering of elements. This is provided by the binary search tree.

When inserting an item into a binary search tree we start to look for a suitable position by first examining the item at the root. If this is equal to the incoming item then the item is already in the tree and the search is terminated; otherwise the search is continued, starting at the left or right child depending upon whether the incoming item is respectively smaller or greater than the root item. Since the left and right children are each the root of a subtree, the same process may be applied at that point. The search continues until either the item is found or an empty left (or right) child position is found at which to insert the item.

For instance, suppose we have the words

    BAT   ANT   ARMADILLO   BEAR   CAT   ANT   BUNNY

to insert into a tree. Alphabetical ordering is an obvious one to use. The first item, BAT, is inserted into the empty tree and becomes its root:

    BAT

ANT comes before BAT in our ordering scheme and so we continue the search by moving down to the left. No node exists in this position, and so the word may be inserted here (Fig. 9.11).

Fig. 9.11

ARMADILLO is less than BAT, so we move down to the left, but it is greater than ANT and so we then move down to its right and insert (Fig. 9.12).

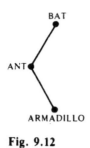

Fig. 9.12

BEAR is greater than BAT, so it is inserted as the right child of BAT (Fig. 9.13).

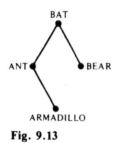

Fig. 9.13

Similarly, CAT is inserted to the right of BEAR, ANT is detected as being already present (and so ignored), and finally BUNNY is placed to the left of CAT (Fig. 9.14).

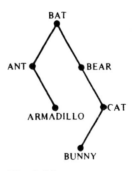

Fig. 9.14

If we wish to determine whether a particular element is present, the same process may be used without the insertion. If a dead end is reached and the item has not been found, we conclude that it is not present. Since, at each node, the size of the search space is roughly divided by two we have a powerful binary search procedure. In addition, the items have been effectively sorted since, using an in-order traversal the items will be accessed in ascending order. (Verify this.)

The applications of this technique include concordance analysis and identifier symbol table management in compilers. The example we shall consider in more detail is the processing of sales in a large store.

In our system the sales of items during the day are registered on a diskette. The information stored includes item number (tag), department, price per item and number sold.

The item structure for file records is defined as follows.

```
type
     purchase =
          record
               tag          : packed array [1..6] of char;
               department : packed array [1..8] of char;
               itemprice,
               numbersold : integer
          end
```

We are interested in the problem of counting the sales of each item and sorting the items into a file ready for updating a stock file, so we shall consider only the tag and numbersold fields.

If a tree structure is used to store information about items and sales, it could be described as follows

```
pointer = ↑tnode;

tnode =
     record
          lchild : pointer;
          data   : sales;
          rchild : pointer
     end
```

where sales is a record structure containing two fields—tag and totalsold.

Program 9.2 illustrates the setting up of the tree structure, the use of the item number as a key to order the elements and the production of the sorted file.

We assume that singlepurchases has already been validated in a separate program and so no checks are required on it. After its elements have been placed in the tree, the tree contents are then transferred, using the in-order search, to the new file.

An alternative approach to this problem would involve sorting the purchase entries and then performing a separate count on items. This would be particularly tedious if the number of sales precluded the use of an internal sort, i.e. one performed in the machine's main memory.

```
Program Sumpurchases ( singlepurchases, accumulatedpurchases );

{***********************************************************************
 *                                                                     *
 * Program 9.2                                                         *
 * The singlepurchases file contains information about individual      *
 * purchases by customers. These are accumulated and stored in a       *
 * binary search tree using the tag of each item as a key. The         *
 * sorted accumulated sales are then transferred to the file called *
 * accumulatedsales.                                                   *
 *                                                                     *
 ***********************************************************************}
```

Program 9.2 (continued opposite)

```
type
     purchase =
        record
           tag          : packed array [1..6] of char;
           department : packed array [1..8] of char;
           itemprice,
           numbersold : integer
        end;

     sales =
        record
           tag          : packed array [1..6] of char;
           totalsold : integer
        end;

     pointer = ↑tnode;

     tnode =
        record
           lchild : pointer;
           data    : sales;
           rchild : pointer
        end;

     purfile = file of purchase;

     salesfile = file of sales;

var
     root : pointer;

     singlepurchases : purfile;

     accumulatedpurchases : salesfile;


procedure createtree ( var singlepurchases : purfile; var root : pointer );

{************************************************************
 *                                                          *
 * Builds up a binary search tree of sales from the file *
 * singlepurchases, using the tag as key.                  *
 *                                                          *
 ***********************************************************}




procedure search ( var item : purchase; var node : pointer );

{************************************************************
 *                                                          *
 * Recursive procedure for inserting item in the binary search *
 * or updating the frequency, as appropriate               *
 *                                                          *
 ***********************************************************}
```

Program 9.2 (continued overleaf)

```
    begin { search }

        if node = nil then
            begin
                new ( node );

                with node↑ do
                    begin
                        data.tag := item.tag;                  { insert  }
                        data.totalsold := item.numbersold;     {  new    }
                        lchild := nil;                         {  item   }
                        rchild := nil                          { in tree }
                    end

            end
        else
            with node↑ do
                if item.tag < data.tag then
                    search ( item, lchild )
                else if item.tag > data.tag then
                    search ( item, rchild )
                else
                    with data do
                        totalsold := totalsold + item.numbersold

    end;  { search }



begin { createtree }

    root := nil;

    while not eof ( singlepurchases ) do
        begin
            search ( singlepurchases↑, root );
            get ( singlepurchases )
        end

end; { createtree }



procedure listtree ( var node : pointer;
                     var accumulatedpurchases : salesfile );

{***************************************************************
 *                                                             *
 * Recursive procedure for accessing each of the elements in   *
 * the tree in ascending order of tag and transmitting them    *
 * to the accumulatedpurchases file.                           *
 *                                                             *
 ***************************************************************}
```

Program 9.2 (continued opposite)

```
begin { listtree }

    if node <> nil then
        with node↑ do
            begin
                listtree ( lchild, accumulatedpurchases );
                accumulatedpurchases↑ := node↑.data;
                put ( accumulatedpurchases );
                listtree ( rchild, accumulatedpurchases )
            end

end;  { listtree }



begin { main program }

    reset ( singlepurchases );
    rewrite ( accumulatedpurchases );

    createtree ( singlepurchases, root );
    listtree ( root, accumulatedpurchases )

end.
```

Program 9.2 (continued)

9.5 Other pointer structures

Any form of interrelationships between items may be built up using pointers. Among the more commonly used ones are multi-level lists (allowing lists *within* lists) and graphs. Graphs allow arbitrary interconnections between nodes, and are useful for representing all kinds of network systems, and structures in which there are many links between items. Data bases make extensive use of the principle of linked storage. By storing each piece of information only once, but allowing each item to be part of multi-linked structures, a fast information retrieval system can be built up.

Summary

By using pointers, a set of items may be linked together in any desired way. This allows accurate modelling of a wide range of data structures. Economy of storage and high speed of operation can be achieved, although care needs to be taken to avoid unduly complicated code—don't use pointer structures if arrays or files would do the job more simply and effectively.

Exercises

1 Write a program to count the number of distinct integers in a file by using a singly-linked list.

2 Symbol tables are used in compilers and assemblers for storing information about identifiers. Write a program to set up a hash table, i.e. a table where a hash function is used to determine the position of each item. The table should be stored as an array of records, and collisions should be handled by associating a linked list with each entry and storing all items with the same hash value in the same list. Assume that each identifier can contain up to eight characters and that its type (constant or variable) is stored, together with its value (in the case of a constant), or its address (in the case of a variable).

3 Another method of storing a symbol table involves using a singly-linked list but, each time an identifier is referenced, it is moved to the beginning of the list (this uses the idea that any reference to an identifier in a program is likely to be followed by others in the same locality). Write and test a program to maintain a symbol table of this form.

4 The *level* of the root of a tree is conventionally 1. The level of any other node is one more than the level of its parent. The *height* of a tree is the maximum level of all of its nodes. Write a recursive procedure to find the height of a binary tree.

An AVL tree is a tree such that, for each node, the height of its left and right subtrees differ by, at most, 1. Write and test a procedure for checking whether a given binary tree is an AVL tree.

5 Write and test a procedure to delete an item from a binary search tree.

6 A list of items and corresponding expected frequencies of access is given. Write a program to insert these items into a binary search tree to minimise the expected average access time.

10

Set structures and tackling a larger problem

Introduction

The last structure that Pascal provides is the set. A set is a collection of objects, and there are explicit Pascal operations for adding elements to sets and also for removing them. Most important of all, there is an operation for testing whether or not an element is in a given set.

To conclude the chapter, we show how all the structures described in the second part of the text may be used in combination to solve a larger problem.

10.1 Sets

Basically, a set consists of a number (possibly 0) of distinct items. The elements must all be of the same scalar type (their base type) and are not assumed to be ordered or interrelated in any way. The base type may not be real but, in theory, may be the whole 'infinite' integer type. In practice, many implementations place an upper limit on the number of items in a set; this may even be as low as 32.

An example of a set type definition and a corresponding variable declaration is shown below.

```
type
        student = ( Thompson, Brown, James, Smith, Jones );

        group = set of student;

var
        historyclass, geographyclass, chemistryclass,

        physicsclass, sciencestream, artsstream, mixedstream : group
```

The identifiers historyclass, geographyclass, and so on, may now be used as names for sets containing any or all of the elements Thompson, Brown, James, Smith, Jones but it is important to note that, like variables of other types, their initial values are undefined. Elements may be placed in the sets by use of assignments. For example, if we wished to indicate that the Geography class contained Jones and Brown then a suitable statement would be

```
        geographyclass := [Jones, Brown]
```

The students in other classes could be specified in a similar fashion:

```
        historyclass    := [Brown, James, Smith];
        chemistryclass := [Thompson, Smith];
        physicsclass    := [Jones, Smith]
```

There are three basic operations that may be used to create new sets from existing ones: union, intersection and difference. The *union* of two sets is the set containing all of the elements present in either set or in both and is indicated in Pascal by placing a '+' between the names of the sets to be combined. After the assignment

```
artsstream := historyclass + geographyclass
```

has been executed, artsstream would contain the elements Brown, James, Jones and Smith. Similarly, after the execution of

```
sciencestream := chemistryclass + physicsclass
```

sciencestream would contain Jones, Thompson and Smith.

If we wish to determine those elements that are common to two sets (their *intersection*) then the '*' operator may be used:

```
mixedstream := artsstream * sciencestream
```

After the execution of this statement, the set mixedstream would contain the names of those who are studying at least one Arts subject and at least one Science subject—in this case Jones and Smith.

The third operation, called *set difference* and denoted by '−' determines all the elements that are in one set (the first named) but not in the other. For example,

```
historyclass - geographyclass
```

would give James and Smith, whereas

```
geographyclass - historyclass
```

is the set containing only Jones.

Notice that the union of these resultant sets is the same as the union of the original two sets, excluding the common element Brown. In general, for any two sets A and B,

$$(A - B) + (B - A) = (A + B) - (A * B)$$

This relationship is not important for our purposes but emphasises the fact that although we are using arithmetic operators to denote set operations they do not, in general, satisfy the normal arithmetic relationships.

Sometimes it turns out that a set has no members at all. For example, Geography and Chemistry have no common students, and so the set

```
geographyclass * chemistryclass
```

does not contain any elements. This is perfectly feasible and the *empty set* produced is denoted by [ ].

A common test that is carried out on sets is that of determining membership. This is performed using the relational operation '**in**'. For example,

```
Jones in chemistryclass
```

will have a Boolean value—in this case false—and may be used in any context where a Boolean value is expected:

```
if Jones in chemistryclass then
   write ( 'student present' )
else
   write ( 'student absent' )
```

in is classified as a relational operator, and has the same precedence in expressions as the other relational operators.

In Program 10.1 below, sets are used to determine the order in which contestants will set off in a skiing competition. random is a function which may be available in your

```
Program Ordergenerator ( output );

{******************************************************************
 *                                                                *
 * Program 10.1                                                   *
 * A set of entrants in a sporting event have competition numbers *
 * in the range 1 to totalentrants. The program uses the function *
 * 'random' to produce a random ordering of competitor numbers.   *
 *                                                                *
 ******************************************************************}

const
      totalentrants = 40;

var
      stilltogo : set of 1..totalentrants;

      x : real;  { used by random number generator }

      position, entrant : integer;

begin

   x := 2.3;    { arbitrary starting value for random number generator}
   stilltogo := [1..totalentrants];

   writeln ( 'Program 10.1  Generation of contestant order' );
   writeln ( '=============================================' );
   writeln;

   writeln ( 'starting     contestant' );
   writeln ( 'position       number' );

   position := 0;

   repeat
      entrant := trunc ( random ( x ) * totalentrants ) + 1; { value in range
                                                             { to totalentrant
      if entrant in stilltogo then
         begin
            position := position + 1;
            writeln ( position :5, entrant :12 );
            stilltogo := stilltogo - [entrant]
         end
   until stilltogo = [ ]

end.
```

Program 10.1

installation, or which may be user-defined, and which gives a real value between 0 and 1. Therefore the expression

```
trunc ( random ( x ) * totalentrants ) + 1
```

gives a random integer value in the range 1 to totalentrants.

Program 10.1 demonstrates the simplicity of the use of the set structure, but also illustrates one of its drawbacks—there is no direct method of checking what elements a set contains except by testing for each possible one. In this case, when there are only two or three contestants left to choose, the program still generates a number between 1 and totalentrants. If this number is not in the set then the process is repeated until a number is produced that does occur. Even when there is only one contestant left to draw, the program will loop round until his number is finally generated. If there were forty contestants to start with then, on average, this will take 20 cycles, but may take many more in a particular case. Even if we use a counter and can therefore check to see if there is only one element left, we still have to determine which element it is.

These considerations do not detract from the usefulness of the program. It is only likely to be run occasionally, with relatively small numbers, and so its overall simplicity and consequent reliability are more important than any efficiency considerations.

A very different, but common, use of sets is in textual manipulation, where we often wish to determine, quickly and effectively, what type each character is. For example, given the declaration

```
var
        alpha, alphanumeric,

        numeric, punctuation : set of char
```

we could define

```
alpha        := ['a'..'z'];
numeric      := ['0'..'9'];
alphanumeric := alpha + numeric;
punctuation  := [';', ',', '''', ':', '.', ' ']
```

Constructions such as

```
while ch in alphanumeric do
```

may then be easily comprehended and effectively carried out.

A procedure skiptonextword which would be more useful in certain contexts than skipblanks, described in Chapter 8 (p. 183), could be defined as follows.

```
procedure skiptonextword;

{*******************************************************************
 *                                                                 *
 * Skips over any punctuation and blanks in the input stream       *
 * stopping in front of the next non-blank or at the end of the file *
 * if this occurs first.                                           *
 *                                                                 *
 *******************************************************************}

var
        nextword : boolean;
```

(continued opposite)

```
begin { skiptonextword }

    nextword := false;

    while not ( eof or nextword ) do
        if input↑ in punctuation then
            get (input)
        else
            nextword := true

end;  { skiptonextword }
```

Readers who are familiar with the theory of sets will have recognised the similarity between the Pascal set type and the mathematical usage. For problems that involve mathematical set manipulation, the Pascal structure is ideal. In addition to the check for membership, there are four other Boolean tests that can be made; see Table 10.1.

Table 10.1

Pascal representation	Definition	Mathematical representation
A = B	true if and only if A and B contain exactly the same members	A $\equiv$ B
A < > B	true if and only if A and B do not contain exactly the same members	A $\neq$ B
A < = B	true if and only if all members of A are also in B	A $\subseteq$ B
A > = B	true if and only if all members of B are also in A	A $\supseteq$ B

It is interesting to consider how the set structure may be implemented in computer systems. Commonly, the bits of a computer word are used to represent the presence (1, say) or absence (0) of a particular item. This usually makes set operations such as union and intersection very easy to implement and fast in execution using the appropriate bit-manipulation instructions available on computers. It also explains why some systems place a low upper limit on the number of elements in a set since many computers only have 32 bits or fewer in each word. Alternative representations include arrays, lists and trees, each with their own advantages and disadvantages. The last of these possibilities is explored further in Problem 10.5 on p. 226.

10.2 Getting it together

As a final example we shall consider a problem in which all the storage structures available in Pascal can be used to advantage. This concerns the processing of entries in a competition.

In many promotional competitions, each entrant is asked to place a number of possibilities in preferred order. So, for example, there may be a list of features of holidays in Greece of the form

- A. Guaranteed summer sun
- B. Good beaches and swimming
- C. Historical interest
- D. Local crafts
- E. Entertainment
- F. Eating out at tavernas
- G. Variety of food
- H. Island excursions
- I. Friendly and helpful locals

```
NAME..........................................................................................

ADDRESS..................................................................................

            ..........................................................................

            ..........................................................................

            ..........................................................................
```

ADVANTAGE	A	B	C	D	E	F	G	H	I
POSITION									

```
SLOGAN (Maximum of 12 words).........................................................

............................................................................................

............................................................................................
```

Fig. 10.1

A panel of judges would decide upon an ideal ordering of these and then each entry would be compared with this. Often, each entrant has to provide a slogan, to be used as a tie-breaker. A typical layout for an entry form is shown in Fig. 10.1.

If a large number of entries was expected then it would be worth using a computer to validate entries and to choose potential winners.

First, we should decide what information needs to be stored in the computer. Obviously, each entrant's solution should be stored. At the end we shall have a list of possible winners for the judges to examine, and so it would be useful to be able to print out the corresponding slogans at the same time. The name and address of each contestant would appear to require storage but would take up a lot of space. A simpler idea would be to stamp each entry, as it is received, with a unique number and file away the entries, so they can be checked when the final winners have been picked. This number is the only identification that needs to be stored for each entry. Assuming that entry information is to be initially typed into a file with 80 characters per line, a suitable layout might be that shown below.

Column	1	2–9	10–20	21–29	30–40	41–80
Contents	#	8 digit entry number	blank	solution	blank	slogan

If the slogan will not fit into the forty-character field, a continuation line may be used. This may be distinguished by an asterisk typed in column 1. Using either the '#' or '*' character in the initial column of a line will simplify error recovery—the program for validating input can easily regain its bearings after detecting an error.

Having decided upon the information to be stored for each entry, we can now write out suitable storage definitions:

```
type
    entrystring = packed array [1..8] of char;

    attempt = array ['a'..'i'] of 1..9;

    stringofwords = packed array [1..119] of char;

    entryrecord =
      record
        entrynumber    : entrystring;
        actualposition : attempt;
        slogan         : stringofwords
      end
```

Since the entries may be arriving over a period of several weeks it may be convenient to accumulate information on disk or magnetic tape, running a reading and validation program each time a sufficiently large batch of entries has been gathered together. This suggests that we should use a file for storing the records after they have been validated.

After the closing date for the competition, and after the last batch of entries has been vetted, the file of entry information could be processed to find possible winners. At the top level the complete process could be described as

> Create empty entry file
> While there are batches left do
>   Validate entries in current batch
> Find and write out possible winning entries

The creation of an empty file can normally be performed by a system command that will vary from machine to machine, and so we shall not describe this task in any more detail; we shall just assume that it has been done. It will also be assumed that, in each run, a new error file is created, which can be printed out by a separate program, whereas valid entries will be added to the entry file. The writing of a program to print out the contents of the error file is left as an exercise. We shall examine in more detail the construction of a program that inputs a new batch of entry information and produces a 'clean' entry file and an error file. Then we shall look at the task of processing this clean file to determine possible winners.

Validation program:

The main steps in the validation program may be stated as follows:

> Create error file
> Copy old entry file to new entry file
> While there are entries left in the batch do
>   Read and validate the next entry
>   If it is valid then
>   Add it to the new entry file
>   Else
>   Add it to the error file

When performing the validation, we should bear in mind the following three principles.

(1) As many errors as possible should be checked for.
(2) No error should cause the program to break down.
(3) The program should be able to recover quickly from processing invalid data, so that no valid entries are ignored or incorrectly dealt with.

As with all validation, we have to decide at what level of detail to halt the checking. At what stage do we say that any further scrutiny is just not worth the effort? Certainly it hardly seems worth examining the slogans for mistyping. Such a check is just about feasible, for most words, by having an English dictionary on file for our program to refer to. The amount of time this would take would be prohibitive and, since the merits of these slogans could only be assessed by the judges anyway, they would be able to pick up any errors rather more effectively than the computer. Another error that is difficult to detect is the typing of the wrong digits in the entry number. A *check digit* system could be employed to reduce the possibility of an undetected error; i.e. an extra digit could be included so that the weighted sum of the digits is divisible by, for example, 11 (although, of course, there may be an error at the point where *this* digit is allocated). We do not include this check here, although in many applications it would be useful.

Having decided upon what *not* to check for, we now list errors that can readily be detected:

 (i)   missing '#' or '*' in column 1;
 (ii) a non-digit in the entry number;
 (iii) a non-digit, zero, or repeated digit in the solution attempt;
 (iv) extraneous characters between the fields.

Since each field has a different layout and requires different checks, we split the reading and validation process into stages:

```
With entry do
   error: = false
   Read in and check entry number
   If not error then
      Read in and check solution
   If not error then
      Read in slogan
valid: = not error
```

Procedures for checking the entry number and solution, and for reading in the slogan are given below.

```
procedure checkentrynumber ( var enumber : entrystring;
                             var error : boolean );

{*****************************************************************
 *                                                              *
 * Reads in and checks the entry number. If its format is       *
 * incorrect then the boolean variable error is set to true.    *
 *                                                              *
 *****************************************************************}

var
     ch : char;

     chnumber, colnumber : integer;

begin { checkentrynumber }

   read ( ch );
   if ch <> '#' then
      error := true;

   for chnumber := 1 to 8 do
      begin
         read ( ch );
         if not ( ch in ['0'..'9'] ) then
            error := true;
         enumber[chnumber] := ch
      end;

   colnumber := 10;
```

Procedure checkentrynumber (continued opposite)

```
    while not error and ( colnumber < 21 ) do
       begin
          read ( ch );
          colnumber := colnumber + 1;        { rest of field }
          if ch <> ' ' then                  { must contain  }
             error := true                    { only spaces   }
       end

end;  { checkentrynumber }
```

Procedure checkentrynumber (continued)

```
procedure checkattempt ( var afield : attempt; var error : boolean );

{*******************************************************************
 *                                                                 *
 * Reads solution attempt into afield, setting error to true if the *
 * field does not consist of 9 distinct digits followed by spaces  *
 *                                                                 *
 *******************************************************************}

var
      digitsleft : set of '1'..'9';

      ch : char;

      letter: 'a'..'j';

      ordzero, colnumber : integer;

begin { checkattempt }

   digitsleft := ['1'..'9'];
   letter := 'a';
   ordzero := ord ( '0' );

   repeat
      read ( ch );
      if not ( ch in digitsleft ) then
         error := true
      else
         begin
            afield[letter] := ord ( ch ) - ordzero;
            letter := succ ( letter );
            digitsleft := digitsleft - [ch]
         end
   until ( letter = 'j' ) or error;

   colnumber := 30;
```

Procedure checkattempt (continued overleaf

```
        while not error and ( colnumber < 41 ) do
          begin
            read ( ch );
            colnumber := colnumber + 1;        { rest of field }
            if ch <> ' ' then                  { must contain  }
              error := true                    { only spaces   }
          end

    end;  { checkattempt }
```

Procedure checkattempt (continued)

```
procedure readslogan ( var sfield : stringofwords;
                       var linenumber : integer );

{**********************************************************************
 *                                                                    *
 * Reads in slogan, continuing on to second line, if necessary *
 *                                                                    *
 **********************************************************************}

var
      asterisk, ch : char;

      colnumber, i : integer;

begin { readslogan }

    for colnumber := 41 to 80 do
      read ( sfield[colnumber - 40] );

    readln;
    linenumber := linenumber + 1;
    if input↑ = '*' then
      begin                                    { read    }
        read ( asterisk );                     { rest of }
        for colnumber := 2 to 80 do            { slogan  }
          read ( sfield[colnumber + 39] );     { from    }
        readln;                                { second  }
        linenumber := linenumber + 1           { line    }
      end
    else                                       { or fill }
      for i := 41 to 119 do                    { up with }
        sfield[i] := ' '                       { blanks  }

end;  { readslogan }
```

Procedure readslogan

First, examine checkentrynumber. Notice how the digits of the number are individually checked before copying to the array enumber. It would be dangerous to read in the entry number as an integer since a mistyping would result in a run-time error. Even if there is an error detected in the entry number the rest of the spurious number is read in since this information will be sent to the error file and will aid location of the incorrect line.

checkattempt uses set structures in two contexts—to look for invalid characters and also to check that each digit occurs only once in the solution.

readslogan has to be carefully written since the slogan may, or may not, continue onto a second line. The lookahead feature provided by the file buffer in textfiles can be used here to examine the first character of the next line without removing it from the input buffer. The variable linenumber is used to count the position of each line in the batch so that the position of any error lines may be more easily located. Incidentally, if the error is found to be due to mistyping, the corresponding entry can be retyped and included in a later batch.

Once these three procedures have been written, the rest of the program falls into place. The main program is shown below.

copy, addnew and adderror are easy to write. The only point that needs further elaboration is the form of the error records:

```
erfile = file of
            record
               entrynumber    : entrystring;
               batchposition : integer
            end


begin { main program }

    rewrite ( errorfile );
    copy ( oldentryfile, newentryfile );
    linenumber := 0;

    while not eof ( input ) do
       begin
          validate ( entry, valid, linenumber );
          if valid then
             addnew ( entry, newentryfile )
          else
             adderror ( entry, errorfile, linenumber )
       end

end.
```

Validation program

Processing valid entries:

Once we have a clean file of entry information, we can concentrate on the main object of the exercise—to find the winning entries. The best method to use for this would depend upon the number of entries and the number of winners. If there were three winners to choose, then the simple technique of scanning the entry file three times, marking the best, second best and third best entry, would seem appropriate. Often in these competitions, however, there are many consolation prizes, and this method soon loses its attraction once the number of winners to be found rises above ten or so. A complete sort of the data is also unattractive if the number of entries is large—we have the same problem of multiple scans of the file.

The number of scans of the data required may be reduced to one with a little thought. For the sake of argument, let us assume that there are twenty-five winners to be chosen. If we form the first twenty-five entries of the file into a list, and keep a note of the worst solution in that list, then as each new entry is examined it can be either added to the list (if it is at least as good as the worst one already there), or otherwise discarded. Obviously, we would have continually to amend this list by deleting the worst entries, so that it does not become too long.

The features required of this temporary storage structure—ease of insertion and deletion—indicate that a linked list would be suitable. The maintenance of this list would be facilitated by storing the entries in descending order of merit, from the best to the worst, thus simplifying the operation of removing the worst entries.

One assumption that we have made and not yet attempted to justify is that the computer can judge how good each attempted solution is. We shall pursue this matter a little later but, for the moment, let's assume that a score can be calculated for each solution attempted. In addition, as a precaution, let us generate rather more potential winners than we need (forty, say) so that, if there are any queries or disqualifications, we have other entries ready, and the program will not have to be run a second time. At the top level, the algorithm for the processing program may be defined as follows.

```
Read in ideal solution
Set up initial list of potential winners
Compute the lowest score of these
While not eof(entryfile) do
    Calculate entry score
    If entry score > = lowest score then
        Insert entry in potential winners list
        Amend potential winners list
    Get next entry
Print list of possible winners, attempts and slogans
```

The setting up of the initial list and the insertion of new entries involves straightforward list operations that we have considered in Chapter 9. Amending the list of potential winners is also fairly straightforward. In most cases it just involves removing the forty-first element. The only exception occurs when the fortieth and forty-first entries (and possibly others) have the same score. In this case the tied entries should be left in the list until further inserted entries make the cut-off possible.

Lastly, we consider the important problem of computing a score for each solution. A simple rule would involve counting the number of positions the contestant has predicted correctly. For example, if the ideal solution is

3   1   7   2   9   6   8   4   5

and one entrant has the solution

2   5   7   4   9   6   8   3   1

then this would score four points, since four advantages have been placed in their correct positions. This is a very crude method and suffers from several drawbacks.

(1)   Since each entry is going to score between 1 and 9 points, we should expect a lot of tied values that have to be distinguished in some other way (e.g. by slogan).

(2)   No account is taken of the relative importance of the advantages placed in their correct positions. An attempt with the first three positions correct is surely better than one that has positions 7, 8 and 9 right.

(3)   No credit is given for attempts that are 'nearly' right (e.g. placing advantage 2 in first position and advantage 1 in second position).

We have used a more elaborate scheme in the program, taking into account these three points. A score is computed by considering the nearness of each position to the ideal, and weighting each result depending upon the position that is being predicted.

Program 10.2 shows the complete processing of the entry file to obtain the list of potential winners. Once this list has been printed, of course, it is up to the judges to make the final decisions on winners.

As your programs get larger it is important to ensure that your main program does not expand at the same rate. Aim for four or five calls to subprograms in the main program with other instructions providing the linkage between them. The subprograms themselves may become difficult to locate. In some languages they can be listed in alphabetical order of name but this is often inconvenient in Pascal where subprograms have to be declared before they are used. In Program 10.2 the problem of subprogram location has been minimised by using extra comments. The comment at the head of each function and procedure has also been more spaciously laid out.

```
Program Findwinners ( input, newentryfile, output );

{**********************************************************************
 *                                                                   *
 * Program 10.2                                                      *
 * The file newentryfile is examined and the forty best entries are *
 * found and printed out.                                           *
 *                                                                   *
 * The procedures used are :                                        *
 *                                                                   *
 *                          readin                                  *
 *                                                                   *
 *                          value                                   *
 *                                                                   *
 *                          print                                   *
 *                                                                   *
 *                          insert                                  *
 *                                                                   *
 *                          setuplist                               *
 *                                                                   *
 *                          amend                                   *
 *                                                                   *
 *                                                                   *
 **********************************************************************}


type
     entrystring = packed array [1..8] of char;

     attempt = array ['a'..'i'] of 1..9;

     stringofwords = packed array [1..119] of char;

     entryrecord =
        record
           entrynumber    : entrystring;
           actualposition : attempt;
           slogan         : stringofwords
        end;

     entryfile = file of entryrecord;
```

Program 10.2 (continued overleaf)

```
        pointer = ↑node;

        node =
          record
            data : record
                      entryinfo : entryrecord;
                      score     : integer
                   end;
            link : pointer
          end;

        solution = array ['a'..'i'] of integer;

var
      newentryfile : entryfile;

      list : pointer;

      lowestscore, entryscore : integer;

      ideal : solution;

      letter : char;



procedure readin ( var ideal : solution );

{**********************************************
 *                                            *
 *          Reads in ideal solution           *
 *                                            *
 **********************************************}

var
      ch : char;

begin { readin }

   for ch := 'a' to 'i' do
      read ( ideal[ch] )

end; { readin }

function value ( var actualposition : attempt;
                 var ideal : solution )  : integer;

{********************************************************************
 *                                                                  *
 * The value of the solution in array 'actualposition' is computed. *
 * This is done by comparing the attempt with the ideal solution    *
 * using a formula that gives higher positions a greater weighting. *
 *                                                                  *
 ********************************************************************}
```

Program 10.2 (continued opposite)

```
const
     maxscore = 450;

var
     sum : integer;

     letter : 'a'..'i';

begin { value }

   sum := 0;

   for letter := 'a' to 'i' do
     sum := sum  +  abs ( actualposition[letter] - ideal[letter] )
                    * ( 10 - ideal[letter] );

   value := maxscore - sum

end;  { value }



procedure print ( list : pointer );

{*****************************************************
 *                                                   *
 *        Prints out list of possible winners        *
 *                                                   *
 ****************************************************}

var
     p : pointer;

     letter : 'a'..'i';

     i : integer;

begin { print }
   writeln ( 'Program 10.2  Competition results' );
   writeln ( '==================================' );
   writeln;

   p := list;

   repeat

     with p↑.data, entryinfo do
        begin
          writeln ( 'entry number :', entrynumber :9 );
          write ( 'attempt       :' );

          for letter := 'a' to 'i' do
            write ( actualposition[letter] :1 );
```

Program 10.2 (continued overleaf)

```
            writeln;
            writeln ( 'score        :', score );
            writeln ( 'slogan :' );
            writeln ( slogan );
            writeln;
            writeln
        end;
    p := p↑.link

  until p = nil

end;  { print }


procedure insert ( var entry : entryrecord; var list : pointer;
                                    entryscore : integer );

{*********************************************************
 *                                                       *
 *       Inserts entry in correct position in list       *
 *                                                       *
 *********************************************************}

var
    p, ppred, pnew : pointer;

    searching : boolean;

begin { insert }

  new ( pnew );
  with pnew↑.data do
    begin
      entryinfo := entry;
      score := entryscore
    end;
  if entryscore >= list↑.data.score then
    begin                                      { insert at }
      pnew↑.link := list;                      { beginning }
      list := pnew                             {  of list  }
    end
  else
    begin
      p := list;
      searching := true;

      while searching do
        if entryscore < p↑.data.score then
          begin
            ppred := p;                        { follow list }
            p := p↑.link;                      {    down     }
            if p = nil then
              searching := false     { end of list reached }
          end
```

Program 10.2 (continued opposite)

```
            else
                searching := false;

            ppred↑.link := pnew;
            pnew↑.link := p
        end

end;  { insert }

procedure setuplist ( var newentryfile : entryfile; var list : pointer;
                      var lowestscore : integer; var ideal : solution );

{*****************************************************************
 *                                                               *
 * Sets up initial list of elements from first forty entries in  *
 * newentryfile. The lowest entry score of these entries is also *
 * computed.                                                     *
 *                                                               *
 *****************************************************************}

var
    element, entryscore : integer;

    p : pointer;

begin { setuplist }

  reset ( newentryfile );
  new ( list );

  with list↑, data do
    begin
      link := nil;                                          { insert }
      entryinfo := newentryfile↑;                           {  first }
      score := value ( newentryfile↑.actualposition, ideal ) { element }
    end;

  get ( newentryfile );

  for element := 2 to 40 do
    begin
      entryscore := value ( newentryfile↑.actualposition, ideal );
      insert ( newentryfile↑, list, entryscore );
      get ( newentryfile )
    end;

  p := list;

  for element := 2 to 40 do
    p := p↑.link;

  lowestscore := p↑.data.score

end;  { setuplist }
```

Program 10.2 (continued overleaf)

```
procedure amend ( list : pointer; var lowestscore : integer );

{*********************************************************************
 *                                                                   *
 * The list is reduced to forty elements if possible. This may not   *
 * be possible if there are several tied entry scores at the end     *
 * of the list.                                                      *
 *                                                                   *
 *********************************************************************}

var
      position : integer;
      p, ppred : pointer;

begin { amend }

   p := list;

   for position := 2 to 40 do
      p := p↑.link;

   lowestscore := p↑.data.score;
   if lowestscore <> p↑.link↑.data.score then
      begin
         ppred := p;                          { if the forty- }
         p := p↑.link;                        { first element }
         ppred↑.link := nil;                  { has a lower   }
         repeat                               { score than    }
            ppred := p;                       { the fortieth  }
            p := p↑.link;                     { then this     }
            dispose ( ppred )                 { element and   }
         until p = nil                        { any successors }
      end                                     { may be removed }

end;   { amend }



{*********************************************************************
 *                                                                   *
 *                         main program                              *
 *                                                                   *
 *********************************************************************}

begin { main program }

   readin ( ideal );
   setuplist ( newentryfile, list, lowestscore, ideal );

   while not eof ( newentryfile ) do
      begin
         entryscore := value ( newentryfile↑.actualposition, ideal );
         if entryscore >= lowestscore then
            begin
               insert ( newentryfile↑, list, entryscore );
```

Program 10.2 (continued opposite)

```
            amend ( list, lowestscore )
        end;
    get ( newentryfile )
  end;

  print ( list )

end.
```

Program 10.2 (continued)

Summary

If you have read up to this point and attempted some of the exercises at the end of each chapter you should be quite adept at solving a range of programming problems. Don't get too complacent, though. Over-confidence may be fine for someone selling computers but not for someone writing software. Now might be a good time to learn a completely different language—Lisp, APL or Prolog, for instance. On the formal side you could find out about the theoretical foundations of programming or read a book that compares programming language features. Other fascinating topics include compiling techniques, programming methodology and data structures. If you have been bitten by the programming bug all of these subjects will be of interest to you. Appendix F contains the titles of a few of the many excellent books on computing that you might like to read to add to your knowledge and enjoyment.

Exercises

1   Given that a set contains integers in the range 1...n write and test procedures for finding the cardinality of the set (i.e. the number of elements it contains), finding the smallest element in the set and printing out the set contents.

2   A directed graph consists of a set of nodes linked by directed branches. A node that has a direct link from another node is said to be a *successor* of the node. For example, in Fig. 10.2, node 1 has two successors—node 2 and node 5.

Fig. 10.2

The information about connections may be represented in several ways. One method involves creating an array of sets where each index represents a node and each set contains a list of successors for that node. Write and test the procedure to list all of the nodes that are accessible from a given node, assuming that the linkage information is stored in this way.

For this example, the sets of accessible nodes are as follows.

Node	Accessible nodes
1	{2,5}
2	Ø
3	{2,3,4,5}
4	{2,3,4,5}
5	Ø

Use this in a program to check whether a directed graph contains any circuits.

3 In touch typing each of the eight fingers covers a range of keys as shown below.

Left-hand fingers	Keys	Right-hand fingers	Keys
2	RTFGVB	2	YUHJNM
3	EDC	3	IK
4	WSX	4	OL
5	QAZ	5	P

To test typing technique it is useful to have sentences that involve using each of the fingers at least once (e.g. 'Now is the time for all good men to come to the aid of the party'). Write a program to input sentences and to indicate which ones involve using all the fingers when typing.

4 Program, using a set structure, the method of Eratosthenes' sieve for finding primes.

5 Set structures may be efficiently represented by using binary search trees. Write a procedure to construct a binary search tree from a list of elements to be placed in the set. Write and test procedures for performing union, intersection and membership operations, ensuring that the trees remain well-balanced.

6 Write a pretty printing program for Pascal. The program should input another Pascal program in any form (assuming that it is valid) and output it with proper indentation and spacing. You should first set out precise rules for dealing with each kind of construction.

7 A newspaper holds a competition to find the all-time top twenty pop records. It lists one hundred tunes and invites readers to submit a list of their twenty favourites in order from this (each reader may only submit one entry). In addition to producing a list of the twenty most popular records from the entries the newspaper wishes to award prizes to the thirty competitors with the best entries. Assuming that there may be up to 20 000 entries, devise a system for processing them and producing the required results. Write the corresponding program(s).

Section 3

Turbo Pascal

Turbo Pascal is probably the most widely used implementation of Pascal on microcomputers. It not only provides a compiler, but also (in Version 6 and above) a state-of-the-art integrated development environment (IDE), with overlapping windows, mouse support, menus, a multi-file editor, and interactive debugging facilities. Space allows us only to discuss its language features, however.

Turbo Pascal has a number of *extensions* to standard Pascal, i.e. additions which are not available in standard Pascal. It also has some *exceptions*, i.e. facilities in standard Pascal which are not available in Turbo Pascal. In this section we look at the major extensions and exceptions with three aims in mind:

(i)   to enable you to run any program in this book under Turbo Pascal, with modifications where necessary;
(ii) to introduce you to some of Turbo Pascal's attractive text and graphics output capabilities;
(iii) to introduce you to Turbo Pascal's file-handling features, and how they differ from those of standard Pascal.

The treatment of Turbo Pascal in this section is therefore not exhaustive, but in the context of these aims.

11

General Turbo Pascal extensions and exceptions

In this chapter we consider most of the Turbo Pascal (Version 6) extensions and exceptions which you need to know about in order to run the programs in this book. (Turbo Pascal files are dealt with separately in Chapter 12.) We will also look at some other useful features which will enhance your programming skills, such as the powerful concept of independently compiled units.

11.1 General syntax

Comments

In Turbo Pascal the symbols (* and *) may be used to enclose comments, as well as the braces { and }. Comments enclosed in one way may contain comments enclosed the other way. This enables you to 'comment out' a whole section of code, including any comments:

```
       m := 1;
   (* c := 297600;
      e := m * c * c {Einstein} *)
```

A $ in the first position of a comment is interpreted as a *compiler directive* (see below).

Program lines

Turbo Pascal program lines may not be longer than 126 characters.

Program heading

Turbo Pascal does not require file parameters (such as input and output) in the program heading, so you can start any program simply with

program test;

In fact, the entire heading may be omitted. However, you should make use of one to improve the readability of your programs, and to maintain compatibility with other compilers.

Order of declarations

Declarations and definitions in program blocks are not generally required to be in a specific order. This allows for greater clarity in declarations or definitions, since related objects may be grouped together.

Symbols

A hexadecimal constant is recognized if prefixed with a dollar symbol:

```
i := $FF;
```

Characters may be represented by their (extended) ASCII codes prefixed with a hash (number symbol):

```
ch := #2;    { smiley face }
writeln( 'Three bells:', #7#7#7 );
```

Codes may be in the range 0–255.

User-defined identifiers

Turbo Pascal identifiers may also contain the underscore character, which can be used to clarify long identifiers:

```
end_of_the_month
```

Identifiers may be of any length, but only the first 63 characters are significant. This is not a serious restriction.

Additional reserved words

Turbo Pascal (Version 6) has the following 13 additional reserved words:

```
asm              interface      string
constructor      object         unit
destructor       shl            uses
implementation   shr            xor
inline
```

Turbo Pascal also has nine predefined *directives*, which may be redefined by the user, although this is not recommended:

```
absolute      far          near
assembler     forward      private
external      interrupt    virtual
```

Additional standard identifiers

In addition to the required standard identifiers (Appendices B and C) Turbo Pascal has over 200 extra 'built-in' identifiers, representing mainly its additional predefined constants, functions and procedures. A number of these are discussed below.

Table 11.1 Turbo Pascal integer data types

Type	Format	Range
shortint	signed 8-bit	−127 to 127
integer	signed 16-bit	−32 768 to 32 767
longint	signed 32-bit	−2 147 483 648 to 2 147 483 647
byte	unsigned 8-bit	0 to 255
word	unsigned 16-bit	0 to 65 535

Standard identifiers not supported

Turbo Pascal does not support the following standard Pascal identifiers:

```
get       page      unpack
pack      put
```

Constant expressions

Turbo Pascal allows certain expressions to be evaluated in **const** declarations. Such expressions are called *constant expressions*. The principle is that the compiler must be able to evaluate the expression without executing the program. Consequently variables and certain standard functions may not appear in constant expressions.

The following functions are allowed in constant expressions (some of these are Turbo Pascal additions to standard Pascal, and are discussed below):

```
abs       odd       sizeof
chr       ord       succ
hi        pred      swap
length    ptr       trunc
lo        round
```

Examples:

```
const
  pi_2      = pi / 2;
  ln2       = 0.693147180559945309417;
  message   = 'Jesus said, "Follow me"';
  mess_leng = length( message );
  mu        = chr( 230 );
  alpha     = ['A'..'Z', 'a'..'z'];
  numeric   = ['0'..'9'];
  alphanum  = alpha + numeric;
```

11.2 Types

Integer types

Turbo Pascal supports five integer types, as shown in Table 11.1. **maxint** is defined as 32 767. Turbo Pascal defines an additional constant **maxlongint** as 2 147 483 647.

Integer overflow

Integer overflow occurs when the intermediate or final result of an integer expression exceeds **maxint**. An error is not generated when this happens; instead Turbo Pascal causes the value to 'wrap around' through the most negative integer value; e.g. if the integer i has the value **maxint**, the operation

```
i := i + 1;
```

produces the result -32768. The best way to avoid this problem is to use real variables if an overflow is likely to occur.

Real types

Turbo Pascal supports five real types, as shown in Table 11.2.
double type is sufficiently accurate for most scientific programming.

Table 11.2   Turbo Pascal real data types

Type	Range	Significant digits	Size in bytes
real	2.9×10^{-39} to 1.7×10^{38}	11–12	6
single	1.5×10^{-45} to 3.4×10^{38}	7–8	4
double	5.0×10^{-324} to 1.7×10^{308}	15–16	8
extended	3.4×10^{-4932} to 1.1×10^{4932}	19–20	10
comp	$-2^{63} + 1$ to $2^{63} - 1$	19–20	8

comp type holds integer values only. It is suitable for representing monetary values as whole numbers of cents (as in dollars and cents) in financial applications. It is considered a real type because all arithmetic done with **comp** type uses the 80x87 coprocessor, which we now discuss briefly.

The **single, double, extended** and **comp** types are sometimes referred to as the IEEE (Institute of Electrical and Electronics Engineers) *floating point types*. These types are supported only if a 80x87 numeric coprocessor is present, or if one is *emulated*.

To use the IEEE floating point types in your code you need to use a combination of the **{$N}** and **{$E}** *compiler directives*. Firstly, the **{$N +}** state must be selected if you want the IEEE types to be supported. However, if a coprocessor is *not* present, an error will be generated. To allow you to use the IEEE types even on machines that do not have a coprocessor, you can alternatively select the **{$E +}** state, which loads special software to *emulate* the coprocessor. Note that these selections are made at compilation, not during execution.

Selecting **{$N +,E +}** therefore guarantees that code with the IEEE types will compile and execute on machines with or without coprocessors. However, the emulation software makes your compiled code much longer. You can avoid unnecessary use of the emulation software, if a coprocessor is present, by making use of a *conditional* directive (see Section 11.13).

Note that **{SN -}** is selected by default. An attempt to use **single, double, extended** or **comp** in this state will therefore generate an error.

{$E}** and **{$N} are *global* directives, and as such must appear before the declaration part of a program.

Array types

Turbo Pascal automatically packs arrays, so the word **packed** may always be omitted.

In Turbo Pascal all the elements of one array may be assigned to another of the same type in a single statement:

```
var
  x, y : array[1..10] of integer;
  ...
  ...            {assigns values to x}
  y := x;   {copy x into y}
```

Turbo Pascal allows you to check the ranges of array index values with the **{$R +}** directive (which is off by default). Since such *range checking* slows down code considerably, it should only be used during program development and testing.

Typed constants

A variable may be initialised at compilation by declaring it as a *typed constant*, e.g.

```
const
  g    : real = 9.8;
  mypi : real = 3.14;
```

Because typed constants are in fact variables, they may be changed during execution of a program. However, being variables, they may not be used in places where only constants are allowed, e.g. in a type declaration. So the following is not allowed:

```
const
   min : integer = 0;
   max : integer = 100;
type
   mark = min..max;
```

Because Turbo Pascal allows multiple **const** keywords in a program, you may have a separate **const** declaration section for typed constants *after* the type declaration section. This allows you to declare your own custom type definitions and then create and initialise variables of your custom type.

Arrays may also be initialised as typed constants:

```
const
   list : array [1..5] of integer = (5, 0, 7, -1, 9);
```

Record constants are handled slightly differently, in that the type must be declared first:

```
type
   student_type =
     record
        name    : string
        sex     : ( female, male );
        married : boolean
     end;
const
   student : student_type =
      (name    : 'Major John';
       sex     : male;
       married : true);
```

Note the use of parentheses in declaring constants of structured types.

11.3 String type

We have defined a type **string** earlier (e.g. Program 6.2) as an array of **char**. Turbo Pascal has such a predefined type, called unsurprisingly, **string**. It is important enough to warrant a section of its own.

The maximum length of such a string is 255 bytes (characters), which is also the default length:

```
var
   a : string;       {255 characters}
   b : string[20];   {20 characters}
```

It is important to distinguish between the physical length and the logical length of a string. The *physical length* is the number of bytes declared; e.g. the physical length of **b** above is 20 bytes, while the physical length of **a** is the maximum 255 bytes.

The *logical length* is the number of bytes currently occupied by the string; this may vary during execution of a program. For example, if **b** is declared as above, the assignment

```
b := 'Mortimer';
```

results in a logical length of eight bytes for **b**.

Note that a *string constant*, such as 'Mortimer', can be assigned directly to a string variable, since both are technically arrays (and Turbo Pascal arrays may be assigned directly).

Particular bytes in a string are accessed with an index in the same way as array elements, so b[4] in the above example contains 't'. However, the first byte of b is not b[1] as you might expect, but b[0], which holds the *string representation* of the current logical length of the string. The logical length is also returned by the Turbo Pascal function length, so length(b) and ord(b[0]) both return the value 8 in this example.

An empty or *null* string (") has a length of 0.

Control characters may be used in strings, as the following example shows:

```
const
  message = #7#7'Error!'#7#7;
begin
  ...
  writeln ( message )
```

Strings may be compared using the six relational operators =, <>, <, >, <= and >=. The results of the comparison are determined by the ASCII *lexical collating sequence* (see Appendix D). For example, the following Boolean expressions are all true:

```
'a' < 'b'
' a' < 'a'
'a ' < 'aa'
'a' < 'aa'
'MCBEAN' < 'McBEAN'
'MC BEAN' < 'MCBEAN'
```

Note that a space (blank) precedes all the letters in the collating sequence, and that uppercase letters all precede the lowercase letters (the function upcase can be used to convert characters from lowercase to uppercase). Note also that 'a' is 'less than' 'aa' because the second character of the first string is technically null, with an ASCII value of 0. This is less than the ASCII value of the second 'a' in the string 'aa'.

You can use read or readln to input mixtures of strings and numeric data as long as you remember that a number of characters equal to the physical length of each string will be read as part of the string. For example, the code fragment

```
var
  name : string [5];
  mark : real;
  ...
  readln ( name, mark );
```

with the data

```
jack90
```

will assign 'jack9' to name and 0 to mark.

The only string operator in Turbo Pascal is +, which concatenates (joins) strings. For example,

```
var
  x, y, z : string;
begin
  x := 'Pilate said, ';
  y := "'What is truth?"';
  z := x + y;
  writeln ( z );
  ...
```

produces the output

```
Pilate said, 'What is truth?'
```

As we saw in Chapter 6, when an array is passed as a parameter to a procedure or function it must be declared with a type which has already been defined, so that the parameter type in the procedure heading can be a simple name. This rule is known as *type identity*. An attempt to pass a Turbo Pascal string as follows will therefore generate a compiler error:

```
procedure plonk ( name : string[20] );
```

The problem is avoided by defining a type for **string[20]**:

```
type
   nametype = string[20];
...
procedure plonk ( name : nametype );
```

Turbo Pascal does, however, allow this type identity rule to be relaxed *in the case of strings only*, with the **{$V−}** compiler directive. Any string variable is then allowed as an actual parameter.

String functions

Turbo Pascal provides five functions which are useful for manipulating strings. The return type is indicated after the function's name in the following list.

copy (strg, start, n) : string
copies **n** bytes from **strg**, beginning at byte **start**, e.g.

```
copy ( 'Napoleon', 5, 4 )
```

returns **'leon'**.

concat (string1, string2, ...) : string
returns the concatenation of its string parameters (of which there may be any number), e.g.

```
concat ( 'c:/', dirname, '\', filename, '.bak' )
```

length (strg) : integer
returns the logical length of **strg**.

pos (substring, strg) : integer
returns the position in **strg** of the first character in **substring** (zero if **substring** does not appear); e.g.

```
pos ( 'pole', 'Napoleon' )
```

returns **3**.

pos is useful for detecting the presence of a character in a string, e.g.

```
pos ( '.', strg ) > 0
```

is **true** if **strg** contains a period.

upcase (char) : char
converts a single character to uppercase, if it is a lowercase letter. Otherwise it has no effect. You can use it to make an uppercase copy of a whole string as follows:

```
function uppercase ( strg : string ) : string;
{ ***********************************
  *                                 *
  * returns uppercase copy of strg  *
  *                                 *
  *********************************** }
```

```
const
  newstr : string = ";
var
  index : integer;
begin { uppercase }

  for index := 1 to length( strg ) do
    newstr := newstr + upcase ( strg[index] );

  uppercase := newstr
end; { uppercase }
```

Note that the local string **newstr** must be initialised to the null string.

When the concatenation operator + is used like this to build up a string, Turbo Pascal automatically increments the logical length of the string in **newstr[0]** (you can see this if you use debugging mode to step through a sample program using this function with, say, newstr[0],5 in the Watch Window).

You might prefer to construct **newstr** element by element:

```
for index := 1 to length( strg ) do
  newstr[index] := upcase ( strg[index] );
```

But then you have to set the logical length in **newstr[0]** explicitly before assigning **newstr** to **uppercase**:

```
newstr[0] := chr ( length ( strg ) );
```

String procedures

Turbo Pascal has four procedures for operating on strings:

delete (strg, start, n)
deletes n characters from **strg** starting at character **start**. For example, if **strg** has the value 'Napoleon',

```
delete ( strg, 1, 4 );
```

changes it to 'leon'.

insert (substring, strg, n)
inserts **substring** into **strg** beginning at character n of **strg**. For example, if **strg** has the value 'leon',

```
insert ( 'Napo', strg, 4 );
```

changes it to 'leoNapon'.

str (x, strg)
converts a real- or integer-type numeric value x, *formatted as for* **write** (Section 11.5), into its string representation. For example,

```
x := -12.34567;
str ( x:7:2, strg );
```

returns **strg** with the value ' −12.35'.

val (strg, x, index)
is the reverse of **str**, and converts **strg** into its numerical equivalent x. **strg** must be a sequence of characters that correctly define a signed whole number. Trailing blanks are not allowed. x must be real or integer. If **strg** is not correctly formatted, the position of the first offending character is returned in **index**.

11.4 Expressions

Boolean expressions

Turbo Pascal includes a fourth Boolean operator, xor (exclusive or). It works like or except that the expression (a xor b) is false if both a and b are true.

Turbo Pascal always *short-circuits* the evaluation of complex Boolean expressions, once their truth value is known. For example, in

        (1 = 1) or (3 + 2 = 6)

the truth value of (3 + 2 = 6) is not evaluated since (1 = 1) is true, and the or makes the whole expression true whatever follows. A program can often be speeded up by rearranging the order of Boolean expressions. If complete evaluation is required, use the {$B+} compiler directive.

Logical (bitwise) operators

The four Boolean operators not, and, or and xor may also operate directly on the internal binary code representation of any integer type. In this context the operators are called *logical* or *bitwise*.

The operators and, or and xor perform their operations on the corresponding bits of their operands, so (in binary) the expression (1001 and 1100) returns 1000.

The operator not (one's complement) flips all the bits of its operand.

There are two additional bitwise operators: shl (shift left) and shr (shift right). They shift the bits of their left operands left and right respectively, according to the value of their right operands, e.g.

        n := n shl 4; {times 16}

Shifting all the bits left (right) by one position is the same as multiplying (dividing) by 2. This provides the fastest way of multiplying and dividing by powers of 2.

The following example shows how to use bitwise operators to output the binary representation of an integer:

```
var
  i, n : integer;
  m : longint;
begin
  write ( 'Number in decimal: ' );
  readln ( n );
  write ( 'Number in binary: ' );
  i := sizeof ( n );
  m := $8000;

  for i := 1 to 8 * sizeof ( n ) do
  begin
    if (n and $8000) = $8000 then
      write ( '1')
    else
      write ( '0' );
    n := n shl 1
  end;
```

Sample output:

```
Number in decimal: 32767
Number in binary: 0111111111111111
```

The hexadecimal constant **$8000** is 2^{16}, i.e. 1 followed by 15 zeros, in binary. The expression (**n** and **$8000**) will therefore be equal to **$8000** only if **n** has a 1 in the first position, in which case **'1'** is output. The statement **n := n shl 1** shifts all the bits in **n** one position to the left, so that the next most significant bit of **n** may be tested against the leading 1 in **$8000**. This process is repeated for each bit in **n**.

sizeof returns the length of its argument in bytes.

Incidentally, if you run this program to see the binary for -32768 (the smallest value of **integer** type) you will see why integer values wrap around between this value and 32767.

With a bit of ingenuity you can use logical **and** and **or** to 'poke' individual bits.

11.5 Standard input and output

Turbo Pascal files are dealt with separately in Chapter 12. This section refers mainly to keyboard input and screen output.

write and *writeln*

Output may be controlled with format specifications, or *write parameters*. The rules are rather complicated, and are best summarised with examples:

```
const
  i : integer = -99;
  name : string[5] = 'Nkosi';
  x : real = -1.2345;
  a : boolean = true;
begin
  writeln ( 'Output:', i:4, x:7:2, x:18, x:8, name:7, a:5 );
```

The output looks like this:

```
Output: -99   -1.23 -1.2345000000E+00-1.2E+00   Nkosi TRUE
```

In the case of an integer, the write parameter specifies the *field width*, right-justified (**4** in the case of **i:4**; remember to leave room for a possible minus sign).

For reals, the write parameter **x:**n specifies scientific notation (floating point form) over a field width of n. Four columns are required for the exponent, one for the decimal point, and one for a possible minus sign. If n is greater than 17, leading blanks are inserted, otherwise the number of decimal places is reduced (as with **x:8**).

The write parameter **x:**n**:**m specifies fixed point form over n columns with m decimal places.

Strings are right-justified over the specified field width. Note that the write parameter **":**n can be used to output n blanks. If a string is output without a field width specifier, trailing blanks are not inserted if its logical length is less than its physical length. If you want to output strings left-justified, with subsequent output starting in a fixed column, e.g. to print a list of names and marks, you can use the following trick:

```
const
  n = 10;
var
  name : string[n];
  mark : integer;
  ...
  writeln ( name, ' ':n - length ( name ), mark:3 );
```

Note that expressions may be used in the format specifications.

If no format specifications are given, integers are output without leading or trailing blanks. Reals are output without trailing blanks, but with one leading blank, which may be used for a minus sign.

eof and eoln with keyboard input

Turbo Pascal's **eof** (end-of-file) function behaves slightly differently with keyboard input to the standard Pascal version.

While you are entering data from the keyboard **eof** remains **false**, until you type the DOS end-of-file character, **Ctrl-z**, followed by **Enter**. The following code allows you to enter numbers from the keyboard, finding their running total, until you type **Ctrl-z**:

```
var
  x, sum : real;
begin
  sum := 0;
  while not eof do    { enter Ctrl-z to end }
    begin
      read ( x );
      sum := sum + x
    end;
  writeln ( 'Total: ', sum );
```

Note that more than one number is allowed per line, and no **readln** is required, as in the standard Pascal example in Section 3.5.

eoln works much the same way as in standard Pascal: it is **true** only when the last character on a line before the end-of-line marker has just been read (or when **eof** is **true**). If you are reading individual characters from the keyboard, **readln** is required to read past the end-of-line marker. The following code shows how to use the **eoln** and **eof** together in order to count the number of (printable) characters typed per line from the keyboard.

```
var
  ch : char;
  n : integer;
begin

  repeat
    n := 0;
    while not eoln do
      begin
        read ( ch );
        n := n + 1
      end;
    readln;    { read past end-of-line marker }
    writeln ( ' ', n, ' characters on that line' )
  until eof;
```

The DOS end-of-line marker actually consists of two control characters, with ASCII codes 13 (carriage return) and 10 (line feed). These are a throw-back to the old days of teletype printers. **read** will read these characters explicitly. The following program segment reads each character entered at the keyboard, and outputs its ASCII code. Two codes are output each time you press **Enter** (because of the way **read** interacts with the keyboard buffer you will not see any of the output for a given line until you press **Enter**). Remember to enter **Ctrl-z** to stop:

```
var
  ch : char;
begin

  repeat
    read ( ch );
    write ( '#', ord ( ch ), ' ' );
  until eof;
```

page

The **page** function is not supported by Turbo Pascal.

11.6 Statements

for

On normal exit from a **for** statement the value of the control variable is defined as its final value. Since this is not standard, it is best not to make use of this feature in code which you might want to run under different compilers.

case

In Turbo Pascal, if there is no label corresponding to a selector value in a **case** statement, the statement following the **case** structure is executed (this situation is undefined in standard Pascal).

In addition Turbo Pascal supports a **case-else** structure. It is demonstrated in the following example, which classifies a 'printable' character (ASCII codes 32–126) entered at the keyboard:

```
var
   ch : char;
begin

repeat
   readln ( ch );
   case upcase ( ch ) of
     'A', 'E', 'I'  , 'O', 'U': writeln ( 'vowel' );
                     '0' .. '9': writeln ( 'digit' );
                     ' ' .. '/': writeln ( 'punctuation/special' );
                     ':' .. '@': writeln ( 'punctuation/special' );
                     '[' .. '`': writeln ( 'punctuation/special' );
                     '{' .. '~': writeln ( 'special' )
   else
      writeln ( 'consonant' )
   end { case }
until eof;
```

11.7 Procedures and functions

Procedural types

Turbo Pascal supports *procedural types*, e.g.

```
type
   integrand = function ( x : real ) : real;
```

This provides a way of passing subprograms (functions and procedures) as parameters. The subprogram to be passed as a parameter must be compiled in the **{$F+}** state. Examples of procedural types are given in Chapter 16, in the contexts of the bisection method and the trapezoidal rule.

11.8 Memory matters

Addresses

It is sometimes useful to know the actual address of an object in memory. An *address* in Turbo Pascal consists of two 16-bit parts: the segment and the offset. The *segment* part of the address points to regions of memory 16 bytes apart, whereas the *offset* part is the distance in bytes into one of the segments.

The standard functions **seg** and **ofs** return the segment and offset of a variable's address, e.g. **ofs (x)**.

Normally when you compile a program Turbo Pascal decides on the addresses of all the variables and data in a program. You can, however, specify a particular address for a variable with an **absolute** clause. For example,

```
var
    herc_screen : array[1..2000] of byte absolute $B000:0000;
```

declares **herc_screen** as a byte array starting at the same address as the Hercules graphics card, which starts at segment **$B000** and offset **$0000**. This trick can be used to save and refresh the screen, as we will see in Section 11.11.

Variables can also be declared on top of each other in this way, e.g.

```
var
    n : integer;
    x : real absolute n;
```

This means that **x** will start at the same address as **n** (although it will take up more memory).

The Turbo Pascal *address operator* **@** returns a pointer to an object (i.e. its address). For example, given the declarations

```
var
    n : integer;
    int_ptr : ^integer;
```

the statement

```
    int_ptr := @n;
```

causes **int_ptr** to point to **n**.

Note that Turbo Pascal uses a circumflex (^) to indicate a pointer.

Dynamic variables and pointers

Turbo Pascal variables may be static or dynamic. A *static* variable is stored in the area of memory called the *stack*. This word is meant to conjure up images of neat stacks of memory locations, used strictly in order, as plates may be taken from a pile in a canteen. Variables that are declared in the usual way we have been doing up to now are static.

In contrast to the stack, Turbo Pascal has a thing called the *heap*. Chunks of memory are grabbed from the heap when needed for some purpose, and thrown back on to the heap when no longer needed, *while the program is still running*. A variable stored in this way is called *dynamic*, and is accessed by means of a pointer, as we have seen in Chapter 9, which points to its address on the heap.

A pointer may be declared with a base type; e.g.

```
var
    ptr_to_real : ^real;
```

declares **ptr_to_real** as a pointer to a variable of real type. Dynamic memory may be allocated, while the program is running, with the function **new**:

```
new ( ptr_to_real );
```

The memory is released with **dispose (ptr_to_real)**. This makes it available for subsequent re-use.

A pointer may also be *generic*. In this case the dynamic variable pointed to is *untyped*, and its size is not fixed at compilation. For example,

```
var
pic : pointer;
   ...
begin
   ...
   getmem ( pic, size ); { e.g. allocate memory to save an image }
   ...
   freemem ( pic, size );
```

getmem allocates **size** bytes of the heap to a variable pointed to by **pic**. This variable is called **pic^**, or **pic**'s *referent*. The largest block that can be allocated in this way is 65 521 bytes.

freemem releases the memory allocated by **getmem**. Note that **freemem** must release *exactly* the number of bytes previously allocated by **getmem**.

The **longint** function **memavail** returns the total amount of free memory remaining on the heap.

The **longint** function **maxavail** returns the size of the largest contiguous free block on the heap. This is the size of the largest dynamic variable that can be allocated at that time. You will have gathered from this that a contiguous block of memory must be allocated to a dynamic variable; it cannot be split over a number of blocks. A large program that creates and destroys dynamic memory haphazardly can lead very rapidly to a fragmented heap; you need to guard against this carefully.

Aliasing with pointers

Sometimes it is convenient to use a pointer to set up an *alias* for a variable, e.g.

```
var
   x : real;
   alias : ^real;
begin
   alias := @x;
   ...
```

Henceforth, the referent **alias^** can be used in the place of **x**, since they both refer to the same memory address. A useful example of aliasing in given in the **driver** modelling program in Chapter 16.

11.9 Units

A *unit* is a separately compiled collection of declarations and subprograms which is only linked with your program after it has been compiled, thus cutting down dramatically on the compilation time of large applications.

Units are the basis of *modular* programming in Turbo Pascal, and are arguably its most valuable extension to standard Pascal. Large programs should generally be broken up into smaller units. This makes for cleaner, more structured programming. It is also possible for your favourite units to be shared by many different programs.

The general structure of a unit is as follows:

```
unit unitname;
interface
   ...
implementation
   ...
begin
   { initialisation code }
   ...
end.
```

Note that the unit's name, like a program name, must be a legal identifier. *The unit must be saved in a file with the same name as the unit.* For example, a unit with name **MyGlobals** must be saved in a file called **myglobals.pas**. It follows that only one unit may be saved in a file.

A unit becomes available to a program (or another unit) by referencing its name in a **uses** clause, e.g.

```
Program theLastOne;
   uses myGlobals;
```

There may be only one **uses** clause in a program; it must be the *first* non-comment line in the program.

The section in a unit between the reserved words **interface** and **implementation** is called the *interface* section. This is the 'public' part of the unit, and must contain the names (with formal parameter lists) of any subprograms in the unit which are to be accessible from the 'outside', i.e. from any program (or unit) using the unit. It may also contain constant, type, or variable declarations. The scope of such declarations extends to all programs using the unit. If any of these subprograms use other units, those units must be mentioned in a **uses** clause in the interface section. There may be *only one* **uses** clause in a unit. It may appear either immediately after the keyword **interface**, or immediately after the keyword **implementation**. Forward declarations are neither necessary nor allowed.

The *implementation* section starts at the reserved word **implementation**. This is the 'private' part of the unit. Everything in the interface section is visible to the implementation section, but the implementation section may have declarations of its own, which will not be visible to any programs using the unit. If subprograms appear in the interface section, the short form of their names must be used in the implementation section (i.e. without parameters).

The *initialisation* section (enclosed in **begin...end.**) is after the implementation section. It looks just like the main body of a program. Any data structures made available by the unit are initialized here; e.g. files may be opened. When a program using a unit is executed, the unit's initialisation code is executed before the main body of the program is run. If a program uses a number of units, the initialisation code of the units is executed in the order in which the units appear in the **uses** clause – and before the main body of the program is run.

The ordering of units in a **uses** clause is not important, except with reference to initialisation, as just mentioned.

If **unit1** uses **unit2**, and a program only needs the declarations in **unit1**, it is only necessary for **unit1** to appear in a **uses** clause in the program.

If **unit1** uses **unit2** and they both declare the same identifier, **ident**, then **unit2**'s **ident** is not normally available to **unit1**. However, if the identifier is qualified with the unit name, it is. So **unit1** can reference its own **ident** and **unit2.ident**.

Although a program or unit may not take up more than 64K of memory, the use of units enables you to write programs which use as much memory as your operating system will allow.

To compile a unit in the Turbo Pascal IDE, set Compile/Destination to Disk before compiling. The compiled code is saved as a **.tpu** file. (An **.exe** version of a complete program is produced in the same way.)

In large applications it is common to group subprograms in units according to their functions, and even to have one unit entirely devoted to global declarations, i.e. constants, types and variables that must be accessible to all units. For example,

```
Program theLastOne;
  uses myGlobals, myInput, myOutput, myGraphics;
```

The file **turbo.tpl** that comes with the Turbo Pascal software contains a library of the standard units: **crt, dos, printer, overlay** and **system**. The **system** unit contains all the standard functions and procedures of Turbo Pascal and is automatically linked to every program. The other units must be mentioned in a **uses** clause if you want to use them. **turbo.tpl** is loaded into memory every time you start up Turbo Pascal. You can move your own units into **turbo.tpl** with **tpumover.exe**. This saves time and disk wear and tear. You can also increase the memory available to your program by removing units that you may not need from **turbo.tpl**.

When changes are made in the interface part of a unit, all other units using that unit need to be recompiled. Turbo Pascal recognises this situation during compilation, and will either report an error or recompile the unit automatically, depending on which options you have selected.

Circular unit references

We noted above that declarations made in the implementation section of a unit are private to that unit. In particular, units used in the implementation section are not visible to users of the unit. This observation makes it possible to construct mutually dependent units (if you really need to). Consider the following two fairly minimal units:

```
unit dum;
interface
implementation uses
   dee;
end.
```

and

```
unit dee;
interface
implementation
uses
   dum;
end.
```

Both can be compiled, under the Turbo Pascal Make or Build option (but *not* under the straight Compile option). This works because Turbo Pascal can compile complete interface sections for both units, since the public interface sections do not depend on each other. You can see this by moving the two **uses** clauses into the interface sections. An attempt to compile now will generate the error

```
Circular unit reference
```

11.10   The *system* unit

Turbo Pascal's standard function and procedures are all implemented in the **system** unit. It is automatically used by any program or unit; it need never be referred to in a **uses** clause.

In this section we describe some **system** unit subprograms not already encountered, which are extensions of standard Pascal (input/output subprograms are discussed in Chapter 12).

Square brackets denote optional parameters.

system **unit procedures**

exit
causes a subprogram to return, or a program to terminate

dec (x[, n])
decrements x (an ordinal-type variable) by 1, or by n (integer-type) if it is specified, i.e. **dec** (x, n) corresponds to x := x − n. Since **dec** generates optimised code it can save execution time in loops.

fillchar (x, count, value)
fills count contiguous bytes of x (any type) with value (any type as long as its representation is no longer than one byte), starting at the first byte occupied by x. If x is an array, an element of the array may be specified as the starting point. No range checking is performed, so beware! This is a high-speed fill since **fillchar** operates directly on memory.

If possible use **sizeof** (see below) for the count parameter, and if x is a string remember to set the length byte yourself. For example,

```
Program test;
var
  x : array[1..10] of real;
  s : string[10];
begin
  ...
  fillchar ( x, sizeof ( x ), #0 );   { full of zeros }
  fillchar (s, sizeof ( s ), 'a' );   { full of a's }
  s[0] := #10;
```

inc (x[, n])
increments in the same way that **dec** decrements.

move (source, dest, count)
copies a block of count bytes starting at the first byte of source to dest, starting at its first byte. If you are not careful with **move** you could overwrite something vital. Since it operates directly on memory it is the fastest way to copy. **move** may be used to good effect in restoring a screen apparently instantaneously (see Section 11.11).

randomize
initialises (seeds) the Turbo Pascal random number generator (**random**) using the system clock. The seed generated by **randomize** is stored in the predeclared **longint** variable **randseed**. By assigning a specific value to **randseed** a specific sequence of random numbers can be generated repeatedly by **random**.

system **unit functions**

Function return types are indicated after their names in the list below. Square brackets denote optional parameters.

frac (x) : real
returns the fractional part of its real argument, i.e. it returns x − int (x) (see below for int).

hi (x) : word
returns the high-order byte of its integer or word argument. It is used, for example, to extract information stored in predeclared variables.

int (x) : real
returns the integer part of its real argument. Note that the return type is real.

lo (x) : word
returns the low-order byte of its integer or word argument. It is used, for example, to extract information stored in predeclared variables.

pi : real
returns the value of π (3.14159 26535 89793 2385)

ptr (seg, ofs) : pointer
returns a pointer to the address given by **seg** and **ofs**.

random[(range)] : real or word
returns a real- or word-type random number, depending on the parameter. If **range** is not specified a real random number x in the range $0 \leqslant x < 1$ is returned. If **range** is specified it must be of integer type, and the result is a word-type random value n in the range $0 \leqslant n < $ **range**.

sizeof (x) : word
returns the number of bytes occupied by **x**, which may be a variable of any type, or a *type identifier*.

11.11 The *crt* unit

The **crt** unit has a number of facilities for handling screen and keyboard operations. A

```
uses crt;
```

statement (the first non-comment line in a program or unit) gives you access to them.

The next program makes a sound like a siren. Try it out. If for some reason you can't stop the noise, try the following trick. Place the cursor on the nearest **nosound** statement. Press **F4**, which executes the code up to the cursor and halts. Then execute the **nosound** statement on its own with **F7** (this all happens in Turbo Pascal Debug mode).

```pascal
program siren;
uses crt;
var
 i, j : integer;
begin

  for j := 1 to 4 do
  begin
    for i := 400 to 500 do
    begin
      sound ( i );
      delay ( 10 );
      nosound
    end;

    for i := 500 downto 400 do
    begin
      sound( i );
      delay( 10 );
      nosound
    end
  end

end.
```

The crt procedure sound(i) makes the computer speaker emit a sound of frequency i hertz. The noise continues until stopped by nosound!

delay (n) causes a delay in program execution of n milliseconds (this is needed after sound so that the sound can be heard).

The next example simulates the ringing of a telephone. The sequence of 'trings' is repeated until you press any key:

```
uses crt;
var
 i : integer;
begin

  repeat
    for i := 1 to 30 do
    begin
      sound ( 600 );
      delay ( 30 );
      nosound;
      sound ( 1500 );
      delay ( 30 );
      nosound
    end;
  delay ( 2000 )
  until keypressed
```

keypressed is a Boolean function which tests whether an input character is waiting to be read from the keyboard buffer. It returns true if a key has been pressed on the keyboard since the last read or readln statement was executed (or since the program started executing), otherwise it returns false. It is useful when you want an operation to continue until the user hits any key.

readkey is another useful crt function. It returns a single character of type char from the keyboard, without echoing it to the screen. The syntax is

```
ch := readkey;
```

This is useful for extracting single-letter responses to a menu.

You can get into a tangle when using readkey and keypressed together. If keypressed was true *before* a call to readkey, the character that made keypressed true is returned by that call to readkey. Otherwise readkey waits for the next character to be input.

Certain keys and key combinations that are not represented by the standard ASCII codes in Appendix E return *two* codes, called *extended key codes*. When such a key (combination) is pressed, a call to readkey returns the null character (#0). The next call to readkey returns the extended key code. Since null characters cannot be generated in any other way, you are guaranteed that the character following a null will be an extended key code; e.g.

```
uses crt;
var
  ch : char;
  pgdn : boolean;
begin
  ...
  pgdn := false;
  writeln ( 'Press PgDn to continue ...' );

  repeat
    ch := readkey;
    if (ch = #0) then
```

```
      begin
        ch := readkey;
        if (ch = #81) then
           pgdn := true
      end
   until pgdn;
   ...
```

There is another example in Section 13.1.

Text windows

The window procedure enables you to define a *text window* anywhere on the screen. All screen output is restricted to this window until the next call to window. This provides the basis for 'pop-up' overlapping windows. The following example demonstrates the basics:

```
uses crt;
   ...
   clrscr;                        { clear the whole screen }
   window( 1, 1, 30, 12 );        { window 1: cols 1-30, rows 1-12 }
   textbackground ( blue );
   clrscr;

   window( 20, 8, 50, 16 );       { window 2: cols 20-50, rows 8-16 }
   textbackground ( magenta );
   clrscr;

   readln;                        { pause to have a look }
   textbackground ( black );
   window( 1, 1, 30, 12 );        { back to window 1 again }
   clrscr;
   readln;                        { pause to have a look }

   window( 20, 8, 50, 16 );       { window 2 again }
   clrscr;
   readln                         { pause for last look }
```

The statement

```
window ( x1, y1, x2, y2 )
```

opens a text window where x1, y1 are the column and row of the top left corner of the window, and x2, y2 are the column and row of the bottom right corner. The default window is the whole screen:

```
window ( 1, 1, 80, 25 )
```

Note that the top left corner is (1, 1).

clrscr sets the current window to its background colour, which is set with **textbackground** (see below).

The quickest way to clear an area of the screen is to define a window on that area and to call clrscr. This is much faster than writing lines of blanks.

The coordinates of the current window are stored in the predeclared variables windmin and windmax. windmin contains the upper left coordinates (i.e. the numerically smaller ones), and windmax contains the lower right ones. The *x*-coordinate is stored in the low byte, and the *y*-coordinate in the high byte. They can be extracted with the functions lo and hi. For example, hi(windmax) returns the *y*-coordinate of the lower right corner. Note that the values returned by windmin and windmax are actually relative to $(0,0)$, and not to $(1,1)$; e.g. after

```
window ( 5, 12, 45, 20 );
```

windmin returns $(4,11)$ and windmax returns $(44,19)$.

Saving the screen buffer

It's very useful (and impressive) to be able to move screen buffers around very quickly, e.g. to get back to your original screen after a help display. The following program shows one way of doing this:

```
program screensaver;
uses crt;
const
  screensize = 80 * 25 * 2;                    { colour monitor }
var
  saveptr   : pointer;
  screenptr : pointer;
  x, y : word;
  ch : char;
begin
  getmem ( saveptr, screensize );       { allocate dynamic memory }
  screenptr := ptr ( $B800, 0 );     { point to starting address }
  clrscr;
  writeln ( 'rhubarb' )'
  write ( 'more rhubarb' );
  x := wherex;                        { record current cursor position }
  y := wherey;
  readln;                                            { pause }
  move ( screenptr^, saveptr^, screensize );        { save screen }
  clrscr;
  readln;                                       { pause again }
  move ( saveptr^, screenptr^, screensize );   { restore screen }
  gotoxy ( x, y );                          { reposition cursor }
  freemem (saveptr, screensize );          { release the memory }
  readln
end.
```

The number of bytes required to hold a colour screen is twice its number of rows multiplied by its number of columns. This information is saved in the constant **screensize**.

The getmem call creates a block of **screensize** bytes of dynamic memory with starting address **saveptr**.

The ptr function is used to create a pointer to the screen buffer (the starting address for colour monitors is $B800:0000; for monochrome monitors it is $B000:0000).

The crt functions wherex and wherey are used to record the *x*- and *y*-coordinates of the current cursor position (column and row).

The move statement copies the contents of the screen buffer into the block **saveptr^**.

The screen is then cleared, so we can see that the next statement works. The following move copies the screen saved in **saveptr^** back to the screen buffer, thus restoring the original screen, apparently instantaneously.

gotoxy(x, y), which moves the cursor to column *x* and row *y*, is used to move the cursor to its original position (otherwise it will go to its 'home' position in the top left corner).

Finally, the dynamic memory used to save the screen buffer is released with **freemem**.

By using an array of such dynamic variables you could save a sequence of screens like this.

This program can be written without using **move**. The alternative version illustrates how to manipulate pointers and their associated memory:

```
program altscreensaver;
uses crt;
const
  screensize = 80 * 25 * 2;                        { colour monitor }
type
  screenbuff = array[ 1..screensize ] of byte;
var
  textscreen : screenbuff absolute $B800:0000;
  screenptr : ^screenbuff;
  x, y : word;
  ch : char;
begin
  new ( screenptr);
  clrscr;
  writeln ( 'rhubarb' );
  write ( 'more rhubarb' );
  x := wherex;                          { record current cursor position }
  y := wherey;
  readln;                                                     { pause }
  screenptr^ := textscreen;                            { save screen }
  clrscr;
  readln;                                              { pause again }
  textscreen := screenptr^;                          { restore screen }
  gotoxy ( x, y );                                 { reposition cursor }
  dispose ( screenptr );                          { release the memory }
  readln
end.
```

In this version an array **textscreen** of **screensize** bytes is declared on top of the video memory, with **absolute**. This ensures that at any moment the contents of **textscreen** is identical to the video memory.

A **new** statement creates a dynamic variable **screenptr^** of the same size as **textscreen**, and the statement

```
screenptr^ := textscreen;
```

stores the screen at that instant in **screenptr^**.

All you have to do to restore the original screen is to reassign **screenptr^** back to **textscreen**.

Table 11.3   Text colour constants

Value	Name	Value	Name
0	black	8	darkgray
1	blue	9	lightblue
2	green	10	lightgreen
3	cyan	11	lightcyan
4	red	12	lightred
5	magenta	13	lightmagenta
6	brown	14	yellow
7	lightgray	15	white
		128	blink

Text colours

The procedures textcolor(colour) and textbackground(colour) may be used to select the text foreground (colours 0–15) and background colours (colours 0–7) from the predefined constants in Table 11.3. Adding blink to a foreground colour makes it blink, e.g. textcolor (red + blink).

Other *crt* procedures

clreol
clears all characters from the cursor position to the end of the line.

delline
deletes the line containing the cursor, moving all lines below it up one line, and clearing the bottom line.

highvideo
selects high-intensity characters.

insline
inserts a blank line at the cursor position.

lowvideo
selects low-intensity characters.

normvideo
selects normal-intensity characters.

wherex
returns the x-coordinate (column) of the current cursor position.

wherey
returns the y-coordinate (row) of the currentcursor position.

11.12   The *dos* unit

The dos unit implements a number of useful operating system routines.

getdate (year, month, day, dayofweek)
returns the system date in its word-type arguments. dayofweek is in the range 0–6 where 0 is Sunday.

gettime (hour, minute, second, sec100)
returns the system time of day in its word-type arguments. sec100 is hundredths of a second.

setdate (year, month, day, dayofweek)
sets the system date (see getdate).

settime (hour, minute, second, sec100)
sets the system time of day (see gettime).

11.13   Compiler directives

Compiler directives are specific instructions to the compiler embodied in your program code as comments.

Switch directives

We have seen examples of one type of compiler directive, the switch directive, such as **{$E +}** to load the coprocessor emulator.

Switch directives which are *global* must appear before the first **uses, const, type, procedure, function** or **begin** keyword. Examples of global switch directives are **$E** (emulation) and **$N** (numeric processing).

Local switch directives may appear anywhere in the code. Examples are **$B** (boolean evaluation), **$I** (input/output checking), **$R** (range checking) and **$V** (**var**-string checking).

Multiple switch directives may appear as a single comment, e.g.

```
{$B+,R-}
```

Conditional directives

Another type of directive is the conditional directive which enables the compiler to produce different compiled code from the same source code, depending on the values of certain conditional symbols. For example,

```
var
    x, y : {$IFDEF CPU87} double {$ELSE} real {$ENDIF};
```

This is similar to the **if-then-else** statement. If an 80x87 numeric coprocessor is present at compile time **x** and **y** are compiled with type **double**, otherwise with type **real**.

CPU87 is a predefined *conditional* symbol, which is defined if an 80x87 coprocessor is present at compilation.

{$IFDEF *name*} compiles the code that follows if *name* is defined.

Conditional compilation is useful in avoiding unnecessary use of the coprocessor emulation software (which produces bigger code). The following directive at the beginning of your code will ensure that you can use the IEEE floating point types, but that the emulation software will only be loaded if an 80x87 is not present:

```
{$N+}
{$IFDEF CPU87}
   {$E-}
{$ELSE}
   {$E+}
{$ENDIF}
```

Summary

This chapter introduces many of the extensions and exceptions in Turbo Pascal.

There are additional integer and real types, and also a predefined **string** type.

Independently compiled units provide a means of modularising large programs. Turbo Pascal has a number of additional standard functions and procedures in predefined units, such as **crt**, **dos** and **system**.

Compiler directives are instructions to the compiler which are embedded in program comments. Some of them support conditional compilation.

12

Turbo Pascal files

One of the major differences between standard and Turbo Pascal is the way files are handled. These differences necessitate rewriting a standard Pascal program that uses files before it can run under Turbo Pascal.

In Turbo Pascal the word *file* has two distinct meanings. It can mean a disk file; we call this a *physical* file. It can also have the meaning it has in standard Pascal, where it means a data structure in a program which does not necessarily have a connection with the real world outside. Such a file is sometimes called a *logical* file, although more often it is simply called a file. Turbo Pascal furthermore allows two distinct types of logical files, *text* files and *binary* files. Text files are accessed *sequentially*, as in standard Pascal. Binary files may be accessed *randomly* (random access files are not supported by standard Pascal).

The differences in Turbo Pascal file syntax can be summarised as follows:

(i)   a (logical) file must be linked to a disk file with an **assign** statement;
(ii) a file is opened with **reset** or **rewrite**, not by referencing its name in the program header;
(iii) **put** and **get** are not supported, neither is the file buffer variable, e.g. as in **ifile↑**;
(iv) forms of **write** and **read** are used to write to a file and read from it directly;
(v)   a file must be explicitly closed with **close**.

12.1   Text files

Turbo Pascal accesses text files sequentially, as does standard Pascal, so we will look at them first.

Reading from text files

Suppose we have a list of students' names and marks in an ASCII (text) disk file called **marks.txt** (its MS-DOS filename):

```
JAPTHA AM          53
NGUBANE MK    67
SMITH JB           9
```

The following code will read this data from the disk file and display it on the screen:

```
const
  n = 15;
var
  textfile : text;
  name     : string[n];
  mark     : integer;
```

```
begin
  assign ( textfile, 'marks.txt' );
  reset ( textfile );

  while not eof ( textfile ) do
  begin
    readln ( textfile, name, mark );
    writeln ( name:n, mark:3 )
  end;

  close ( textfile );
```

The output is:

```
JAPTHA AM     53
NGUBANE MK    67
SMITH JB       9
```

Note the following:

(i)   **assign** links the file variable **textfile** to the disk file **marks.txt**.
(ii) **reset** opens an existing file for reading. The file window (Figure 8.3) is placed over the first item in the file.
(iii) **eof** is used with a parameter to read a file of unknown length.
(iv) Because **name** is declared as a string with length 15, the first 15 characters of each line in the file are read into **name**. The disk file must be set up so that the mark appears after column 15.

The absence of a file buffer variable in Turbo Pascal is highlighted when one tries to examine a character in a file before reading it. In Section 8.6 the procedure **skipblanks** is used as part of the procedure **getword** to skip over non-blanks in the input stream. **getword** then reads the following group of non-blanks as a single word. The standard Pascal version there uses the file buffer **input↑** to peep ahead at the next character in the stream. Only if it is a blank is it read with **get**:

```
if input↑ = ' ' then
  get ( input )
else
  blank := false;
```

In Turbo Pascal the character must be read before it can be examined:

```
read ( textfile, ch );
if (ch <> ' ') then
  blank := false;
```

where **ch** is of type **char**, and **textfile** is the file variable. But the important difference now is that when **skipblanks** returns, **ch** will be the first character of the next word. This must be taken into account if we want to amend **getword** to run under Turbo Pascal. Furthermore, if we want **getword** to handle more than one line of text we must prevent **skipblanks** from reading the end-of-line marker. We can therefore rewrite **skipblanks** as follows:

```
procedure skipblanks ( var ch : char; var textfile : text );

{ ************************************************************
  *                                                        *
  * Skips over non-blanks in textfile, reading first non-blank *
  * into ch unless end of line or end of file occurs       *
  *                                                        *
  ************************************************************ }
```

```
var
  blank : boolean;

begin { skipblanks }
  blank := true;

  while not eof ( textfile ) and not eoln ( textfile ) and blank do
  begin
    read ( textfile, ch );
    if (ch <> ' ') then
      blank := false
  end

end; { skipblanks }
```

Note the following changes:

(i) Recall that **eoln** (here used with a file variable parameter) is **true** only when the last character *before* the end-of-line marker has been read. Its use here prevents **skipblanks** from actually reading the end-of-line marker.

(ii) **skipblanks** now *returns* the last character read (as **ch**). The reason for this will become clear below.

getword may then be rewritten as follows:

```
procedure getword ( var inword : string; var ch : char;
                    var textfile : text );

{ ***********************************************************
  *                                                         *
  * The next word in textfile is read in to inword assuming that *
  * words are separated by at least one blank. ch is the first   *
  * letter of the word, returned by skipblanks                   *
  *                                                         *
  ***********************************************************}

var
  i : integer;
  endofword : boolean;

begin { getword }
  i := 2;
  endofword := false;
  inword[1] := ch;
              { first letter of word already read by skipblanks }

  repeat
    if (i <= maxwordsize) then
      begin
        read ( textfile, ch );
        if (ch <> ' ' ) then
          begin
            inword[i] := ch;
            i := i + 1
          end
      end
    else
      read ( textfile, ch );
                            { if more than maxwordsize characters in}
                            { word then these are ignored           }
```

```
          if (eof ( textfile )) or (ch = ' ') or (eoln ( textfile )) then
             endofword := true
       until endofword;

       inword[0] := chr ( i-1 );   { set inword[0] to logical length }

       for i := i to maxwordsize do              { fill out with blanks }
          inword[i] := ' ';

       skipblanks ( ch, textfile )
    end; { getword }
```

Note the following:

(i)   The new version of **getword** must assign ch (as returned by **skipblanks** and passed to it as a parameter – see below) to inword[1] (so i must be initialised to 2 instead of 1).

(ii)   Assuming that words are not split between lines, **endofword** must also be set to **true** if eoln is **true**.

(iii) The character representation of the logical length of **inword** must be assigned to inword[0].

A program using these two amended procedures could be as follows:

```
program test_TP_getword;
const
   maxwordsize = 3;
var
   textfile : text;
   ch : char;
   inword : string;
procedure skipblanks ( var ch : char; var textfile : text );
      ...
end; { skipblanks }

procedure getword ( var inword : string; var ch : char;
                    var textfile : text );
      ...
end; { getword }

begin
   assign ( textfile, 'text.' );
   reset ( textfile );
   writeln ( 'Output:' );

   while not eof ( textfile ) do
      begin
         skipblanks ( ch, textfile );
                                    { skip leading blanks on new line }

         while not eoln ( textfile ) do
            begin
               getword ( inword, ch, textfile);
               writeln ( inword )                { display the word }
            end;

         readln ( textfile )              { read end-of-line marker }
      end;

   close ( textfile )
end.
```

Note:

(i) **skipblanks** must be called at the beginning of each line since **getword** now relies on it to pass it the first character of the new word.

(ii) The **while** statement ensures that **getword** is used only on the current line.

(iii) **readln(textfile)** reads the end-of-line marker.

(iv) **skipblanks** must be external to **getword**, since both procedures need to be called in the main program when processing more than one line of text. The first character **ch** of a new word must therefore be passed between them to avoid having to declare it as a global variable.

eof and *eoln* with files

Turbo Pascal defines a *current file position*, which is the same as the file window of Section 8.2.

    eof(file), where **file** is a file variable of any type, returns **true** if the current file position is beyond the last component of the file (or if the file is empty).

    eoln(file), where **file** is a text-file variable, returns **true** if the current file position is at the end-of-line marker, or if **eof(file)** is **true**.

Writing to text files

Writing to a text file is simply the reverse of reading, except that **rewrite** or **append** are used instead of **reset**. The following example reads a name of up to 10 letters and a mark from the keyboard (until **Ctrl-z/Enter** are pressed). The mark must not start before the 11th column, otherwise it is read as part of the name. The name and mark is then written to a file **text** (any existing file of that name is destroyed):

```
var
   textfile : text;
   name : string[10];
   mark : integer;

begin
   assign ( textfile, 'text.' );
   rewrite ( textfile );

   while not eof do
      begin
         read( name );
         readln( mark );
         writeln( textfile, name, ' ', mark );
      end;

   close ( textfile );
```

Appending text files

New material may be added to the end of an existing text file (*appended*) if it is opened with **append** instead of **rewrite**. The current file position is then set to the end of the file. Try this out with the above example.

reset, *rewrite* and *append* with text files

An existing file may be opened for reading with **reset**.

A new file can be created and opened for writing with **rewrite**. If **rewrite** is used to open an existing file, *the file is destroyed, and a new one is created with the same name.*

An existing file may be opened for appending with **append**. The current file position is set to the end of the file.

Text files opened with **reset** are read-only, while text files opened with **reset** and **append** are write-only. In other words, you cannot *update* a text file (easily).

Sending output to the printer

The standard unit **printer** declares a special text-file variable **Lst** which is assigned to the printer:

```
uses printer;
...
writeln( Lst, 'rhubarb rhubard on the printer … ' );
```

A text-file filter

A *filter* is a program that reads a file, does something to it, and writes the result to another file, or back to the original file. In the example below, the filter converts the text in a text file to lowercase. The program also introduces two other important features: input/output error checking, and command line parameters. Discussion follows the program:

```
program filter;
uses crt;
var
  f, infile, outfile : text;
  ans, ch : char;
  name : string;
begin
  ans := ' ';                                    { initialize }
  name := paramstr( 1 );       { read filename from command line }
  assign( infile, name );                        { master file }
  reset( infile );

  assign( outfile, 'scratch.txt' );              { scratch file }
  {$I-}
  reset( outfile );                         { it may already exist }
  {$I+}
  if IOresult = 0 then
    begin
      write( 'scratch file already exists',
             ' – do you want to overwrite it (y/n)? ' );
      ans := upcase( readkey );
      writeln
    end;

  if ans <> 'N' then
    begin
      rewrite( outfile );                     { create or overwrite }

      while not eof( infile ) do
        begin
          read( infile, ch );                  { read from master }
          if (ch in ['A' .. 'Z']) then
            ch := chr( ord(ch) + 32 ); { convert to lowercase }
          write( outfile, ch )                 { write to scratch }
        end;
```

```
            close ( infile );
            close ( outfile );
            assign ( f, name );
            erase ( f );                          { delete master }
            assign ( f, 'scratch.txt' );
            rename ( f, name )          { rename scratch as master }
        end
    else
        begin
            close ( infile );                { close them anyway }
            close ( outfile );
        end
end.
```

Note:

(i) The standard function **paramstr(n)** is discussed below.

(ii) The output (lowercase version) is first to be written to a temporary text file, **scratch.txt**. However, this file may already exist, so we first need to check for its existence. The easiest way of doing this is to attempt to read from it. Normally, if you try to read from a non-existent file Turbo Pascal crashes. However, you can suspend normal input/output (I/O) checking with the **{$I-}** compiler directive. If you then attempt to open a non-existent file with **reset** no crash occurs, but an error number is generated by the standard function **IOresult**. If it is not zero an error occurred. You can then use the value of **IOresult** to program further action (after switching I/O error checking back on with **{$I+}**).

(iii) A character from the input file is converted to lowercase with

```
if (ch in ['A' .. 'Z']) then
    ch := chr ( ord (ch) + 32 );
```

since 32 is the difference between the ASCII codes for an uppercase letter and its lowercase counterpart.

(iv) When the filtering is finished, the master file is deleted with **erase** and the temporary file **scratch.txt** renamed with the name of the master file using **rename**.

You might well be nervous about deleting your master file – there might be a power failure at the crucial moment! It is wise to make a backup first. The following code makes a copy of any text tile, giving the copy the extension **.zzz**:

```
var
    name, backupname : string;
    dot : word;
    ch : char;
    infile, outfile : text;

begin
    name := paramstr ( 1 ); { get filename from command line }
    dot := pos ( '.', name );
                        { find position of period in filename }
    if (dot = 0) then        { there might not be a period … }
        dot := length ( name ) + 1;
    backupname := copy ( name, 1, dot-1 ) + '.ZZZ'; { backup name }
    assign ( infile, name );
    reset ( infile );
    assign ( outfile, backupname );
    rewrite ( outfile );
```

```
while not eof( infile ) do
   begin
      read( infile, ch );
      write( outfile, ch )
   end;

close( infile );
close( outfile )
```

Command line parameters

The standard function paramstr(n) returns the nth command line parameter (entered from DOS) as a string. For example, if the .exe version of the filter example above is called filter, the DOS command

```
filter text
```

will cause paramstr(1) to return the filename text.

You can enter command line parameters from within the Turbo Pascal IDE when developing a program by selecting Run/Parameters. Enter the parameters in the dialogue box exactly as you would in DOS, with spaces between them.

The function paramcount returns the number of parameters passed to a program from the command line.

I/O error checking and *IOresult*

The function IOresult returns the error code of the last I/O operation (zero means no error). If I/O checking is off – {$I-} – and an I/O error occurs, the program does not crash, and all subsequent I/O operations are ignored until a call is made to IOresult. A call to IOresult resets it to zero, so its value may need to be assigned to a variable for subsequent reference.

When I/O error checking is active – {$I+} – the program crashes if there is an I/O error. This is the default state.

12.2   Random access with typed files

As we have seen, Turbo Pascal text files (like standard Pascal files) may only be accessed sequentially, i.e. the current file position may only be advanced one position at a time. This can be inefficient; for example, to access something near the end of a text file, you have to read almost the entire file. Text files are also restricted in that they may be opened either for reading or writing, but not both.

Turbo Pascal *typed* and *untyped* files (also called *binary* files) may be accessed at random for both reading and writing. This mode of file access is also known as *random access*.

If a Turbo Pascal file is typed, its components must all be of the same type (the *component type*). The components may be any type except a file type or a structured type with a file type component.

The next three programs demonstrate the use of typed files. Detailed discussion follows the last one.

The first program, SetUp, sets up a file of records (student_type), each record containing the name and mark of a student. Names and marks are read from the keyboard and written to the disk file student.bin:

```
Program SetUp;
type
   student_type = record
                     name: string;
                     mark: integer;
                  end;
```

```
var
   student : student_type;
   student_file: file of student_type;
begin

   assign ( student_file, 'student.bin' );
   rewrite ( student_file );
   write ( 'name and mark on separate lines (ctrl-z/enter to end): ' );

   with student do
      while not eof do
         begin
            readln ( name );
            readln ( mark );
            write ( student_file, student );
            write ( 'name and mark on separate lines ',
                    '(ctrl-z/enter to end): ' );
         end;

   close ( student_file );
end.
```

The next program, **Display**, reads the records from the file and displays them on the screen:

```
Program Display;
type
   student_type = record
                     name: string;
                     mark: integer;
                  end;
var
   student: student_type;
   student_file: file of student_type;
   i : integer;

begin
   assign ( student_file, 'student.bin' );
   rest ( student_file );
   writeln ( 'student', ' ':20-length ( 'student' ), ' mark' );
   writeln;

   while not eof ( student_file ) do
      with student do
         begin
            read ( student_file, student );
            writeln ( name, ' ':20-Length ( name ), mark:6 )
         end;

readln;
   close ( student_file )
end.
```

The third program, **UpDate**, asks you which record you want to update (starting at record 0), and then lets you alter that student's mark. This demonstrates that any record may be read and rewritten at random:

```
Program Update;
type
   student_type = record
                     name: string;
                     mark: integer;
                  end;
```

```
var
   student: student_type;
   student_file: file of student_type;
   newmark : real;
   recnum : integer;

begin
   assign( student_file, 'student.bin' );
   reset( student_file );

   repeat
      write( 'Which record to update (<0 to end): ' );
      readln( recnum);
      if (recnum >= 0) then
         with student do
            begin
               seek( student_file, recnum );
               read( student_file, student );
               writeln( name, ' ':20-length( name ), mark:6 );
               write( 'corrected mark: ' );
               readln( mark );
               seek( student_file, filepos( student_file ) - 1 );
               write( student_file, student )
            end
   until (recnum < 0);

   close( student_file )
end.
```

Note the following:

(i)   Data are written to (and read from) a typed file with **read** and **write** (**readln** and **writeln** apply only to text files).

(ii) Each component in the file is referred to as a *record*. This is not to be confused with the Turbo Pascal **record** data type. Typed files must have records of fixed length (as opposed to text files), which is why each record must contain the same data type. In the case of **student_file** above, each record happens to contain exactly one Turbo Pascal **record** structure. However, the component type could just as easily be an array, say, in which case each file record would contain an entire array, e.g.

```
type
   arraytype = array[1..10] of integer;
var
   arrayfile : file of arraytype;
   x : arraytype;
begin
   assign ( arrayfile, 'junk.' );
   rewrite ( arrayfile );
   ...
   write( arrayfile, x ); { write the entire array to the file }
   close ( arrayfile );
```

(iii) A file's records are numbered sequentially from zero, so the first record is number 0. **read** or **write** advances the current file position one record, so if you read a record and immediately want to overwrite it, you have to move the current file position back one record. This may be done with **filepos** and **seek**:

```
seek( filevar, filepos( filevar - 1 ) ); { go back 1 record }
```

filepos(file) returns the record number of the next record in **file** to be read or written. **seek(file, recnum)** moves **file**'s current file position in such a way that record number **recnum** is the next record to be read or written. Neither **filepos** nor **seek** may be used with text files.

(iv) You should never try to display a non-text file on the screen. At best you'll get garbage, and at worst your machine will hang up.

reset and *rewrite* with typed files

An existing file can be opened with **reset**.

A new file can be created and opened with **rewrite** (an existing file will be destroyed, and a new one will be created with the same name).

Typed files always allow both reading and writing regardless of whether they were opened with **reset** or **rewrite**.

12.3 Untyped files

An *untyped* file in Turbo Pascal is simply a continuous stream of bytes, regardless of the component type of any physical (disk) file which may be associated with it. Its declaration omits the type:

```
var
   chunk : file;
```

The advantage of untyped files is that they may be used to move information around very quickly, with the help of the standard procedures **blockread** and **blockwrite**. Their use is demonstrated in the next example, which also illustrates how to handle file date stamps.

Foolproof file copy: date stamps

You may have fallen into the trap of backing up a valuable file in the 'wrong direction'. For example, suppose you are working on your *magnus opus*, **nobel.doc**, in the current directory. At the end of a session you would normally make a backup on to a disk in drive A, say, with the DOS command

```
copy nobel.doc a:
```

to make a backup of the same name. However, you might accidentally type

```
copy a:nobel.doc
```

which will replace your master copy with the last backup, which may be from months ago!

This problem can be prevented if you check the *date stamps* on the files first, and make sure you never copy an older version into a newer one. The program **scopy** shows you how to check the date stamps first, before using **blockread** and **blockwrite** to make a copy (since these procedures use untyped files, the program will work on any sort of file, no matter how it was created). As it presently stands you have to give the full names of the master and the backup, e.g.

```
scopy nobel.doc a:nobel.doc
```

You may like to modify it so that it mimics the DOS **copy** command more closely:

```
Program scopy;
uses dos;

const
   buffsize = 2048;
```

```
var
  masterfile, backupfile : file;
  masterstamp, backupstamp : longint;
  master, backup : string;
  numread, numwritten : word;
  buff : array[1..buffsize] of byte;
  io : integer;
begin
  master := paramstr( 1 );
  backup := paramstr( 2 );
  assign( masterfile, master );
  assign( backupfile, backup );
  reset( masterfile, 1 );                 { record length of 1 byte }
  getftime( masterfile, masterstamp );       { master datestamp }
  {$I-}
  reset( backupfile, 1 );                 { check if it exists first }
  {$I+}

  io := IOresult;              { can only reference IOresult once }

  if io = 0 then { backup already exists, so get its date stamp }
    getftime( backupfile, backupstamp );

  if (io = 0) and (backupstamp > masterstamp) then
    writeln( #8'target is mor recent than master -
                                     copy not made ...' )
  else
    begin
      rewrite( backupfile, 1 );              { create new backup }

      repeat
        blockread( masterfile, buff, buffsize, numread );
        blockwrite( backupfile, buff, numread, numwritten )
      until (numread = 0) or (numwritten <> numread);

      setftime( backupfile, masterstamp )
                                     { update backup's date stamp }
    end;

  close( masterfile );
  close( backupfile )
end.
```

Note:

(i) The **dos** unit procedure **getftime(file, datestamp)** returns the file date stamp in its second parameter as a packed **longint**. Such date stamps may be compared in Boolean expressions; the larger date stamp is more recent.

  The **dos** procedure **setftime(file, datestamp)** works in reverse; it sets a file's date stamp according to the second parameter.

(ii) When **blockread** and **blockwrite** are used on untyped files the record length is assumed to be 128 bytes. This length can be changed with an optional second parameter to **reset** and **rewrite** (only with *untyped*) files). Normally the record length should be as large as possible to achieve as fast a transfer of data as possible. However, when the length of the file is unknown, as in this case, it is best to set the record length to 1 byte, as in:

```
reset( masterfile, 1 );
```

The procedure call

```
blockread ( masterfile, buff, buffsize, numread );
```

reads **buffsize** or less records (of length 1 here) from **masterfile** into the variable **buff** (which may be any convenient variable). The actual number of complete records read (≤ **buffsize** here) is returned in the optional parameter **numread**. This information is needed in case the end of the file is reached before the transfer is completed. Then, if the record size is greater than 1, **numread** returns the number of complete records read; a possible last partial record is not included in **numread**.

The procedure call

```
blockwrite ( backupfile, buff, numread, numwritten );
```

works like **blockread** except that data is transferred from the variable **buff** to **backupfile**. The optional parameter **numwritten** returns the number of records actually written. If **numwritten** is less than **numread** it means that the disk became full before the transfer was completed. You could test for such a condition and report that an incomplete transfer took place.

12.4   Device files

Switching output between screen and printer

You may sometimes want to write a program which will produce a lot of output on a printer. However, while you are developing and debugging it, it is much more convenient for the output to go to the screen (or a file). But when the program is finally ready, it is a great nuisance to have to change every **write(** *rhubarb* **)** to **write(Lst,** *rhubarb***)**.

The following code shows you how to switch an entire program's output from the screen to a printer (or a file), and vice versa, with a single keystroke:

```
uses crt;
var
  out : text;
  ch : char;

begin
  write ( 'Output to screen (S) or printer (P)? ' );
  writeln;
  ch := readkey;
  ch := upcase ( ch );

  if (ch = 'S') then
    assign ( out, 'CON' )
  else
    assign ( out, 'PRN' );

  rewrite ( out );
  writeln ( out, 'Output is on chosen device!' );
  close ( out );
```

Device files

CON and PRN are the names of two DOS hardware devices. They are treated by Turbo Pascal as files, and so are sometimes called *device files*. The standard I/O procedures and functions can all operate on device files.

CON is the console, and PRN is a synonym for LPT1, the printer. You may also use two further printers with device names LPT2 and LPT3.

COM1 and COM2 refer to the standard serial communication ports. AUX may be used instead of COM1.

NUL is a device which ignores everything written to it, and generates an immediate end-of-file when read from. It is useful when you don't want to create a particular file, but the program syntax requires a filename.

Summary

This chapter introduces Turbo Pascal files, which differ from standard Pascal files to the extent that a program which uses standard Pascal files must usually be rewritten before it can run under Turbo Pascal.

Turbo Pascal files are linked to disk files with the **assign** statement.

Turbo Pascal files are opened with **reset** or **rewrite** and not by referencing their names in the program header.

Turbo Pascal does not support **get**, **put** or the file buffer variable.

Turbo Pascal files must be explicitly closed with **close**.

Turbo Pascal text files are similar to standard Pascal files, and are accessed sequentially. New material may be added to the end of a text file with **append**.

Turbo Pascal typed and untyped files (also called binary files) may be accessed randomly as opposed to sequentially.

A number of useful file handling facilities are introduced.

13

Turbo Pascal graphics

A picture, it has been said, is worth a thousand words. If you are serious about scientific and engineering programming, you will doubtless want to draw graphs. In this chapter we look at the basics of Turbo Pascal graphics, and also introduce a useful unit for drawing 'mathematical' graphs, myworld, with a minimum of fuss.

13.1 Some basics

Without further ado, you should enter and run the following program, which draws a rectangle with diagonals, covering the screen.

```
Program testgraph;
uses graph;
var
   grdriver, grmode, xmax, ymax : integer;
begin
   grdriver := detect;
   initgraph( grdriver, grmode, 'c:\tp6\bgi' );
   xmax := getmaxx;
   ymax := getmaxy;
   rectangle( 0, 0, xmax, ymax );              { draw rectangle }
   line( 0, 0, xmax, ymax );                   { draw diagonals ... }
   line( 0, ymax, xmax, 0 );
   readln;
   closegraph
end.
```

Note:

(i)   The Turbo Pascal graph unit contains all the predeclared graphics paraphernalia. It must be referenced in a uses clause in any program (or unit) that uses graphics.

(ii) The third argument of initgraph must be a string giving the path to the Borland .bgi files, which are needed to run Turbo Pascal graphics. All graphics examples assume that the .bgi files are stored in the subdirectory c:\tp6\bgi.

Autodetection of graphics hardware

initgraph initialises graphics, by actually calling another function detectgraph, which in turn detects which of the many types of graphics hardware cards (if any) is installed on your computer. Calling initgraph with its first parameter grdriver set to the predeclared constant detect, as above, means we are requesting *autodetection*. This means that the parameters grdriver and grmode are set (by the invisible call to detectgraph) to the *driver code* and *mode code* of the graphics device detected. Incidentally, these codes may be found with the

Help menu by selecting Contents/Units/Graph. Then select Constants and Types/Graphics Modes, etc.

For example, if you have a VGA card installed, the value of **grdriver** returned will be the value of the predeclared constant **VGA (9)**, and the value returned for **grmode** will be **VGAHi (2)**. This allows for a resolution of 640 pixels horizontally by 480 pixels vertically. A *pixel* (picture element) is the smallest point addressable on the graphics screen with a particular graphics card.

By the way, since **initgraph** expects a variable as its first parameter you cannot pass **detect** directly as that parameter. You must first assign it to a variable, and then pass the variable.

Having detected your graphics card, the compiler will then attempt to find and load the appropriate *graphics driver* – a file with a **.bgi** extension. BGI stands for Borland Graphics Interface. As the name implies, a graphics driver handles the details of the interface between your Turbo Pascal graphics program and the hardware device.

If a graphics driver can't be loaded, well and good, because **initgraph** doesn't attempt to do any graphics; it simply tries to load the driver. However, attempting to do any graphics if the driver is not loaded could cause a disaster. Therefore you should always use the standard **graph** unit function **graphresult** to return the error code. If it is zero **(grOk)** you may proceed. Otherwise you should halt the program (or exit the subprogram) after calling **grapherrormsg** to interpret the error code, e.g.

```
initgraph( grdriver, grmode, 'c:\tp6\bgi' );
errorcode := graphresult;
if (grerror <> grOk) then
  begin
    writeln( 'graphics error: ', grapherrormsg( errorcode ) );
    writeln( 'graphics aborted … ' );
    halt( 1 )
  end;
  …
```

All graphics programs should have this error trapping code!

Having got through all that, we can now draw some pictures. Pixels are numbered from the top down, and to the right. So the top left corner of the screen is (0, 0) (PC graphics was not designed by mathematicians!). **getmaxx** returns the maximum horizontal (*x*) coordinate. This will be 639 in **VGAHi** mode, since the left-most coordinate is 0. **getmaxy** similarly returns 479. The point at the bottom right of the screen will therefore be (639, 479).

```
rectangle( x1, y1, x2, y2 );
```

draws a rectangle with top left corner at (**x1, y1**), and bottom right corner at (**x2, y2**). (Parameters representing pixels are integers.)

```
line( x1, y1, x2, y2 );
```

draws a straight line from (**x1, y1**) to (**x2, y2**).

You must call **closegraph** when you have finished graphics, since DOS doesn't take kindly to being left hanging in graphics mode.

Overriding autodetection

Some graphics cards cannot be autodetected (in which case graphics is done in default CGA mode), or you may specifically want to override autodetection. You do this by passing a particular driver and mode code to **initgraph**, e.g.

```
grdriver := IBM8514;            { IBM 8514 card not autodetected }
grmode := IBM8514Hi;
initgraph( grdriver, grmode, 'c:\tp6\bgi' );
```

Toggling between graphics and text mode

The function **restorecrtmode** restores the screen to its original state before **initgraph** was called. Similarly, **setgraphmode(grmode)** restores the graphics screen after a call to **restorecrtmode**. You can therefore use these two functions to toggle back and forth between text and graphics (e.g. to prompt for data) without having to call **initgraph** and **closegraph** each time:

```
uses graph;
var
   grdriver, grmode : integer;
   ...
begin
   grdriver := detect;
   initgraph ( grdriver, grmode, 'c:\tp6\bgi' );
   outtext ( 'graphics mode ... ' );
   readln;
   restorecrtmode;
   writeln ( 'text mode ... ' );
   readln;
   setgraphmode ( grmode );
   outtext ( 'back in graphics ... ' );
   readln;
   closegraph;
```

Bars, pies, etc.

The following code draws boxes in different coloured *fill patterns* at random:

```
uses crt, graph;
var
   grdriver, grmode : integer;
   x1, y1, x2, y2, pattern, colour : integer;
begin
   grdriver := detect;
   initgraph ( grdriver, grmode, 'c:\tp6\bgi' );
   randomize;
repeat
   x1 := random ( getmaxx );
   x2 := random ( getmaxx );
   y1 := random ( getmaxy );
   y2 := random ( getmaxy );
   pattern := random ( 12 );
   colour := random ( 15 ) + 1;
   setfillstyle ( pattern, colour );
   bar3d ( x1, y1, x2, y2, 0, false );
   delay ( 10 )
until keypressed;
```

The function

```
setfillstyle ( style, colour );
```

sets the fill pattern and colour to **pattern** (0–11) and **colour** (0–15). Use the Help menu, or **Ctrl-F1** (context-sensitive help) with the cursor under **setfillstyle**, to see the possible patterns and colours available.

```
bar3d ( x1, y1, x2, y2, depth, topflag );
```

draws a three-dimensional box with opposite corners at $(x1, y1)$ and $(x2, y2)$ filled with the current fill pattern and colour. depth is the depth in pixels (0 if you want a two-dimensional bar). If topflag is true, a three-dimensional lid is drawn on top of the bar.

There is also a two-dimensional version:

```
bar( x1, y1, x2, y2);
```

It is filled with the current fill pattern and colour. The difference between rectangle and bar is that rectangle is not filled with the current fill pattern.

To fill other shapes like a rectangle use

```
floodfill( x, y, border );
```

to flood an enclosed area. (x, y) is a seed point within the enclosed area to be filled. The area bounded by the colour border is flooded with the current fill pattern and fill colour. If the seed point is inside an enclosed area, the inside will be filled. If the seed is outside the area, the exterior will be filled.

The function

```
pieslice( x, y, startangle, endangle, radius );
```

draws a pie slice centred at (x, y) with radius radius filled with the current fill pattern. The angles are in degrees, and are measured counter-clockwise from 0° at 3 o'clock.

Current pointer and functions relating to it

The *current pointer* (CP) is the graphics equivalent of the cursor position on the text screen: it is the point on the graphics screen where the next output will go (if appropriate). Functions like rectangle and line don't update the CP. Others, however, do.

```
lineto( x, y );
```

draws a line from the CP to the point (x, y) updating the CP.

```
linerel( dx, dy );
```

draws a line *relative* to the CP, updating the CP. That is, if the CP is (x, y), linerel(dx, dy) draws a line from the CP to $(x+dx, y+dy)$.

```
moveto( x, y );
```

moves the CP to (x, y), without drawing on the way.

```
moverel( dx, dy );
```

moves the CP dx pixels horizontally and dy pixels vertically, again without drawing on the way.

getx and gety return the *x*- and *y*-coordinates of the CP respectively.

Line style

```
setlinestyle( style, 0, thickness );
```

enables you to change the style and thickness of all subsequent lines drawn, e.g. by rectangle, line, etc. Use Help for possible values for style and thickness.

Text on the graphics screen

The function

```
outtextxy( x, y, strg );
```

displays the text in the string strg in such a way that the smallest box containing the text will have its top left corner at the position (x, y). outtextxy does not update the CP.

A related function,

```
outtext( strg );
```

outputs **strg** at the CP, updating the CP at the same time.

The style, orientation and magnification of text on the graphics screen is controlled by **settextstyle**, e.g.

```
settextstyle( SansSerifFont, HorizDir, 7 );
outtextxy( 1, 100, 'Turbo P is for me!' );
```

The first parameter specifies the *font*, the second the orientation (horizontal or vertical), and the third the magnification, on a scale of 1–10.

To output numeric data on the graphics screen, first use the procedure **str(v, strg)** to convert the value **v** into its string representation **strg**.

Viewports

A *viewport* is a 'window' on the graphics screen set up with the function

```
setviewport( left, top, right, bottom, clip );
```

The opposite corners of the viewport are (**left, top**) and (**bottom, right**). If **clip** is **true**, drawing is clipped off at the viewport boundary. All subsequent graphics coordinates are relative to this viewport; the point (0, 0) will be plotted at the top left corner of the viewport. The exceptions to this rule are **getmaxx** and **getmaxy** which always return *absolute* coordinates (otherwise you could never enlarge a viewport).

If **clip** is **false**, points with negative coordinates may be plotted.

When you change viewports, the original viewport is not cleared. You can clear a viewport with **clearviewport**.

Clearing the graphics screen

The whole graphics screen (as opposed to the current viewport) is cleared with

```
cleardevice;
```

Note that **clrscr** clears the *text* screen. If you attempt to **clrscr** the graphics screen you will get garbage on the screen.

Colour

Colour is an intriguing and fairly complicated subject. The 16 predeclared EGA/VGA colour constants are the same as those numbered 0–15 in Table 11.3. Integers in this range may also be used for the colours.

The current drawing colour is set with

```
setcolor( colour );
```

(note the American spelling in the function name) where **colour** may be one of the predeclared constants (if that colour is available for the graphics card in the current mode) or an integer in the range 0 to **getmaxcolor**.

The background colour is set with

```
setbkcolor( colour );
```

These remarks apply to the default *palette* on a VGA card. A palette controls which of the many colours you can choose from when drawing. On a VGA card this runs into a few hundred thousand (defined with **setrgbpalette**, which allows you to set the monitor's red, green and blue electron 'guns'). The Turbo Pascal manuals explain how to use palettes.

Plotting points

An individual pixel may be drawn with

```
putpixel( x, y, colour );
```

Animation

Animation is achieved by repeatedly drawing and moving an image. There are very sophisticated ways of doing this. The following code demonstrates the easiest (and crudest) form of animation. The motion of a small box is directed by the **Up-, Down-, Right-** or **Left-arrow** keys. Pressing any other cursor movement key makes the box stop. (The cursor movement keys return extended key codes as described in Chapter 11.) The program stops when **Enter** is pressed.

```
Program movebox;
uses crt, graph;
const
  wait = 3;                             { milliseconds between moves }
var
  grdriver, grmode, w, h, dx, x, dy, y: integer;
  pic : pointer;
  ch : char;

begin
  grdriver := detect;
  initgraph( grdriver, grmode, 'c:\tp6\bgi' );
  x := 0;                                        { location }
  y := getmaxy div 2;
  w := 2;                                           { width }
  h := 2;                                           { height }

  rectangle( x, y, x+w, y+h );                   { draw rectangle }
  getmem( pic, imagesize( x, y, x+w, y+h ) );
                                          { allocate enough memory }
  getimage( x, y, x+w, y+h, pic^ );                { save image }
  putimage( x, y, pic^, xorput );                  { rub it out }
  dx := 1;                                 { initialize direction }
  dy := 0;

  repeat
    repeat
      x := x + dx;                                    { move }
      y := y + dy;

      putimage( x, y, pic^, xorput );            { draw image }
      delay( wait );                                 { pause }
      putimage( x, y, pic^, xorput )             {rub out }
    until keypressed;

    ch := readkey;
    if (ord( ch ) = 0) then              { test for extended code }
```

```
      begin
        ch := readkey;
        dx := 0;
        dy := 0;
        case ord( ch ) of              { decide on direction }
          72: dy := -1;                         { up arrow }
          80: dy := 1;                          { down arrow }
          75: dx := -1;                         { left arrow }
          77: dx := 1                           { right arrow }
        end; { case }
      end
    until ord( ch ) = 13;                       { hit enter }

    closegraph
  end.
```

imagesize returns the number of bytes required to save a copy of the graphics image in the given rectangular area, i.e. bounded by the points (x, y) and $(x+w, y+h)$ in this case. (Not more than one 64K segment of dynamic memory can be addressed by default; **imagesize** returns zero if more than this is requested.)

rectangle draws the image, and **getimage** copies the part of the graphics screen specified (called a *bitmap image*) into the memory addressed by **pic**.

The **repeat** loop then uses **putimage** to copy the saved bitmap image addressed by **pic** to the screen. The coordinates specify where the top left corner of the image must be drawn. The effect of **xorput** is to draw a pixel if there isn't one there already, and to rub one out if there is one there already. So after a short delay, the image is rubbed out by **xor**ing it in the same place. The position is then updated, before the loop **xor**s it in a new place.

Saving a graphics image to disk

A bitmap image can be written to disk, and read back again, as the following example shows. An image of PacMan is written to disk, and read back to demonstrate that it got there and back safely:

```
    Program graphsaver;
    uses graph;
    var
      grmode, grdriver : integer;
      picsize : integer;
      pic : pointer;                 { points to any dynamic variable }
      f : file; { untyped file }

    begin
      grdriver := detect;
      initgraph( grdriver, grmode, 'c:\tp6\bgi' );
      picsize := imagesize( 0, 0, 40, 40 );
      assign( f, 'a:pic.' );
      rewrite( f, picsize );
                      { record length = picsize for fastest write }
      getmem( pic, picsize );        { create dynamic variable pic^ }
      setfillstyle( 5, green );
      pieslice( 20, 20, 30, 330, 20 );              { draw PacMan }
      getimage( 0, 0, 40, 40, pic^ );  { save it in dynamic memory }
      readln;
      blockwrite( f, pic^, 1 );    { write it to disk as 1 record }
      cleardevice;                          { clear screen }
      readln;
```

```
      freemem ( pic, picsize );
                                  { throw away dynamic memory to make sure! }
      getmem ( pic, picsize );    { get some new memory from the heap }
      reset ( f, picsize );
      blockread ( f, pic^, 1 );                  { read image from disk }
      putimage ( 0, 0, pic^, xorput );    { put it back on the screen }
      freemem ( pic, picsize );              { release the memory again }

      readln;
      closegraph;
      close ( f )
   end.
```

13.2   *myworld*: a world coordinate graphics unit

Having struggled with a few graphics programs you will readily appreciate that drawing even fairly simple mathematical functions poses a non-trivial challenge. For example, try to draw the graph of

$$y(t) = e^{-0.1t} \sin t \qquad\qquad (13.1)$$

for t from 0 to 8π, in steps of $\pi/20$. Also draw in the y- and t-axes (where t is the horizontal coordinate usually represented by x).

The main problem is that a point with conventional Cartesian or *world* coordinates (t, y) must be transformed into a plottable pixel somewhere on the screen. An additional slight irritation is that you might get your graph upside down, because the vertical pixels increase downwards, whereas Cartesian coordinates normally increase upwards.

What we need is a set of routines which will transform our more natural world coordinates into absolute screen coordinates. This is achieved by the unit **myworld**, the listing of which appears immediately below. An example and explanation follow the listing.

myworld listing

The complete listing of the **myworld** unit is as follows:

```
{-myworld-----------------------------------------------------------}
{ }
{ Procedures and functions in this unit                             }
{ assist in scaling the user's more convenient world coordinates }
{ into absolute screen coordinates.                                 }
{ }
{-----------------------------------------------------------------}

unit myworld;

interface
uses crt, graph;

function h ( x: real): integer;
procedure setwindow ( xmin, xmax, ymin, ymax: real );
function v ( y: real): integer;
procedure wbar ( x1, y1, x2, y2 : real );
procedure wbar3d ( x1, y1, x2, y2: real; depth : word; top : boolean );
procedure wline ( x1, y1, x2, y2 : real );
procedure wlineto ( x, y : real );
procedure wmoveto ( x, y : real );
procedure wouttextxy ( x, y : real; textstring: string );
```

```
procedure wputpoint( x, y : real; colour : word );
procedure wrectangle( x1, y1, x2, y2 : real );
function xrange: integer;
function yrange: integer;

implementation

var
   xleft, xright, ydown, yup : real;          { world coordinates }
   currentport               : viewporttype;

function h;
{ scales world x-coordinate into h absolute coordinate }
var
   tempx : real;
begin
   tempx := xrange * (x - xleft) / (xright - xleft);
   if tempx > maxint then
     tempx := maxint
   else if tempx < -maxint then
     tempx := -maxint
   else
     h := round( tempx )
end; { h }

procedure setwindow;
{ passes world coordinates from calling program }
begin
   xleft  := xmin;          { smallest world x-coordinate }
   xright := xmax;          { largest world x-coordinate }
   ydown  := ymin;          { smallest world y-coordinate }
   yup    := ymax           { largest world y-coordinate }
end; { setwindow }

function v;
{ scales world y-coordinate into v absolute coordinate }
{ vertical axis is inverted }
var
   tempy : real;
begin
   tempy := yrange * (y - yup ) / (ydown - yup);
   if tempy > maxint then
     tempy := maxint
   else if tempy < -maxint then
     tempy := -maxint
   else
     v := round( tempy )
end; { v }

procedure wbar;
{ world coordinate analogue of bar }
begin
   bar( h( x1), v( y1 ), h( x2 ), v( y2 ) )
end; { wbar }

procedure wbar3d;
{ world coordinate analogue of bar3d }
```

```
begin
  bar3d( h( x1 ), v( y1 ), h( x2 ), v( y2 ), depth, top )
end; { wbar3d }

procedure wline;
{ world coordinate analogue of line }
begin
  line( h( x1 ), v( y1 ), h( x2 ), v( y2 ) )
end; { wline }

procedure wlineto;
{ world coordinate analogue of lineto }
begin
  lineto( h( x ), v( y ) )
end; { wlineto }

procedure wmoveto;
{ world coordinate analogue of moveto }
begin
  moveto( h( x ), v( y ) )
end; { wmoveto }

procedure wouttextxy;
{ world coordinate analogue of outtextxy }
begin
  outtextxy( h( x ), v( y ), textstring )
end; { wouttextxy }

procedure wputpoint;
{ world coordinate analogue of putpixel }
begin
  putpixel( h( x ), v( y ), colour )
end; { wputpoint }

procedure wrectangle;
{ world coordinate analogue of wrectangle }
begin
  rectangle( h( x1 ), v( y1 ), h( x2 ), v( y2 ) )
end; { wrectangle }

function xrange;
{ calculates xrange for use in function h }
begin
  getviewsettings( currentport );
    with currentport do
      xrange := x2 - x1
end; { xrange }

function yrange;
{ calculates yrange for use in function v }
begin
  getviewsettings( currentport );
    with currentport do
      yrange := y2 - y1
end; { yrange }


end. { myworld }
```

myworld explained

A program which uses the myworld unit to draw the attenuated sine graph of Equation (13.1) is as follows. Note that it must reference both graph and myworld in a uses clause:

```
Program damping;
uses graph, myworld;
var
   grdriver, grmode : integer;
   y, t : double;
begin
   grdriver := detect;
   initgraph ( grdriver, grmode, 'c:\tp6\bgi' );
   setwindow ( 0, 8 * pi, -1, 1 );          { set the scales }
   wline ( 0, -2, 0, 2 );                         { y-axis }
   wline ( 0, 0, 8 * p, 0 );                      { x-axis }
   wmoveto ( 0, 0 );                      { move to world origin }
   t := 0;

   while t <= 8.01 * pi do      { 8.01 allows for rounding error }
      begin
         wlineto ( t, exp ( -0.1 * t ) * sin ( t ) );
         t := t + pi/20
      end;

   readln;
   closegraph
end.
```

First, let's just see what the program does, before looking into the messy details of myworld. The fundamental procedure in myworld is

```
setwindow ( left, right, bottom, top );
```

This sets up a world coordinate system running from left to right horizontally (the *t*-direction here), and from bottom to top vertically. So this particular call to setwindow sets up horizontal world coordinates from 0 to 8π, and vertical world coordinates from -1 to 1.

wline is the myworld counterpart of the standard graph unit procedure line (generally, myworld routines simply prefix the corresponding graph routines with a w). So

```
wline ( x1, y1, x2, y2 );
```

draws a line between world points (x1, y1) and (x2, y2) (all world coordinates are real type).

The two wline calls draw the axes. You could add your own axes-drawing functions to myworld – why not add tic marks as well?

wmoveto sets the current pointer at the world origin, ready for drawing

wlineto draws incremental lines from the current pointer to the specified world point.

Note that myworld does not initialise or close graphics. You must still do this.

Now we need to look at myworld in a little more detail. As already mentioned, setwindow is the crucial function that holds it all together. It sets four variables, xleft, xright, ydown and yup, declared in the *implementation* section of myworld, to its parameters received from the calling program. The scope of these variables, which are needed in the subsequent scaling, extends to all routines in the implementation section, so they must be global to myworld. However, because they are declared in the implementation section, as opposed to the interface section, they are private to myworld and not visible to any programs using the unit. Consequently, a user cannot accidentally modify their values (and interfere with the scaling).

Two other fundamental functions are h and v. They respectively transform x and y world coordinates into absolute horizontal and vertical screen coordinates. v also inverts the vertical axis.

Let's take a closer look at the essential part of h, for example:

```
function h;
{ scales world x-coordinate into h absolute coordinate }
var
   tempx : real;
begin
   tempx := xrange * (x - xleft) / (xright - xleft);
   ...
      h := round( tempx )
end; { h }
```

It makes use of xleft and xright, as expected, and invokes a further function xrange which also warrants closer examination:

```
function xrange;
{ calculates xrange for use in function h }
begin
   getviewsettings( currentport );
      with currentport do
         xrange := x2 - x1
end; { xrange }
```

xrange calls a standard graph function getviewsettings with the parameter currentport declared in the implementation section of myworld with type viewporttype. This is a type declared in the graph unit as follows

```
type
   ViewPortType = record
      X1, Y1, X2, Y2 : Integer;
      Clip : Boolean;
   end;
```

On return currentport will hold the absolute coordinates of the top left and bottom right corners of the current viewport in the fields X1, Y1, X2 and Y2. What is returned therefore by xrange is the width of the current viewport in absolute terms, and this is used in turn by h to scale correctly.

The effect of this is that world coordinate graphs may be drawn in several viewports, because setwindow works in the *current* viewport. If you have different world coordinate limits in different viewports, you will have to remember to call setwindow after each call to setviewport.

After that, the remaining functions are pretty straightforward. Look at wline, for example:

```
procedure wline( x1, y1, x2, y2 : real );
{ world coordinate analogue of line }
begin
   line( h( x1 ), v( y1 ), h( x2 ), v( y2 ) )
end; { wline }
```

Its parameters are world coordinates. Each parameter (e.g. x1) is converted into the appropriate absolute screen coordinate (e.g. h(x1)), and these absolute coordinates are passed to the standard function line to do the actual drawing.

You can make your own world coordinate counterpart of any of the other graph unit routines in a similar way, simply by transforming the world coordinates first with h and v.

Examples

All the examples in this section use the myworld unit.

Fourier square wave approximation

A square wave of period T may be defined by the function $f(t)$ which is 1 for $0 < t < T$ and -1 for $-T < t < 0$. The Fourier series for $f(t)$ is given by

$$\frac{4}{\pi} \sum_{k=0}^{\infty} \frac{1}{2k+1} \sin\left[\frac{(2k+1)\pi t}{T}\right]$$

It is of interest to know how many terms are needed for a good approximation to this infinite sum. The following program takes $T = 1$, and displays the sum to n terms of the series for t from -1 to 1 in steps of 0.1. The program stops when a negative value for n is entered. Try some different values of n, between 0 and 30, say.

```pascal
Program drawfourier;
uses graph, myworld;
function foursqu ( n: integer; t: real ): real;
  var
    k  : word;
    sum  : real;
  begin
    sum := 0;
    for k := 0 to n do
      sum := sum + sin( (2 * k + 1) * pi * t) /(2 * k + 1);
    foursqu := sum * 4 /pi
  end; { foursqu }

var
  t    : real;
  nstr : string;
  grdriver, grmode, n : integer;
begin
  grdriver := detect;
  initgraph( grdriver, grmode, 'c:\tp6\bgi' );
  setwindow( -2, 2, -2, 2 );

  repeat
    restorecrtmode;              { back to text for readln with echo }
    write( 'value of n? ' );
    readln( n );
    if n < 0 then
      begin
        closegraph;
        exit
      end;
    setgraphmode( grmode );   { back to graphics }
    t := -1;
    outtext( 'value of n: ' );
    str( n, nstr );
    outtext( nstr );
    wmoveto( t, foursqu( n, t ) );

    while t <= 1 do              { draw the Fourier approximation }
```

```
      begin
        wlineto( t, foursqu( n, t ) );
        t := t + 0.05
      end;

    readln
  until n < 0;

  closegraph
end.
```

Fractal trees with Turtle graphics

The unit **turtle** below simulates LOGO Turtle graphics. The turtle (which is not shown, although its path can be drawn) can turn left or right a specified number of degrees, and can move forward or back a specified distance. It uses world coordinates. Since **forward** is a reserved word, **fwd** is used instead as a procedure name:

```
unit turtle;
{ uses myworld coordinates set by setwindow in calling program }

interface
uses graph, myworld;
procedure back( d: real );
procedure clearscreen;
procedure fwd( d: real );
procedure left( da: real );
procedure right( da: real );

implementation

var a, { angular heading in degrees }
    x, y : real;                                    { current position }

procedure back;
begin
  fwd( - d )
end; { back }

procedure clearscreen;
begin
  clearviewport;
  x := 0;
  y := 0;
  a := 90  { heading up }
end; { clearscreen }

procedure fwd;
var
  dx, dy, newx, newy: real;
begin
  dx := d * cos( a * pi /180 );
  dy := d * sin( a * pi /180 );
  newx := x + dx;
  newy := y + dy;
  wline( x, y, newx, newy );
  x := newx;
  y := newy
end; { fwd }
```

```
procedure left;
begin
  a := a + da
end; { left }

procedure right;
begin
  left( - da )
end; { right }

end. { turtle }
```

The following program uses the **turtle** unit to draw a tree using a recursively defined shape, which is an example of a *fractal*. (A fractal can be thought of as an object with fractional dimensions, e.g. 1.2, and which is characterised by infinite structure, often with self-replicating features.) The program draws a tree with a vertical stem of height **leng**, which branches symmetrically, so that **ang** is half the angle between the branches. Each branch is made a fraction**frac** of the stem, and branches in the same way as the stem. New branches are always a fraction **frac** of their 'parent' branches. This pattern is repeated while the branches remain longer than two units. With a little thought you should be able to see how the recursive procedure **tree** does this. Values of 50, 0.6 and 20 for **leng**, **frac** and **ang**, respectively, give a fairly common or garden tree, while values of 60, 0.7 and 90, for example, give a slightly less usual tree.

```
Program growtree;
uses graph, myworld, turtle;
var
   grdriver, grmode: integer;
   oldcolor : world;

procedure tree( leng, frac, ang: real );
begin
  if leng < 2 then
    exit;
  fwd( leng );
  left( ang );
  tree( frac * leng, frac, ang );
  right( 2 * ang );
  tree( frac * leng, frac, ang );
  left( ang );
  back( leng )
end; { tree }

begin
  grdriver := detect;
  initgraph( grdriver, grmode, 'c:\tp6\bgi' );
  setwindow( -140, 140, -120, 120 );
  clearscreen;              { turtle at origin of world coordinates }
  oldcolor := getcolor;            { record current drawing colour }
  setcolor( getbkcolor );
                       { set drawing color to background color }
  back( 120 );                          { plant it on the ground }
  setcolor( oldcolor ); { re-instate the previous drawing colour }
  tree( 50, 0.6, 20 );                        { draw the tree }
  readln;
  closegraph
end.
```

Lissajous boxes

This program, which is also purely for fun, draws a series of coloured boxes based on Lissajous figures:

```
Program lissabox;
{ lissajous boxes }
uses crt, graph, myworld;

var
   color, clock, nx, ny, style, grdriver, grmode : integer;
   i, x, y : real;

procedure reset;
begin
   clearviewport;
   nx := round( 7 * random + 1 );
   ny := round( 9 * random + 1 );
   if nx = 1 then
      nx := 3;
   if ny = 1 then
      ny := 3;
   if nx = ny then
      nx := nx + 1
end; { reset }
begin
   randomize;
   grdriver := detect;
   initgraph( grdriver, grmode, 'c:\tp6\bgi' );
   setwindow( -1.3, 1.3, -1.3, 1.3 );
   clock := 0;
   i := 0;
   nx := 1;
   ny := 3;

   repeat
      if clock mod 700 = 0 then
         reset;
      x := sin( 1.1 * nx * i );
      y := cos( 1.1 * ny * i );
      i := i + 0.01;
      clock := clock + 1;
      color := round( 15 * random + 1 );
      style := clock mod 15;
      setcolor( color );
      setfillstyle( style, color );
      wbar3d( x, y, x + 0.22, y + 0.22, 0, false );
   until keypressed

end.
```

13.3 Fractals

The discovery of fractals in the past few years has led to a wealth of coffee table books with the most beautiful and fascinating pictures of the Julia and Mandelbrot sets.

The Julia set

We give below a simple program for drawing the Julia set of the complex polynomial

$$z^2 - \mu, \tag{13.2}$$

where z is a complex variable, $z = x + iy$, and μ is a complex constant (parameter), $\mu = a + ib$.

A working definition of the Julia set of this family of polynomials is as follows. Take a region of the complex plane. For every point z_0 in this region calculate the *iterated function sequence* (IFS) of the polynomial (13.2):

$$z_1 = z_0^2 - \mu,$$
$$z_2 = z_1^2 - \mu,$$
$$\dots$$
$$z_n = z_{n-1}^2 - \mu.$$

If an n can be found such that $z_n^2 > R$, where R is the radius of a (large) disk in the complex plane, z_0 is said to have *escaped*. The set of all points z_0 in the region of interest which do not escape is the Julia set of the polynomial.

One way to compute the IFS requires the real and imaginary parts of the polynomial $z^2 - \mu$, which are $x^2 - y^2 - a$, and $2xy - b$, respectively.

The code below draws the Julia set of $z^2 - 1.1$, so $a = 1.1$ and $b = 0$. Ideally R should be as large as possible, but we will take it as 4, since this gives quite a reasonable picture. You can experiment with larger values if you have the time! If z_0 has not escaped by the time n has reached the value of **maxits** (40), we will assume that it will never escape. The program checks each pixel in the world coordinate range $-2 \le x \le 2$, $-2 \le y \le 2$, to see if it escapes (applying the reverse of the transformation used in **myworld** to change world coordinates to absolute coordinates). If the pixel escapes it is lit up, in a different colour according to how quickly it escapes. The Julia set is then the set of pixels shaded in the background colour. (Strictly speaking, the Julia set is the *boundary* of the region in the background colour, and the region itself is the *filled* Julia set.) Note that the program does not need the **myworld** unit:

```
Program julia;
{ draws the Julia set of the family: z * z - mu }
uses graph;

const
  maxits : word = 40;                     { maximum no. of iterations }
  r : real = 4;                                       { infinity }
var
  a, b,                            { real and imaginary parts of mu }
  xmin, xmax, ymin, ymax : real;   { range of world coordinates }
  x, y, x0, y0, newx, newy : real;           { world coordinates }
  colour, grdriver, grmode : integer;     { graphics variables }
  n : integer;                                        { counter }
  xp, yp : integer;                        { absolute coordinates }

begin
  xmin := -2;
  xmax := 2;
  ymin := -2;
  ymax := 2;
  a := 1.1;
  b := 0;
  grdriver := detect;
  initgraph( grdriver, grmode, 'c:\tp6\bgi' );
```

```
for xp := 0 to getmaxx do
   for yp := to getmaxy do
      begin
         x0 := (xmax - xmin) * xp /getmaxx + xmin;
         y0 := (ymin - ymax) * yp /getmaxy + ymax;
         x := x0;
         y := y0;
         n := 0;

         while (n < maxits) and (x * x + y * y <= r) do
            begin
               n := n + 1;
               newx := x * x - y * y - a;
               newy := 2 * x * y - b;
               x := newx;
               y := newy
            end;

         if x * x + y * y > r then
            begin
               n := (n + 1) mod getmaxcolor;
               putpixel( xp, yp, n )
            end
      end;

   readln;
   closegraph
end.
```

You can speed up the drawing of this particular picture by a factor of 4 by observing that it has symmetry about both the *x*- and *y*-axes (the code in uppercase is what needs to be inserted):

```
for xp := 0 to getmaxx DIV 2 do
   for yp := 0 to getmaxy DIV 2 do
   ...
      if x * x + y * y > r then
         begin
            n := (n + 1) mod getmaxcolor;
            putpixel( xp, yp, n );
            PUTPIXEL( GETMAXX - XP, YP, N );
            PUTPIXEL( XP, GETMAXY - YP, N );
            PUTPIXEL( GETMAXX - XP, GETMAXY - YP, N )
         end
```

The boundary of the filled Julia set has the self-replicating property characteristic of fractals. Change the program (by adjusting xmin, xmax, etc.) to 'zoom' in on one of the 'spires' sticking out of the main body of the set. A little patience will be richly rewarded.

The Mandelbrot set

The Mandelbrot set was discovered by Benoit Mandelbrot, and has been described as the most complicated object known to man (?). It is related to the Julia set, and is drawn in much the same way, although it is more difficult to think about.

The Julia set above is for the polynomial $z^2 - \mu$, with $\mu = 1.1$. If you run the program for a different value of the parameter μ, the set will look different. The Mandelbrot set is concerned with μ, and is drawn in the *parameter* space of the polynomial. The Mandelbrot set is in fact the set of all values of μ for which the origin does not escape.

Recall that $\mu = a + ib$. For all possible values of a and b now (as opposed to x and y for the Julia set) we compute the IFS of $z^2 - \mu$, starting at $z = 0$ each time. If z_n (the nth iterate) for a particular μ does not escape it belongs to the Mandelbrot set. The program is very similar to the one for the Julia set. Only the relevant lines are shown here:

```
maxits   : word = 20;                    { maximum no. of iterations }
r : real = 10;                                         { infinity }
...
xmin := -0.5;
xmax := 1.5;
ymin := -1;
ymax := 1;
...
for xp := 0 to getmaxx do
  for yp := 0 to getmaxy do
    begin
      a := (xmax - xmin) * xp / getmaxx + xmin;
      b := (ymin - ymax) * yp / getmaxy + ymax;
      x := 0;
      y := 0;
    ....
```

The Mandelbrot set is a 'fuzzy' fractal. If you enlarge one of the little 'snowmen' on its boundary (coastline) you will see a figure which is similar but not identical (zooming on the Julia set coastline reveals identical replicas of the Julia set). In fact the structures on the boundaries of the Mandelbrot set resemble Julia sets. It is as if the coastline of the Mandelbrot set is made by stitching together microscopic copies of the Julia sets which it represents.

Zooming in on the 'sea' outside the Mandelbrot set may be rewarding too. You may find islands there that no-one else has ever seen.

13.4 Some other graphics goodies

Some other useful **graph** procedures are the following. Angles are counter-clockwise in degrees with 0° at 3 o'clock.

arc (x, y, start, finish, radius)
draws a circular arc centred at (x, y), from **start** angle to **finish** angle, with a radius of **radius**.

circle (x, y, radius)
draws a circle centred at (x, y) with a radius of **radius**.

ellipse (x, y, start, finish, xradius, yradius)
draws an elliptical arc centred at (x, y), from **start** angle to **finish** angle, with **xradius** and **yradius** as the horizontal and vertical (major) axes.

Consult the Turbo Pascal Library Reference Manual for the many more **graph** facilities that are available.

Summary

This chapter introduces many of the features of Turbo Pascal graphics available in the **graph** unit.

Graphics hardware may be autodetected with **initgraph**, or autodetection may be overridden. According to your graphics hardware, Turbo Pascal will attempt to load the appropriate graphics driver with a .**bgi** extension (for Borland Graphics Interface).

All parameters of **graph** routines involving screen pixels are of **integer** or **word** type.

The **myworld** unit is introduced. It converts conventional Cartesian (world) coordinates into screen pixels, thus enabling you to program graphics more conveniently.

Exercises

Most of the exercises are much easier if you use the **myworld** unit developed in this chapter.

1 Write a program to set up world coordinates from −1 to 1 horizontally, and from −1 to 1 vertically. Draw a border around the perimeter of the screen, and draw the x- and y-axes. Now draw the graph of your favourite function.

2 Draw a graph of the population of the USA from 1790 to 2000, using the (logistic) model

$$P(t) = \frac{197\,273\,000}{1 + e^{-0.03134(t - 1913.25)}}$$

where t is the date in years.

Actual data (in 1000s) for the years 1790 to 1950 are as follows: 3929, 5308, 7240, 9638, 12866, 17069, 23192, 31443, 38558, 50156, 62948, 75995, 91972, 105711, 122775, 131669, 150697. Superimpose this data on the graph of $P(t)$. Plot the data either as single characters, or as little rectangles.

3 The Spiral of Archimedes may be represented in polar coordinates by the equation

$$r = at$$

where r is the distance along a ray from the origin making an angle t radians with the x-axis, and a is some constant. (The shells of a class of animals called nummulites grow in this way.) Write a program to draw the spiral for some values of a. (If a point has polar coordinates (r, θ), its Cartesian coordinates are $x = r \cos \theta$, $y = r \sin \theta$.)

4 Another type of spiral is the logarithmic spiral, which describes the growth of shells of animals like the periwinkle and the nautilis. Its equation is

$$r = aq^t,$$

where r and t are as in Exercise 3 and $a > 0$, $q > 1$. Write a program to draw this spiral.

5 The arrangement of seeds in a sunflower head (and other flowers, like daisies) follows a fixed mathematical pattern. The nth seed is at position

$$r = \sqrt{n},$$

with angular coordinate $\pi dn/180$ radians, where d is the constant angle of divergence (in degrees) between any two successive seeds, i.e. between the nth and $(n + 1)$th seeds. A perfect sunflower head is generated by $d = 137.51°$. Write a program to plot the seeds (either use a point for each seed, or construct a symbol to represent each seed). A remarkable feature of this is that the angle d must be exact to get proper sunflowers. Experiment with some different values, e.g. 137.45° (spokes, fairly far out), 137.65° (spokes all the way), 137.92° (Catherine wheels).

6 The equation of an ellipse in polar coordinates is given by

$$r = a(1 - e^2)/(1 - e \cos \theta),$$

where a is the semi-major axis and e is the eccentricity, if one focus is at the origin, and the semi-major axis lies on the x-axis.

Halley's Comet, which visited us recently moves in an elliptical orbit about the Sun (at one focus) with a semi-major axis of 17.9 AU. (AU stands for Astronomical Unit, which is the mean distance of the Earth from the Sun: 149.6 million km.) The eccentricity of the orbit is 0.967276. Write a program which draws the orbit of Halley's Comet and the Earth (assume the Earth is circular).

7 A very interesting iterative relationship that has been studied a lot recently is defined by

$$y_{k+1} = ry_k(1 - y_k)$$

(this is a discrete form of the logistic model). Given y_0 and r, successive y_k may be computed very easily, e.g. if $y_0 = 0.2$ and $r = 1$, then $y_1 = 0.16$, $y_2 = 0.1334$, and so on. This formula is often used to model population growth in cases where the growth is not unlimited, but is restricted by shortage of food, living area, etc.

y_k exhibits fascinating behaviour, known as *mathematical chaos*, for values of r between 3 and 4 (independent of y_0). Write a program which plots y_k against k (as individual points). The horizontal range should be from 0 to **getmaxx**, and the vertical range from 0 to 1.

Values of r that give particularly interesting graphs are 3.3, 3.5, 4.5668, 3.575, 3.5766, 3.738, 3.8287, and many more that can be found by patient exploration.

A two-dimensional form of this problem is related to the Mandelbrot set.

8 Have a look at the Julia sets of $z^2 - \mu$, for $\mu = 1.25$, and $\mu = -0.27334 + 0.007421i$. You may need to use a slightly smaller region than the one in the program above for the best effect.

9 Zoom in on some parts of the coastline of the Mandelbrot set, e.g. the region $0.04 \le a \le 0.06$. $0.98 \le b \le 1$, where $\mu = a + ib$.

Section 4

Mathematical applications of Turbo Pascal

In this section we see how Turbo Pascal may be used to solve interesting problems in the areas of simulation, matrices and numerical methods. Most of the programs can be run under a standard Pascal compiler with very few changes.

14

Simulation

An extremely powerful application of modern computers is in the field of simulation, which was mentioned briefly in Chapter 9. A simulation is a *computer experiment* which mirrors some aspect of the real world that appears to be based on random processes, or is too complicated to understand properly. (Whether events can be really random is actually a philosophical or theological question.) Some examples are: radioactive decay, bacteria division and traffic flow. The essence of a simulation program is that the programmer is unable to predict beforehand exactly what the outcome of the program will be, which is true for the event being simulated. For example, when you spin a coin, you do not know exactly what the result will be.

14.1 Random number generation

Random events are easily simulated in Turbo Pascal with the standard function random, which returns a *uniformly distributed pseudo-random* number in the range $0 \leq$ random < 1. (A computer cannot generate truly random numbers, but they can be practically unpredictable.) For example,

```
for i := 1 to 5 do
    writeln ( random );
```

Output:

```
4.65661287307739E-0010
6.27598790451884E-0002
2.77903065551072E-0001
4.05161930248141E-0001
5.45842534396797E-0001
```

Of course, if you re-use this piece of code again, you will get exactly the same sequence of 'random' numbers, which is rather disappointing (and not true to life, as every gambler knows). To produce a different sequence each time, the generator can be *seeded* by calling the Turbo Pascal function randomize to initialise the random generator with a 'random' value, obtained from the system clock.

If you do not have access to Turbo Pascal, you can use the following code for random number generation, based on the *linear congruential method*:

```
function myrand ( var seed: longint ) : real;

{ returns a random value between 0 and 1                          }
{ initialize seed before first call                              }
{ reseed after each call                                          }
```

```
begin
  myrand := seed / 65536;
  seed := (25173 * seed + 13849) mod 65536
end; { myrand }
```

Note that **myrand** needs to be reseeded on each call, so you would use it as follows:

```
seed := 0; { or whatever }
for l := 1 to 10 do
  writeln ( myrand ( seed ) );
```

This method will only work on installations where $maxint \geq 2^{31} - 1$ (so to run it under Turbo Pascal **seed** must be **longint**).

14.2   Spinning coins

When a fair (unbiased) coin is spun, the probability of getting heads or tails is 0.5 (50%). Since a value returned by Turbo Pascal's **random** is equally likely to lie anywhere in the interval [0, 1) we can represent heads, say, with a value of less than 0.5, and tails otherwise.

Suppose an experiment calls for a coin to be spun 50 times, and the results recorded. In real life you are likely to want to repeat such an experiment a number of times; this is where computed simulation is handy. The following code simulates spinning a coin 50 times:

```
randomize;
for i := 1 to 50 do
  if (random > 0.5) then
    write ( 'H' )
  else
    write ( 'T' );
```

The call to **randomize** ensures that each time the program runs, the output will be different, e.g.

```
HTTHTTHTHTTHHTHHTHHTHTHTHHHHTTTTTTTTTTTHHHHTHHTTHHTTTH
TTHTTHHTTHHTTHHTHHTTTHTTHHHHTTTTTHTTTTHHHHHHHHHHHTTTHHT
```

Note that it should be impossible in principle to tell from the output alone whether the experiment was simulated or real (if the random number generator is sufficiently random).

14.3   Rolling dice

When a fair die is rolled, the number uppermost is equally likely to be any integer from 1 to 6. If **random** is called with a single **word** argument n, it returns a random integer r in the range $0 \leq r < n$. The following code simulates 20 rolls of a die. The output from two successive runs is shown.

```
randomize;
for i := 1 to 20 do
  write ( random ( 6 ) + 1:3 );
```

Output:

```
6  2  3  2  5  3  1  1  5  1  5  2  5  4  2  6  6  3  5  6
1  5  3  1  2  5  5  5  2  3  6  6  2  5  1  6  1  1  2  4
```

We can do statistics on our simulated experiment, just as if it were a real one. For example, we could estimate the mean of the number obtained when the die is rolled 100 times, and the probability of getting a six.

14.4   A random walk

A drunken sailor has to negotiate a jetty to get to his ship. The jetty is 50 paces long and 20 wide. A mate places him in the middle of the jetty at the quay-end, and points him toward the ship. Suppose at every step he has a 60% chance of lurching toward the ship, but a 20% chance of lurching to the left or right (he manages to be always facing the ship). If he reaches the ship-end of the jetty, he is hauled aboard by waiting mates.

The problem is to simulate his progress along the jetty, and to estimate his chances of getting to the ship without falling into the sea. To do this correctly, we must simulate one *random walk* along the jetty, find out whether or not he reaches the ship, and then repeat this simulation 100 times, say. The proportion of simulations that end with the sailor safely in the ship will be an estimate of his chances of making it to the ship. For a given walk we assume that if he has not either reached the ship or fallen into the sea after, say, 10 000 steps, he dies of thirst on the jetty.

To represent the jetty, we set up coordinates so that the *x*-axis runs along the middle of the jetty with the origin at the quay-end. *x* and *y* are measured in steps. The sailor starts his walk at the origin each time. The algorithm, program, and output from two successive runs are as follows:

Initialise variables
Repeat 100 simulated walks down the jetty
   Start at the quay-end of the jetty
   While still on the jetty and still alive do
      Get a random number *R* for the next step
      If *R* < 0.6 then
         Move forward (to the ship)
      Else if *R* < 0.8 then
         Move port (left)
      Else
         Move starboard
   If he got to the ship then
      Count that walk as a success
Compute and print estimated probability of reaching the ship
Stop.

```
Program walk_the_plank;
const
  safe : word = 0;                     { number of times he makes it }
  sims : word = 1000;                      { number of simulations }
  steps  : word = 0      { number of steps taken on a given walk }
var
  prob : real;                      { probability of reaching ship }
  r  : real;                               { random number }
  walks  : word;                              { counter }
  x, y : integer;                      { position on jetty }

begin
  randomize

  for walks := 1 to sims do
    begin
      steps := 0;                              { each new walk … }
      x := 0;                      { … starts at the origin }
      y := 0;

      while (x <= 50) and (abs( y ) <= 10) and (steps < 10000) do
          { continue walking until he arrives, falls off or dies }
```

```
      begin
        steps := steps + 1;                    { that's another step }
        r := random;                 { random number for that step }
        if r < 0.6 then                    { which way did he go? }
          x := x + 1                           { maybe forward ... }
        else if r < 0.8 then
          y := y + 1                           { maybe to port ... }
        else
          y := y - 1                         { maybe to starboard }
      end;

    if x > 50 then
      safe := safe + 1                        { he actually made it! }
  end;

  prob := 100.0 * safe / sims;
  writeln( 'probability of reaching ship: ', prob: 6:1, '%' );
  readln
end.
```

Output:

```
probability of reaching ship:  87.6%
probability of reaching ship:  88.1%
```

14.5 Traffic flow

A major application of simulation is in modelling the traffic flow in large cities, in order to test different traffic-light patterns before inflicting them on the real traffic (this has been done on a large scale in Leeds in the United Kingdom, for example). In this example we look at a very small part of the problem: how to simulate the flow of a single line of traffic through one set of traffic-lights. We make the following assumptions (you can make additional or different ones if you like):

(i)   Traffic travels straight, without turning.
(ii)   The probability of a car arriving at the lights in a particular second is independent of what happened during the previous second. This is called a *Poisson process*. This probability (call if p) may be estimated by watching cars at the intersection and monitoring their arrival pattern. In this simulation we take $p = 0.3$.
(iii) When the lights are green, assume the cars move through a steady rate of, say, eight every ten seconds.
(iv)   In the simulation, we will take the basic time interval to be ten seconds, so we want a display showing the length of the queue of traffic (if any) at the lights every ten seconds.
(v)   We will set the lights red or green for variable multiples of ten seconds.

The situation is modelled with a record **traffic** of type **trafficstatus** with fields for all the relevant information. This record is passed between procedures.

In the sample run below the lights are red for 40 seconds (**traffic.redints** = 4), green for 20 seconds (**traffic.greenints** = 2). The simulation runs for 480 seconds (**numints** = 48).

```
Program trafficsimulation;
uses crt;

type
  trafficstatus =
    record
      cars        : integer;                      { cars in queue }
      greenints   : word;                  { period lights are green }
```

```
          greentimer : word;              { counter for green lights }
          lights     : char;                 { colour of lights }
          redints    : word;              { period lights are red }
          redtimer   : word;              { counter for red lights }
          sim        : word                 { simulation counter }
      end;

var
   traffic   : trafficstatus;     { record of all relevant info }
   p         : real;    { probability a car arrives in any second }
   numints   : word;    { number of simulated 10-second intervals }
   t         : word;                         { time in seconds }

procedure showqueue ( var traffic : trafficstatus ); forward;
procedure go ( var traffic: trafficstatus );
{ lights are green here }
begin
   with traffic do
      begin
         greentimer := greentimer + 1;             { advance timer }
         cars := cars - 8;                  { let 8 cars through }
         if cars < 0 then           { may have been less than 8! }
            cars := 0;
         showqueue ( traffic );            { display traffic queue }
         if greentimer = greenints then
            begin
               lights := 'r';                   { change lights … }
               greentimer := 0              { … and reset timer }
         end end
end; { go }


procedure showquene;
{ display the queue of cars }
var
   i : integer;     { car counter }
begin
   with traffic do
      begin
         write( sim:3 );
         write( lights:2, '   ' );
         for i := 1 to cars do
            write( '*' );
         writeln
      end
end; { showqueue }

procedure stop ( var traffic : trafficstatus );
{ lights are red here }
begin
   with traffic do
      begin
         redtimer := redtimer + 1;              { advance timer }
         showqueue ( traffic );            { display traffic queue }
         if redtimer = redints then
            begin
               lights := 'g';                   { change lights … }
               redtimer := 0;                { … and reset timer }
```

```
          end
      end
end; { stop }

begin
  clrscr;
  randomize;
  p := 0.3;
  numints := 48;

  with traffic do
    begin                                          { initialize }
      cars := 0;
      greenints := 2;              { green for 2 10-second intervals }
      greentimer := 0;
      lights := 'r';                          { red to start with }
      redtimer := 0;
      redints := 4;                  { red for 4 10-second intervals }

      for sim := 1 to numints do
                            { run for numints 10-second intervals }
        begin
          for t := 1 to 10 do
            if random < p then
              cars := cars + 1;             { another car arrives }
          if lights = 'g' then
            go ( traffic )
          else
            stop ( traffic )
        end

    end;

end.
```

Output:

```
 1 r ***
 2 r *******
 3 r **********
 4 r *************
 5 g **********
 6 g ****
 7 r ******
 8 r ******
 9 r ********
10 r ********
 ...
45 r ************************
46 r **************************
47 g *********************
48 g **************
```

From this particular run it seems that a traffic jam is building up, although more and longer runs are needed to see if this is really so. In that case, one can experiment with different periods for red and green lights in order to get an acceptable traffic pattern before setting the real lights to that cycle (try it). Of course, we can get closer to reality by considering two-way traffic, and allowing cars to turn in both directions, and occasionally to break down, but this program gives the basic ideas.

Summary

This chapter introduces simulation as a computer experiment which mimics some aspect of reality. The basis of simulation is the random number generator. Turbo Pascal supplies such a random number generator, random. It may be initialised randomly with the function randomize.

A number of examples of simulations are presented.

Exercises

1 In a game of Bingo the numbers 1–99 are drawn at random from a bag. Write a program to simulate the draw of the numbers (each number can be drawn only once), printing them ten to a line.

2 A one-dimensional *random walk* may be simulated as follows. A gas molecule is constrained to move along the x-axis. It starts at the origin. It moves randomly a large number of times, to the left or right (with equal probability), one unit at a time. Let the frequency f(x) be the number of times it is at position x. Write a program to compute these frequencies, and to print a bar chart representing them. Assume that the molecule never moves outside some given range −xmax to xmax.

3 A random number generator can be used to estimate π as follows (such a method is called a *Monte Carlo* method). Write a program which generates random points in a square of length 2, say, and which counts what proportion of these points falls inside the circle of unit radius that fits exactly into the square. This proportion will be the ratio of the area of the circle to that of the square. Hence estimate π. (This is not avery efficient method, as you will see from the number of points required to get even a rough approximation.)

4 The aim of this exercise is to simulate bacteria growth. Suppose that a certain type of bacterium divides or dies according to the following assumptions:

(a) during a fixed time interval, called a *generation*, a single bacterium divides into two identical replicas with probability p;
(b) if it does not divide during that interval, it dies;
(c) the offspring (called daughters) will divide or die during the next generation, independently of the past history (there may well be no offspring, in which case the colony becomes extinct).

Start with a single individual and write a program which simulates a number of generations. Take $p = 0.75$. The number of generations which you can simulate will depend on your computer system. Carry out a large number (e.g. 100) of such simulations. The probability of ultimate extinction, $p(E)$, may be estimated as the proportion of simulations that end in extinction. You can also estimate the mean size of the nth generation from a large number of simulations. Compare your estimate with the theoretical mean of $(2p)^n$.

Statistical theory shows that the expected value of the extinction probability $p(E)$ is the smaller of 1, and $(1 - p)/p$. So for $p = 0.75$, $p(E)$ is expected to be $\frac{1}{3}$. But for $p \le 0.5$, $p(E)$ is expected to be 1, which means that extinction is certain (a rather unexpected result). You can use your program to test this theory by running it for different values of p, and estimating $p(E)$ in each case.

5 Dribblefire Jets Inc. makes two types of aeroplane, the two-engined DFII, and the four-engined DFIV. The engines are terrible and fail with probability 0.5 on a standard flight (the engines fail independently of each other). The manufacturers claim that the planes can fly if at least half of their engines are working, i.e. the DFII will crash only if both its engines fail, while the DFIV will crash if all four, or if any three, engines fail.

You have been commissioned by the Civil Aviation Board to ascertain which of the two models is less likely to crash. Since parachutes are expensive, the cheapest (and safest!) way to do this is to simulate a large number of flights of each model. For example, two calls of random could represent one standard DFII flight: if both random numbers are less than 0.5, that flight crashes, otherwise it doesn't. Write a program which simulates a large number of flights of both models, and estimates the probability of a crash in each case. If you can run enough simulations, you may get a surprising result. (Incidentally, the probability of n engines failing on a given flight is given by the binomial distribution, but you do not need to use this fact in the simulation.)

6   Two players, A and B, play a game called *Eights*. They take it in turns to choose a number 1, 2 or 3, which may not be the same as the last number chosen (so if A starts with 2, B may only choose 1 or 3 at the next move). A starts, and may choose any of the three numbers for the first move. After each move, the number chosen is added to a common running total. If the total reaches 8 exactly, the player whose turn it was wins the game. If a player causes the total to go over 8, the other player wins. For example, suppose A starts with 1 (total 1), B chooses 2 (total 3), A chooses 1 (total 4) and B chooses 2 (total 6). A would like to play 2 now, to win, but he can't because B cunningly played it on the last move, so A chooses 1 (total 7). This is even smarter, because B is forced to play 2 or 3, making the total go over 8 and thereby losing.

Write a program to simulate each player's chances of winning, if they always play at random.

15

Matrices and their applications

In this chapter we will see how to write programs to solve problems involving matrices, with examples from such areas as networks, populations dynamics, Markov processes and linear algebra.

15.1 Matrices

A *matrix* is a two-dimensional array, as mentioned briefly in Chapter 6, which may be used in a wide variety of representations. For example, a distance array representing the lengths of direct connections in a network is a matrix. We will deal mainly with *square* matrices in this chapter (i.e. matrices having the same number of rows as columns), although in principle a matrix can have any number of rows or columns.

A matrix is usually denoted by a bold capital letter, e.g. *A*. Each entry, or element, of the matrix is denoted by the small letter of the same name followed by two subscripts, the first indicating the row of the element, and the second indicating the column. So a general element of the matrix *A* is called a_{ij}, meaning it may be found in row *i* and column *j*. If *A* has three rows and columns – (3×3) for short – it will look like this in general:

$$\begin{bmatrix} a_{11} & a_{12} & a_{13} \\ a_{21} & a_{22} & a_{23} \\ a_{31} & a_{32} & a_{33} \end{bmatrix}.$$

A matrix may be represented by a two-dimensional array in Pascal, e.g.

```
Program mat;
type
   matrix = array [1..3, 1..3] of real;
const
   m : matrix = ((1, 2, 3), (4, 5, 6), (7, 8, 9));
```

Note that in Turbo Pascal a matrix may be initialised *by row* as a typed constant.

Turbo Pascal lacks the optional feature of *conformant array parameters* as discussed in Section 6.3. To pass a matrix as a parameter to a procedure its maximum size must therefore be specified in a type declaration. Additional parameters indicating its actual size must also be passed. For example, the following code calls a procedure **matread** to read a (3×3) matrix from the keyboard (by row):

```
type
   matrix = array [1..10, 1..10] of real;

procedure matread ( var a : matrix; n, m : integer );
var
   i, j : integer;
```

```
begin
  for i := 1 to n do                              { rows }
    for j := 1 to m do                            { columns }
      read( a[i,j] );
  readln
end; { matread }


var
  a : matrix;
begin
  matread( a, 3, 3 );
  ...
```

You could write a similar procedure, **matwrite**, to output a matrix.

The type declaration which sets the maximum size of matrices could of course be in a unit which is used by the calling program.

Matrix multiplication

Probably the most important matrix operation is matrix multiplication. It is used widely in areas as diverse as network theory, solution of linear systems of equations, transformation of coordinate systems, and population modelling.

When two matrices A and B are multiplied together, their product is a third matrix C. The operation is written as

$$C = AB,$$

and the general element c_{ij} of C is formed by taking the *scalar product* of the ith row of A with the jth column of B. (The scalar product of two *vectors* x and y is $x_1 y_1 + x_2 y_2 + \cdots$, where x_i and y_i are the components of the vectors.)

It follows that A and B can be successfully multiplied (in that order) only if the number of columns in A is the same as the number of rows in B.

The general definition of matrix multiplication is as follows: if A is an $(n \times m)$ matrix and B is an $(m \times p)$ matrix, their product C will be an $(n \times p)$ matrix such that the general element c_{ij} of C is given by

$$c_{ij} = \sum_{k=1}^{m} a_{ik} b_{kj}$$

Note that in general AB is not equal to BA (matrix multiplication is not *commutative*). Example:

$$\begin{bmatrix} 1 & 2 \\ 3 & 4 \end{bmatrix} \times \begin{bmatrix} 5 & 6 \\ 0 & -1 \end{bmatrix} = \begin{bmatrix} 5 & 4 \\ 15 & 14 \end{bmatrix}$$

If you are serious about scientific and engineering programming it's part of your education to code a matrix multiplication on your own. The following example includes a procedure to multiply matrices and some code which uses it. A is $(n \times m)$, B is $(m \times p)$ and their product C is $(n \times p)$.

```
const
  maxsize = 10;
type
  matrix = array [1..maxsize, 1..maxsize] of real;
```

```
procedure matmult ( var a, b, c : matrix; n, m, p : integer );
{------matmult---------------------------------------------------- }
{                                                                  }
{ multiplies matrices A (n x m) by B (m x p) and returns product }
{ C (n x p) }
{                                                                  }
{---------------------------------------------------------------- }

var
   i, j, k : integer;
begin
   for i := 1 to n do                    { for every row in A }
      for j := 1 to p do                 { for every column in B }
         begin
            c[i,j] := 0;
            for k := 1 to m do { for every column in A and row in B }
               c[i,j] := c[i,j] + a[i,k] * b[k,j]
         end
end; { matmult }
...


var
   a, b, c : matrix;
begin
   matread( a, 2, 2 );                          { as above }
   matread( b, 2, 2 );
   matmult( a, b, c, 2, 2, 2 );
   matwrite( c, 2, 2 );                         { write your own }
...
```

To make the function foolproof you should check that the matrix *A* has the same number of *columns* as the matrix *B* has *rows*.

Try it out on the example given above.

Since a vector is a matrix with one column, our procedure matmult should be able to multiply a matrix by a vector, as in

$$\begin{bmatrix} 1 & 2 \\ 3 & 4 \end{bmatrix} \times \begin{bmatrix} 2 \\ 3 \end{bmatrix} = \begin{bmatrix} 8 \\ 18 \end{bmatrix}$$

Try matmult out on this example also ($m = 2$, $n = 2$, $p = 1$).

15.2   Reachability of spies

In our first application of matrix multiplication we consider a problem which at first glance appears to have nothing at all to do with it.

Suppose five spies in an espionage ring have the code names Alex, Boris, Cyril, Denisov and Eric (whom we can label A, B, C, D and E respectively). The hallmark of a good spy network is that no agent is able to contact all the others. The arrangement for this particular group is:

(i)   Alex can contact only Cyril;
(ii) Boris can contact only Alex or Eric;
(iii) Denisov can contact only Cyril;
(iv) Eric can contact only Cyril or Denisov.

(Cyril can't contact anyone in the ring: he takes information out of the ring to the spymaster. Similarly, Boris brings information in from the spymaster: no-one in the ring can contact him.) The need for good spies to know some matrix theory becomes apparent when we spot that the

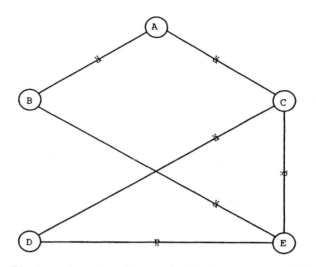

Fig. 15.1 The network represented by the adjacency matrix A

possible paths of communication between the spies can be represented by a (5×5) matrix, with the rows and columns representing the transmitting and receiving agents respectively, thus:

	A	B	C	D	E
A	0	0	1	0	0
B	1	0	0	0	1
C	0	0	0	0	0
D	0	0	1	0	0
E	0	0	1	1	0

We will call this matrix A. It represents a *directed network* with the spies at the *nodes*, and with *arcs* of length 1, where a network is a collection of points called nodes. The nodes are joined by lines called arcs. In a directed network, movement (e.g. of information) is only possible along the arcs in one direction (see Fig. 15.1).

The matrix A is known as an *adjacency* matrix, with a 1 in row i and column j if there is an arc from node i to node j, or a 0 in that position if there is no arc between those two nodes. The diagonal elements of A (i.e. a_{11}, a_{22}, etc.) are all zero because good spies do not talk to themselves (since they might then talk in their sleep and give themselves away). Each 1 in A therefore represents a path which is 1 arc long.

If we multiply the adjacency matrix A by itself, we get A^2. The rules of matrix multiplication enable us to interpret the entry in row i and column j of A^2 as representing the number of paths of length 2 between nodes i and j (on the understanding that all arcs in the network are of length 1).

In general, the element in row i and column j of the kth power of an adjacency matrix is equal to the number of paths consisting of k arcs linking nodes i and j.

The *reachability* matrix R of a network with n nodes may be defined as the sum of the first $(n-1)$ powers of its associated adjacency matrix A. You may be wondering why we can stop at the $(n-1)$th power of A. The elements of $A^{(n-1)}$ will be the number of paths that have $(n-1)$ arcs, i.e. that connect n nodes (since each arc connects two nodes). Since there are no further nodes that can be reached, it is not necessary to raise A to the nth power (assuming that the network has no cycles).

In our example, the reachability matrix is

$$R = A + A^2 + A^3 + A^4.$$

The elements of **R** give the total number of paths of communication between the agents. Carrying out the calculations by hand gives

$$R = \begin{bmatrix} 0 & 0 & 1 & 0 & 0 \\ 1 & 0 & 3 & 1 & 1 \\ 0 & 0 & 0 & 0 & 0 \\ 0 & 0 & 1 & 0 & 0 \\ 0 & 0 & 2 & 1 & 0 \end{bmatrix}$$

So we can read off from the reachability matrix **R** the fact that there are, for example, three different paths between Boris and Cyril, but only two between Eric and Cyril (the actual lengths of these paths will have been calculated in finding the powers of *A*). The name 'reachability' is used because the non-zero elements of **R** indicate who may contact whom, directly or indirectly, or, for a general distance network, which nodes can be reached from each node.

The following code shows the essential parts of a program to compute the reachability matrix **R** for any network given the adjacency matrix *A*. It uses the arrays b and c for the intermediate powers of a, adding them to r each time:

```
const
   maxsize = 10;
   n : integer = 5;
type
   matrix = array [1..maxsize, 1..maxsize] of real;

procedure matsum ( var a, b, sum : matrix; n, m : integer );
var
   i, j : integer;
begin
   for i := 1 to n do
      for j := 1 to m do
         sum[i,j] := a[i,j] + b[i,j]
end; { matsum }
...

var
   a, b, c, r : matrix;                    { b, c for working space }
   i : integer;
begin
   matread( a, n, n );
   r := a;                                 { initialize r and b }
   b := a;                                 { first power of a }

   for i := 1 to n-2 do
      begin
         matmult( a, b, c, n, n, n );      { next power of a in c }
         b := c;                           { increasing powers of a }
         matsum( b, r, r, n, n )           { update r }
      end;

   matwrite( r, n, n );                    { output r }
   ...
```

The new procedure matsum returns the sum of its first two parameters (matrix addition of two matrices *A* and *B* is defined in the obvious way: $c_{ij} = a_{ij} + b_{ij}$).

It may help to go through the code by hand for $n = 5$ to see how it works. Keep track of the contents of b, c and r in terms of the adjacency matrix a.

You may be tempted to call

```
matmult( a, b, b, n, n, n );
```

to avoid the use of an additional array c. However, because of the nature of matrix multiplication, this will interfere with the way the product b is formed. The same problem does not occur in matsum.

15.3 Leslie matrices: population growth

Another very interesting and useful application of matrices is in population dynamics.

Suppose we want to model a population of rabbits, in the sense that, given their number at some moment, we would like to estimate the size of the population in a few years' time.

One approach is to divide the rabbit population into a number of age classes, where the members of each age class are one time unit older than the members of the previous class, the time unit being whatever is convenient for the population being studied (days, months, etc.).

If X_i is the size of the ith age class, we define a *survival factor* P_i as the proportion of the ith class that survive to the $(i + 1)$th age class, i.e. the proportion that 'graduate'. F_i is defined as the *mean fertility* of the ith class. This is the mean number of newborn individuals expected to be produced during one time interval by each member of the ith class at the beginning of the interval (only females count in biological modelling, since there are always enough males to go round!).

Suppose for our rabbit model we have three age classes, with x_1, x_2 and x_3 members respectively. We will call them young, middle-aged and old-aged for convenience. We will take our time unit as one month, so x_1 are the number that were born during the current month, and which will be considered as youngsters at the end of the month. x_2 are the number of middle-aged rabbits at the end of the month, and x_3 the number of oldsters. Suppose the youngsters cannot reproduce, so that $F_1 = 0$. Suppose the fertility rate for middle-aged rabbits is 9, so $F_2 = 9$, while for oldsters $F_3 = 12$. The probability of survival from youth to middle-age is one third, so $P_1 = \frac{1}{3}$, while no less than half the middle-aged rabbits live to become oldsters, so $P_2 = 0.5$ (we are assuming for the sake of illustration that all old-aged rabbits die at the end of the month – this can be corrected easily). With this information we can quite easily compute the changing population structure month by month, as long as we have the population breakdown to start with.

If we now denote the current month by t, and next month by $(t + 1)$, we can refer to this month's youngsters as $x_1(t)$, and to next month's as $x_1(t + 1)$, with similar notation for the other two age classes. We can then write a scheme for updating the population from month t to month $(t + 1)$ as follows:

$$x_1(t + 1) = F_2 x_2(t) + F_3 x_3(t),$$
$$x_2(t + 1) = P_1 x_1(t),$$
$$x_3(t + 1) = P_2 x_2(t).$$

We now define a population vector $x(t)$, with three components, $x_1(t)$, $x_2(t)$, and $x_3(t)$, representing the three age classes of the rabbit population in month t. The above three equations can then be rewritten as

$$\begin{bmatrix} x_1 \\ x_2 \\ x_3 \end{bmatrix}_{(t+1)} = \begin{bmatrix} 0 & F_2 & F_3 \\ P_1 & 0 & 0 \\ 0 & P_2 & 0 \end{bmatrix} \times \begin{bmatrix} x_1 \\ x_2 \\ x_3 \end{bmatrix}_t$$

where the subscript at the bottom of the vectors indicates the month. We can write this even more concisely as the matrix equation

$$x(t + 1) = L \, x(t) \tag{15.1}$$

where L is the matrix

$$\begin{bmatrix} 0 & 9 & 12 \\ \frac{1}{3} & 0 & 0 \\ 0 & \frac{1}{2} & 0 \end{bmatrix}$$

in this particular case. L is called a *Leslie matrix*. A population model can always be written in the form of Equation (15.1) if the concepts of age classes, fertility, and survival factors, as outlined above, are used.

Now that we have established a matrix representation for our model, we can easily write a program using matrix multiplication and repeated application of Equation (15.1):

$$x(t+2) = L\ x(t+1),$$
$$x(t+3) = L\ x(t+2), \text{ etc.}$$

However, we only need a single vector x in the program, because after each matrix multiplication we can assign the product back to x.

We will assume to start with, that we have one old (female) rabbit, and no others, so $x_1 = x_2 = 0$, and $x_3 = 1$.

The relevant part of the program is then:

```
const
  n = 3;                              { number of age classes }
  maxsize = 10;
type
  matrix = array [1..maxsize, 1..maxsize] of real;

function total ( var x : matrix; n : integer ) : real;
var
  i    : integer;
  sum  : real;
begin
  sum := 0;
  for i := 1 to n do
    sum := sum + x[ i,1 ];                    { first column only }
  total := sum
end; { total }
  ...

var

  l : matrix;                              { leslie matrix }
  x : matrix;                            { population vector }
  d : matrix;                        { dummy for multiplication }
  i, t : integer;                     { age class counter, time }

begin
  matread ( l, n, n );
  matread ( x, n, 1 );
  t := 0;
  writeln ( 'month', 'young':14, 'middle':15, 'old':14, 'total':14);
  writeln;

  for t := 1 to 24 do
    begin
      matmult ( l, x, d, n, n, n );
      x := d;
      write ( t:5 );
```

```
for i := 1 to 3 do
    write( x[ i,1 ]:14:0 );

writeln( total( x, n ):14:0 )
end;
```

Note that a one-dimensional array could be used for the population vector in place of the (10×10) array defined by the type **matrix**, if it is necessary to save space. **matmult** would then have to be rewritten, since both operands in the matrix multiplication are assumed to be of type **matrix**.

A function **total**, has been written to return the total population.

The output of the program, over a period of 24 months, is:

month	young	middle	old	total
0	0	0	1	1
1	12	0	0	12
2	0	4	0	4
3	36	0	2	38
4	24	12	0	36
5	108	8	6	122
6	144	36	4	184
...				
22	11184615	1864145	466016	13514776
23	22369496	3728201	932073	27029771
24	44738685	7456491	1864101	54059277

'Fractional' rabbits should be kept, and not rounded (and certainly not truncated). They occur because the fertility rates and survival probabilities are averages.

If you look carefully at the output you may spot that after some months the total population doubles every month. This factor is called the *growth factor*, and is a property of the particular Leslie matrix being used (for those who know about such things, it's the *dominant eigenvalue* of the matrix). The growth factor is 2 in this example, but if the values in the Leslie matrix are changed, the long-term growth factor changes too (try it and see).

You probably didn't spot that the numbers in the three age classes tend to a limiting ratio of 24:4:1. This can be demonstrated very clearly if you run the model with an initial population structure having this limiting ratio. This limiting ratio is called the *stable age distribution* of the population, and again it is a property of the Leslie matrix (in fact, it is the *eigenvector* belonging to the dominant eigenvalue of the matrix). Different population matrices lead to different stable age distributions.

The interesting point about this is that a given Leslie matrix always eventually gets a population into the same stable age distribution, which increases eventually by the same growth factor each month, no matter what the initial population breakdown is. For example, if you run the above model with any other initial population, it will always eventually get into a stable age distribution of 24:4:1 with a growth factor of 2 (try it and see).

15.4   Markov chains

Often a process that we wish to model may be represented by a number of possible *discrete* (i.e. discontinuous) states that describe the outcome of the process. For example, if we are spinning a coin, then the outcome is adequately represented by the two states 'heads' and 'tails' (and nothing in between). If the process is random, as it is with spinning coins, there is a certain probability of being in any of the states at a given moment, and also a probability of changing from one state to another. If the probability of moving from one state to another depends on the present state only, and not on any previous state, the process is called a *Markov chain.* Markov chains are used widely in such diverse fields as biology and business decision making, to name just two.

A random walk

Suppose a street in a university suburb has six intersections. An inebriated student wanders down the street. His home is at intersection 1, and his favourite bar at intersection 6. At each intersection other than his home or the bar he moves in the direction of the bar with probability $\frac{2}{3}$, and in the direction of his home with probability $\frac{1}{3}$. He never wanders down a side street. If he reaches his home or the bar, he disappears into them, never to reappear (when he disappears we say in Markov jargon that he has been *absorbed*).

We would like to know: what are the chances of our student ending up at home or in the bar, if he starts at a given corner (other than home or the bar, obviously)? He can clearly be in one of six states, with respect to his random walk, which can be labelled by the intersection number, where state 1 means Home and state 6 means Bar. We can represent the probabilities of being in these states by a six-component *state vector* $x(t)$, where $x_i(t)$ is the probability of him being at intersection i at moment t. The components of $x(t)$ must sum to 1, since he has to be in one of these states.

We can express this Markov process by the following *transition probability matrix*, P, where the rows represent the next state (i.e. corner), and the columns represent the present state:

	Home	2	3	4	5	Bar
Home	1	$\frac{1}{3}$	0	0	0	0
2	0	0	$\frac{1}{3}$	0	0	0
3	0	$\frac{2}{3}$	0	$\frac{1}{3}$	0	0
4	0	0	$\frac{2}{3}$	0	$\frac{1}{3}$	0
5	0	0	0	$\frac{2}{3}$	0	0
Bar	0	0	0	0	$\frac{2}{3}$	1

The entries for Home–Home and Bar–Bar are both 1 because he stays put there with certainty.

Using the probability matrix P we can work out his chances of being, say, at intersection 3 at moment $(t+1)$ as

$$x_3(t+1) = \tfrac{2}{3}x_2(t) + \tfrac{1}{3}x_4(t).$$

To get to 3, he must have been at either 2 or 4, and his chances of moving from there are $\frac{2}{3}$ and $\frac{1}{3}$, respectively.

Mathematically, this is identical to the Leslie matrix problem. We can therefore form the new state vector from the old one each time with a matrix equation:

$$x(t+1) = P\,x(t).$$

If we suppose the student starts at intersection 2, the initial probabilities will be $(0; 1; 0; 0; 0; 0)$. The Leslie matrix program may be adapted with very few changes to generate future states:

```
const
  n = 6;
  maxsize = 10;
type
  matrix = array [1..maxsize, 1..maxsize] of real;
  ...

var
  d, p, x : matrix;
  i, j, t : integer;
```

```
begin
   for i := 1 to n do
      for j := 1 to n do
         begin
            p[i,j] := 0; x[i,j] := 0; { initialize p and x to zero }
         end;

   for i := 3 to 6 do              { generate non-zero elements of p }
      begin
         p[i,i-1] := 2.0 /3;
         p[i-2,i-1] := 1.0 / 3
      end;

   p[1,1] := 1; p[6,6] := 1;
   x[2,1] := 1;

   t := 0;
   writeln( 'Time', 'Home':9, '2':9, '3':9, '4':9, '5':9, 'Bar':9 );
   writeln;

   for t := 1 to 50 do
      begin
         matmult( p, x, d, n, n, n );
         x := d;
         write( t:4 );

         for i := 1 to 6 do
            write( x[ i,1 ]:9:4 );

         writeln
      end;
```

Note that because of the symmetries in the probability matrix we can construct it with a **for** loop (the same applies to Leslie matrices).

Output is as follows:

Time	Home	2	3	4	5	Bar
1	0.3333	0.0000	0.6667	0.0000	0.0000	0.0000
2	0.3333	0.2222	0.0000	0.4444	0.0000	0.0000
3	0.4074	0.0000	0.2963	0.0000	0.2963	0.0000
4	0.4074	0.0988	0.0000	0.2963	0.0000	0.1975
5	0.4403	0.0000	0.1646	0.0000	0.1975	0.1975
6	0.4403	0.0549	0.0000	0.1756	0.0000	0.3292
7	0.4586	0.0000	0.0951	0.0000	0.1171	0.3292
8	0.4586	0.0317	0.0000	0.1024	0.0000	0.4073
9	0.4692	0.0000	0.0553	0.0000	0.0683	0.4073
10	0.4692	0.0184	0.0000	0.0596	0.0000	0.4528
...						
40	0.4839	0.0000	0.0000	0.0000	0.0000	0.5161
...						
50	0.4839	0.0000	0.0000	0.0000	0.0000	0.5161

By running the program for long enough, we soon find the limiting probabilities: he ends up at home about 48% of the time, and at the bar about 52% of the time. Perhaps this is a little surprising; from the transposition probabilities, we might have expected him to get to the bar rather more easily. It just goes to show that you should never trust your intuition when it comes to statistics!

Note that the Markov chain approach is not a simulation: we get the theoretical probabilities each time. But it is interesting to confirm the limiting probabilities by simulating the student's progress, using a random number generator (see Exercise 3 below).

15.5 Solution of linear equations

A problem that often arises in scientific applications is the solution of a system of linear equations, e.g.

$$2x - y + z = 4 \qquad (15.2)$$
$$x + y + z = 3 \qquad (15.3)$$
$$3x - y - z = 1. \qquad (15.4)$$

One method of solution is by *Gauss reduction*.

Gauss reduction

In Gauss reduction a matrix is constructed from the coefficients of the left-hand sides of the n equations to be solved. The right-hand side constants form the $(n + 1)$th column of the matrix, e.g.

$$\begin{bmatrix} 2 & -1 & 1 & \bigm| & 4 \\ 1 & 1 & 1 & \bigm| & 3 \\ 3 & -1 & -1 & \bigm| & 1 \end{bmatrix}$$

for the system above. This matrix is sometimes called the *augmented matrix A* of the system of equations. A series of arithmetic operations is performed on the rows of A, involving the subtraction of multiples of the rows from each other. If the equations have a unique solution, A will end up with the identity matrix (ones on the main diagonal, zeros everywhere else) in the first n columns, and the solution in the right-most column:

$$\begin{bmatrix} 1 & 0 & 0 & \bigm| & 1 \\ 0 & 1 & 0 & \bigm| & 0 \\ 0 & 0 & 1 & \bigm| & 2 \end{bmatrix}$$

The solution may therefore be read off as $x = 1$, $y = 0$, $z = 2$.

Two other situations could arise in Gauss reduction:

(i) A row of zeros could appear right across the array. In this case the system of equations is *indeterminate* and the solution can only be determined down to as many arbitrary constants as there are rows of zeros.

(ii) A row of the array could be filled with zeros, except for the extreme right-hand element. In this case the equations are *inconsistent*, which means there is no solution.

The following code uses a procedure **gauss** to perform a Gauss reduction on a system of equations, assuming a unique solution. It makes use of the procedures **matread** and **matwrite** described earlier. You should try it out on Equations (15.2)–(15.4):

```
const
   n         = 3;                    { actual number of equations }
   maxsize   = 10;
type
   matrix = array [1..maxsize, 1..maxsize] of real;

var
   a : matrix; { augmented matrix }
```

```
procedure gauss( var a: matrix; n : integer );

{------gauss--------------------------------------------------}
{                                                             }
{ performs a gauss reduction on the n equations in the augmented }
{ matrix a. the solution will be in the last column on return.   }
{-------------------------------------------------------------}

   var
      j, k, pivrow, tarrow : integer;
      pivelt, tarelt : real;
      dum : ^matrix;                          { pointer to matrix type }
   begin


      { make each row the pivot row in turn, and divide each element }
      { in the pivot row by the pivot element.                       }


      for pivrow := 1 to n do
      begin
         pivelt := a[pivrow, pivrow];

         if pivelt = 0 then                   { check for zero pivot }
            begin
               k := pivrow + 1; { run down rows to find non-zero pivot }
               while (pivelt = 0) and (k <=n) do
                  begin
                     pivelt := a[k, pivrow];
                     k := k + 1               { k will be too big by 1 }
                  end;

               if (pivelt = 0) then           { if it's still zero … }
                  begin
                     writeln( 'Can't find non-zero pivot' );
                     exit
                  end
               else
                  begin                       { non-zero pivot in row k …
                                                so swop pivrow and row k }
                     new( dum );         { temporary matrix for row swop }
                     k := k - 1;
                     dum^ := a;                     { make a copy of a }
                     for j := 1 to n+1 do
                        a[pivrow, j] := a[k, j];            { swop rows }
                     for j := 1 to n+1 do
                        a[k, j] := dum^[ pivrow, j];
                     dispose( dum )      { free the dynamic memory used }
                  end
            end;

         for j := 1 to n+1 do { now proceed with the non-zero pivot }
            a[pivrow, j] := a[pivrow, j] /pivelt;

{ then replace all other rows (target rows) by target row      }
{ minus pivot row minus pivot row times element in target row }
{ and pivot column.                                            }
```

```
        for tarrow := 1 to n do
            if tarrow <> pivrow then
            begin
                tarelt := a[tarrow, pivrow];
                for j := 1 to n+1 do
                    a[tarrow, j] := a[tarrow, j] - a[pivrow, j] * tarelt
            end
    end
end; { gauss }
begin
    writeln( 'Enter augmented matrix by rows:' );
    matread( a, n, n+1 );
    gauss( a, n );
    writeln( 'Solution is in last column:' );
    matwrite( a, n, n+1 );
    readln
end.
```

Summary

This chapter introduces the use of matrices in a number of useful applications. A matrix is represented in Pascal as a two-dimensional array. If a matrix is to be passed as a parameter to a procedure its maximum size must be specified in a type declaration. Additional parameters indicating its actual size may also need to be passed.

Most of the examples in the chapter involve matrix multiplication.

Exercises

1 Write a procedure

```
transpose ( var a : matrix; n, m : integer );
```

which replaces the $(n \times m)$ matrix A by its own transpose – an $(m \times n)$ matrix with a_{ij} replaced by a_{ji}.

2 Compute the limiting probabilities for the student in Section 15.4 when she starts at each of the remaining intersections in turn, and confirm that the closer she starts to the bar, the more likely she is to end up there.

3 Write a program to simulate the progress of the student in Section 15.4 down the street. Start her at a given intersection, and generate a random number to decide whether she moves toward the bar or home, according to the probabilities in the transition matrix. For each simulated random walk, record whether she ends up at home or in the bar. Repeat a large number of times. The proportion of walks that end up in either place should approach the theoretical limiting probabilities computed using the Markov model in Section 15.4.

Hint: if the random number in the range $[0; 1)$ is less than $\frac{2}{3}$ she moves toward the bar (unless already at home or the bar), otherwise she moves toward home.

4 Suppose we want to *invert* the matrix

$$A = \begin{bmatrix} 2 & 2 & 2 \\ 3 & 2 & 2 \\ 3 & 2 & 3 \end{bmatrix}$$

Construct the augmented matrix $A \mid I$, where I is the identity matrix:

$$\begin{bmatrix} 2 & 2 & 2 & 1 & 0 & 0 \\ 3 & 2 & 2 & 0 & 1 & 0 \\ 3 & 2 & 3 & 0 & 0 & 1 \end{bmatrix}$$

Now perform a Gauss reduction until the identity matrix has appeared to the left of the vertical line, so that the augmented array finally looks as follows:

$$\begin{bmatrix} 1 & 0 & 0 & -1 & 1 & 0 \\ 0 & 1 & 0 & \frac{3}{2} & 0 & -1 \\ 0 & 0 & 1 & 0 & -1 & 1 \end{bmatrix}$$

The matrix to the right of the line is the inverse of A. You can check by multiplying it by A; you should get the identity. If A is not invertible, the process breaks down and a row of zeros appears.

Write a procedure based on the procedure **gauss** that inverts a square matrix by Gauss reduction.

5   *Ill-conditioning* is a situation in numerical analysis where a small change in the coefficients of a problem causes a large change in the solution. The following system, suggested by T.S. Wilson, illustrates this very nicely:

$$10x + 7y + 8z + 7w = 32$$
$$7x + 5y + 6z + 5w = 23$$
$$8x + 6y + 10z + 9w = 33$$
$$7x + 5y + 9z + 10w = 31.$$

Use the procedure **gauss** to show that the solution is $x = y = z = w = 1$. Then change the right-hand side constants to 32.01, 22.99, 32.99 and 31.01 (a change of about 1 in 3000) and find the new solution. Finally, change the right-hand side constants to 32.1, 22.9, 32.9 and 31.1 and observe what effect this has on the 'solution'.

16

Introduction to numerical methods

A major scientific use of computers is in finding numerical solutions to mathematical problems which have no analytical solutions, i.e. solutions which may be written down in terms of polynomials and the known mathematical functions. In this chapter we look briefly at three areas where numerical methods have been highly developed: solving equations, evaluating integrals, and solving differential equations.

16.1 Equations

In this section we consider how to solve equations in one unknown numerically. The general way of expressing the problem is to say that we want to solve the equation $f(x) = 0$, i.e. we want to find its *root* (or roots) x. There is no general method for finding roots analytically for any given $f(x)$.

Newton's method

Newton's method is the easiest numerical method for solving equations. It is an *iterative* method, meaning that it repeatedly attempts to improve an estimate of the root, as follows: if x_k is an approximation to the root, the next approximation x_{k+1} is given by

$$x_{k+1} = x_k - \frac{f(x_k)}{f'(x_k)}$$

where $f'(x)$ is df/dx.

Newton's method may be described algorithmically as follows:

Read in starting value x_0 and required accuracy e
While $|f(x_k)| \geq e$ repeat up to $k = 20$ times, say
   $x_{k+1} = x_k - f(x_k)/f'(x_k)$
   Print x_{k+1} and $f(x_{k+1})$
Decide whether the process converged
Stop.

Note that there are two conditions that will stop the loop: convergence of the process, or the completion of, say, 20 iterations. A test is therefore required to see why the loop stopped.

To solve the equation $x^3 + x - 3 = 0$, we must have $f(x) = x^3 + x - 3$, which means that $f'(x) = 3x^2 + 1$. A program which implements Newton's method to solve this equation is as follows:

```
Program newton;

function f ( x : real ) : real;
{ the equation to be solved }
```

```
begin
  f := x * x * x + x - 3
end; { f }

function df ( x : real ) : real;
{ derivatives of f(x) }
begin
  df := 3 * x * x + 1
end; { df }

const
  eps : real = 1e-6;                    { maximum error }
  its : integer = 0;                   { iteration counter }
  max : integer = 20;                  { maximum iterations }

var
  converged  : boolean;                { convergence flag }
  x          : real;                          { unknown }

begin
  readln( x);                          { read the initial guess }
  converged := abs( f(x) ) <= eps;

  while (not converged) and (its < max) do
    begin
      x := x - f(x) /df(x);
      writeln( x:10:6, ' ', f(x):11 );
      its := its + 1;
      converged := abs( f(x) ) <= eps
    end;

  writeln;
  if converged then
    writeln( 'convergence achieved' )
  else
    writeln( 'convergence not achieved' );
  readln
end.
```

If we start with $x_0 = 2$, the output is as follows:

```
1.461538      1.58E+0000
1.247788      1.91E-0001
1.214185      4.19E-0003
1.213412      2.17E-0006
1.213412     -4.03E-0013

convergence achieved
```

As an exercise, try running the program with different starting values of x_0 to see whether the algorithm always converges.

Also try finding a non-zero root of $2x = \tan(x)$, using Newton's method. You might have some trouble with this one. If you do, you will have demonstrated the one serious problem with Newton's method: it converged to a root only if the starting guess is 'close enough'. Since 'close enough' depends on the nature of $f(x)$ and on the root, one can obviously get into difficulties here. The only remedy is some intelligent trial-and-error work on the initial guess – this is made considerably easier by sketching $f(x)$ carefully.

If Newton's method fails to find a root, the bisection method, discussed below, may be used.

The bisection method

Consider again the problem of solving the equation $f(x) = 0$, where

$$f(x) = x^3 + x - 3$$

We attempt to find by inspection, or trial-and-error, two values of x, call them x_L and x_R, such that $f(x_L)$ and $f(x_R)$ have different signs, i.e. $f(x_L)f(x_R) < 0$. If we can find two such values, the root must lie somewhere in the interval between them, since $f(x)$ changes sign on this interval (see Fig. 16.1). In this example, $x_L = 1$ and $x_R = 2$ will do, since $f(1) = -1$ and $f(2) = 7$. In the bisection method, we estimate the root by x_M, where x_M is the midpoint of the interval $[x_L, x_R]$, i.e.

$$x_M = (x_L + x_R)/2 \tag{16.1}$$

Then if $f(x_M)$ has the same sign as $f(x_L)$, as drawn in the figure, the root clearly lies between x_M and x_R. We must then redefine the left-hand end of the interval as having the value of x_M, i.e. we let the new value of x_L be x_M. Otherwise, if $f(x_M)$ and $f(x_L)$ have different signs, we let the new value of x_R be x_M, since the root must lie between x_L and x_M in that case. Having redefined x_L or x_R, as the case may be, we bisect the new interval again according to Equation (16.1) and repeat the process until the distance between x_L and x_R is as small as we please.

The neat thing about this method is that we can calculate *before* starting how many bisections are needed to obtain a certain accuracy, given initial values of x_L and x_R. Suppose we start with $x_L = a$, and $x_R = b$. After the first bisection the worst possible error (E_1) in x_M is $E_1 = |a - b|/2$, since we are estimating the root as being at the midpoint of the interval $[a, b]$. The worst that can happen is that the root is actually at x_L or x_R, in which case the error is E_1. Carrying on like this, after n bisections the worst possible error E_n is given by $E_n = |a - b|/2^n$. If we want to be sure that this is less than some specified error E, we must see to it that n satisfies the inequality $|a - b|/2^n < E$, i.e.

$$n > \frac{\log(|a - b|/E)}{\log(2)} \tag{16.2}$$

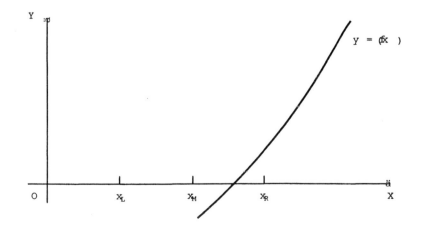

Fig. 16.1 The bisection method

Since n is the number of bisections, it must be an integer. The smallest integer n that exceeds the right-hand side of inequality (16.2) will do as the maximum number of bisections required to guarantee the given accuracy E.

The following scheme may be used to program the bisection method. It will work for any function $f(x)$ that changes sign (in either direction) between the two values a and b, which must be found beforehand by the user. The program follows below.

Read a, b and E
Initialise x_L and x_R
Compute maximum bisections n from inequality (16.2)
Repeat n times:
    Compute x_M according to Equation (16.1)
    If $f(x_L)f(x_M) > 0$ then
      Let $x_L = x_M$
    Else
      Let $x_R = x_M$
Print root x_M
Stop.

We have assumed that the procedure will not find the root exactly; the chances of this happening with real variables are infinitesimal.

Passing subprograms as parameters

In Section 5.4 we mentioned that Pascal allows subprograms (functions or procedures) to be passed as parameters. Turbo Pascal implements this feature by means of *procedural types*. The following program demonstrates the use of procedural type with the bisection method:

```
Program test;

type
   fung = function ( x : real ) : real;

function bisect ( a, b, e : real; var n : integer; f : fung ) : real;
{ function f to be solved is passed as a procedural parameter }
var
   xL, xM, xR : real;
   i : integer;
begin
   sL := a;
   xR := b;
   n := trunc( ln( abs(a - b)/e ) / ln( 2 ) ) + 1;

   for i := 1 to n do
     begin
       xM := (xL + xR) /2;
       if f(xL) * f(xM) > 0 then
         xL := xM
       else
         xR := xM
     end

     bisect := xM;                              { return the root }
   end; { bisect }

{$F+}
function y ( x : real ) : real;
{ this function will be passed to bisect as a procedural parameter }
```

```
begin
   y := x * x * x + x - 3
end; { y }
{$F-}

var
   a, b, e, x : real;
   n : integer;

begin
   readln( a, b, e );
   x := bisect( a, b, e, n, y );
   writeln( 'Bisections: ', n );
   writeln( x:8:4, ' ', y ( x ):10 );
   readln
end.
```

Note

(i)   A procedural type **fung** is declared.

(ii) The function **bisect** has a parameter **f** of this procedural type.

(iii) The subprogram to be passed as a parameter (**y** in this example) must be compiled in the **{$F+}** state.

(iv) The effect of **bisect**'s procedural parameter **fung** is that it may be passed by any real function whose header contains a single real parameter.

(v)   The declaration of **fung** and the code for **bisect** could be compiled independently as a unit.

Here is some output from a sample run:

```
Bisections: 14
   1.2134    1.5E-0004
```

16.2   Integration

Although most 'respectable' mathematical functions can be differentiated analytically, the same cannot be said for integration. There are no general rules for integrating, as there are for differentiating. For example, the indefinite integral of a function as simple as e^{-x^2} cannot be found analytically. We therefore need a numerical method for evaluating integrals.

This is quite easy to do, and depends on the well-known fact that the definite integral of a function $f(x)$ between the limits $x = a$ and $x = b$ is equal to the area under $f(x)$ bounded by the x-axis and the two vertical lines $x = a$ and $x = b$. So all numerical methods for integrating simply involve more or less ingenious ways of estimating the area under $f(x)$.

The trapezoidal rule

One of the standard methods is the trapezoidal (or trapezium) rule. The area under $f(x)$ is divided into vertical panels each of width h, called the *step-length*. If there are n such panels, then $nh = b - a$, i.e. $n = (b - a)/h$. If we join the points where successive panels cut $f(x)$, we can estimate the area under $f(x)$ as the sum of the area of the resulting trapezia. If we call this approximation the integral S, then

$$S = \frac{h}{2}\left[f(a) + f(b) + 2\sum_{i=1}^{n-1} f(x_i)\right] \tag{16.3}$$

where $x_i = a + ih$. Equation (16.3) is the trapezoidal rule, and provides an estimate for the integral

$$\int_a^b f(x)\, \mathrm{d}x$$

The following code passes the function $y(x) = x^3$ to the procedure **trap** which implements the trapezoidal rule to integrate it between the limits 0 and 4.

```
Program integrator;
type
   integral = function ( x : real ) : real;
var
   a, b, h, s: real;

{$F+}
function y( x: real ): real;
{ integrand }
begin
   y := x * x * x
end; { y }
{$F-}


procedure trap( var s : real; a, b, h : real; f : integrand );
{ Trapezoidal rule to integrate f(x) from a to b with step-length h }
var
   i, n : integer;
begin
   s := 0;
   n := round( (b - a) /h );
   for i := 1 to n-1 do
      s := s + f( a + i * h );
   s := h /2 * (f( a ) + f( b ) + 2 * s)
end; { trap }


begin
   a := 0;
   b := 4;
   write( 'h? ' );
   readln( h );
   trap( s, a, b, h, y );
   writeln( 'integral by trapezoidal rule: ', s:8:4 );
   readln
end.
```

With $h = 0.01$, the estimate is 64.0004 (the exact integral is 64). You will find that as h gets smaller, the estimate gets more accurate.

Simpson's rule

Simpson's rule is a method of numerical integration which is a good deal more accurate than the trapezoidal rule, and should always be used before you try anything fancier. It also divides the area under the function to be integrated, $f(x)$, into vertical panels, but instead of joining the points $f(x_i)$ with straight lines, every set of three such successive points is fitted with a parabola. To ensure that there are always an even number of panels, the step-length n is usually chosen so that there are $2n$ panels, i.e. $n = (b - a)/(2h)$.

Using the same notation as above, Simpson's rule estimates the integral as

$$S = \frac{h}{3}\left[f(a) + f(b) + 2\sum_{i=1}^{n-1} f(x_{2i}) + 4\sum_{i=1}^{n} f(x_{2i-1}) \right]$$

This rule can be coded as a function Simp() to join your growing stable of numerical utilities:

```
type
   integrand = function ( x : real ) : real;
   ...

procedure simp( var s : real; a, b, h : real; f : integrand );
{ uses Simpson's rule to integrate f(x) from a to b with
                                              step-length h }
var
   i, n : integer;
begin
   s := 0;
   n := round( (b - a) / (2 * h) );              { 2n panels now }
   for i := 1 to n-1 do
     s := s + 2 * f( a + 2 * i * h );
   for i := 1 to n do
     s := s + 4 * f( a + (2 * i - 1) * h );

   s := h /3 * ( f( a ) + f( b ) + s )
end; { simp }
```

Note that n is half its previous value.

If you try out Simpson's rule on $f(x) = x^3$ between any limits, you will find rather surprisingly that it gives the same result as the exact mathematical solution. This is a nice extra benefit of the rule: it integrates cubic polynomials exactly (which can be proved).

16.3 Numerical differentiation

The *Newton quotient* for a function $f(x)$ is given by

$$\frac{f(x + h) + f(x)}{h}$$

where h is 'small'. As h tends to zero, this quotient approaches the first derivative, df/dx. The Newton quotient may therefore be used to estimate a derivative numerically.

The next program uses the Newton quotient to draw the derivative df of a given function f. A procedural type is used, so that either f or df may be passed to drawfunc. You will be surprised at the effect different values of h, between 2 and 0.0001, say, have on the numerical derivative of the particular function used here.

```
Program derivatives;
uses crt, graph, myworld;
type
   func = function( x : real ) : real;
const
   xmin : real = 0;
   xmax : real = 10;
   ymin : real = -8;
   ymax : real = 8;
var
   h, x : real;
   grdriver, grmode : integer;

procedure axes;
begin
   wline( xmin, 0, xmax, 0 );
   wline( 0, ymin, 0, ymax )
end; { axes }
```

```
{$F+}
function f ( x : real ) : real;
begin
  f := 4 * sin ( x ) + cos ( 4 * x )
end; { f }

function df ( x: real ): real;
begin
  df := (f ( x + h ) - f ( x )) /h
end; { df }
{$F-}

procedure drawfunc ( f: func );
begin
  x := 0;
  wmoveto ( x, f ( x ) );
  while x < xmax do
  begin
    wlineto ( x, f ( x ) );
    x := x + pi / 40
  end
end; { drawfunc }
begin
  grdriver := detect;
  initgraph ( grdriver, grmode, 'c:\tp6\bgi' );
  setviewpoint ( 0, 0, getmaxx, getmaxy div 2 - 10, true );
  setwindow ( xmin, xmax, ymin, ymax );
                                    { upper window for function }
  axes;
  drawfunc ( f );
  outtextxy ( 5, 5, 'h? ' );
  gotoxy ( 5, 1 );
  readln ( h );
  setviewport ( 0, getmaxy div 2 - 5, getmaxx, getmaxy - 10, true );
  setwindow ( xmin, xmax, ymin, ymax );
                                    { lower window for derivative }
  axes;
  drawfunc ( df );
  readln;
  closegraph
end.
```

16.4 First-order differential equations

The most interesting situations in real life that we may want to model, or represent quantitatively, are usually those in which the variables change in time (e.g. biological, electrical or mechanical systems). If the changes are continuous, the system can often be represented with equations involving the derivatives of the dependent variables. Such equations are called *differential* equations. Very few differential equations can be solved analytically, so once again numerical methods are required. We will look at the simplest method of numerical solution in this section: Euler's method. We will also consider briefly how to improve it.

Euler's method for air resistance

To illustrate Euler's method, we will take an example from Newtonian dynamics, of motion under gravity against air resistance. Suppose a skydiver steps out of a hovering helicopter, but does not open his parachute for 24 seconds. We would like to find his velocity as a function of time during this period. Assuming air resistance cannot be neglected (ask any skydiver!), he falls subject to two opposing vertical forces: gravity acting downward, and air resistance acting upward. The air resistance force is assumed to be proportional to the square of his velocity (this is fairly accurate). Applying Newton's second law to the skydiver, we arrive at

$$\frac{dv}{dt} = g - kv^2 \tag{16.4}$$

where g is the acceleration due to gravity and v his velocity at time t after opening the parachute. Equation (16.4) is the differential equation describing the motion of the skydiver under gravity. The constant k varies with shape and mass, and may be found experimentally from the *terminal velocity* of the falling object. This terminal velocity (v_T) is reached when the object stops accelerating, and may be found by equating the right-hand side of Equation (16.4) to zero. Thus

$$v_T = \sqrt{g/k}$$

For a man wearing an unopened parachute, k is found to be about 0.004 in SI units. Before we proceed with the numerical solution of Equation (16.4) we should note that this particular differential equation can be solved analytically, since it is of the type called variables separable:

$$v(t) = \frac{a(C - e^{-2akt})}{C + e^{-2akt}} \tag{16.5}$$

where $a = v_T$ and $C = [a + v(0)]/[a - v(0)]$.

Euler's method for solving Equation (16.4) numerically consists of approximating the derivative on the left-hand side by its Newton quotient. After a slight rearrangement of terms, we get

$$v(t + h) \approx v(t) + h[g - kv^2(t)] \tag{16.6}$$

If we divide up the time period t into n intervals of h, then $t = nh$. If we define v_n as $v(t)$, then $v_{n+1}(t + h)$. We can therefore replace Equation (16.6) with the iterative scheme

$$v_{n+1} = v_n + h(g - kv_n^2) \tag{16.7}$$

Since we are given the initial condition $v_0 = 0$, Equation (16.7) provides a numerical scheme for finding the Euler approximation v_n in general.

It is very easy to program Euler's method. We can also test its accuracy by trying different values of h and comparing the results with the exact solution. The following program uses Euler's method as implemented in Equation (16.7) to estimate v for the first 24 seconds of the skydiver's motion. It also computes the exact solution for comparison.

```
Program euler; { rhymes with boiler }
const
   g : real = 9.8;
var
   h k, t, t0, tend, v, v0 : real;
function vexact ( t, v0, k : real ) : real;
{ exact formula for skydiver's velocity }
var
   a, c : real;
```

```
begin
   a := sqrt( g / k );
   c := (a + v0) / ( a - v0);
   vexact := a * (c - exp(-2 * a * k * t)) / (c + exp(-2 * a * k * t))
end; { vexact }

begin
   writeln ( 'Enter k, h, t0, v(t0), tend: ' );
   readln ( k, h, t, v0, tend );
   v := v0;
   writeln ( 'Time':10, 'Euler':10, 'Exact':10 );

   while t <= tend do
      begin
         writeln ( t:10:2, v:10:2, vexact( t, v0, k ):10:2 );
         v := v + h * (g - k * v * v);
         t := t + h
      end;

   readln
end.
```

Taking $h = 2$ and $k = 0.004$ we get:

Time	Euler	Exact
0.00	0.00	0.00
2.00	19.60	18.64
4.00	36.13	32.64
6.00	45.29	41.08
8.00	48.48	45.50
10.00	49.28	47.65
12.00	49.45	48.65
14.00	49.49	49.11
16.00	49.50	49.32
18.00	49.50	49.42
20.00	49.50	49.46
22.00	49.50	49.48
24.00	49.50	49.49

Euler's method gets more accurate if you reduce h, e.g. with $h = 0.5$ the worst error is only about 3%. Note that the errors get smaller as terminal velocity approaches.

Now let's see what happens when the skydiver opens his parachute. The air resistance term will be different now. For an open parachute, $k = 0.3$ is quite realistic. We can use the same program as before, although we need to supply a new starting value of 49.49 for v. Since $h = 0.5$ worked well before, we try the same value now. The results are rather surprising. Not only does Euler's solution show that the man flies upward, he does so with tremendous speed, and soon exceeds the speed of light! The results make nonsense physically. Fortunately, in this example our intuition tells us that something is wrong. The only remedy is to reduce h. Some experimenting will reveal that the results for $h = 0.01$ are much better.

Finally, note that Euler's method will be just as easy to compute if the air resistance term is not kv^2, but $kv^{1.8}$ (which is more realistic), although now an analytic solution cannot be found.

Euler's method for bacteria growth

Euler's method performs quite adequately in the skydiver problem once we have got the right value of the step-length h. In case you think that the numerical solution of all differential equations is just as easy, we will now consider an example where Euler's method doesn't do too well.

Suppose a colony of 1000 bacteria are multiplying at the rate of $r = 0.8$ per hour per individual (i.e. an individual produces an average of 0.8 offspring every hour). How many bacteria are there after 10 hours? Assuming that the colony grows continuously and without restriction, we can model this growth with the differential equation

$$\frac{dN}{dt} = rN, \qquad N(0) = 1000 \tag{16.8}$$

where $N(t)$ is the population size at time t. This process is called *exponential growth*. Equation (16.8) may be solved analytically to give the well-known formula for exponential growth, $N(t) = N(0)e^{rt}$. To solve Equation (16.8) numerically, we apply Euler's algorithm to it to get

$$N_{k+1} = N_k + rhN_k$$

where $N_k = N(t)$, and $N_0 = 1000$. Taking $h = 0.5$ gives the results shown in Table 16.1, where the exact solution is also given.

This time the numerical solution (in the column headed Euler) is not too good. In fact, the error gets worse at each step, and after 10 hours of bacteria time it is about 72%. Of course, the numerical solution will improve if we take h smaller, but there will still always be a value of t where the error exceeds some acceptable limit.

You may wonder why Euler's method works so well with the skydiver, but so badly with the bacteria. The answer is to do with the second derivative of v; in the first case it gets smaller as time increases, whereas in the second case it grows without bound.

There are better numerical methods for overcoming these sorts of problems. Two of them are discussed below. More sophisticated methods may be found in most textbooks on numerical analysis. However, Euler's method may always be used as a first approximation as long as you realise where and why errors may arise.

A predictor–corrector method

One improvement on the solution of

$$\frac{dy}{dx} = f(x, y), \qquad y(0) \text{ given}$$

Table 16.1   Bacteria growth

Time	Euler	Predictor corrector	Exact
0.0	1 000	1 000	1 000
0.5	1 400	1 480	1 492
1.0	1 960	2 190	2 226
1.5	2 744	3 242	3 320
2.0	3 842	4 798	4 953
...			
5.0	28 925	50 422	54 598
...			
8.0	217 795	529 892	601 845
...			
10.0	836 683	2 542 344	2 980 958

is as follows. The Euler approximation, which we are going to denote by an asterisk, is given by

$$y_{k+1}^* = y_k + hf(x_k, y_k) \tag{16.9}$$

But this formula favours the old value of y in computing $f(x_k, y_k)$ on the right-hand side. Surely it would be better to say

$$y_{k+1}^* = y_k + h[f(x_{k+1}, y_{k+1}^*) + f(x_k, y_k)]/2 \tag{16.10}$$

where $x_{k+1} = x + h$, since this also involves the new value y_{k+1}^* in computing f on the right-hand side? The problem of course is that y_{k+1}^* is as yet unknown, so we can't use it on the right-hand side of Equation (16.10). But we could use Euler to estimate (predict) y_{k+1}^* from Equation (16.9) and then use Equation (16.10) to correct the prediction by computing a better version of y_{k+1}^*, which we will call y_{k+1}. So the full procedure is:

Repeat as many times as required:
    Use Euler to predict: $y_{k+1}^* = y_k + hf(x_k, y_k)$
    Then correct y_{k+1}^* to: $y_{k+1} = y_k + h[f(x_{k+1}, y_{k+1}^*) + f(x_k, y_k)]/2$

This is called a *predictor–corrector* method. The program above can easily be adapted to this problem. The relevant lines of code, which will generate all the entries in Table 16.1 at once, are:

```
while t <= 10 do
  begin
    writeln ( t:5:1, ne:12:0, nc:12:0, n0 * exp ( r * t ):12:0 );
    ne := ne + r * h * ne;                    { straight Euler }
    np := nc + r * h * nc;                     { predictor }
    nc := nc + r * h * (np + nc) / 2;          { corrector }
    t := t + h
  end;
```

ne stands for the 'straight' (uncorrected) Euler solution, np is the Euler predictor, and nc is the corrector. They must all be initialised to N_0. The worst error is now only 15%. This is much better than the uncorrected Euler solution, although there is still room for improvement.

16.5 Runge–Kutta methods

There are a variety of algorithms, under the general name of Runge–Kutta, which can be used to integrate ordinary differential equations. The *fourth-order* formula is given below, for reference. A derivation of this and the other Runge–Kutta formulae can be found in most books on numerical analysis.

Runge–Kutta fourth-order formulae

The general first-order differential equation is

$$\frac{dy}{dx} = f(x, y), \qquad y(0) \text{ given.} \tag{16.11}$$

The fourth-order Runge–Kutta estimate y^* at $x + h$ is given by

$$y^* = y + (k_1 + 2k_2 + 2k_3 + k_4)/6$$

where

$$k_1 = hf(x, y)$$
$$k = hf(x + 0.5h, y + 0.5k_1)$$
$$k_3 = hf(x + 0.5h, y + 0.5k_2)$$
$$k_4 = hf(x + h, y + k_3)$$

Systems of differential equations: a predator–prey model

The Runge–Kutta formulae may be adapted to integrate systems of first-order differential equations. Here we adapt the fourth-order formulae to integrate the well-known Lotka–Volterra predator–prey model:

$$\frac{dx}{dy} = px - qxy \qquad\qquad (16.12)$$

$$\frac{dy}{dt} = rxy - sy \qquad\qquad (16.13)$$

where $x(t)$ and $y(t)$ are the prey and predator population sizes at time t, and p, q, r and s are biologically determined parameters. We define $f(x, y)$ and $g(x, y)$ as the right-hand sides of Equations (16.12) and (16.13), respectively. In this case, the Runge–Kutta estimates x^* and y^* at time $(t + h)$ may be found from x and y at time t with the formulae

$$x^* = x + (k_1 + 2k_2 + 2k_3 + k_4)/6$$
$$y^* = y + (m_1 + 2m_2 + 2m_3 + m_4)/6$$

where

$$k_1 = hf(x, y)$$
$$m_1 = hg(x, y)$$
$$k_2 = hf(x + 0.5k_1, y + 0.5m_1)$$
$$m_2 = hg(x + 0.5k_1, y + 0.5m_1)$$
$$k_3 = hf(x + 0.5k_2, y + 0.5m_2)$$
$$m_3 = hg(x + 0.5k_2, y + 0.5m_2)$$
$$k_4 = hf(x + k_3, y + m_3)$$
$$m_4 = hg(x + k_3, y + m_3)$$

It should be noted that in this example x and y are the dependent variables, and t (which does not appear explicitly in the equations) is the independent variable. In Equation (16.11) y is the dependent variable, and x is the independent variable.

16.6 A differential equation modelling package

This section implements a skeleton *interactive modelling* program, **driver**. Its basis is a fourth-order Runge–Kutta procedure to integrate a time-based system of first-order differential equations. The example used below is the predator–prey model of the previous section, with $x(0) = 105$, $y(0) = 8$, $p = 0.4$, $q = 0.04$, $r = 0.02$, and $s = 2$.

A brief discussion follows the program listing.

```
Program driver;
{ interactive solution of differential equations }
{ email author at bdh@maths.uct.ac.za
    for complete version plus user manual }

uses crt, graph, myworld;
const
    first : boolean  = true;
    nvar             = 2;              { number of variables }
    npar             = 4;              { number of parameters }
    outwidth         = 10;
```

```pascal
type
  str2    = string[2];
  str8    = string[8];
  vartype = record
        name : str8;
        inval, val, lobound, upbound : real
            end;
  partype = record
            name : str8;
            val : real
          end;
var
  ans                  : str2;
  t, dt                : real;                    { model time }
  xmin, xmax, ymin, ymax : real;
  opintscr             : longint; { output interval on screen }
  optype               : byte;    { 1 : table; 2: phase plane }
  grdriver, grmode, i  : integer;
  runtime, time        : longint;            { iteration count }

  params : array[ 1..npar ] of partype;

  varias: array[ 1..nvar ] of vartype;

procedure header; forward;
procedure model: forward;
procedure out1( which : integer ); forward;
procedure out2; forward;

procedure carryon;
{ continue running model from current values of variables }
begin
  header;
  first := false;
  model
end; { carryon }

procedure change;
{ allows certain changes }
begin
  writeln ( 'present values of runtime and dt are: ', runtime,
        ' ', dt:11 );
  write( 'enter new values: ' );
  readln( runtime, dt )
end; { change }

procedure header;
{ headings for table output }
{ sets up graphics for phase plane output }
begin
  if optype = 1 then                              { table output}
    begin
      writeln;
      writeln( 'time', varias[1].name:outwidth,
          varias[2].name:outwidth );
      writeln
    end
  else if optype = 2 then                    { phase plane output }
```

```
    begin
      setgraphmode( grmode );
      xmin := varias[1].lobound;
      xmax := varias[1].upbound;
      ymin := varias[2].lobound;
      ymax := varias[2].upbound;
      setwindow( xmin, xmax, ymin, ymax );
      wline( xmin, ymin, xmax, ymin );
      wline( xmin, ymin, xmin, ymax );
      wouttextxy( (xmin + xmax) /2, ymin + 0.05 * (ymax - ymin),
            varias[1].name );
      settextstyle( defaultfont, vertdir, 1 );
      wouttextxy( xmin + 0.02 * (xmax - xmin), (ymin + ymax) /2,
                  varias[2].name );
      wmoveto( varias[1].val, varias[2].val )
    end
end;

procedure initial;
{ initialize everything }
begin
  params[1].val := 0.4;
  params[2].val := 0.04;
  params[3].val := 0.02;
  params[4].val := 2;
  varias[1].name := 'prey';
  varias[2].name := 'pred';
  varias[1].inval := 105;
  varias[2].inval := 8;
  varias[1].val := 105;
  varias[2].val := 8;
  varias[1].lobound := 85;
  varias[1].upbound := 115;
  varias[2].lobound := 7;
  varias[2].upbound := 13;
  dt := 1;
  t := 0;
  time := 0;
  runtime := 10;
  opintscr := 1;
  optype := 1
end; { initial }

procedure intervals;
{ allows change of output interval }
begin
  writeln( 'present screen output interval is: ', opintscr );
  write( 'enter new screen output interval (0 for no output): ' );
  readln( opintscr )
end; { intervals }

procedure model;
var
  itime : longint;
  f : array[ 1..nvar ] of real;

  procedure diffeqns;
  { model differential equations }
```

```
var
  prey, pred : ^real;                              { variable aliases }
  p, q, r, s : ^real;                              { parameter aliases }
begin
  prey := @varias[1].val;
  pred := @varias[2].val;
  p := @params[1].val;
  q := @params[2].val;
  r := @params[3].val;
  s := @params[4].val;
  f[1] := p^ * prey^ - q^ * prey^ * pred^;
  f[2] := r^ * prey^ * pred^ - s^ * pred^
end; { diffeqns }

procedure runge4;
{ fourth-order runge-kutta }
var
  h, z : real;
  a, b, c, d, x : array[ 1..nvar ] of real;   { working space }
  i : byte;

begin
  for i := 1 to nvar do
    x[i] := varias[i].val;
  diffeqns;
  for i := 1 to nvar do
    a[i] := dt * f[i];
  for i := 1 to nvar do
    varias[i].val := x[i] + a[i] / 2;
  diffeqns;
  for i := 1 to nvar do
    b[i] := dt * f[i];
  for i := 1 to nvar do
    varias[i].val := x[i] + b[i] /2;
  diffeqns;
  for i := 1 to nvar do
    c[i] := dt * f[i];
  for i := 1 to nvar do
    varias[i].val := x[i] + c[i];
  diffeqns;
  for i := 1 to nvar do
    begin
      d[i] := dt * f[i];
      varias[i].val := x[i] + (a[i] + 2 * b[i] + 2 * c[i] + d[i]) /6
    end
  end { runge4 };

begin
  out1( -1 );                                     { display initial values }
  for itime := 1 to runtime do
    begin
      time := time + 1                            { total iteration count }
      t := t + dt;                           { model time if we need it }
      runge4;
      out1( 0 )
    end;
  out2

end; { model }
```

```
procedure opengraphics;
begin
  grdriver := detect;
  initgraph( grdriver, grmode, 'c:\tp6\bgi' );
end;

procedure out1;
{ organizes output }
var
  screen : boolean;
  frscr : real;
begin
  screen := false;
  if which = -1 then
    screen := true
  else
    begin
      frscr := frac( abs( time ) /opintscr );
      if (1 - 1e-7 < frscr) or (frscr < 1e-7) then
        screen := true
    end;
  case optype of
    1: if screen then
        writeln( t:4:1, varias[1].val:outwidth:2,
                        varias[2].val:outwidth:2 );
    2: if screen then
        wlineto( varias[1].val, varias[2].val )
  end
end; { out1 }

procedure out2;
{ tidies up at end of run }
begin
  if optype = 2 then
    begin
      readln;
      restorecrtmode
    end;
end; { out2 }

procedure run;
{ runs model from initial values }
begin
  t := 0;
  time := 0;
  for i := 1 to nvar do
    varias[i].val := varias[i].inval;
  header;
  model
end; { run }

procedure upper;
{ converts user response to uppercase }
var
  dum : str2;
begin
  for i := 1 to 2 do
    insert( upcase( ans[i] ), dum, i );
  ans := dum
end; { upper }
```

```
begin { driver }
  initial;
  clrscr;
  opengraphics;
  restorecrtmode;
  writeln( 'pocket version of driver: the interactive modelling tool' );

  repeat
    ans := '';
    writeln;
    write( 'what shall I do now? ' );
    readln( ans );
    upper;
    if ans = 'CA' then
      carryon
    else if ans = 'CH' then
      change
    else if ans = 'GO' then
      run
    else if ans = 'IN' then
      intervals
    else if ans = 'P' then
      begin
        optype := 2;
        writeln( 'phase plane output')
      end
    else if ans = 'TA' then
      begin
        optype := 1;
        writeln( 'table output' )
      end
  until ans = 'KI';

  closegraph
end. { driver }
```

Each model variable is represented by an element of a global array **varias**, of type **vartype**, which has fields for various properties of the variable, such as its common name (e.g. 'pred'), initial value, current value, etc. The current value is kept so that the user may run the model either from the initial values, or the current values. The model parameters are represented by a similar array **params** of type **partype**.

There are a number of other global variables, which are described in comments.

The part of the program which implements the model is the procedure **model**, and in particular its local procedure **diffeqns**, which evaluates the right-hand side of the ith model differential equation in the ith element of the array **f**. To enable the user to have more meaningful symbolic names for parameters and variables, *aliases* are set up between the user's symbolic names and the **driver** arrays **varias** and **params**. This is done with pointers, e.g. **prey** and **pred**, declared ^**real**. The addresses of **driver** variables are assigned to these pointers with the Turbo Pascal address operator **@**. The variables addressed by the pointers, or referents, e.g. **prey^**, are then aliases for the respective **driver** variables. In other words, **prey^** and **varias[1].val**, for example, refer to the same memory location.

driver is driven by commands from the user. It allows you to start integrating the model equations from the initial conditions ('GO'), or from the current values ('CA' for Carry On). The 'TA' command sets the output mode to table form. 'PH' sets the output mode to phase plane trajectories, i.e. a graph of $x(t)$ against $y(t)$ as t increases. You can change ('CH') the values of the integration step-length and the total running time (number of step-lengths). 'IN' enables you to set the output interval in multiples of the step-length. The sample output below shows the response to 'GO' and 'TA' mode with the data as given.

We will look at some of the other procedures roughly in the order in which they are executed.

initial sets up model variable and parameter names, values and graph bounds, and also initialises other global variables. Note that all this information could be read from a disk file (which itself could be set up by another procedure), and written back to the file at the end of a session. In this way you could start a new session from where the previous one left off.

opengraphics initialises graphics.

Suppose you choose the 'GO' option from the main menu. This invokes the procedure run. Model time t is set to zero, the current values of the model variables are reset to their initial values, header sets up headings for table output or draws axes for phase plane output, and finally model actually runs the model by calling runge4.

model also calls out1 to generate appropriate output at the end of each time step. out1 includes a piece of code to ensure that output occurs at the correct multiple of the step-length, as set by 'IN'.

When the run is complete, out2 is called to terminate output neatly.

The data in the program produce the following output in response to 'GO':

time	prey	pred
0.0	105.00	8.00
1.0	110.88	9.47
2.0	108.32	11.65
3.0	98.83	12.57
4.0	91.12	11.26
5.0	90.30	9.24
6.0	95.81	7.98
7.0	104.30	7.99
8.0	110.45	9.34
9.0	108.61	11.48
10.0	99.58	12.52
...		

Depending on your enthusiasm, you could extend this skeleton a great deal. For example, you could also allow for parameter changes, and you could even write a procedure for setting up a new model, which asks the user for symbolic names of variables and parameters, and which generates the aliasing code for subsequent inclusion into diffeqns. This is very useful for large models.

The code of this mini-version of driver, or the much more powerful complete version, which includes a user manual, will be emailed on request to bdh@maths.uct.ac.za

16.7 Partial differential equations: a tridiagonal system

The numerical solution of partial differential equations (PDEs) is a vast subject. Space only permits one example, which serves two important purposes. It demonstrates a powerful method of solving a class of PDEs called *parabolic*. It also illustrates a method of solving *tridiagonal* systems of linear equations.

Heat conduction

The conduction of heat along a thin uniform rod may be modelled by the partial differential equation

$$\frac{\partial U}{\partial t} = \frac{\partial^2 U}{\partial x^2} \qquad (16.14)$$

where $U(x, t)$ is the temperature distribution a distance x from one end of the rod at time t. It is assumed that no heat is lost from the rod along its length.

Half the battle in solving PDEs is mastering the notation. We set up a rectangular grid, with step-lengths of h and k in the x and t directions, respectively. A general point on the grid has coordinates $x_i = ih$, $y_j = jk$. A concise notation for $U(x, t)$ at x_i, y_j is then simply $U_{i,j}$.

Now $U_{i,j}$ is of course the exact solution of the PDE. Exact solutions can only be found in a few special cases; we want a general method for finding approximate solutions. This is done by using truncated Taylor series to replace the PDE by a *finite difference scheme*. We define $u_{i,j}$ as the solution of the finite difference scheme at the grid point x_i, y_j. We now attempt to find numerical solutions for $u_{i,j}$, which will therefore be our approximation to the exact solution $U_{i,j}$.

The left-hand side of Equation (16.14) is usually approximated by a *forward difference*:

$$\frac{\partial U}{\partial t} = \frac{u_{i,j+1} - u_{i,j}}{k}$$

One way of approximating the right-hand side of Equation (16.14) is as follows:

$$\frac{\partial^2 U}{\partial x^2} = \frac{u_{i+1,j} - 2u_{i,j} + u_{i-1,j}}{h^2} \qquad (16.15)$$

This leads to a scheme, which although easy to compute, is only conditionally stable.

If, however, we replace the right-hand side of the scheme in Equation (16.15) by the mean of the finite difference approximation on the jth and $(j + 1)$th time rows, we get the following scheme for Equation (16.14):

$$-ru_{i-1,j+1} + (2 + 2r)u_{i,j+1} - ru_{i+1,j+1} = ru_{i-1,j} + (2 - 2r)u_{i,j} + ru_{i+1,j}, \qquad (16.16)$$

where $r = k/h^2$. This is known as the Crank–Nicolson *implicit* method, since it involves the solution of a system of simultaneous equations, as we shall see.

To illustrate the method numerically, let's suppose that the rod has a length of 1 unit, and that its ends are in contact with blocks of ice, i.e. the *boundary conditions* are $U(0, t) = U(1, t) = 0$. Suppose also that the initial temperature is given by the *initial condition*

$$U(x, 0) = \begin{cases} 2x, & 0 \leqslant x \leqslant \frac{1}{2} \\ 2(1 - x), & \frac{1}{2} \leqslant x \leqslant 1 \end{cases}$$

This situation could come about by heating the centre of the rod for a long time, with the ends kept in contact with the ice, removing the heat source at time $t = 0$. This particular problem has symmetry about the line $x = \frac{1}{2}$; we exploit this fact in finding the solution.

If we take $h = 0.1$ and $k = 0.01$, we will have $r = 1$, and Equation (16.16) becomes

$$-u_{i-1,j+1} + 4u_{i,j+1} - u_{i+1,j+1} = u_{i-1,j} + u_{i+1,j}$$

Putting $j = 0$ then generates the following set of equations for the unknowns $u_{i,1}$ up to the midpoint of the rod, represented by $i = 5$, i.e. $x = ih = 0.5$. Exact and approximate solutions coincide on the boundaries and at time $t = 0$. The subscript $j = 1$ has been dropped for clarity:

$$0 + 4u_1 - u_2 = 0 + 0.4$$
$$-u_1 + 4u_2 - u_3 = 0.2 + 0.6$$
$$-u_2 + 4u_3 - u_4 = 0.4 + 0.8$$
$$-u_3 + 4u_4 - u_5 = 0.6 + 1.0$$
$$-u_4 + 4u_5 - u_6 = 0.8 + 0.8$$

Symmetry then allows us to replace u_6 in the last equation by u_4. This system can be written in matrix form as

$$\begin{bmatrix} 4 & -1 & 0 & 0 & 0 \\ -1 & 4 & -1 & 0 & 0 \\ 0 & -1 & 4 & -1 & 0 \\ 0 & 0 & -1 & 4 & -1 \\ 0 & 0 & 0 & -2 & 4 \end{bmatrix} \begin{bmatrix} u_1 \\ u_2 \\ u_3 \\ u_4 \\ u_5 \end{bmatrix} = \begin{bmatrix} 0.4 \\ 0.8 \\ 1.2 \\ 1.6 \\ 1.6 \end{bmatrix} \tag{16.17}$$

The matrix (A) on the left of Equation (16.17) is known as a *tridiagonal* matrix. Such a matrix can be represented by three one-dimensional arrays: one for each diagonal. The system can then be solved very efficiently by Gauss elimination (implemented by the procedure **tridiag** below).

Care needs to be taken with the matrix representation. The following form is often chosen:

$$A = \begin{bmatrix} b_1 & c_1 & & & & \\ a_2 & b_2 & c_2 & & & \\ & a_3 & b_3 & c_3 & & \\ & & & \ddots & & \\ & & & a_{n-1} & b_{n-1} & c_{n-1} \\ & & & & a_n & b_n \end{bmatrix}$$

Take note of the subscripts!

The following program implements the Crank–Nicolson method to solve this particular problem over 10 time steps of $k = 0.01$. The step-length h is specified by N in the relationship $h = 1/(2N)$ because of the symmetry. r is therefore not restricted to the value 1, although it takes this value in the program.

```
Program cranknicolson;

const
   n = 5;                       { number of unique internal x grid points }
   tsteps = 10;                               { number of time steps }

type
   vector = array[ 0 .. n+2 ] of real;

var
   i, j : integer;
   h k, r, t : real;
   a, b, c, u, g, ux : vector;

procedure tridiag ( var x : vector; a b, c, g : vector; n : integer );
{ solves a tridiagonal system: a, b, c as in text, rhs in g,
   solution in x }
var
   i, j : integer;
   d : real;
   w : vector;                                     { working space }
begin
   for i := 1 to n do
      w[i] := b[i];
```

```
      for i := 2 to n do
        begin
          d := a[i] /w[i-1];
          w[i] := w[i] - c[i-1] * d;
          g[i] := g[i] - g[i-1] * d;
        end;
      x[n] := g[n] /w[n];                          { start back substitution }
                                                   { solution will be in x }
      for i := 1 to n-1 do
        begin
          j := n-i;
          x[j] := (g[j] - c[j] * x[j+1]) /w[j];
        end
    end; { tridiag }

begin
  k := 0.01;
  h := 1.0 / (2 * n);                              { symmetry assumed }
  r := k / (h * h);

  { some elements at either end of arrays are assigned unnecessarily,
                                            to simplify coding }
    for i := 1 to n do
      begin
        a[i] := -r;
        b[i] := 2 + 2 * r;
        c[i] := -r;
      end;

    a[n] := -2 * r;                                { from symmetry }

    for i := 0 to n do                             { initial conditions }
      u[i] := 2 * i * h;

    u[n+1] := u[n-1];

    t := 0;
    write( ' ':3, 'x =' );                         { headings}
    for i := 1 to n do
      write( (i * h):8:4);
    writeln;
    writeln( ' t' );
    write( t:6:2 );
    for i := 1 to n do                             { initial conditions }
      write( u[i]:8:4 );
    writeln;

    for j := 1 to tsteps do                        { solution will be in ux }
    begin
        t := t + 0.01;
        for i := 1 to n do
          g[i] := r * (u[i-1] + u[i+1]) + (2 - 2 * r) * u[i];
        tridiag( ux, a, b, c, g, n );

        write( t:6:2 );
        for i := 1 to n do
          write( ux[i]:8:4 );
        writeln;
```

```
            for i := 1 to n do              { get ready for next round }
               u[i] := ux[i];
               u[n+1] := u[n-1];
            end;
        end.
```

Output:

x =	0.1000	0.2000	0.3000	0.4000	0.5000
t					
0.00	0.2000	0.4000	0.6000	0.8000	1.0000
0.01	0.1989	0.3956	0.5834	0.7381	0.7691
0.02	0.1936	0.3789	0.5397	0.6461	0.6921
...					
0.10	0.0948	0.1803	0.2482	0.2918	0.3069

Notethat the procedure tridiag can be used to solve any tridiagonal system, and could be made part of a general utility unit.

Summary

A number of numerical methods are introduced in this chapter.

Turbo Pascal's procedural type may be used to pass subprogram names as parameters.

The driver interactive modelling package may be used to integrate systems of time-based ordinary differential equations.

Exercises

1   Use Newton's method in a program to solve some of the following (you may have to experiment a bit with the starting value):

(a) $x^4 - x = 10$ (two real and two complex roots);
(b) $e^{-x} = \sin x$ (infinitely many roots);
(c) $x^3 - 8x^2 + 17x - 10 = 0$ (three real roots);
(d) $\log x = \cos x$;
(e) $x^4 - 5x^3 - 12x^2 + 76x - 79 = 0$ (two real roots near 2; find the complex roots as well).

2   Use the bisection method to find the square root of 2, taking 1 and 2 as initial values of x_L and x_R. Continue bisecting until the maximum error is less than 0.05. Use inequality (16.2) to determine how many bisections are needed.

3   Use the trapezoidal rule to evaluate $\int_0^4 x^2 \, dx$, using a step-length of $h = 1$.

4   A human population of 1000 at time $t = 0$ grows at a rate given by

$$\frac{dN}{dt} = aN$$

where $a = 0.025$ per person per year. Use Euler's method to project the population over the next 30 years, working in steps of (a) $h = 2$ years, (b) $h = 1$ year and (c) $h = 0.5$ years. Compare your answers with the exact mathematical solution.

5   The basic equation for modelling radioactive decay is

$$\frac{dx}{dt} = -rx$$

where x is the amount of the radioactive substance at time t, and r is the decay rate. Some radioactive substances decay into other radioactive substances, which in turn also decay. For example, Strontium 92 ($r_1 = 0.256$ per hour) decays into Yttrium 92 ($r_2 = 0.127$ per hour), which in turn decays into Zirconium. Write down a pair of differential equations for Strontium and Yttrium to describe what is happening.

Starting at $t = 0$ with 5×10^{26} atoms of Strontium 92 and none of Yttrium, use the Runge–Kutta formulae to solve the equations up to $t = 8$ hours in steps of $1/3$ hours. Also use Euler's method for the same problem, and compare your results.

6   The impala population $x(t)$ in the Kruger National Park in South Africa may be modelled by the equation

$$\frac{dx}{dt} = (r - bx \sin at)x$$

where r, b, and a are constants. Write a program which

(a) reads values for r, b, a and the step-length $h \leq 1$ (in months);
(b) reads the initial value of x;
(c) uses Euler's method to compute the impala population;
(d) prints the population at monthly intervals over a period of 2 years.

7   The luminous efficiency (ratio of the energy in the visible spectrum to the total energy) of a black-body radiator may be expressed as a percentage by the formula

$$E = 64.77T^{-4} \int_{4 \times 10^{-5}}^{7 \times 10^{-5}} x^{-5}(e^{1.432/Tx} - 1)^{-1} \, dx$$

where T is the absolute temperature in degrees Kelvin, x is the wavelength in cm, and the range of integration is over the visible spectrum. Taking $T = 3500$ K, use Simpson's rule to compute E, firstly with 10 intervals ($n = 5$), and then with 20 intervals ($n = 10$), and compare your results.

8   Van der Pol's equation is a second-order non-linear differential equation which may be expressed as two first-order equations as follows:

$$\frac{dx_1}{dt} = x_2$$

$$\frac{dx_2}{dt} = \varepsilon(1 - x_1^2)x_2 - b^2 x_1$$

The solution of this equation has a stable limit cycle, which means that if you plot the phase trajectory of the solution (the plot of x_1 against x_2) starting at any point in the positive x_1–x_2 plane, it always moves continuously into the same closed loop. Use the Runge–Kutta method to solve this system numerically, with $h = 0.1$, $x_1(0) = 0$, and $x_2(0) = 1$. If you have access to graphics facilities, draw the phase trajectory for $b = 1$ and ε ranging between 0.01 and 1.0.

Appendix A
Syntax diagrams for Pascal

Program

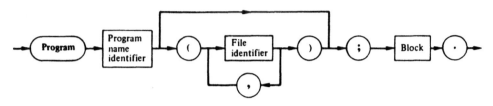

Block

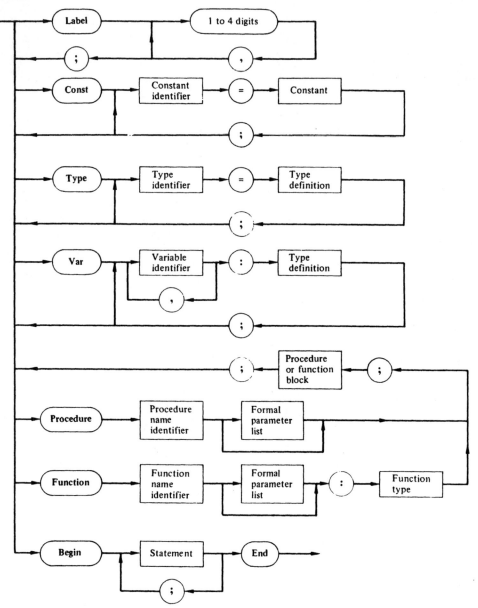

Type definition

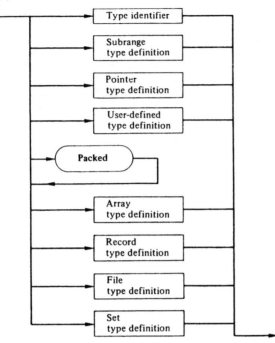

Subrange type definition

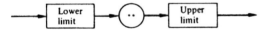

Pointer type definition

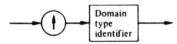

User-defined type definition

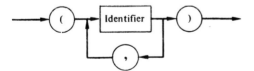

Array type definition

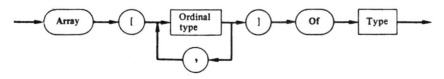

Record type definition

Field list

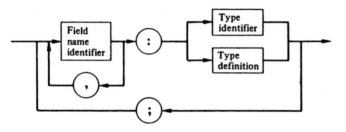

Fixed part

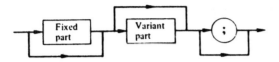

Variant part

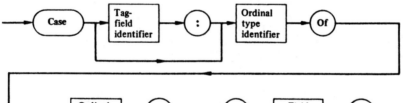

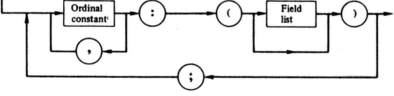

File type definition

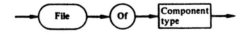

Set type definition

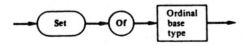

Formal parameter list

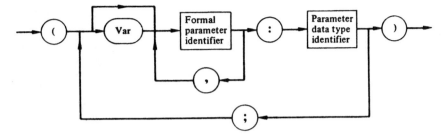

Statement

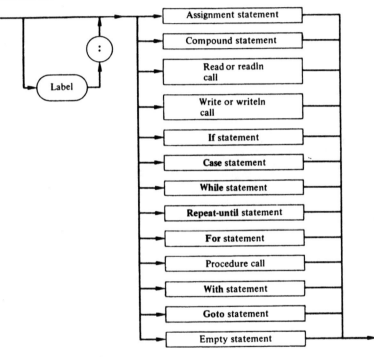

Assignment statement

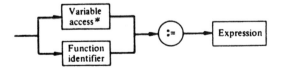

*Note that a 'variable access' is a name that denotes a variable. This may be a variable identifier, a compound or a structured variable, an element referenced by a pointer variable or a buffer variable.

Compound statement

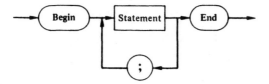

read call

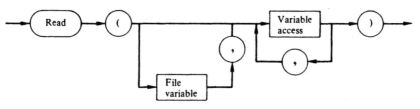

readln call

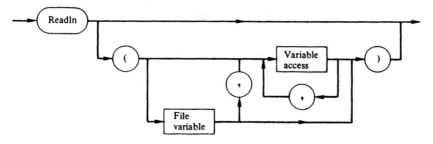

write call

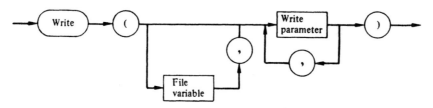

writeln call

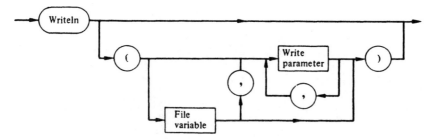

Write parameter

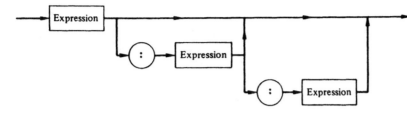

If statement

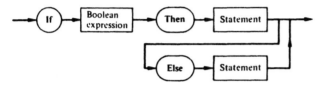

Case statement

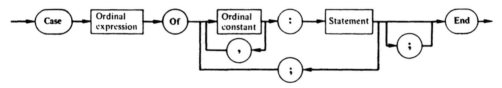

While statement

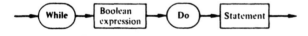

Repeat-until statement

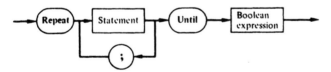

For statement

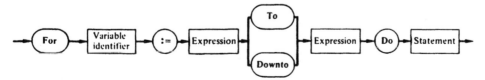

Procedure or function call

Actual parameter list

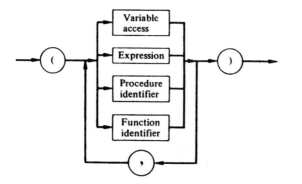

With statement

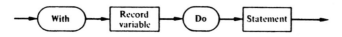

Expression

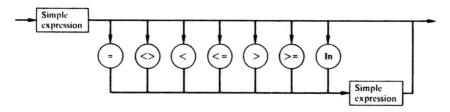

Simple expression

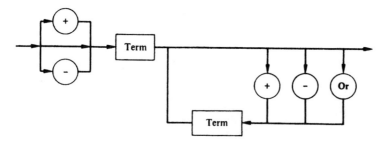

Term

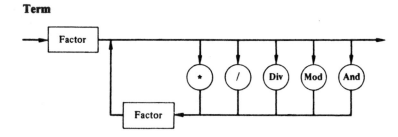

Factor

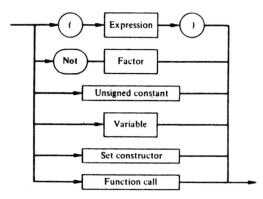

Array reference

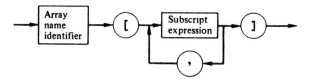

Set constructor

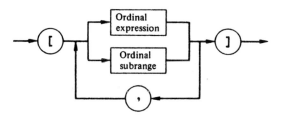

Identifier

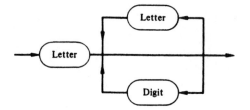

Constant

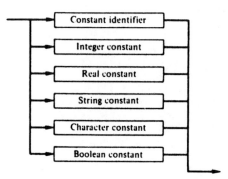

Integer constant

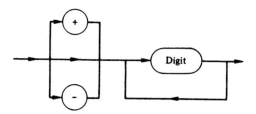

Real constant

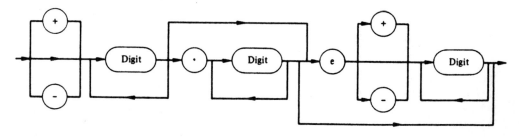

String or character constant

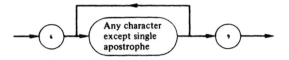

Boolean constant

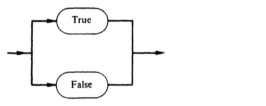

Comment

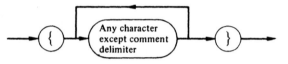

Appendix B
Reserved words and required identifiers

Reserved words (word delimiters) are words that always have a predefined meaning in Pascal programs; they cannot be redefined by the user. They may be listed as follows:

and	end	nil	set
array	file	not	then
begin	for	of	to
case	function	or	type
const	goto	packed	until
div	if	procedure	var
do	in	program	while
downto	label	record	with
else	mod	repeat	

Required identifiers also have a predefined meaning but the user may, if he wishes, redefine any of these within program declarations. These identifiers include required function and procedure names (see Appendix C) and the following words.

> false   true   maxint
> integer   boolean   real   char   text
> input   output

(The identifier maxint takes the value of the largest integer available in the implementation being used.)

Exceptions to this rule are input and output which cannot be redefined in the program block if they occur in the list of files in the program heading.

The word **forward** is not reserved but is a directive to the Pascal processor.

Appendix C
Required functions and procedures

Functions

Function	Parameter type	Result type	Effect
abs(x)	real or integer	Same as parameter	Computes the magnitude of x (e.g. abs(-5) = 5)
arctan(x)	real or integer	real	Computes the inverse tangent of x
chr(x)	integer	char	Returns the character with the ordinal number x
cos(x)	real or integer	real	Computes the cosine of x
eof(f)	File	boolean	Returns the value true if the file window is over end-of-file and false otherwise
eoln(f)	Textfile	boolean	Returns the value true if the file window is over the line-separator and false otherwise
exp(x)	real or integer	real	Exponential function
ln(x)	real or integer	real	Natural logarithm
odd(x)	integer	boolean	true if x is an odd number, otherwise false
ord(x)	Any scalar type except real	integer	Returns the value of the ordinal number of x within the set of values x may take
pred(x)	Any scalar type except real	Same as parameter	Returns the value of the predecessor of x in the set of values x may take
round(x)	real	integer	Returns the value of the closest integer to x
sin(x)	real or integer	real	Computes sine of x
sqr(x)	real or integer	Same as parameter	Computes x^2
sqrt(x)	real or integer	real	Computes $\sqrt{x}$
succ(x)	Any scalar type except real	Same as parameter	Returns the value of the successor of x in the set of values x may take
trunc(x)	real	integer	Returns the value of the whole number part of x

Procedures

Procedure	Parameter type	Effect
dispose(p)	Pointer	Indicates that the space occupied by p↑ is no longer needed
dispose(p,t1,....tn)	p is a pointer t1,... tn are constants	Indicates that the space occupied by the record p↑ with tag field values t1,....tn is no longer needed
get(f)	File	Moves the file window to the next component of the file and assigns the value of this component to the buffer variable f↑
new(p)	Pointer	Allocates a new variable to which p now refers
new(p,t1,....tn)	p is a pointer t1,...tn are constants	Allocates a new variable with tag field values to which p now refers
pack(a,i,b)	a is an array i is of any scalar type except real b is a packed array	Copies components stored in array a into packed array b starting with A[i]
page(f)	Textfile	Causes skipping to the top of the next page when f is printed
put(f)	File	Appends the value of the buffer variable f↑ to the file f
read ⎫ readln ⎭ see below		
reset(f)	File	Sets the file window over the first component of the file ready for reading
rewrite(f)	File	File f becomes empty, ready for writing to
unpack(b,a,i)	a is an array b is a packed array	Copies contents of packed array b into array a starting at a[i]
write ⎫ writeln ⎭ see below		

Most of these functions and procedures are discussed in more detail in the main text. In particular read, readln, write and writeln are too involved to describe in brief here. Refer to the index to find further information on these.

Appendix D
Turbo Pascal functions and procedures

The following Turbo Pascal functions and procedures are described in the text. Use the index to find the descriptions. All Turbo Pascal items are indexed under the heading Turbo Pascal.

D.1 *system* unit

append opens an existing text file for appending.

assign assigns the name of an external file to a file variable.

blockread reads one or more records from an untyped file into a variable.

blockwrite writes one or more records to an untyped file from a variable.

close closes an open file.

concat concatenates a sequence of strings.

dec decrements its argument.

delete deletes a substring from a string.

dispose destroys a dynamic variable.

erase deletes an external file.

exit exits immediately from the current block.

filepos returns the current file position of a file. Not used for text tiles.

fillchar fills a specified number of contiguous bytes with a specified value.

frac returns the fractional part of its argument.

freemem destroys a dynamic variable of given size.

getmem creates a new dynamic variable of given size and sets a pointer variable to point to it.

halt stops program execution and returns to the operating system. It has an optional word-type parameter which may be examined on return to the operating system, e.g. in a DOS batch file.

hi returns the high-order byte of its argument.

inc increments its argument.

insert inserts a substring into a string.

IOresult returns an integer code for the status of the last I/O (input/output) operation performed.

length returns the dynamic length of a string.

lo returns the low-order byte of its argument.

maxavail returns the size of the largest contiguous free block in the heap, corresponding to the size of the largest dynamic variable that can be allocated at that moment.

memavail returns the number of free bytes of heap storage available.

move copies a specified number of contiguous bytes from a source range to a destination range.

new creates a new dynamic variable and sets a pointer variable to point to it.

ofs returns the offset of a specified object.

paramcount returns the number of parameters passed to the program from the command line.

paramstr returns the specified command-line parameters.

pi returns the value of π (3.14159 26535 89793 2385).

pos returns the position of a substring in a string.

ptr converts a segment base and an offset address to a pointer-type value.

random returns a random number.

randomize initialises the built-in random number generator with a random seed.

rename renames an external file.

reset opens an existing file.

rewrite creates and opens a new file.

seek moves the current file position to the specified component. Not used with text files.

seg returns the segment of a specified object.

sizeof returns the number of bytes occupied by its argument.

str returns the string representation of a given numeric value.

upcase converts a character to uppercase.

val converts a string value to its numeric representation.

D.2   *crt* unit

clreol clears all characters from the cursor position to the end of the line.

clrscr clears the text screen and homes the cursor.

delay delays program execution a specified number of milliseconds (approximately).

delline deletes the line containing the cursor and moves all lines below it one line up.

gotoxy moves the cursor to the specified position on the text screen.

highvideo selects high-intensity characters.

insline inserts an empty line at the cursor position.

keypressed returns **true** if a key has been pressed on the keyboard, and **false** otherwise.

lowvideo selects low-intensity characters.

normvideo selects normal-intensity characters.

nosound turns off the internal speaker.

readkey reads a character from the keyboard without echoing it to the screen.

sound starts the internal speaker.

textbackground selects the background character colour on the text screen.

textcolor selects the foreground character colour on the text screen.

wherex returns the *x*-coordinate (column) of the current cursor position.

wherey returns the *y*-coordinate (row) of the current cursor position.

window defines a window on the textscreen.

D.3 *dos* unit

getdate gets the current date set by the operating system.

getftime gets the date and time a file was last written.

gettime gets the current time from the operating system.

setdate sets the current date in the operating system.

setftime sets a file's date stamp, i.e. the date and time a file was last written.

settime sets the current time in the operating system.

D.4 *graph* unit

arc draws a circular arc

bar draws a bar using the current fill style and colour.

bar3d draws a three-dimensional bar using the current fill style and colour.

circle draws a circle.

cleardevice clears the graphics screen and homes the current pointer.

clearviewport clears the current viewport.

closegraph shuts down the graphics system.

detectgraph checks hardware and decides which graphics driver and mode to use.

ellipse draws an elliptical arc.

getimage saves a bit image of the specified graphics region into a buffer.

getmaxcolor returns the highest colour that can be passed to setcolor.

getmaxx returns the maximum *x*-coordinate of the current graphics driver and mode.

getmaxy returns the maximum *y*-coordinate of the current graphics driver and mode.

getviewsettings gets the current viewport parameters.

getx returns the *x*-coordinate of the current pointer.

gety returns the *y*-coordinate of the current pointer.

grapherrormsg returns an error message for the specified graphics error code.

graphresult returns an error code for the last graphics operation.

imagesize returns the number of bytes required to store a rectangular region of the graphics screen.

initgraph initialises the graphics system and puts the hardware into graphics mode.

line draws a line between two specified points.

linerel draws a line to a point a relative distance from the current pointer.

lineto draws a line from the current pointer to a specified point.

moverel moves the current pointer a relative distance from its current position.

moveto moves the current pointer to the specified position.

outtext writes a string on the graphics screen at the current pointer.

outtextxy writes a string on the graphics screen at the specified position.

pieslice draws and fills a pie-slice of specified size at the specified position.

putimage puts a bit image on to the graphics screen.

putpixel plots a pixel at the specified point.

rectangle draws a rectangle of specified size using the current line style and colour.

restorecrtmode restores the screen mode before graphics was initialised.

setbkcolor sets the current graphics background colour.

setcolor sets the current graphics drawing colour.

setfillstyle sets the fill pattern and colour.

setgraphmode sets the system to graphics mode and clears the screen.

setlinestyle sets the current line width and pattern.

settextstyle sets the current text font, style and character magnification factor for text on the graphics screen.

setviewport sets the current graphics viewport. E

Appendix E
Common codes

ASCII (American Standard Code for Information Interchange)

Left digit(s) \ Right digit	0	1	2	3	4	5	6	7	8	9
3			□	!	"	#	$	%	&	'
4	(	)	*	+	,	−	.	/	0	1
5	2	3	4	5	6	7	8	9	:	;
6	<	=	>	?	@	A	B	C	D	E
7	F	G	H	I	J	K	L	M	N	O
8	P	Q	R	S	T	U	V	W	X	Y
9	Z	[	\	]	^	_	'	a	b	c
10	d	e	f	g	h	i	j	k	l	m
11	n	o	p	q	r	s	t	u	v	w
12	x	y	z	{	|	}	~			

EBCDIC (Extended Binary Coded Decimal Interchange Code)

Left digit(s) \ Right digit	0	1	2	3	4	5	6	7	8	9
7					¢	.	<	(	+	
8	&									
9	!	$	*	)	;	¬	−	/		
10							∧	,	%	−
11	>	?								
12			:	#	@	'	=	"		a
13	b	c	d	e	f	g	h	i		
14						j	k	l	m	n
15	o	p	q	r						
16			s	t	u	v	w	x	y	z
17							¦	{	}	
18	[	]								
19				A	B	C	D	E	F	G
20	H	I								J
21	K	L	M	N	O	P	Q	R		
22							S	T	U	V
23	W	X	Y	Z						
24	0	1	2	3	4	5	6	7	8	9

Appendix F
Portability

One of the attractions of using a high level language is that programs written in such a language can, in theory, be moved from one computer to another with the minimum of fuss, and with every expectation that results will be consistent. Unfortunately, this has not been the case for most of the popular languages that have been developed. Modifications that are needed when moving a program from one machine to another vary from minor but irritating changes to the character set used to wholesale rewriting of sections of code.

Niklaus Wirth was aware of these problems when he developed Pascal and sought to minimise them in two ways. First he designed his new language to be consistent and versatile. This discourages compiler designers from tampering with the specifications, adding features in one compiler that may not be available in another. Secondly, in association with Kathleen Jensen, he produced a manual and report which defined precisely what facilities should be available in the language, how they should be represented and what they should mean. The first edition of this book was published in 1975 and the latest edition (*Pascal User Manual and Report*, K Jensen, N Wirth, Springer-Verlag 1985) incorporates minor changes to conform with the International Standards Organization (ISO) requirements for standard Pascal. The variations that are likely to be found from system to system fall into two categories—those due to differences in input character sets and those due to the idiosyncrasies of the compilers.

Programs reproduced in the original user manual and report look very different from those in this book. Examine the piece of code below that is written in the same style as in the report:

```
E.1   begin {main program}
        reset(oldmaster);
        reset(transaction);
        rewrite(newmaster);
        rewrite(errorfile);

        while (oldmaster↑.accnumber < > maxkey)
              or (transaction↑.accnumber < > maxkey) do
          begin
            setupcurrentrecord;
            processtranswithsamekey;
            if not emptycurrentrecord then
              begin
                newmaster↑: = currentrecord;
                put(newmaster)
              end
          end;

        newmaster↑: = oldmaster↑;        {dummy key at end}
        put(newmaster)                   {    of newmaster   }
      end.
```

In many systems underline characters are not available, some systems do not allow lower case letters and some do not have an up-arrow. Still other versions do not allow braces and use, instead '(*' and '*)' to denote opening and closing of comments respectively. And so the list goes on. Minor problems in themselves but they involve irritating changes to programs when transferring them from one computer to another.

Arguably the most satisfactory systems are ones where the reserved words are automatically highlighted as they are typed in. There are now excellent systems on the market which, in addition to highlighting reserved words, perform automatic formatting of programs including indentation of nested statements. These are particularly suitable for naive users.

Of more significance than the variations between character sets are the differences in behaviour that are observed when the same program is run with different compilers. The problems that occur fall into four main groups:

(i)   limitations of the compiler (or compiler writers)
(ii)   enhancements of the language
(iii) differences of interpretation of constructions
(iv)   compiler bugs

(i) *Limitations of the compiler*

There are often great difficulties in designing compilers to fit the architecture of particular machines. For example, one could design a compiler that imposed no limit on the size of integer values that could be manipulated. This would be adding a facility of little benefit to the great majority of users but might add considerably to the processing time. Pascal has a standard identifier maxint which is implementation-dependent and takes the value of the largest integer available on the system in use. This may vary from 32 767 on some microcomputers to over 10^{14} on larger main-frame computers. Another common restriction is that imposed on the size of identifiers or, at least, on the number of characters of identifiers that are distinguished. Most compilers would allow identifier1 and identifier2 but would not necessarily distinguish between them. Often, only the first eight characters are examined (although the ISO and ANSI standards require all characters to be significant). These restrictions are not unduly inconvenient for the most part, as long as the user is aware of them. Other restrictions that may be imposed are more serious and seem difficult to justify.

Although Pascal contains only a modest set of standard procedures and functions it is quite common to find some of them omitted—pack and unpack are sometimes left out. One of the most popular (and in other ways highly commendable) implementations of Pascal on micros—Turbo Pascal—omits the procedures page, get and put. The Microsoft and Macintosh versions of the languages are among the most scrupulous in including the standard features of Pascal.

Possibly the most inconsistent feature of implementations is in the treatment of files. Sometimes the only type of file available is the textfile, or perhaps files of records. The number of systems that treat files as directed in the user manual actually seem to be in the minority. The manual specified that any files that exist prior to the running of a program or are to be retained after the termination of its execution should be declared in the program parameter list. In practice, most systems ignore these parameters or may positively prohibit them. Often a lock or close instruction is needed to ensure that a file is retained after a program has terminated. Sometimes the external name (in the system) of a file has to be linked to its internal name (in the program) by using a special instruction or by modifying the reset and rewrite instructions, e.g.

    reset(internalname,'externalname')

(ii) *Enhancements of the language*

Whatever the language, there is always a temptation for compiler designers to introduce extra features to 'improve' it. The most common enhancements include the modification of the **case** statement to allow an **else** part to deal with the situation when none of the case labels apply; see the following example.

```
case mark div 10 of
    0,1,2,3,4 : write ('fail');
    5,6       : write ('pass');
    7,8,9,10  : write('distinction');
      else: write('error in data')
end
```

Some compilers allow input and output of *any* scalar value, not just standard ones. Both of these facilities seem sensible although it may be argued that using any facilities that make a program less portable should be discouraged. In addition, there is the danger that a new feature may have slightly different effects in two different systems.

The most tempting enhancements of all are the ones that use special facilities available on a particular machine such as the graphics capabilities. If these features are used then care should be taken not to intersperse them with the rest of the program but only to use them in special purpose subroutines that can be substituted for if the program is transferred to another machine.

(iii)   *Differences of interpretation of constructions*
The possibility of slightly different interpretations of the same construction is not so much of a problem in standard Pascal as in other languages, because of its precise definition. The loopholes in the original definition were, for the most part, unlikely to affect most programmers at all. A key article that pinpointed some of the problems is 'Ambiguities and insecurities in Pascal' by Welsh, Sneeringer and Hoare, published in *Software— Practice and Experience*, **7**, pp. 685–96 (1977).

These and other problems were addressed by the ISO's Pascal committee and after three years they published a draft proposal in 1980 clarifying some of the finer points of interpretation. The single new addition to the language that was proposed was confor- mant arrays (see page 130), but this is only available in some implementations ('level 1'). Level 0—implementations (approved by the American National Standards Institute— ANSI) do not have conformant arrays.

(iv)   *Compiler bugs*
Although Pascal was designed to allow efficient compilation and effective error checking there are still many compilers exhibiting undesirable characteristics. This is particularly so with regard to compilers on microcomputers. Sometimes a syntactic error will cause compilation to stop and require the re-initialising of the system. More frequently, run- time errors such as integer overflow or subscripted variable outside array limits remain undetected and cause the wrong answers to be output.

So is Pascal truly portable? If, by this, we mean can we take a program run with one compiler and hope, with any degree of confidence, that it will run first time with another compiler and give the same results then the answer must be no. However, many problems are minor ones and as long as programs are carefully written with non-standard features localized to specialised sub-programs any changes that will be necessary will be small or, at least, easy to pinpoint.

Lastly, it would seem appropriate to pay tribute to two projects that greatly helped the advancement of Pascal in the early days and contributed to its reliability. First, the UCSD project at the University of California has promoted the use of a relatively machine- independent Pascal system that has been adopted on many computers. Secondly, the work done at the University of Tasmania in producing a test bed of programs for checking the reliability of Pascal compilers gives a useful yardstick for comparing different systems.

Appendix G
Glossary

Algorithm

A set of directions that describe the steps in the solution of a problem. The directions must be clear and unambiguous and will often be used as the basis of a computer program* for solving the problem. Often the algorithmic steps are described in English and embedded in a diagram that indicates the order in which the steps are to be carried out. Flowcharts* used to be a popular method of representing algorithms but they have largely been replaced by other techniques that encourage a structured approach to producing a solution such as structure diagrams* and Nassi-Shneiderman diagrams.

Arithmetic and logic unit (alu)

The part of the computer that performs high-speed operations on its inputs generally producing a single result. It carries out, for example, simple arithmetic operations and comparisons of values.

Compiler

A program that takes as data another program written in a high-level programming language* and translates it into an equivalent program in a low-level programming language*. They usually have an option allowing the printing of a copy of the program itself—the 'source listing'. If the high-level 'source' program is incorrect then most compilers will produce a listing of errors. The 'object' program produced by a correct source program can be run or 'executed' directly by the computer with appropriate data*. The two stage process is illustrated in Fig. G.1.

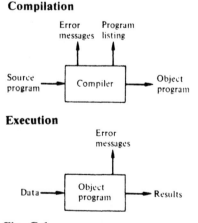

Fig. G.1

Computer program

A set of instructions for directing the activity of a computer.

Data

This word has different meanings depending upon the context. For our purposes it is the input that is processed by a computer program. This may, for instance, be a set of numbers, a list of names or even (if the program is a compiler*) another program.

Documentation

Information that serves to explain the purpose of a program. Documentation may be internal—in the form of comments and appropriately named variables and constants etc. or may be external in the form of a written description and structure diagrams*, for instance.

File

In Pascal*, a sequence of components that are considered as a unit and that have certain operations that can be performed on them. Components can be read in order from a file by a computer program* or can be added or 'written' to the end of a file. The input to a program may be considered as a 'read-only file'. Similarly the results may be regarded as an output file.

Floating point

A notation for representing real numbers that is particularly convenient for expressing very large or very small values. The number is written in two parts. The first part is the 'mantissa', and the second part is the 'exponent'. The exponent (an integer) indicates the power of ten by which the mantissa is to be multiplied in order to get the normal decimal representation of the number. In Pascal programs the two parts are separated by an 'e'. For example the floating point value 2.4e6 would be written 2 400 000 as a decimal numeral and the decimal numeral 0.000 064 2 could be represented as 6.42e−5 in floating point form.

Flowchart (flow diagram)

A diagrammatic representation of an algorithm*. Individual actions to be carried out are enclosed in rectangular boxes. Boxes are linked by arrowed lines to indicate the order in which the steps are to be carried out. At a point where there are alternative courses of action a diamond shaped box (decision box) contains a question and the box has two or more labelled arrowed lines leading from it indicating which route to follow in what circumstances. Oval boxes are used to denote start and finish points for the algorithm and various other exotic boxes are often introduced depending upon the application.

A flowchart for playing a golf hole is given in Fig. G.2.

Hardware

The physical parts of a computer, including its electronic, electrical and mechanical components. Often contrasted with software*.

High-level programming language

A computer language that is written in a form that humans can readily understand rather than in a form that the computer can easily execute. Commonly used high-level languages

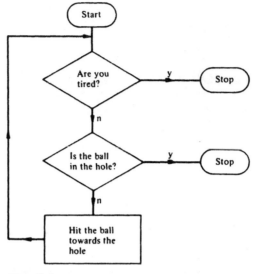

Fig. G.2

include Pascal*, Cobol and PL/1. Each language needs its own compiler* before it can be run on a computer.

Input unit (device)

A device that transfers data, programs, or signals into the computer. Keyboards have more-or-less supplanted card readers as the most common input device.

Low-level programming language

A programming language that is readily executed by a computer. Each type of computer has its own low-level languages containing instructions that take advantage of the machine's hardware* features. Consequently programming in such languages is time consuming and difficult. Ultimately every piece of software run on the computers must be translated into a low-level language before it is executed. Fortunately programs such as compilers* usually perform this task for us.

Output unit (device)

A device that converts signals from the computer into a form suitable for usage outside the computer. Often this is a device such as a vdu* or printer* that converts the signals to a readable form.

Pascal

A high-level programming language* developed in the 1970s to aid the teaching of programming concepts. It was developed from Algol 60, and inherits many of the features of that language.

Printer

An output device* that converts the output from the computer into a printed form on paper. A commonly used form in large installations is the line printer where the whole of one line is printed simultaneously.

Programming language

A notation for writing computer programs*. Most programming languages can be categorized as high-level* or low-level* depending upon how far removed from the computer's own language (its 'machine language') they are.

Software

The instructions that make the computer perform its tasks, usually meaning the computer programs* that run on the machine. It is often contrasted with hardware*.

Structure diagram

A method of representing an algorithm* in a diagram so that the structure of the solution procedure is readily appreciated. Each step of the process is enclosed in a rectangular box and one or more branches may lead below it to other boxes. These lower boxes describe the step in the 'parent' box in more detail. (See Fig. G.3.)

Fig. G.3

Note that the ordering of the activities is implicitly from left to right. The lower boxes may themselves require a fuller description in which case they may have their own 'children'. An algorithm may in this way be represented at several levels of detail in a single diagram.

Other boxes to represent conditions and repetition may be introduced. A structure diagram illustrating their use for the problem of playing a hole of golf is shown in Fig. G.4. Compare this solution with that using a flowchart*.

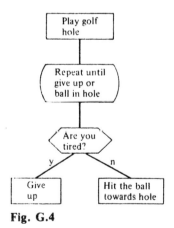

Fig. G.4

Syntax diagram (syntax chart)

A method of describing valid constructions in programming languages. For each construction a diagram indicates all permissible elements of that construction and also

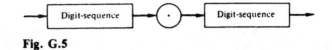

Fig. G.5

the possible orders in which they may occur. For instance a syntax diagram to describe valid real numbers in a certain programming language could be represented as in Fig. G.5. In a syntax diagram a box denotes a set of elements. For instance the box containing the phrase 'Digit-sequence' denotes the set containing all possible sequences of one or more digits (0, 56, 1962 etc.). A sequence of elements is built from the diagram by following the arrowed lines and, when a box is encountered, by adding one of its elements to the sequence. As the box is passed any element from it can be selected. For example, when the first box containing 'Digit-sequence' is passed we might pick up 596. The next box contains only a decimal point and so we add this to the sequence to get '596.'. Lastly from the second 'Digit-sequence' box we could pick up 29 giving the final result '596.29'. Effectively this diagram is saying that a real number must consist of a sequence of digits followed by a decimal point and terminated by a sequence of digits.

If an element is enclosed in a rectangular box then this means that a more detailed description of the structure can be found in another syntax diagram. A syntax diagram for 'Digit-sequence' is shown in Fig. G.6.

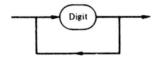

Fig. G.6

Here there is a loop which can be traversed any number of times. Each time the digit box is encountered another digit is picked up. Notice that the digit box is oval which means that the definition of the construction is not to be found in another diagram. This is used when it is obvious what elements it contains.

Alternative courses of action can be easily included. So if we wanted to indicate that a sign may precede the first digit-sequence in a real number the diagram could be modified as shown in Fig. G.7.

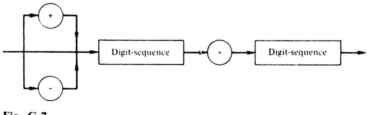

Fig. G.7

Depending upon which direction is taken at the first junction either ' + ', ' − ' or no sign will precede the number.

Teletype

A device for receiving messages from the computer which are then printed onto a roll of paper. Messages can usually be sent back to the computer via a keyboard and these messages are normally also printed (also known as a teleprinter or teletypewriter).

Terminal

A device attached to the computer and used for inputting data or for receiving results. It is normally remote from the computer and is most often a vdu* or a teletype*.

Vdu

The abbreviation for visual display unit. A terminal* that displays output from the computer on a screen (usually a cathode-ray tube). The screen can often display graphical in addition to textual information. Usually there is an associated keyboard for transmitting information back to the computer and this information can also be displayed on the screen.

Index

Turbo Pascal items are indexed under the heading Turbo Pascal.

Printed in the United Kingdom
by Lightning Source UK Ltd.
118690UK00001B/21